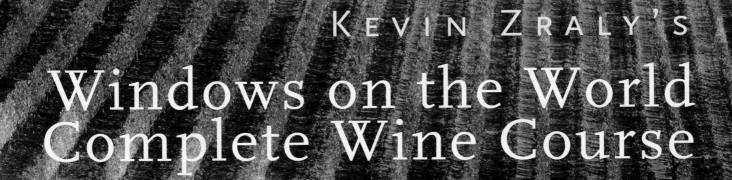

# Kevin Zraly's
# Windows on the World
# Complete Wine Course

STERLING EPICURE
New York

## DEDICATION

The 2014 edition is dedicated to all the teachers who helped me (and everyone else) to learn the art of language, pronunciation, and communication. I have always said to my wine students, "If you can't say it, you can't buy it."

I hope you all enjoy the new pronunciation guides that I firmly believe will help immensely on your worldwide wine journey.

Thank you to my first teachers, my parents, who guided me in those early wonder years by not only helping me to say words correctly, but defining all that I needed to, so that I could understand their meaning and context.

To all the good nuns and teachers at St. Thomas School in Pleasantville, New York, who continued the work of my parents. Those years will forever remain as some of the most meaningful and magical in my life.

To my parish priest, Father Matarazzo, who taught me Latin, and who also introduced to me to the beautiful Italian language.

To my French and Spanish teachers in high school and college who paved the way for my first wine journeys to Europe. Thank you for giving me the knowledge and confidence to speak with people in their own language.

And finally my oldest son, Anthony, who turned twenty-one and we can now "legally" share wine together.

The signatures on the endpapers of the book represent some of the winery owners, vineyardists, winemakers, and marketing and public relations professionals whose help has been invaluable to me.

I welcome questions and comments. Please visit my website at www.kevinzraly.com for updates and wine news.

STERLING EPICURE
New York

An Imprint of Sterling Publishing
387 Park Avenue South
New York, NY 10016

STERLING EPICURE is a trademark of Sterling Publishing Co., Inc. The distinctive Sterling logo is a registered trademark of Sterling Publishing Co., Inc.

ISBN 978-1-4549-0909-5

Distributed in Canada by Sterling Publishing
c/o Canadian Manda Group, 165 Dufferin Street
Toronto, Ontario, Canada M6K 3H6
Distributed in the United Kingdom by GMC Distribution Services
Castle Place, 166 High Street, Lewes, East Sussex, England BN7 1XU
Distributed in Australia by Capricorn Link (Australia) Pty. Ltd.
P.O. Box 704, Windsor, NSW 2756, Australia

For information about custom editions, special sales, premium and corporate purchases, please contact Sterling Special Sales Department at 800-805-5489 or specialsales@sterlingpublishing.com.

Manufactured in China
2  4  6  8  10  9  7  5  3
www.sterlingpublishing.com

*A Tribute to the Wines of America: The Journey Continues*

Forty years ago, I was underway with my career in wine. I had already taught my first wine class, was the manager of a *New York Times* four-star restaurant, and only a sophomore in college. Lucky for me the drinking age in New York was eighteen, which allowed me to taste and teach about wine at the time. I had been to all of the vineyards of my home state of New York, which were primarily located in the Finger Lakes District—Long Island had not even started to plant grapes yet. But I couldn't go to California to taste the wines there since the drinking age was twenty-one years old. It's difficult for someone to teach about something they have never seen or experienced.

Even though I had a really good job, like most college students I didn't have a lot of money. I couldn't afford to fly to California, so in the summer of my twenty-first year I began my journey on Route 209 in Stone Ridge, New York, with my thumb in the air! California or bust. Joining me was my friend Bill, who was and still is a photographer and who wanted to take pictures from the perspective of a hitchhiker crossing America, and also as my "official" photographer of the wineries. On our first day, we made it to Route 80 and State College, Pennsylvania. As the sun was setting, we were getting ready to pull out our sleeping bags and call it a night when we saw a pickup truck backing up toward us. As it got closer, we could make out the license plate: California! The person who picked us up was in the military and in a hurry to get home to see his girlfriend. Three days later we were in Santa Cruz, California.

I am still amazed that at twenty-one years old I was smart enough to write ahead to the wineries to set up visits. I spent that summer soaking up everything I could learn about wine: winemaking, vineyard production, how to taste, etc. For a twenty-one-year-old, this was an experience of a lifetime.

After hitchhiking back to New York I continued with my restaurant job and received my college degree. Right after graduating with New York and California under my belt, I headed off to the great wine regions of Europe, which gave me a totally different perspective on wine.

From both of these experiences I was able to see firsthand the differences between the Old World and the New World of wine. All of these travel experiences gave me a sense of what was to come in California. Little did I realize that the wine explosion would continue into Washington, New York, and Oregon. And today all fifty states have wineries and some are making spectacular wines.

This edition is expanding outside of the four major states. I have added Virginia, Texas, Pennsylvania, Ohio, Missouri, North Carolina, Michigan, and Illinois to round out the top twelve states in number of wineries. As of this past year, the United States became the number-one consumer of wines in the world; forty years ago I would never have predicted this. And the future for American wines is very exciting.

In last year's edition, we added smart tags, so you can now download videos to watch before you read each chapter. I remember how difficult it was for me in my early days of studying wine to have the correct pronunciation of the hundreds of wine villages, vineyards, grape varieties, and winemaking terminology. So I am happy to say that for this edition we also added smart tags so you will now have a native speaker giving the pronunciation of more than 1,300 words.

Good luck on your wine journey! May your glass always be half full.

# Contents

Look for links and tags you can scan with your smartphone throughout the book to access video introductions and pronunciation guides for the wine terms in each chapter.

This picture was taken from the 107th floor of One World Trade Center overlooking the East River and the Brooklyn Bridge.

# Witness to the Wine Revolution

In 1970 when I began my journey in wine, I studied only French wines and a little German wine. Then it started to happen: California began to produce some really outstanding wines, especially Cabernet Sauvignon from the Napa Valley. Next, not in any specific order, the wines of Chile, Australia, Oregon, New Zealand, South Africa, Washington State, Argentina, New York State, and more, came into the quality category. Wine has become a global community. This is the golden age of wine.

Here are the changes that I have seen since 1970 that have significantly altered the course of winemaking and viticulture. Also, wherever possible throughout the book, I have included a Past and Present sidebar, comparing wine statistics in 1970 to 2013.

## Winemaking and Viticulture

Wine quality has improved significantly over the last four decades. Vast strides have been made in the science and technology of winemaking, growers have readapted back-to-the-earth farming techniques, and there has been widespread planting of international grapes, all of which have led to wine's rise in popularity.

Here are some of the specific changes in winemaking and viticulture that I have witnessed in my career.

- More attention is being paid to the individual vineyards, clonal selection, and trellis systems

- More care is taken to match grape varieties with specific sites

- There is far less filtering of wine, leading to a fuller, more complex, and natural taste

- Oak is used far more judiciously

- Even though wine alcohol levels have reached historic highs, the majority of winemakers have adjusted their winemaking techniques to keep all components in balance

- "Sustainability" has become the international buzz-word in viticulture: Grape growers are using fewer herbicides and pesticides and many are going organic. While there are still very few producers of biodynamic wines, elite wineries such as Benziger, Grgich Hills, J. Phelps, Quintessa, Chapoutier, Domaine Leflaive, Zind Humbrecht, Domaine Leroy, and Araujo are practicing biodynamic techniques.

- The number of vines planted per acre (vine density) has increased dramatically. This has allowed the viticulturalist more freedom to produce better grapes.

- Screw caps are gradually replacing corks on more than just inexpensive wines: screw caps seal 75 percent of Australian and 93 percent of New Zealand wines

- Global warming: Between 1960 and 1969, grape harvesting in Burgundy, France, on average began September 27. From 2000 to 2013, grape harvesting began closer to the first week of September. To help offset the effects of a shorter growing season, some viticulturists have begun planting grapes vertically rather than horizontally to avoid excess sun.

- Chaptalization (the addition of sugar) is now rarely used

- Winemakers increasingly are using natural rather than laboratory yeasts

- The European Union has standardized basic wine labeling rules for member nations, and countries exporting to the EU (and worldwide) are following their regulations. For example, one new law states that if a grape is on the label, the wine must contain a minimum of 85 percent of that grape.

## The Business of Wine

Besides the tremendous elevation in wine quality, the business of wine has also benefited greatly from the global planting of *Vitis vinifera* grapes. Cabernet Sauvignon, Merlot, Pinot Noir, Chardonnay, Riesling, Sauvignon Blanc, and other familiar grapes are now grown throughout the world, making it easier for consumers to buy unfamiliar wines with the expectation that they will be getting a wine that is familiar in style and of a fairly consistent quality.

Here are a few of the most significant advances in the business of wine:

- Most wines sold in the United States (about 70 percent) retail for $7 or less

- China is now the fifth biggest wine consumer in the world. Imports in that country have doubled over the last few years, and they are now the number-one importer of Bordeaux. The Chinese are primarily drinking red (their lucky color) wine. Consumption has increased more than 150% from 2007 to 2013.

- When I began my study of wine in 1970, Europe was by far the number-one producer of wine in the world, with 78 percent of the total. In 2013, Europe dropped to 63 percent and the United States increased from 16 percent to 18.5 percent of worldwide wine production.

- Wine has enjoyed the largest growth rate of all alcoholic beverages since 2001

- American wine names are becoming more creative, for example: Ménage à Trois, Gnarly Head, Red Truck, Pinot Evil, Killer Juice, Marilyn Merlot, Kick Ass Red, and Mad Housewife

- In 2005, the U.S. Supreme Court approved the interstate shipping of wine directly to consumers, causing most states to rewrite their wine laws. FedEx and UPS are delivering wine directly to consumers, which is now legal in at least 42 states.

- The quality of American wine lists has never been better. Although some restaurants have created "monster" lists for promotional purposes (and intimidating "new" wine drinkers), others list only the best wines in each category. You can now find wine lists in diners all across America!

- Costco sells annually over $1.4 billion in wine, making it the largest retailer of wine in the United States. In 2010, Costco spent over $22 million to help get Washington State's laws changed away from state control to privitization of wine sales.

- Consolidation has reduced the number of U.S. wine wholesalers by 50 percent: two companies, Southern Wine & Spirits and the Charmer Sunbelt Group, control 38 percent of U.S. liquor and wine distribution

- Celebrity branding is big, from baseball stars (Tom Seaver) to race-car drivers (Jeff Gordon, Mario Andretti) to musicians (Bob Dylan, Dave Matthews) to golf players (Greg Norman) to actors (Drew Barrymore) to politicians (Nancy Pelosi). Celebrity wine sales exceeded $50 million in 2013.

- Thanks to Wine 2.0—and wine blogs—now everyone can become a wine critic or ask the critics questions on eRobertParker.com, *Wine Spectator*'s blog index, winelibrary.com, *Wine Enthusiast*'s UnReserved, or Dr. Vino, to name just a few

- Wine in a box is becoming more popular, especially among California jug wine producers, to reduce greenhouse emissions and lower carbon footprints due to the high cost of making and shipping glass

- Exports of American wine went from almost nothing in 1970 to over $1.39 billion in 2013!

## Wine Consumers

Combining better quality, familiar varietals, and expert marketing has given consumers worldwide some of the best wines ever produced at some of the most reasonable prices. Consumers today have a better selection of wine at all price points than ever before. And it promises to get even better in the future!

Here are my picks for the wine consumer highlights of the last forty years:

- Americans are drinking more and better wine than ever before. Wine consumption in the United States has reached a record 856 million gallons—an increase of over 600 million gallons since 1970. In 2012, the United States became the world's largest market with sales over $40 billion. The per capita consumption went from 1.31 gallons in 1970 to 3.03 gallons in 2012.

- 2012 was the nineteenth consecutive year of growth in U.S. wine consumption, with total wine sales reaching over 347 million cases

- The millennial generation (ages 21–34), with 70 million people strong, has shown the largest percentage increase in wine consumption over generation X (ages 34–44, 44 million) and the baby boomers (ages 45–63, 77 million). Baby boomers account for 40 percent of wine consumed, millenials 26 percent.

- U.S. wine events proliferate, and almost all donate some proceeds to charity. In 2012, Auction Napa Valley raised more than $8 million, and in 2013, the Naples, Florida, wine festival raised $8.6 million.

- Wine lovers turn increasingly to auctions: worldwide auction sales totaled $389 million in 2012, compared to $33 million in 1994. U.S. auction sales in 2012 were over $131.8 million, and Internet auction sales exceeded $39.3 million.

- Buyer beware: Fraudulent wines have become more prevalent! (Read *The Billionaire's Vinegar*.)

- The best châteaux of Bordeaux have been priced out of reach for the average consumer. Some 2009 Bordeaux sell at over $3,500 a bottle! You can "thank" China for their new interest in Bordeaux wines.

- In France, Spain, and Italy, wine consumption has dropped more than 50 percent since 1970

- Since his first review in 1978, American wine critic Robert Parker has become an international icon with his 100-point scoring method. In 2013 he sold the *Wine Advocate* to three investors from Singapore but will continue to write about Bordeaux and the Rhône Valley.

- *Super Wines*
  - California started producing super-premium wines, such as Opus One and Harlan Estate

  - "Super Tuscans," such as Sassicaia and Ornellaia, have become collector's items

  - "Super Everywhere" wines priced over $100 are now available from wine regions in Australia, Chile, Argentina, and South Africa, but are they selling?

# Prelude
# to Wine

WINE FLAVORS • GRAPES • FERMENTATION • MATURATION AND AGING •

ON TASTING WINE • THE 60-SECOND WINE EXPERT •

WHITE GRAPES OF THE WORLD • RED GRAPES OF THE WORLD

VIDEO
http://bit.ly/fRjujW

PRONUNCIATIONS
http://bit.ly/ApAJ1q

*At the beginning of each class, and at various points throughout the book, you will see links like the ones above. Use your smartphone or web browser to access videos of Kevin guiding you through the book and pronunciation guides.*

SCIENTISTS ARE beginning to be able to identify the aroma compounds in wine by name, but tasters are likely to stick with existing lingo. Who would want to remember methoxypyrazine for "green bell pepper," or linalool and geraniol for "floral"?

A BOTTLE of wine (750 ml) is 86% water.

A BOTTLE of wine contains 600–800 grapes (2.4 lbs.).

**A SAMPLING OF THE MAJOR GRAPES**

*Vitis vinifera*
Chardonnay
Cabernet Sauvignon

*Vitis labrusca*
Concord
Catawba

*Hybrids*
Seyval Blanc
Baco Noir

# Wine Flavors

WHAT CAUSES the tastes, aromas, and flavors of wine? How does a wine made from grapes smell of cherries, lemongrass, or apples if those things are not added to the fermentation vat and no artificial flavorings are used?

The biology and chemistry of each of these sources give us the main tastes of wine—sweet, sour, and sometimes bitter—and the aroma compounds that we associate with different foods, spices, or minerals. These aroma compounds are often the same as those in actual cherries, lemongrass, or apples, but they form due to the complicated biology of grapes, or the metabolic action of yeast, or the many other chemical interactions of the winemaking and aging process.

Wine's flavors come from three main sources:

**GRAPES**
**FERMENTATION**
**MATURATION AND AGING**

Following the winemaking process from grape to bottle will give us a chance to see just how tastes and aromas form in our wine.

## FLAVORS FROM GRAPES

### Is all wine made from the same kind of grape?

No. The major wine grapes come from the species *Vitis vinifera*. All over the world, winemakers use *Vitis vinifera*, which includes many different varieties of grapes—both red and white. However, there are other grapes also used for winemaking. The most important native grape species in America is *Vitis labrusca*, which is grown widely in New York State as well as other East Coast and Midwest states. Hybrids, which are also used, are a cross between *Vitis vinifera* and native American grape species such as *Vitis labrusca*.

### Do all grapes have the same flavor?

The grape variety has a huge influence on wine flavor. Varietal character—the usual or expected taste and aroma of a particular grape—is an important concept in winemaking, and each type of grape has typical characteristics to offer. For example, black grapes with thick skins tend to produce wines high in tannin, which equates to bitterness and astringency when a wine is young. Riesling grapes tend to produce wines high in acidity (sourness and tartness) and Muscat grapes produce highly aromatic wines that smell of orange flowers. Many different aspects of varietal character come through in the wine. One of the challenges of the winemaker is to either preserve or tame the distinctive qualities of grapes to create a wine that is well balanced.

## Does it matter where grapes are planted?

Yes, it does. Grapes are agricultural products that require specific growing conditions.

Just as you wouldn't try to grow oranges in Maine, you wouldn't try to grow grapes at the North Pole. There are limitations on where vines can be grown. Some of these limitations are the growing season, the number of days of sunlight, the angle of the sun, the average temperature, and rainfall. Soil is of primary concern, and adequate drainage is a requisite. The right amount of sun ripens the grapes properly to give them their sugar.

## Where are the best locations to plant grapes?

Traditionally, many grape varieties produce better wines when planted in certain locations. For example, most red grapes need a longer growing season than do white grapes, so red grapes are usually planted in warmer locations. In colder northern regions—in Germany and northern France, for instance—most vineyards are planted with white grapes. In the warmer regions of Italy, Spain, and Portugal, and in California's Napa Valley, the red grape thrives.

## What is terroir?

The concept of terroir can be difficult to grasp because it is conceptual rather than scientific. It is the "somewhereness" of a particular region or vineyard, including the soil makeup and geography; sunlight, weather, and climate; rainfall; the natural plant life of the area; and many other elements. Many winemakers believe that terroir has an impact on the flavor of wine, and in

VITIS is Latin for "vine."
VINUM is Latin for "wine."

**THREE HIGH-TANNIN GRAPES**

Nebbiolo
Cabernet Sauvignon
Syrah/Shiraz

**THREE AROMATIC GRAPES**

Muscat
Gewürztraminer
Torrontés

*"And Noah began to be a husbandman and he planted a vineyard, and he drank of the wine."* —GENESIS 9:20–21

PLANTING OF vineyards for winemaking began more than 8,000 years ago near the Black Sea in places like Georgia.

VINES ARE planted during their dormant periods, usually in the months of April and May. Most vines will continue to produce good-quality grapes for 40 years or more.

WINEMAKERS SAY that winemaking begins in the vineyard with the growing of the grapes.

**KEVIN ZRALY'S BEST WINE REGIONS ON EARTH**

| | |
|---|---|
| Bordeaux | Piedmont |
| Burgundy | Rhein |
| Champagne | Rhône Valley |
| Douro (Port) | Rioja |
| Mosel | Sonoma |
| Napa | Tuscany |

fact, the effects on grape quality of certain aspects of terroir, such as sunlight and soil drainage, are measurable.

**The "taste" of soil:** Soil type is one aspect of terroir that is widely believed to carry through into the finished wine. In general terms, this flavor can be described as "minerality." Certain wine regions are famous for the apparent effect of their soil on the wines they produce, which are said to taste of that soil type. German Rieslings may taste of the slate they grow in; likewise, in Burgundy the Chardonnay grapes, which grow in limestone, may show aromas of gunflint or wet river pebbles. Grapevines do not absorb soil through their roots, and the minerals they take in are in trace amounts that may be available in any soil, making it more likely that minerality is a result of some other aspect of terroir or regional winemaking processes. Still, proponents of terroir swear by the flavor of the land in wine. The mystery deepens when you consider that a sea brine aroma may be apparent in Muscadet, grown at the mouth of the Loire River in France.

**The taste of nearby plants:** On the other hand, the aromas of regional plants in wine are likely to come from the plants themselves. Eucalyptus aroma in wine has been shown in some cases to come from the transfer of eucalyptus oil from nearby trees to the grapes. The aroma of garrigue, the scrubby mixture of evergreen plants and herbs such as rosemary and wild thyme that grows in the southern Rhône Valley and around the Mediterranean, may find its way into wine in the same way.

## When is the harvest?

Grapes are picked when they reach the proper sugar/acid ratio for the style of wine the vintner wants to produce. Go to a vineyard in June and taste one of the small green grapes. Your mouth will pucker because the grape is so tart and acidic. Return to the same vineyard—even to that same vine—in September or October, and the grapes will taste sweet. All those months of sun have given sugar to the grape as a result of photosynthesis.

June
3% acid
0 Brix

July
2.3% acid
10 Brix

August
1.7% acid
15 Brix

Harvest
September
0.9% acid
22 Brix

## What effect does weather have on the grapes?

Weather can interfere with the quality of the harvest, as well as its quantity. In the spring, as vines emerge from dormancy, a sudden frost may stop the flowering, thereby reducing the yields. Even a strong windstorm can affect the grapes adversely at this crucial time. Not enough rain, too much rain, or rain at the wrong time can also wreak havoc.

Rain just before the harvest will swell the grapes with water, diluting the juice and making thin, watery wines. Lack of rain will affect the wine's balance by creating a more powerful and concentrated wine, but will result in a smaller crop. A severe drop in temperature may affect the vines even outside the growing season. Case in point: In New York State the winter of 2003–04 was one of the coldest in fifty years. The result was a major decrease in wine production, with some vineyards losing more than 50 percent of their crop for the 2004 vintage.

## What can the vineyard owner do in the case of adverse weather?

A number of countermeasures are available to the grower. Some of these measures are used while the grapes are on the vine; others are part of the winemaking process.

| PROBLEM | RESULTS IN | SOME SOLUTIONS |
| --- | --- | --- |
| Frost | Reduced yield | Various frost protection methods: wind machines, sprinkler systems, and flaming heaters |
| Not enough sun | Underripe, green herbal, vegetal character, high acid, low sugar | Chaptalization (see pages 9–10) |
| Too much sun | Overripe, high-alcohol, prune character | Amelioration (the addition of water) |
| Too much rain | Thin, watery wines | Pray for drier weather! |
| Mildew | Rot | Spray with copper sulfate |
| Drought | Scorched grapes | Irrigate or pray for rain |
| High alcohol | Change in the balance of the components | De-alcoholize |
| High acidity | Sour, tart wine | De-acidify |
| Phylloxera (see page 6) | Dead vines | Graft vines onto resistant rootstock |

STORM STORIES

- The 2011 vintage was a challenging one around the world, from too much rain, heat waves, frost, and cool weather, especially in the regions of Bordeaux, Burgundy, and Tuscany.
- In 2010, an earthquake in Chile devastated that year's vintage. Most of the damage came when the earthquake caused large storage tanks to topple over, resulting in a loss of an estimated 125 million liters. That, combined with electricity outages at wineries and the damage to warehouses and irrigation structures, caused huge losses.
- In 2009, major fires hit the Yarra Valley during the start of the harvest
- In 2008, a spring frost damaged vineyards all over the state of California. It was the worst frost since the early seventies.
- In 2008, Australia got hit with everything—the worst drought ever and scorching heat in South Australia and record-breaking rain and major flooding in the Hunter Valley
- In Alsace, France, a hailstorm in June 2007 destroyed entire vineyards
- In 2007, hailstorms in Mendoza, Argentina, from December to February dramatically reduced yields
- In 2004, Burgundy suffered major hailstorms in July and August that damaged or destroyed at least 40% of the grapes
- The historic 2003 heat wave in Europe changed the balance of the traditional style of wines produced in most regions
- A spring frost damaged 80% of the 2002 vintage Champagne grapes
- Poor weather conditions for the 2002 vintage in Tuscany resulted in no production of Chianti Classico Reserva
- In 2002, the Piedmont region of Italy (Barolo, Barbaresco) was hit with a September hailstorm that destroyed some of the best vineyards in the region

(continued)

• A rainy September made the 2001 Champagne harvest the wettest since 1873
• From 1989 to 1999 in Bordeaux, France, it rained during the harvest of eight out of ten vintages, which affected picking dates, yields, and the quality of the wine
• An April frost in Bordeaux destroyed more than 50% of 1991's grape harvest

GRAPEVINES can grow and produce limited quantities of fruit for more than 100 years. The Champagne house Bollinger still harvests vines planted in the mid-1800s.

ALTHOUGH THE words "old vines" or "vieilles vignes" on a wine label are not legally regulated, most winemakers agree that vines must be at least 35 years old to qualify.

A VINE doesn't usually produce grapes suitable for winemaking until the third year.

ONE OF the few countries to escape phylloxera is Chile. Chilean wine producers imported their vines from France in the 1860s, before phylloxera attacked the French vineyards.

IN THE early 1980s, phylloxera became a problem in the vineyards of California. Vineyard owners were forced to replant their vines at a cost of $15,000 to $25,000 per acre, costing the California wine industry over $1 billion.

## Why is ripeness important?

The concept of vintage in wine—as in "2009 was a great vintage in Bordeaux"—involves all the weather and other events in the vineyard during the growing season, but in the end it comes right back to the ripeness of the grapes at harvest. Were the grapes picked at the perfect moment in their development, when acidity, sugars, and flavors had peaked? And did this happen before the first killing frost and before a heavy rain could dilute the juice or cause rot?

When grapes are ripe, they contain higher sugar levels, which generally translate to higher alcohol at fermentation and fuller body in the final wine. The flavors and aromas of ripe grapes are also fully developed for the possibility of greater richness and complexity in the wine. Green (unripe) grapes may result in wine with high acidity that is out of balance with the wine's flavors, and high tannin from grape skins that have not fully developed. The winemaker may also have trouble achieving an acceptable level of alcohol from fermentation. Measures may be taken in the winery to correct these problems, but often it is not possible to completely undo the effects of green grapes.

## Does the age of the vines matter?

Older grapevines produce fewer bunches of grapes that tend to have smaller berries and concentrated flavors—a greater intensity of aroma and flavor that is apparent in the wine made from these grapes.

## What is phylloxera?

Phylloxera, a grape louse, is one of the grapevine's worst enemies because it eventually kills the entire plant. An epidemic infestation in the 1870s came close to destroying all the vineyards of Europe. Luckily, the roots of native American vines are immune to this louse. After this was discovered, all the European vines were pulled up and grafted onto phylloxera-resistant American rootstocks.

## What is "noble rot"?

For almost all wines, rot is undesirable—and can be disastrous. But a few of the world's finest sweet wines couldn't be made without the presence of *Botrytis cinerea,* or "noble rot." The classic sweet wines of Sauternes, German

Beerenauslese and Trockenbeerenauslese, and the Hungarian Tokaji Aszú all have a distinctive honeyed flavor due to the presence of this type of rot. Because *Botrytis* decreases the water content of the grape berries before harvest, wines made from grapes with noble rot also have an intensity of flavor not found in conventionally harvested wines. The rot affects grape bunches gradually, so growers have the option of picking when grapes are only partially affected, or waiting for a thorough onset. This means it is possible to taste only slight *Botrytis* in a wine, or to get the full impact.

# FLAVORS FROM FERMENTATION

## What is fermentation and how long does it take?

Fermentation is the process by which the grape juice turns into wine. The simple formula for fermentation is:

$$\text{Sugar} + \text{Yeast} = \text{Alcohol} + \text{Carbon Dioxide (CO}_2\text{)}$$

The fermentation process begins when the grapes are crushed and ends when all of the sugar has been converted to alcohol or the alcohol level has reached around 15 percent, the point at which the alcohol kills off the yeast. Sugar is naturally present in the ripe grape through photosynthesis. Yeast also occurs naturally as the white bloom on the grape skin. However, this natural yeast is not always used in today's winemaking. Laboratory strains of pure yeast have been isolated and may be used often, each strain contributing something unique to the style of the wine. The carbon dioxide dissipates into the air, except in Champagne and other sparkling wines, in which this gas is retained through a special process which we will discuss in Class Eight.

The winemaking process, in which yeast consumes sugars in the grape must and produces alcohol and carbon dioxide, is also crucial to creating flavors and aromas in wine. Depending on the temperature of the fermentation, it may take less than a week (for red wines) or a few weeks or even months (for white and sweet wines). The temperature—"hot fermentation" or "cold fermentation"—also affects the types of flavors created.

Many other factors come into play in creating flavor, such as whether the wine is fermented in stainless steel tanks (which are inert; they impart no

IN THE United States, "table wine" is considered to have at least 7% alcohol, but at least 11% is optimal for grape wine.

**NEW WINEMAKING AND GRAPE-GROWING CATCH PHRASES**

Reductive winemaking
Cold soaking of grapes
Phenolic ripening
Green harvesting

**TYPICAL ALCOHOL CONTENT OF SELECTED WINES**

German Riesling 8–12.5%
Champagne 12%
Most white wines 11.5–13.5%
Most red wines 12–14.5%
California Cabernet Sauvignon 13–15%
Sherry 15–22%
Port 20%

FOR WINES sold in the United States, the percentage alcohol listed on the label is allowed a margin of 1.5% above or below the percentage stated, up to 14%. So, a wine labeled 13.5% alcohol could be as low as 12% or as high as 15%.

ALCOHOL, when consumed in moderation, will increase HDL (good cholesterol) and decrease LD (bad cholesterol).

MOG MEANS material other than grapes.

MUST IS the juice and skin mixture that comes from the grapes.

PRESSING OF white grape must is a delicate process usually done with high-tech equipment which prevents a forceful pressing that will extract bitter tannins from the skins and seeds.

aroma) or oak vats (which may add a slight oak flavor and tannin to the wine), as well as the type of yeast the winemaker uses for fermentation.

## Does the alcohol content in wine affect the tastes, flavors, and body of wine?

Yes, the more alcohol there is in a wine, the more body (weight) there will be.

Alcohol is more viscous than water, so the higher a wine's alcohol content, the fuller-bodied it is likely to be. Riper grapes at harvest contain more natural sugar, which gives the yeast more to ferment into alcohol.

"Extract"—the total solid material present in the liquid of wine—also contributes to body. Extract includes tannins, proteins, and other microscopic solids, and can be increased by macerating (see page 9) the grapes before or after fermentation, and by choosing not to filter the wine. Residual sugar remaining in the wine after fermentation is also part of the extract and contributes greatly to body—sweet wines usually have more body than dry wines.

## What's the first step in the fermentation process?

The grapes are brought in from the vineyards, ideally packed carefully in small crates so they don't get crushed and begin fermentation before their time. When making great wine, the fruit is hand-sorted on a conveyor belt to remove sticks, leaves, stones, and other mog.

The first decision of the winemaker is whether to destem the grapes. White grapes almost always go through the destemming machine. For red wine, leaving some or all of the stems intact will add tannin when the juice, skins, and stems are soaked together. The grapes may also be put through a crusher, which breaks the berries.

## Are red wines and white wines made the same way?

After the grapes are sorted and destemmed and possibly crushed, red and white winemaking follow different paths, primarily due to the grape skins. All grape skins contain flavor compounds that are essential to the success of the wine. But skins (and seeds) also contain tannin, which can cause bitterness and astringency in young wines. Past a certain point, tannin is undesirable in white wines. For this reason, after crushing, the white grape must is usually pressed immediately to separate the juice for fermentation.

Some types of white grapes may be allowed to soak for a certain time with the skins, a process called skin contact. This allows varietal flavors and aromas—those specific to the grape variety—to be extracted from the skins, and creates a richer flavor in the wine.

## Can white wine be made from red grapes?

Yes. The color of wine comes primarily from the grape skins. By removing the skins immediately after picking, no color is imparted to the wine, and it will be white. In the Champagne region of France, a large percentage of the grapes grown are red, yet most of the resulting wine is white. California's White Zinfandel is made from red Zinfandel grapes.

## What is maceration?

Unlike white skins and juice, which are separated before fermentation, the must of black grapes goes directly to the fermentation vats. There, it may undergo "maceration," or soaking to extract aromas, tannins, and color from the skins. Maceration increases aroma intensity and the wine's mouth-feel—the weight and texture of the wine in your mouth. The winemaker may choose to macerate the must before and/or after fermentation.

## What is carbonic maceration?

You may have noticed that Beaujolais, from Burgundy, France, has a particularly light and fruity flavor, with an aroma of fresh crushed strawberries or red raspberries. This is due to a process called carbonic maceration, in which the grape berries are carefully left whole and undergo a type of fermentation *inside each berry*, without the assistance of yeast. Eventually, normal fermentation takes place, but the initial, whole-berry fermentation gives the wines a brighter color and that distinctive tutti-frutti.

## Is sugar ever added to wine?

Sometimes, sugar is added to wine before fermentation in regions where this is permitted. The process is called chaptalization (after Jean-Antoine Chaptal, a proponent of it in the early 1800s), and it allows sugar to be added to grape must so the yeast is able to generate more alcohol in the final wine. The sugar

**WHAT IS RESIDUAL SUGAR?**

Some of the natural sugars in ripe grapes remain undigested by yeast after fermentation. This is referred to as residual sugar in the wine, or RS. A wine with no RS, or RS below a certain legal level, is a "dry" wine.

THE EUROPEAN UNION RULES that a wine labeled "dry" can have up to 4 grams of sugar per liter. A wine labeled "sweet" can have 45 grams per liter.

SUR LIE, a French term, is used when a wine is left aging with its sediment, such as dead yeast cells and grape skins and seeds.

WILD YEAST is airborne in vineyards all over the world, and it is possible to conduct a fermentation using only the yeast present on the grape skins at harvest. Some winemakers choose to use cultured yeast, however, which can give a more predictable flavor.

is used to compensate for grapes that do not have enough of their own natural sugars to produce a wine of sufficient alcohol—basically, to compensate for underripe grapes. Chaptalization does not result in a sweet wine, since all of the sugars are converted into alcohol.

## Does the yeast have a flavor?

Yeast does have a flavor, as you know if you have ever smelled or eaten freshly baked bread. In winemaking, the yeast always has some impact on the flavor of the wine, but whether it is detectable depends on choices made by the winemaker. There is one sure way to create a yeasty aroma in wine: lees contact.

Lees are the dead yeast cells and other solids that settle to the bottom of the wine after fermentation. Often in white winemaking, when fermentation takes place in barrels, the wine will be left in the barrels with the lees for up to a year after fermentation has ended. This lees contact gives the wine a rich mouthfeel and a brioche or bread-roll aroma—the same effect yeast has in Champagne making. The influence of lees can be increased by stirring the lees in the barrels, a process called *bâtonnage*.

## What is tannin, and is it desirable in wine?

WALNUTS AND TEA also contain tannin.

BESIDES TANNIN, red wine contains resveratrol, which in medical studies has been associated with anticancer properties.

KING TUTANKHAMEN, who died in 1327 B.C., apparently preferred the taste of red wine, according to scientists who found ancient residues of red-wine compounds (tannins) in jars found in his tomb.

Tannin is a natural preservative and is one of the many components that give wine its longevity. It comes from skins, pits, and stems of the grapes. Another source of tannin is wood, such as the oak barrels in which some wines are aged or fermented. Generally, red wines have a higher level of tannin than whites because red grapes are usually left to ferment with their skins.

A word used to describe the sensation of tannins is "astringent." Especially in young wines, tannin can be very astringent and make the wine taste bitter. Tannin is not a taste, however—it's a tactile sensation.

Tannin is also found in strong tea. And what can you add to tea to make it less astringent? Milk—the fat and the proteins in milk soften the tannin. And so it is with a highly tannic wine. If you take another milk by-product, such as cheese, and have it with wine, it softens the tannin and makes the wine more appealing. Enjoy a beef entrée or one served with a cream sauce and a young, tannic red wine to experience it for yourself.

## Is acidity desirable in wine?

All wine will have a certain amount of acidity. Generally, white wines have more perceived acidity than reds, though winemakers try to have a balance of fruit and acid. An overly acidic wine is also described as tart or sour. Acidity is a very important component in the aging of wines.

## What is malolactic fermentation?

Malolactic fermentation ("malo") takes place after the alcoholic fermentation and any lees contact. Almost all red wines undergo malo for an increased stability after bottling, but it is used very selectively for whites.

Grapes have a high level of tart malic acid at harvest, the same acidity as in green apples. For most red wines and some whites, the winemaker will allow lactic bacteria naturally present to start a malolactic fermentation and convert some amount of that puckery malic acid into softer lactic acid. Malo is avoided for most white wines, except for some Chardonnays, because a tart acidity is often desirable, and because malo tends to give wines a buttery flavor. If you have ever had a rich, buttery California Chardonnay, you have tasted the effects of malo.

# FLAVORS FROM MATURATION AND AGING

## How does aging in barrels affect the flavor of wine?

Barrels have been used to ferment, mature, and ship wine for thousands of years. Early in the history of barrel use, it was discovered that different kinds of barrels, or different sizes, could be used for varying amounts of time to impart certain flavors to wine. These flavors range from woody or cedar to vanilla, clove, or coconut, depending on the source of the barrels and how they were made.

Relatively recent alternatives to barrels, such as cement vats or stainless steel tanks, allow wines to remain free of oak flavors, for a bright, fruity effect.

Most wines in the world are made with no oak aging, and it is up to the winemaker to determine the type and amount of oak influence in wine.

---

**FIVE HIGH-ACID GRAPES**

Riesling (white)
Chenin Blanc (white)
Barbera (red)
Sangiovese (red)
Pinot Noir (red)

AS SUGAR levels increase, the "perceived" taste of acidity decreases.

THE NAME *malic acid* comes from the Latin word for apple, *mālum*.

*Large barrels versus small:* The larger the barrel, the lower the ratio of barrel surface area to volume: less of the wine by volume will be in direct contact with the surface of the barrel. Barrels range in size from 1,000- or 1,200-liter giants down to less than 100 liters. The largest barrels will have little if any flavor impact on the wine. The barrel size most recognizable to consumers is the 225-liter *barrique* used in Bordeaux.

*Oak flavor:* The wood cells inside the barrel impart their flavors and tannins when they come into contact with the alcohol in wine, adding an oak flavor. New barrels impart more flavor; as barrels are used again and again, the wine leaches much of the flavor and tannin from the cells, leaving the barrel "neutral." It is not only flavor and tannin that come from barrels, however—they also allow more oxygen contact with the wine. Barrels used in their first three years to impart flavor may be kept for many more simply to give wines a very slow oxidation. Winemakers often age a percentage of a given wine in new barrels and the rest in neutral barrels, then blend the two to achieve the desired wine style.

*Toast:* When barrels are formed, they are held over a heat source (fire) which makes the wood pliable and easier to bend. It also will toast the wood inside the barrel. The more the flame chars the interior, the more of a barrier there will be between the cells of the oak and the wine. This means less tannin and wood flavor will leach into the wine. But the toasting process imparts flavors of its own. Winemakers can order barrels with different degrees of toast depending on what flavors they want. Light toast gives few flavors of its own, but still allows the wine access to heavy tannin from the oak cells. Medium toast often gives the wine a vanilla or caramel flavor. Heavy toast can taste like cloves, cinnamon, smoke, or coffee.

*American oak, French oak, or Eastern European oak:* Oak for barrels comes from all over the United States and Europe. American oak barrels are less expensive, but European oak adds a different intensity and flavor to the wine. Winemakers source barrels according to what flavor and tannin profile they want for the wine. Differences in flavor are due to the different species of oak, different grains of the wood, and variations in barrel making.

## What does "unfiltered" mean on the label?

After any barrel aging and before the wine is bottled, it may be filtered to remove stray yeast cells or bacteria, microscopic bits of grape material, and other potentially unstable solids. The winemaker can choose to give the wine a light filtration or a heavier one. Heavy filtration can strip out so much of the solid matter from the wine that flavor and texture are also lost—and some winemakers and consumers believe that wine should remain unfiltered, in its more natural state, for a fuller, truer flavor experience. "Unfiltered" wine may be slightly less clear-looking than filtered wine, and have a fuller body and richer mouthfeel, a more intense flavor, and even some sediment on the bottom of the bottle.

## What is meant by "vintage"? Why is one year considered better than another?

A vintage indicates the year the grapes were harvested, so every year is a vintage year. A vintage chart reflects the weather conditions for various years. Better weather usually results in a better rating for the vintage, and therefore a higher likelihood that the wine will age well.

THE FIRST known reference to a specific vintage was made by Roman scientist Pliny the Elder, who rated the wines of 121 B.C. "of the highest excellence."

2005 WAS a great vintage year in every major wine region on earth!

## Are all wines meant to be aged?

No. It's a common misconception that all wines improve with age. In fact, more than 90 percent of all the wines made in the world should be consumed within one year, and less than 1 percent of the world's wines should be aged for more than five years. Wines change with age. Some get better, but most do not. The good news is that the 1 percent represents more than 350 million bottles of wine every vintage.

## What impact does aging have on the flavor of red wine?

Wine is like a living organism that is always changing from the moment it is made. Even once it is bottled, it ages due to the effects of oxygen, and due to various reactions that cause tannins to drop to the bottom of the bottle as grainy sediment, new flavors to develop, and color goes from pale slowly toward brown.

TO IDENTIFY the flavor of oxidation in wine, think of Sherry, which is intentionally oxidized during winemaking.

As tannins become sediment, the tannin in the wine itself is decreased, so the wine tastes gentler, with more fruit, tannin, and acid balance. When wine is young, its fruit flavors are fresh; as it ages, the fruit may taste dried (dried cherries, prunes, dates) and the wine may develop vegetal aromas (mushrooms, canned peas, or asparagus). Oxygen also makes itself known in the form of a gradual browning of the wine's color and a gradual nutty flavor.

## What makes a wine last more than five years?

**The color and the grape:** Red wines, because of their tannin content, will generally age longer than whites. And certain red grapes, such as Cabernet Sauvignon, tend to have more tannin than, say, Pinot Noir.

**The vintage:** The better the weather conditions in one year, the more likely the wines from that vintage will have a better balance of fruits, acids, and tannins, and therefore have the potential to age longer.

**Where the wine comes from:** Certain vineyards have optimum conditions for growing grapes, including such factors as soil, weather, drainage, and slope of the land. All of this contributes to producing a great wine that will taste better after aging.

**How the wine was made (vinification):** The longer the wine remains in contact with its skins during fermentation (maceration), and if it is fermented and/or aged in oak, the more of the natural preservative tannin it will have, which can help it age longer. These are just two examples of how winemaking can affect the aging of wine.

**Wine storage conditions:** Even the best-made wines in the world will not age well if they are improperly stored. (Best storage conditions: 55°F and 75 percent humidity).

## What are some examples of bad flavors?

Successful winemaking depends on the cooperation of certain microorganisms—and equally on the good behavior of others. Occasionally, things go wrong. Here are the five most common wine faults or flaws, and what they taste like.

    **Corked wine:** A common misconception about corked wine is that it has to do with bits of cork floating in the glass. In fact, "corked" is a term used to describe a musty aroma in wine caused by the organic compound commonly called trichloroanisole (TCA). There are many theories of how TCA affects the cork. But we do know that when TCA in the cork comes into contact with wine in the bottle, it causes a smell similar to wet or mildewed cardboard. This can range in strength from almost undetectable (when it merely dulls the flavor of the wine) to a strong reek that can be smelled from across the room.

There is no remedy for corked wine. Because it causes huge losses in the wine industry each year, many winemakers are switching to screw-cap closures instead of natural cork.

**Oxidation:** Just as a cut apple oxidizes when exposed to air, grape juice undergoes a transformation through contact with oxygen. Oxygen begins its interaction with grape juice the moment the grapes are harvested and brought to the winery, and much of winemaking is about carefully protecting the wine from oxygen. Many winemakers, depending on the style of wine they produce, allow controlled oxidation to add an additional layer of flavor in their wine. Accidental overexposure to oxygen results in browning of the wine and a nutty, sherrylike flavor.

**Sulfur:** Sulfur dioxide is a natural antioxidant, preservative, and disinfectant used by most winemakers at various stages of the winemaking process to prevent unwanted oxidation of the grape juice and to inhibit the action of bacteria or wild yeast. If the level of sulfur in the finished wine is not carefully monitored, you will know by the smell (burnt match) if the sulfur was overused. If there is any hint of sulfur dioxide in the wine, I consider that to be a flaw.

**Brett:** If you have ever tasted a wine with an aroma of a barnyard, or more specifically, sweaty saddle, or sweaty horse, you've tasted Brett. Brett is short for *Brettanomyces*, a yeast that may grow in the winery—particularly on equipment or in barrels that have not been carefully cleaned—and will infect wine that comes into contact with it. For some, Brett is not all that bad: it is considered by many tasters to add a desirable complexity to the flavor of wine when it is present at low levels.

**Volatile acidity:** There is a certain level of desirable volatile acidity, or VA, in all wines, but VA becomes a fault when the bacteria acetobacter—the bacteria used to create vinegar—goes to work. Acetobacter creates excess acetic acid in wine, which in high concentrations causes the wine to smell like vinegar.

**FOR FURTHER READING**

I recommend *From Vines to Wine* by Jeff Cox, *The Art and Science of Wine* by James Halliday, and *The Vintner's Apprentice* by Eric Miller.

93% OF all wines of New Zealand and 75% of all wines from Australia are bottled with screw caps.

SHERRY WINE is made by allowing the wine to be in contact with oxygen.

WHILE IT is possible for winemakers to avoid adding any sulfur during winemaking, all wines contain at least a small amount because sulfur is produced by the yeast during fermentation.

SULFUR IS a common preservative in foods such as dried fruit.

ACCORDING TO *Wines & Vines*, the value of wine sold worldwide is now more than $100 billion.

THERE ARE over 800 wine regions in the world.

THERE ARE more than 60 wine-producing countries in the world.

THE SIX major wine importers into the United States in 2012:
1. Italy (30%)
2. France (24%)
3. Australia (14%)
4. Chile (7%)
5. Argentina (6%)
6. Spain (6%)
These six countries account for over 86% of the total wines imported into the United States.

THE TOP ten producers of wine in the world in 2012:
1. France          6. Australia
2. Italy           7. Germany
3. Spain           8. South Africa
4. United States   9. Chile
5. Argentina      10. Portugal
Over 50% of all wine production in the world is from Italy, France, Spain, and the United States.

## WINDOWS ON WINE 2012

World production: 39 billion bottles
World consumption: 33 billion bottles
Acres of vineyards: 19.6 million

THE TOP three countries in wine grape acreage worldwide:
1. Spain
2. France
3. Italy

# GRAPE VARIETIES AND THEIR FLAVORS

| GRAPE VARIETY | GRAPE FLAVORS | WINEMAKING FLAVORS |
|---|---|---|
| **Cabernet Sauvignon** | Cassis (black currant) Blackberry Violets | Pencil shavings Toast Tobacco—dead leaf |
| **Grenache** | Cherries Raspberries Spicy | Concentrations Extraction |
| **Merlot** | Blackberries Black olive Plum | Pencil shavings Toast |
| **Nebbiolo** | Plum Raspberries Truffle Acidity | Strong tea Nutmeg Gamey |
| **Pinot Noir** | Perfumed Raspberries Red cherry Acidity | Smoky Earthy |
| **Sangiovese** | Black cherries Blackberries Violets Spice | Cedar Plum Vanilla |
| **Syrah/Shiraz** | Spicy Black fruits Blueberry | Toasty Vanilla Coffee |
| **Tempranillo** | Fruity Cherries | Oak (American) Tobacco |
| **Zinfandel** | Spicy Ripe berries Cherries | Savory Tar Chocolate |
| **Chardonnay** | Apple Melon Pear | Vanilla Toast Butterscotch |
| **Riesling** | Minerality Citrus Tropical fruit Acidity | Steely Green apples Petrol |
| **Sauvignon Blanc** | Tomato stalk Cut grass Grapefuit Citrus Aromatic | Coconut Smoky Vanilla |

MATURATION AND AGING FLAVORS
As wines get older (20+ years), no matter what grapes they are made with, they all take on a similar aroma. Some descriptors often used are: cigar box, dusty, meaty, gamey, leather, and tobacco.

# ON TASTING WINE

You can read all the books (and there are plenty) written on wine to become more knowledgeable on the subject, but the best way to truly enhance your understanding of wine is to taste as many wines as possible. Reading is the more academic side of wine, while tasting is more enjoyable and practical. A little of each will do you the most good.

The following are the necessary steps for tasting wine. You may wish to follow them with a glass of wine in hand.

Wine tasting can be broken down into five basic steps: color, swirl, smell, taste, and savor.

## Color

The best way to get an idea of a wine's color is to get a white background—a napkin or tablecloth—and hold the glass of wine on an angle in front of it. The range of colors that you may see depends, of course, on whether you're tasting a white or red wine. Here are the colors for both, beginning with the youngest wine and moving to an older wine:

| WHITE WINE | RED WINE |
|---|---|
| Pale yellow-green | Purple |
| Straw yellow | Ruby |
| Yellow-gold | |
| Gold | Red |
| Old gold | |
| Yellow-brown | Brick red |
| Maderized | Red-brown |
| Brown | Brown |

**THE TOP 3 WAYS AMERICANS BUY THEIR WINE**

1. Tasted before
2. Recommended
3. By grape variety

*"There are no standards of taste in wine, cigars, poetry, prose, etc. Each man's own taste is the standard, and a majority vote cannot decide for him or in any slightest degree affect the supremacy of his own standard."*

—MARK TWAIN, 1895

IF YOU can see through a red wine, it's generally ready to drink!

AS WHITE wines age, they gain color. Red wines, on the other hand, lose color as they age.

**TYPES OF TASTINGS**

| HORIZONTAL | Tasting wines from the same vintage |
|---|---|
| VERTICAL | Comparing wines from different vintages |
| BLIND | The taster does not have any information about the wines |
| SEMI-BLIND | The taster knows only the style of wine (grape) or where it comes from |

Color tells you a lot about the wine. Since we start with the white wines, let's consider three reasons why a white wine may have more color:

1. It's older.
2. Different grape varieties give different color. (For example, Chardonnay usually gives off a deeper color than does Sauvignon Blanc.)
3. The wine was aged in wood.

In class, I always begin by asking my students what color the wine is. It's not unusual to hear that some believe that the wine is pale yellow-green, while others say it's gold. Everyone begins with the same wine, but color perceptions vary. There are no right or wrong answers, because perception is subjective. So you can imagine what happens when we actually taste the wine!

## Swirl

Why do we swirl wine? To allow oxygen to get into the wine. Swirling releases the esters, ethers, and aldehydes that combine with oxygen to yield a wine's bouquet. In other words, swirling aerates the wine and releases more of the bouquet and aroma.

## Smell

This is the most important part of wine tasting. You can perceive just four tastes—sweet, sour, bitter, and salty—but the average person can identify more than 2,000 different scents, and wine has more than 200 of its own. Now that you've swirled the wine and released the bouquet, I want you to smell the wine at least three times. You may find that the third smell will give you more information than the first smell did. What does the wine smell like? What type of nose does it have? Smell is the most important step in the tasting process and most people simply don't spend enough time on it.

Pinpointing the nose of the wine helps you to identify certain characteristics. The problem here is that many people in class want me to tell them what the wine smells like. Since I prefer not to use subjective words, I may say that the wine smells like a French white Burgundy. Still, I find that this doesn't satisfy the majority of the class. They want to know more. I ask these people to describe what steak and onions smell like. They answer, "Like steak and onions." See what I mean?

I LIKE TO have my students put their hands over the glass of wine when they swirl to create a more powerful bouquet and aroma.

BOUQUET IS the total smell of the wine. Aroma IS the smell of the grapes. "Nose" is a word that wine tasters use to describe the bouquet and aroma of the wine.

THIS JUST IN: It is now known that each nostril can detect different smells.

THE OLDEST part of the human brain is the olfactory region.

THE 2004 Nobel Prize for Medicine was awarded to two scientists for their research on the olfactory system and the discovery that there are more than 10,000 different smells!

ONE OF THE most difficult challenges in life is to match a smell or a taste with a word that describes it.

The best way to learn what your own preferences are for styles of wine is to "memorize" the smell of the individual grape varieties. For white, just try to memorize the three major grape varieties: Chardonnay, Sauvignon Blanc, and Riesling. Keep smelling them, and smelling them, and smelling them until you can identify the differences, one from the other. For the reds it's a little more difficult, but you still can take three major grape varieties: Pinot Noir, Merlot, and Cabernet Sauvignon. Try to memorize those smells without using flowery words, and you'll understand what I'm talking about.

For those in the Wine School who remain unconvinced, I hand out a list of 500 different words commonly used to describe wine. Here is a small excerpt:

| | | | |
|---|---|---|---|
| acetic | character | legs | seductive |
| aftertaste | corky | light | short |
| aroma | developed | maderized | stalky |
| astringent | earthy | mature | sulfury |
| austere | finish | metallic | tart |
| baked-burnt | flat | nose | thin |
| balanced | fresh | nutty | tired |
| bitter | grapey | off | vanilla |
| body | green | oxidized | woody |
| bouquet | hard | pétillant | yeasty |
| bright | hot | rich | young |

You're also more likely to recognize some of the defects of a wine through your sense of smell.

Following is a list of some of the negative smells in wine:

| SMELL | WHY |
|---|---|
| Vinegar | Too much acetic acid in wine |
| Sherry* | Oxidation |
| Dank, wet, moldy, cellar smell | Wine absorbs the taste of a defective cork (referred to as "corked wine") |
| Sulfur (burnt matches) | Too much sulfur dioxide |

* Authentic Sherry, from Spain, is intentionally made through controlled oxidation.

All wines contain some sulfur dioxide since it is a by-product of fermentation. Sulfur dioxide is also used in many ways in winemaking. It kills bacteria in wine, prevents unwanted fermentation, and acts as a preservative. It sometimes causes a burning and itching sensation in your nose.

WHAT KIND of wine do I like? I like my wine bright, rich, mature, developed, seductive, and with nice legs!

### NEED MORE WORDS?

*WineSpeak* by Bernard Klem includes 36,975 wine-tasting descriptions. Who knew?

OXYGEN CAN be the best friend of a wine, but it can also be its worst enemy. A little oxygen helps release the smell of the wine (as with swirling), but prolonged exposure can be harmful, especially to older wines.

EVERY WINE contains a certain amount of sulfites. They are a natural by-product of fermentation.

EACH PERSON has a different threshold for sulfur dioxide, and although most people do not have an adverse reaction, it can be a problem for individuals with asthma. To protect those who are prone to bad reactions to sulfites, federal law requires wineries to label their wines with the warning that the wine contains sulfites.

THE AVERAGE person has 10,000 taste buds. (That means that some of you have 20,000 and some of you have none!)

TASTING WINE is confirming what the color and smell are telling you.

THERE IS now evidence that people may perceive five tastes: sweet, sour, bitter, salty, and possibly umami.

OTHER SENSATIONS associated with wine include numbing, tingling, drying, cooling, warming, and coating.

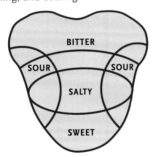

BITTER: Think endive or arugula.
TANNIN: Think gritty.

*"One not only drinks wine, one smells it, observes it, tastes it, sips it, and—one talks about it."*

—KING EDWARD VII OF ENGLAND

## Taste

To many people, tasting wine means taking a sip and swallowing immediately. To me, this isn't tasting. Tasting is something you do with your taste buds. You have taste buds all over your mouth—on both sides of the tongue, underneath, on the tip, and extending to the back of your throat. If you do what many people do, you take a gulp of wine and bypass all of those important taste buds. When I taste wine I leave it in my mouth for three to five seconds before swallowing. The wine warms up, sending signals about the bouquet and aroma up through the nasal passage then on to the olfactory bulb, and then to the limbic system of the brain. Remember, 90 percent of taste is smell.

## What should you think about when tasting wine?

Be aware of the most important sensations of taste and your own personal thresholds of those tastes. Also, pay attention to where they occur on your tongue and in your mouth. As I mentioned earlier, you can perceive just four tastes: sweet, sour, bitter, and salty (but there's no salt in wine, so we're down to three). Bitterness in wine is usually created by high alcohol and high tannin. Sweetness occurs only in wines that have some residual sugar left over after fermentation. Sour (sometimes called "tart") indicates the acidity in wine.

*Sweetness:* The highest threshold is on the tip of the tongue. If there's any sweetness in a wine whatsoever, you'll get it right away.

*Acidity:* Found at the sides of the tongue, the cheek area, and the back of the throat. White wines and some lighter-style red wines usually contain a higher degree of acidity.

*Bitterness:* Tasted on the back of the tongue.

*Tannin:* The sensation of tannin begins in the middle of the tongue. Tannin frequently exists in red wines or white wines aged in wood. When the wines are too young, tannin dries the palate to excess. If there's a lot of tannin in the wine, it can actually coat your whole mouth, blocking the fruit. Remember, tannin is not a taste: it is a tactile sensation.

*Fruit and varietal characteristics:* These are not tastes, but smells. The weight of the fruit (the "body") will be felt in the middle of the tongue.

*Aftertaste:* The overall taste and balance of the components of the wine that lingers in your mouth. How long does the balance last? Usually a sign of a high-quality wine is a long, pleasing aftertaste. The taste of many of the great wines lasts anywhere from one to three minutes, with all their components in harmony.

## Savor

After you've had a chance to taste the wine, sit back for a few moments and savor it. Think about what you just experienced, and ask yourself the following questions to help focus your impressions.

- Was the wine light, medium, or full-bodied?
- For a white wine: How was the acidity? Very little, just right, or too much?
- For a red wine: Is the tannin in the wine too strong or astringent?
- What is the strongest component (residual sugar, fruit, acid, tannin)?
- How long did the balance of the components last (ten seconds, sixty seconds, etc.)?
- Is the wine ready to drink? Or does it need more time to age?
- What kind of food would you enjoy with the wine?
- To your taste, is the wine worth the price?
- This brings us to the most important point. The first thing you should consider after you've tasted a wine is whether or not you like it. Is it your style?

You can compare tasting wine to browsing in an art gallery. You wander from room to room looking at the paintings. Your first impression tells whether or not you like something. Once you decide you like a piece of art, you want to know more: Who was the artist? What is the history behind the work? How was it done? And so it is with wine. Usually, once oenophiles (wine aficionados) discover a wine that they like, they want to learn everything about it: the winemaker; the grapes; exactly where the vines were planted; the blend, if any; and the history behind the wine.

## How do you know if a wine is good or not?

The definition of a good wine is one that you enjoy. I cannot emphasize this enough. Trust your own palate and do not let others dictate taste to you!

## When is a wine ready to drink?

This is one of the most frequently asked questions. The answer is very simple: when all components of the wine are in balance to your particular taste.

WINE TEXTURES:
Light: skim milk
Medium: whole milk
Full: heavy cream

*"The key to great wine is balance, and it is the sum of the different parts that make a wine not only delicious but complete and fascinating as well as worthy of aging."*
—FIONA MORRISON, M.W.

*"A wine goes in my mouth, and I just see it. I see it in three dimensions. The textures. The flavors. The smells. They just jump out at me. I can taste with a hundred screaming kids in a room. When I put my nose in a glass, it's like tunnel vision. I move into another world, where everything around me is just gone, and every bit of mental energy is focused on that wine."*
—ROBERT M. PARKER JR., *author and wine critic, in the* Atlantic Monthly

### WHAT MAKES A GREAT WINE GREAT?

Varietal character
Balance of components
Complexity
Sense of place
Emotional response

*"Great wine is about nuance, surprise, subtlety, expression, qualities that keep you coming back for another taste. Rejecting a wine because it is not big enough is like rejecting a book because it is not long enough, or a piece of music because it is not loud enough."*
—KERMIT LYNCH, Adventures on the Wine Route

*"Wine makes daily living easier, less hurried, with fewer tensions and more tolerance."*
—BENJAMIN FRANKLIN

Step One: Look at the color of the wine.
Step Two: Smell the wine three times.
Step Three: Put the wine in your mouth and leave it there for three to five seconds.
Step Four: Swallow the wine.
Step Five: Wait and concentrate on the wine for 60 seconds before discussing it.

**THE CELEBRATION OF WINE AND LIFE: THE TOAST**

To complete the five senses (sight, hearing, smell, taste, and touch), don't forget to toast your family and friends with the clinking of the glasses. This tradition started in ancient times when the Greeks, afraid of being poisoned by their enemies, shared a little of their wine with one another. If someone had added something to the wine, it would be a short evening for everyone! The clinking of the glasses also is said to drive away the "bad spirits" that might exist and cause the next-day hangover!

*"Wine is the best of all beverages . . . because it is purer than water, safer than milk, plainer than soft drinks, gentler than spirits, nimbler than beer, and ever so much more pleasant to the educated senses of sight, smell, and taste than any of the drinkable liquids known to us."*

—ANDRE L. SIMON, *author and founder of the Wine & Food Society*

I WILL make my decision about whether or not I like the style of a wine within 45 to 60 seconds.

# THE 60-SECOND WINE EXPERT

Over the last few years I have insisted that my students spend one minute in silence after they swallow the wine. I use a "60-second wine expert" tasting sheet in my classes for students to record their impressions. The minute is divided into four sections: 0 to 15 seconds, 15 to 30 seconds, 30 to 45 seconds, and the final 45 to 60 seconds. Try this with your next glass of wine.

Please note that the first taste of wine is a shock to your taste buds. This is due to the alcohol content, acidity, and sometimes the tannin in the wine. The higher the alcohol or acidity, the more of a shock. For the first wine in any tasting, it is probably best to take a sip and swirl it around in your mouth, but don't evaluate it. Wait another thirty seconds, try it again, and then begin the 60-second wine expert tasting.

*0 to 15 seconds:* If there is any residual sugar/sweetness in the wine, I will experience it now. If there is no sweetness in the wine, the acidity is usually at its strongest sensation in the first fifteen seconds. I am also looking for the fruit level of the wine and its balance with the acidity or sweetness.

*15 to 30 seconds:* After the sweetness or acidity, I am looking for great fruit sensation. After all, that is what I am paying for! By the time I reach thirty seconds, I am hoping for balance of all the components. By this time, I can identify the weight of the wine. Is it light, medium, or full-bodied? I am now starting to think about what kind of food I can pair with this wine (see pages 273–280).

*30 to 45 seconds:* At this point I am beginning to formulate my opinion of the wine, whether I like it or not. Not all wines need sixty seconds of thought. Lighter-style wines, such as Rieslings, will usually show their best at this point. The fruit, acid, and sweetness of a great German Riesling should be in perfect harmony from this point on. For quality red and white wines, acidity—which is a very strong component, especially in the first thirty seconds—should now be in balance with the fruit of the wine.

*45 to 60 seconds:* Very often wine writers use the term "length" to describe how long the components, balance, and flavor continue in the mouth. I concentrate on the length of the wine in these last fifteen seconds. In big, full-bodied red wines from Bordeaux and the Rhône Valley, Cabernets from California, Barolos and Barbarescos from Italy, and even some full-bodied Chardonnays, I am concentrating on the level of tannin in the wine. Just as the acidity and fruit balance are my major concerns in the first thirty seconds, it is now the tannin and fruit balance I am looking for in the last thirty seconds. If the fruit, tannin, and acid are all in balance at sixty seconds, then I feel that the wine is probably ready to drink. Does the tannin overpower the fruit? If it does at the sixty-second mark, I will then begin to question whether I should drink the wine now or put it away for more aging.

It is extremely important to me that if you want to learn the true taste of the wine, you take at least one minute to concentrate on all of its components. In my classes it is amazing to see more than a hundred students silently taking one minute to analyze a wine. Some close their eyes, some bow their heads in deep thought, others write notes.

One final point: Sixty seconds, to me, is the minimum time to wait before making a decision about a wine. Many great wines continue to show balance well past 120 seconds. The best wine I ever tasted lasted more than three minutes—that's three minutes of perfect balance of all components!

*"I like to think about the life of wine, how it is a living thing. I like to think about what was going on the year the grapes were growing. How the sun was shining, if it rained. I like to think about all the people who tended and picked the grapes. And if it's an old wine, how many of them must be dead by now. I like how wine continues to evolve, like if I opened a bottle of wine today it would taste different than if I'd opened it on any other day, because a bottle of wine is actually alive. And it's constantly evolving and gaining complexity, that is until it peaks, like your '61. And then it begins its steady inevitable decline."*
—MAYA, *from the movie* Sideways *(2004)*

Part of the 60-second wine expert tasting worksheet I give out in my class:

---

## TASTING WORKSHEET

**60-Second Wine Expert:**

Identify the major component in each time slot.

0–15 seconds _____

15–30 seconds _____

30–45 seconds _____

45–60 seconds _____

**Color:**

_____

**Aroma/Bouquet:**

_____

_____

_____

|  | Low | Medium | High |
|---|---|---|---|
| Residual Sugar |  |  |  |
| Fruit |  |  |  |
| Acid |  |  |  |
| Tannin |  |  |  |

Light-Bodied _____ Medium-Bodied _____ Full-Bodied _____

Ageability: Ready to Drink? _____ Needs more time? _____ Past its prime? _____

Personal Rating/Comments _____

---

**FOR FURTHER READING**

I recommend Michael Broadbent's *Pocket Guide to Wine Tasting*, Jancis Robinson's *Vintage Timecharts*, and Alan Young's *Making Sense of Wine*.

VIDEO
http://bit.ly/gKfLvn

MORE THAN 50 major white-wine grape varieties are grown throughout the world.

OTHER WHITE grapes and regions you may wish to explore:

| GRAPES | WHERE THEY GROW BEST |
|---|---|
| Albariño | Spain |
| Chenin Blanc | Loire Valley, France; California |
| Gewürztraminer, Pinot Blanc, Pinot Gris | Alsace, France |
| Grüner Veltliner | Austria |
| Pinot Grigio (aka Pinot Gris) | Italy; California; Oregon |
| Sémillon | Bordeaux (Sauternes); Australia |
| Viognier | Rhône Valley, France; California |

## NEW WORLD VERSUS OLD WORLD

Wines from the United States, Australia, Chile, Argentina, New Zealand, and South Africa usually list the grape variety on the label. French, Italian, and Spanish wines usually list the region, village, or vineyard where the wine was made—but not the grape.

# White Grapes of the World

NOW THAT YOU KNOW THE BASICS of how wine is made and how to taste it, you're almost ready to begin the first three classes on white wines.

Before you do, simplify your journey by letting me answer the question most frequently asked by my wine students on what will help them most in learning about wine. The main thing is to understand the major grape varieties and where they are grown in the world.

The purpose of this book is not to overwhelm you with information about every grape under the sun. My job as a wine educator is to try to narrow down this over-abundance of data. So let's start off with the three major grapes you need to know to understand white wine. More than 90 percent of all quality white wine is made from these three grapes. They are listed here in order from the lightest style to the fullest:

Riesling          Sauvignon Blanc          Chardonnay

This is not to say that world-class white wine comes from only these grapes, but knowing these three is a good start.

One of the first things I show my students in Class One is a list indicating where these three grape varieties grow best. It looks something like this:

| GRAPES | WHERE THEY GROW BEST |
|---|---|
| *Riesling* | Germany; Alsace, France; New York State; Washington State |
| *Sauvignon Blanc* | Bordeaux, France; Loire Valley, France; New Zealand; California (Fumé Blanc) |
| *Chardonnay* | Burgundy, France; Champagne, France; California; Australia |

There are world-class Rieslings, Sauvignon Blancs, and Chardonnays made in other countries, but in general the above regions specialize in wines made from these grapes.

# Red Grapes of the World

VIDEO
http://bit.ly/hOTs1d

**C**lasses Four through Seven will delve into the great red wines of the world. It is important that you review the major red-grape varieties and where in the world they produce the best wines.

In Class Four, I start with a list of what I consider to be the major red-wine grapes, ranked from lightest to fullest-bodied style, along with the region or country in which the grape grows best. By looking at this chart, you will not only get an idea of the style of the wine, but also a feeling for gradations of weight, color, tannin, and ageability.

THERE ARE hundreds of different red-wine grapes planted throughout the world. California alone grows 31 different red-wine grape varieties.

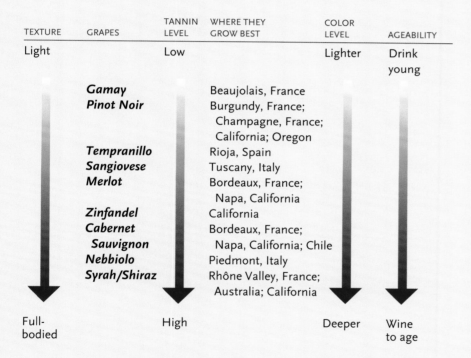

| TEXTURE | GRAPES | TANNIN LEVEL | WHERE THEY GROW BEST | COLOR LEVEL | AGEABILITY |
|---|---|---|---|---|---|
| Light | | Low | | Lighter | Drink young |
| | *Gamay* | | Beaujolais, France | | |
| | *Pinot Noir* | | Burgundy, France; Champagne, France; California; Oregon | | |
| | *Tempranillo* | | Rioja, Spain | | |
| | *Sangiovese* | | Tuscany, Italy | | |
| | *Merlot* | | Bordeaux, France; Napa, California | | |
| | *Zinfandel* | | California | | |
| | *Cabernet Sauvignon* | | Bordeaux, France; Napa, California; Chile | | |
| | *Nebbiolo* | | Piedmont, Italy | | |
| | *Syrah/Shiraz* | | Rhône Valley, France; Australia; California | | |
| Full-bodied | | High | | Deeper | Wine to age |

IN GENERAL, the lighter the color, the more perceived the acidity.

ONCE YOU have become acquainted with these major red-wine grapes, you may wish to explore the following:

| GRAPES | WHERE THEY GROW BEST |
|---|---|
| Barbera | Italy |
| Dolcetto | Italy |
| Cabernet Franc | Loire Valley and Bordeaux, France |
| Grenache/ Garnacha | Rhône Valley, France Spain |
| Malbec | Bordeaux and Cahors, France; Argentina |

To put this chart together is extremely challenging, given all the variables that go into making wine and the many different styles that can be produced. Remember, there are always exceptions to the rule, just as there are other countries and wine regions not listed here that produce world-class wine from some of the red grapes shown. You'll begin to see this for yourself if you do your homework and taste a lot of different wines. Good luck!

# Questions for Prelude

# The White Wines of France

❦

UNDERSTANDING FRENCH WINE • ALSACE • LOIRE VALLEY •

WHITE WINES OF BORDEAUX • GRAVES • SAUTERNES/BARSAC • WHITE WINES OF BURGUNDY

• CHABLIS • CÔTE DE BEAUNE • CÔTE CHÂLONNAISE • MÂCONNAIS

FRANCE

CHAMPAGNE

Paris ★

LOIRE VALLEY

ALSACE

BURGUNDY

*Atlantic Ocean*

BORDEAUX

CÔTES DU RHÔNE

LANGUEDOC

PROVENCE

ROUSSILLON

*Mediterranean Sea*

o  Miles          100          200

o  Kilometers          200

# Understanding French Wine

FRANCE IS the number-two producer of wines in the world.

BEFORE WE BEGIN OUR FIRST CLASS, "The White Wines of France," I think you should know a few important points about all French wines. Take a look at a map of France to get familiar with the main wine-producing areas. As we progress, you'll understand why geography is so important.

Here's a quick rundown of which areas produce which styles of wine:

| WINE REGIONS | STYLES | MAJOR GRAPES |
|---|---|---|
| **Alsace** | Mostly white | Riesling, Gewürztraminer |
| **Bordeaux** | Red and white | Sauvignon Blanc, Sémillon, Merlot, Cabernet Sauvignon, Cabernet Franc |
| **Burgundy** | Red and white | Pinot Noir, Gamay, Chardonnay |
| **Champagne** | Sparkling wine | Pinot Noir, Chardonnay |
| **Côtes du Rhône** | Mostly red | Syrah, Grenache |
| **Languedoc/ Roussillon** | Red and white | Carignan, Grenache, Syrah, Cinsault, Mourvèdre |
| **Loire Valley** | Mostly white | Sauvignon Blanc, Chenin Blanc, Cabernet Franc |
| **Provence** | Red, white, and rosé | Grenache, Syrah |

WHY WOULD Georges Duboeuf, Louis Latour, and many other famous wine-makers start wineries in Languedoc and Roussillon? For one thing, the land is much less expensive compared to regions such as Burgundy or Bordeaux, so the winemakers can produce moderately priced wines and still get a good return on their investment.

IN THE SOUTHERN French region of Provence, look for these producers:
Domaine Tempier
Château Routas

Anyone who is interested in wine is bound to encounter French wine at one time or another. Why? Because of the thousands of years of history and winemaking tradition, because of the great diversity and variety of wines from the many different regions, and because French wines have the reputation for being among the best in the world. There's a reason for this, and it goes back to quality control.

French winemaking is regulated by strict government laws that are set up by the Appellation d'Origine Contrôlée. If you don't want to say "Appellation d'Origine Contrôlée" all the time, you can simply say "AOC." This is the first of many wine lingo abbreviations you'll learn in this book.

***Vins de Pays***: This is a category that's growing in importance. A 1979 French legal decision liberalized the rules for this category, permitting the use of nontraditional grapes in certain regions and even allowing vintners to label wines with the varietal rather than the regional name. For exporters to the American market, where consumers are becoming accustomed to buying wines by grape variety—Cabernet Sauvignon or Chardonnay, for example—this change makes their wines much easier to sell.

THE REGIONS most active in the production of Vin de Pays varietal wines is Languedoc and Roussillon, in southwest France. Called in the past the "wine lake" because of the vast quantities of anonymous wine made there, the Languedoc has more than 700,000 acres of vineyards, and produces more than 200 million cases a year, about a third of the total French crop.

ONLY 35% of all French wines are worthy of the AOC designation.

THERE ARE more than 465 AOC French wines.

## TOP FRENCH WINE BRANDS

Georges Duboeuf: Beaujolais
Louis Jadot: Burgundy
Fat Bastard
B&G
Red Bicyclette

HECTARE—metric measure
1 hectare = 2.471 acres

HECTOLITER—metric measure
1 hectoliter = 26.42 U.S. gallons

FAMOUS NON-AOC French wines that are available in the United States include: Moreau, Boucheron, Chantefleur, and René Junot.

CHAMPAGNE IS another major white-wine producer, but that's a chapter in itself.

## FRENCH CONTROL LAWS

*Established in the 1930s, the Appellation d'Origine Contrôlée (AOC) laws set minimum requirements for each wine-producing area in France. These laws also can help you decipher French wine labels, since the AOC controls the following:*

|  | EXAMPLE | EXAMPLE |
|---|---|---|
| *Geographic origin* | *Chablis* | *Pommard* |
| *Grape variety: Which grapes can be planted where* | *Chardonnay* | *Pinot Noir* |
| *Minimum alcohol content: This varies depending upon the particular area where the grapes are grown* | *10%* | *10.5%* |
| *Vine-growing practices: For example, a vintner can produce only so much wine per acre* | *40 hectoliters/ hectare* | *35 hectoliters/ hectare* |

*Vins de Table:* These are ordinary table wines and represent almost 35 percent of all wines produced in France.

Most French wine is meant to be consumed as a simple beverage. Many of the *vins de table* are marketed under proprietary names and are the French equivalent of California jug wines. Don't be surprised if you go into a grocery store in France to buy wine and find it in a plastic wine container with no label on it! You can see the color through the plastic—red, white, or rosé—but the only marking on the container is the alcohol content, ranging from 9 to 14 percent. You choose your wine depending on how sharp you need to be for the rest of the day!

When you buy wines, keep these distinctions in mind, because there's a difference not only in quality but also in price.

## What are the four major white wine–producing regions of France?

**ALSACE     LOIRE VALLEY     BORDEAUX     BURGUNDY**

Let's start with Alsace and the Loire Valley, because these are the two French regions that specialize in white wines. As you can see from the map at the beginning of this chapter, Alsace, the Loire Valley, and Chablis (a white wine–producing region of Burgundy) have one thing in common: they're all located in the northern region of France. These areas produce white wines predominantly, because of the shorter growing season and cooler climate that are best suited for growing white grapes.

# ALSACE

I often find that people are confused about the difference between wines from Alsace and those from Germany. Why do you suppose this is?

First of all, your confusion could be justified since both wines are sold in tall bottles with tapering necks. Just to confuse you further, Alsace and Germany grow the same grape varieties. But when you think of Riesling, what are your associations? You'll probably answer "Germany" and "sweetness." That's a very typical response, and that's because the German winemaker adds a small amount of naturally sweet unfermented grape juice back into the wine to create the distinctive German Riesling. The winemaker from Alsace ferments every bit of the sugar in the grapes, which is why 90 percent of all Alsace wines are totally dry.

Another fundamental difference between wine from Alsace and wine from Germany is the alcohol content. Wine from Alsace has 11 to 12 percent alcohol, while most German wine has a mere 8 to 9 percent.

## What are the white grapes grown in Alsace?

The four grapes you should know are:

*Riesling:* accounts for 22 percent
*Pinot Blanc:* accounts for 21 percent
*Gewürztraminer:* accounts for 19 percent
*Pinot Gris:* accounts for 15 percent

FROM 1871 TO 1919, Alsace was part of Germany.

ALL WINES produced in Alsace are AOC-designated and represent nearly 20% of all AOC white wines in France.

ALSACE PRODUCES 8% of its red wines from the Pinot Noir grape. These generally are consumed in the region and are rarely exported.

WINE LABELING in Alsace is different from the other French regions administered by the AOC, because Alsace is the only region that labels its wine by varietal. All Alsace wines that include the name of the grape on the label must be made entirely from that grape.

**GREAT SWEET (LATE HARVEST) WINES FROM ALSACE**

**Vendange Tardive**
**Sélection de Grains Nobles**

IN THE LAST 20 years, there have been more Pinot Blanc and Riesling grapes planted in Alsace than any other variety.

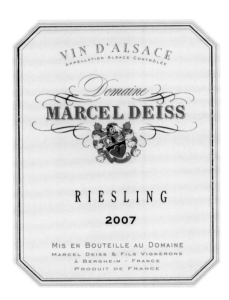

THERE ARE 35,000 acres of grapes planted in Alsace, but the average plot of land for each grower is only five acres.

THE ALSACE region has little rainfall, especially during the grape harvest, and the town of Colmar—the Alsace wine center— is the second driest in France. That's why they say a "one-shirt harvest" will be a good vintage.

SOMETIMES YOU'LL see "Grand Cru" on an Alsace label. This wine can be made only from the best grape varieties of Alsace. There are more than 50 different vineyards entitled to the Grand Cru label.

## What types of wine are produced in Alsace?

As mentioned earlier, virtually all the Alsace wines are dry. Riesling is the major grape planted in Alsace, and it is responsible for the highest-quality wines of the region. Alsace is also known for its Gewürztraminer, which is in a class by itself. Most people either love it or hate it, because Gewürztraminer has a very distinctive style. *Gewürz* is the German word for "spice," which aptly describes the wine.

Pinot Blanc and Pinot Gris are becoming increasingly popular among the growers of Alsace.

## How should I select an Alsace wine?

Two factors are important in choosing a wine from Alsace: the grape variety and the reputation and style of the shipper. Some of the most reliable shippers are:

DOMAINE DOPFF AU MOULIN    DOMAINE F. E. TRIMBACH
DOMAINE MARCEL DEISS        DOMAINE HUGEL & FILS
DOMAINE WEINBACH            DOMAINE LÉON BEYER
DOMAINE ZIND-HUMBRECHT

## Why are the shippers so important?

The majority of the landholders in Alsace don't grow enough grapes to make it economically feasible to produce and market their own wine. Instead, they sell their grapes to a shipper who produces, bottles, and markets the wine under his own name. The art of making high-quality Alsace wine lies in the selection of grapes made by each shipper.

## What are the different quality levels of Alsace wines?

Quality of Alsace wines is determined by the shipper's reputation rather than any labeling on the bottle. That said, the vast majority of any given Alsace wine is the shipper's varietal. A very small percentage is labeled with a specific vineyard's name, especially in the appellation "Alsace Grand Cru." Some wines are labeled "Réserve" or "Réserve Personelle," terms that are not legally defined.

## Should I lay down my Alsace wines for long aging?

In general, most Alsace wines are made to be consumed young—that is, one to five years after they're bottled. As in any fine-wine geographic area, in

Alsace there is a small percentage of great wines produced that may be aged for ten years or more.

## How have Alsace wines changed in the past forty years?

Forty years later I am enjoying the same producers, such as Trimbach and Hugel, as I did then. A dry, crisp acidic Riesling is still one of my favorite wines to have at the beginning of a meal, especially with a fish appetizer. Pinot Blanc is a perfect summer picnic wine, or at a restaurant for wine by the glass, and the famous Gewürztraminer is one of the most unique and flavorful wines in the world.

The best part about Alsace wines is that they are still very affordable, of good quality, and available throughout the United States.

### BEST BETS FOR RECENT VINTAGES FROM ALSACE

2005* 2007* 2008** 2009* 2010 2011 2012

*Note: * signifies exceptional vintage    ** signifies extraordinary vintage*

### FOR FURTHER READING

I recommend *Alsace and Its Wine Gardens* by S. F. Hallgarten and *Alsace Wines and Spirits* by Pamela Vandyke Price.

ALSACE IS also known for its fruit brandies, or *eaux-de-vie*:
Fraise: strawberries
Framboise: raspberries
Kirsch: cherries
Mirabelle: yellow plums
Poire: pears

### FOR THE TOURISTS

Visit the beautiful wine village of Riquewihr, whose buildings date from the fifteenth and sixteenth centuries.

### FOR THE FOODIES

Alsace is not just about great wine. There are over 26 Michelin-rated restaurants, with three of them having three stars.

## WINE AND FOOD

During a visit to Alsace, I spoke with two of the region's best-known producers to find out which types of food they enjoy with Alsace wines. Here's what they prefer:

ÉTIENNE HUGEL: *"Alsace wines are not only suited to classic Alsace and other French dishes. For instance, I adore Riesling with such raw fish specialties as Japanese sushi and sashimi, while our Gewürztraminer is delicious with smoked salmon and brilliant with Chinese, Thai, and Indonesian food."*

Mr. Hugel describes Pinot Blanc as *"round, soft, not aggressive . . . an all-purpose wine . . . can be used as an apéritif, with all kinds of pâté and charcuterie, and also with hamburgers. Perfect for brunch—not too sweet or flowery."*

HUBERT TRIMBACH: *"Riesling with fish—blue trout with a light sauce."* He recommends Gewürztraminer as an apéritif, or with foie gras or any pâté at meal's end; with Muenster cheese, or a stronger cheese such as Roquefort.

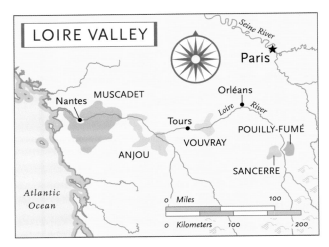

LOIRE VALLEY

# LOIRE VALLEY

Starting at the city of Nantes, a bit upriver from the Atlantic Ocean, the Loire Valley stretches inland for six hundred miles along the Loire River.

There are two white-grape varieties you should be familiar with:

### SAUVIGNON BLANC    CHENIN BLANC

Rather than choosing by grape variety and shipper, as you would in Alsace, choose Loire Valley wines by style and vintage. Here are the main styles:

**Pouilly-Fumé:** A dry wine that has the most body and concentration of all the Loire Valley wines. It's made with 100 percent Sauvignon Blanc.

**Muscadet:** A light, dry wine, made from 100 percent Melon de Bourgogne grapes.

**Sancerre:** Striking a balance between full-bodied Pouilly-Fumé and light-bodied Muscadet, it's made with 100 percent Sauvignon Blanc.

**Vouvray:** The "chameleon" can be dry, semisweet, or sweet. It's made from 100 percent Chenin Blanc.

## How did Pouilly-Fumé get its name, and what does *fumé* mean?

Many people ask me if Pouilly-Fumé is smoked, because they automatically associate the word *fumé* with smoke. Two of the many theories about the origin of the word come from the white morning mist that blankets the area. As the sun burns off the mist, it looks as if smoke is rising. Others say it is the "smokelike" bloom on Sauvignon Blanc grapes.

## When are the wines ready to drink?

Generally, Loire Valley wines are meant to be consumed young. The exception is a sweet Vouvray, which can be laid down for a longer time.

Here are more specific guidelines:

**Muscadet:** one to two years

**Pouilly-Fumé:** three to five years

**Sancerre:** two to three years

IN THE LOIRE VALLEY, over 50% of the AOC wines produced are white, and 96% of those are dry.

THE LOIRE VALLEY is famous not only for its wines, but also as a summer retreat for royalty. Elegant and sometimes enormous châteaux embellish the countryside.

FOR RED wines look to Bourgueil, Chinon, and Saumur, all made from the Cabernet Franc grape.

THE DISTINCT nose, or bouquet, of Pouilly-Fumé comes from a combination of the Sauvignon Blanc grape and the soil of the Loire Valley.

MOST POUILLY-FUMÉ and Sancerre wines are not aged in wood.

THE LOIRE VALLEY is the largest white-wine region in France and second largest in sparkling-wine production.

OTHER SAUVIGNON BLANC wines from the Loire to look for: Menetou-Salon and Quincy. For Chenin Blanc try Savennières.

## What's the difference between Pouilly-Fumé and Pouilly-Fuissé?

My students often ask me this, expecting similarly named wines to be related. But Pouilly-Fumé is made from 100 percent Sauvignon Blanc and comes from the Loire Valley, while Pouilly-Fuissé is made from 100 percent Chardonnay and comes from the Mâconnais region of Burgundy.

## Forty years later in the Loire Valley

I am still enamored of the quality and diversity of the white wines of the Loire Valley. The wines have maintained their style and character, representing great value for the consumer. Forty years ago the most important Loire Valley wine was Pouilly-Fumé. Today Sancerre is the most popular Loire wine in the United States. Both wines are made from the same grape variety, 100 percent Sauvignon Blanc, both are medium-bodied with great acidity and fruit balance, and both are perfect food wines.

Muscadet continues to be a great value, and Vouvray is still the best example of the quality that the grape Chenin Blanc can achieve.

### BEST BETS FOR RECENT VINTAGES FROM THE LOIRE VALLEY

2005* 2009* 2010* 2011

*Note: * signifies exceptional vintage*

## WINE AND FOOD

**BARON PATRICK DE LADOUCETTE**
*suggests the following combinations:*
**Pouilly-Fumé:** *"Smoked salmon; turbot with hollandaise; white meat chicken; veal with cream sauce."*
**Sancerre:** *"Shellfish, simple food of the sea, because Sancerre is drier than Pouilly-Fumé."*
**Muscadet:** *"All you have to do is look at the map to see where Muscadet is made: by the sea where the main fare is shellfish, clams, and oysters."*
**Vouvray:** *"A nice semidry wine to have with fruit and cheese."*

**MARQUIS ROBERT DE GOULAINE**
*suggests these combinations:*
**Muscadet:** *"Muscadet is good with a huge variety of excellent and fresh 'everyday' foods, including all the seafood from the Atlantic Ocean, the fish from the river— pike, for instance—game, poultry, and cheese (mainly goat cheese). Of course, there is a must in the region of Nantes: freshwater fish with the world-famous butter sauce, the beurre blanc, invented at the turn of the century by Clémence, who happened to be the chef at Goulaine. If you prefer, try Muscadet with a dash of crème de cassis (black currant); it is a wonderful way to welcome friends!"*

SAUVION
PRODUCE OF FRANCE
*Sancerre*
APPELLATION SANCERRE CONTRÔLÉE
MIS EN BOUTEILLE PAR SAUVION
LE CLÉRAY · 44194 VALLET · FRANCE

**KEVIN ZRALY'S FAVORITE PRODUCERS**

**Muscadet:** Marquis de Goulaine, Sauvion, Métaireau
**Pouilly-Fumé:** Guyot, Michel Redde, Château de Tracy, Dagueneau, Ladoucette, Colin, Jolivet, Jean-Paul Balland
**Sancerre:** Archambault, Roblin, Lucien Crochet, Jean Vacheron, Château de Sancerre, Domaine Fournier, Henri Bourgeois, Sauvion
**Savennières:** Nicolas Joly
**Vouvray:** Huët

IF YOU see the phrase "sur lie" on a Muscadet wine label, it means that the wine was aged on its lees (sediment).

THE LOIRE VALLEY also produces the world-famous Anjou Rosé.

de Ladoucette
Pouilly-Fumé
APPELLATION POUILLY-FUMÉ CONTRÔLÉE
ALC. 12,5% BY VOL. PRODUCT OF FRANCE 750 ML
MIS EN BOUTEILLE PAR de LADOUCETTE
AU CHATEAU DU NOZET, POUILLY-S/-LOIRE (NIÈVRE) FRANCE

BORDEAUX PRODUCTION:
85% red
13% white
2% sweet wine

THE NAME "Graves" means "gravel"—the type of soil found in the region.

WHEN PEOPLE think of dry white Bordeaux wines, they normally think of the major areas of Graves or Pessac-Léognan, but some of the best value/quality white wines produced in Bordeaux come from the Entre-Deux-Mers area.

CLASSIFIED WHITE château wines make up only 3% of the total production of white Graves.

# THE WHITE WINES OF BORDEAUX

## Doesn't Bordeaux always mean red wine?

That's a misconception. Actually, two of the five major areas of Bordeaux—Graves and Sauternes—are known for their excellent white wines. Sauternes is world-famous for its sweet white wine.

The major white-grape varieties used in both areas are:

**SAUVIGNON BLANC**      **SÉMILLON**

## GRAVES

### How are the white Graves wines classified?

There are two levels of quality:

**GRAVES**      **PESSAC-LÉOGNAN**

The most basic Graves is simply called Graves. The best wines are produced in Pessac-Léognan. Those labeled "Graves" are from the southern portion of the region surrounding Sauternes, while Pessac-Léognan is in the northern half of the region, next to the city of Bordeaux. The best wines are known by the name of a particular château, a special vineyard that produces the best-quality grapes. The grapes grown for these wines enjoy better soil and better growing conditions overall. The classified château wines and the regional wines of Graves are always dry.

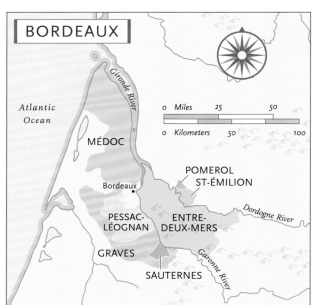

### How should I select a Graves wine?

My best recommendation would be to purchase a classified château wine.

The classified châteaux are:

CHÂTEAU BOUSCAUT*
CHÂTEAU CARBONNIEUX*
CHÂTEAU COUHINS-LURTON
DOMAINE DE CHEVALIER
CHÂTEAU HAUT-BRION
CHÂTEAU LA LOUVIÈRE*

CHÂTEAU LA TOUR-MARTILLAC
CHÂTEAU LAVILLE-HAUT-BRION
CHÂTEAU MALARTIC-LAGRAVIÈRE
CHÂTEAU OLIVIER*
CHÂTEAU SMITH-HAUT-LAFITTE

*The largest producers and the easiest to find.*

## Forty years later in white Bordeaux

The dry white wines of Bordeaux were never considered equal to the great red châteaux and sweet whites of Sauternes. That has all changed over the last forty years. Millions of dollars have been spent on state-of-the-art winemaking equipment, and new vineyard management has created great white-wine production, especially in the Pessac-Léognan.

There are very few other regions in the world that blend Sauvignon Blanc and Sémillon and age them in oak. The winemakers have also been very careful to integrate the fruit and oak together to maintain the freshness and crispness of the wine. Recent vintages have been outstanding.

### BEST BETS FOR RECENT VINTAGES OF WHITE GRAVES

2000*  2005*  2007*  2008  2009*  2010*  2011

*Note: \* signifies exceptional vintage*

## WINE AND FOOD

DENISE LURTON-MOULLÉ (*Château La Louvière, Château Bonnet*): With Château La Louvière Blanc: grilled sea bass with a beurre blanc, shad roe, or goat cheese soufflé. With Château Bonnet Blanc: oysters on the half-shell, fresh crab salad, mussels, and clams.

JEAN-JACQUES DE BETHMANN (*Château Olivier*): "Oysters, lobster, Rouget du Bassin d'Arcachon."

ANTHONY PERRIN (*Château Carbonnieux*): "With a young Château Carbonnieux Blanc: chilled lobster consommé, or shellfish, such as oysters, scallops, or grilled shrimp. With an older Carbonnieux: a traditional sauced fish course or a goat cheese."

THE STYLE of classified white château wines varies according to the ratio of Sauvignon Blanc and Sémillon used. Château Olivier, for example, is made with 65% Sémillon, and Château Carbonnieux with 65% Sauvignon Blanc.

WHEN THE original edition of the *Complete Wine Course* came out in 1985, the appellation "Pessac-Léognan" had not yet been established. Since 1987, this "new" appellation is your guarantee of the finest dry white wines in Bordeaux.

WHEN BUYING regional Sauternes look for these reputable shippers: Baron Philippe de Rothschild and B&G.

THERE ARE more Sémillon grapes planted in Bordeaux than there are Sauvignon Blanc.

OTHER SWEET-WINE producers in Bordeaux: Ste-Croix-du-Mont and Loupiac.

SAUTERNES is expensive to produce because several pickings must be completed before the crop is entirely harvested. The harvest can last into November.

NOT CLASSIFIED, but of outstanding quality: Château Fargues, Château Gilette, and Château Raymond Lafon.

### WORLD RECORD

In 2011, one bottle of Château d'Yquem 1811 sold for $117,000, the most money ever paid for a white wine.

SAUTERNES IS A wine you can age. In fact, most classified château wines in good vintages can easily age for 10 to 30 years.

# SAUTERNES/BARSAC

French Sauternes are always sweet, meaning that not all the grape sugar has turned into alcohol during fermentation. A dry French Sauternes doesn't exist. The Barsac district, adjacent to Sauternes, has the option of using Barsac or Sauternes as its appellation.

## What are the two different quality levels in style?

1. Regional ($)
2. Classified château ($$$–$$$$)

Sauternes is still producing one of the best sweet wines in the world. With the great vintages of 2003, 2005, 2007, and 2009, you'll be able to find excellent regional Sauternes if you buy from the best shippers. These wines represent a good value for your money, considering the labor involved in production, but they won't have the same intensity of flavor as that of a classified château.

## What are the main grape varieties in Sauternes?

**SÉMILLON**      **SAUVIGNON BLANC**

## If the same grapes are used for both the dry Graves and the sweet Sauternes, how do you explain the extreme difference in styles?

First and most important, the best Sauternes is made primarily with the Sémillon grape. Second, to make Sauternes, the winemaker leaves the grapes on the vine longer. He waits for a mold called *Botrytis cinerea* ("noble rot") to form. When noble rot forms on the grapes, the water within them evaporates and they shrivel. Sugar becomes concentrated as the grapes "raisinate." Then, during the winemaking process, not all the sugar is allowed to ferment into alcohol: hence, the high residual sugar.

### BEST BETS FOR VINTAGES OF SAUTERNES

1986*  1988*  1989*  1990*  1995  1996  1997*  1998  2000
2001*  2002  2003*  2005*  2006  2007*  2008  2009*  2010*

*Note: * signifies exceptional vintage*

## How are Sauternes classified?

### FIRST GREAT GROWTH—GRAND PREMIER CRU

Château d'Yquem*

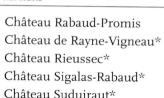

CHÂTEAU D'YQUEM did not produce a wine in 2012 due to poor weather conditions.

### FIRST GROWTH—PREMIERS

Château Climens* (Barsac)
Château Clos Haut-Peyraguey*
Château Coutet* (Barsac)
Château Guiraud*
Château Lafaurie-Peyraguey*
Château La Tour Blanche*

Château Rabaud-Promis
Château de Rayne-Vigneau*
Château Rieussec*
Château Sigalas-Rabaud*
Château Suduiraut*

CHÂTEAU RIEUSSEC is owned by the same family as Château Lafite-Rothschild.

### SECOND GROWTHS—DEUXIÈMES CRUS

Château d'Arche
Château Broustet (Barsac)
Château Caillou (Barsac)
Château Doisy-Daëne (Barsac)
Château Doisy-Dubroca (Barsac)
Château Doisy-Védrines* (Barsac)
Château Filhot*

Château Lamothe
Château Lamothe-Guignard
Château de Malle*
Château Myrat (Barsac)
Château Nairac* (Barsac)
Château Romer du Hayot*
Château Suau (Barsac)

* These are the châteaux most readily available in the United States.

## JUST DESSERTS

*My students always ask me, "What do you serve with Sauternes?" Here's a little lesson I learned when I first encountered the wines of Sauternes.*

*Many years ago, when I was visiting the Sauternes region, I was invited to one of the châteaux for dinner. Upon arrival, my group was offered appetizers of foie gras, and, to my surprise, Sauternes was served with it. All the books I had ever read said you should serve drier wines first and sweeter wines later. But since I was a guest, I thought it best not to question my host's selection.*

*When we sat down for the first dinner course (fish), we were once again served*

*a Sauternes. This continued through the main course—which happened to be rack of lamb—when another Sauternes was served.*

*I thought for sure our host would serve a great old red Bordeaux with the cheese course, but I was wrong again. With the Roquefort cheese was served a very old Sauternes.*

*With dessert soon on its way, I got used to the idea of having a dinner with Sauternes, and waited with anticipation for the final choice. You can imagine my surprise when a dry red Bordeaux— Château Lafite-Rothschild—was served with dessert!*

*Their point was that Sauternes doesn't have to be served only with dessert. All the Sauternes went well with the courses, because all the sauces complemented the wine and food.*

*By the way, the only wine that didn't go well with dinner was the Château Lafite-Rothschild with dessert, but we drank it anyway!*

*Perhaps this anecdote will inspire you to serve Sauternes with everything. Personally, I prefer to enjoy Sauternes by itself; I'm not a believer in the "dessert wine" category. This dessert wine is dessert in itself.*

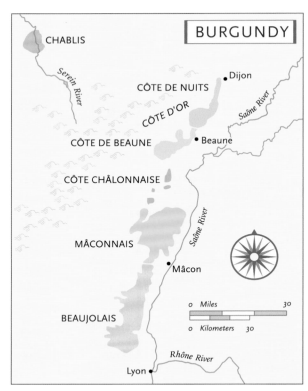

CHABLIS

Serein River

CÔTE DE NUITS  • Dijon

CÔTE D'OR

Saône River

CÔTE DE BEAUNE  • Beaune

CÔTE CHÂLONNAISE

Saône River

MÂCONNAIS

• Mâcon

0  Miles  30

0  Kilometers  30

BEAUJOLAIS

Rhône River

Lyon •

BURGUNDY

FRANCE

Paris ★

Atlantic
Ocean

BURGUNDY

THE LARGEST CITY in Burgundy is known not
for its wines but for another world-famous
product. The city is Dijon, and the product
is mustard.

# THE WHITE WINES OF BURGUNDY

## Where is Burgundy?

Burgundy is a region located in central eastern France. Its true fame is as one of the finest wine-producing areas in the world.

## What is Burgundy?

Burgundy is one of the major wine-producing regions that hold an AOC designation in France. However, over the years, I have often found that people are confused about what a Burgundy really is, because the name has been borrowed so freely.

Burgundy is *not* a synonym for red wine, even though the color known as burgundy is obviously named after red wine. Many of the world's most renowned (and expensive) white wines come from Burgundy. Adding to the confusion (especially going back twenty-plus years) is that many red wines around the world were simply labeled "Burgundy" even though they were ordinary table wines. There are still some wineries, especially in the United States, that continue to label their wines as Burgundy, but these wines have no resemblance to the style of authentic French Burgundy wines.

## What are the main regions within Burgundy?

CHABLIS      CÔTE D'OR { CÔTE DE NUITS
                        CÔTE DE BEAUNE

CÔTE CHÂLONNAISE      MÂCONNAIS      BEAUJOLAIS

Before we explore Burgundy region by region, it's important to know the types of wine that are produced there. Take a look at the chart on the next page: it breaks down the types of wine and tells you the percentage of reds to whites.

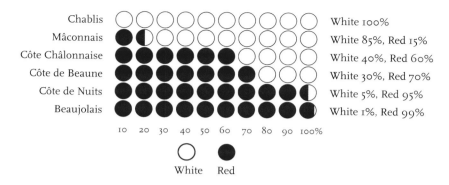

| | | | | | | | | | | |
|---|---|---|---|---|---|---|---|---|---|---|
| Chablis | ◯ ◯ ◯ ◯ ◯ ◯ ◯ ◯ ◯ ◯ | | | | | | | | | White 100% |
| Mâconnais | ◐ ◯ ◯ ◯ ◯ ◯ ◯ ◯ ◯ ◯ | | | | | | | | | White 85%, Red 15% |
| Côte Châlonnaise | ● ● ● ● ◯ ◯ ◯ ◯ ◯ ◯ | | | | | | | | | White 40%, Red 60% |
| Côte de Beaune | ● ● ● ● ● ● ● ◯ ◯ ◯ | | | | | | | | | White 30%, Red 70% |
| Côte de Nuits | ● ● ● ● ● ● ● ● ● ◐ | | | | | | | | | White 5%, Red 95% |
| Beaujolais | ● ● ● ● ● ● ● ● ● ● | | | | | | | | | White 1%, Red 99% |

10 20 30 40 50 60 70 80 90 100%

◯ White   ● Red

CÔTE D'OR production:
78% red
22% white

Burgundy is another region so famous for its red wines that people may forget that some of the finest white wines of France are also produced there. The three areas in Burgundy that produce world-famous white wines are:

**CHABLIS     CÔTE DE BEAUNE     MÂCONNAIS**

ALTHOUGH CHABLIS is part of the Burgundy region, it is a three-hour drive south from there to the Mâconnais area.

If it's any comfort to you, you need to know only one white-grape variety: Chardonnay. All the great white Burgundies are made from 100 percent Chardonnay.

## Is there only one type of white Burgundy?

Although Chardonnay is used to make all the best French white Burgundy wines, the three areas produce many different styles. Much of this has to do with where the grapes are grown and the vinification procedures. For example, the northern climate of Chablis produces wines with more acidity than those in the southern region of Mâconnais.

With regard to vinification procedures, after the grapes are harvested in the Chablis and Mâconnais areas, most are fermented and aged in stainless steel tanks. In the Côte de Beaune, after the grapes are harvested, a good percentage of the wines are fermented in small oak barrels and also aged in oak barrels. The wood adds complexity, depth, body, flavor, and longevity to the wines.

White Burgundies have one trait in common: they are dry.

ANOTHER WHITE grape found in the Burgundy region is the Aligoté. It is a lesser grape variety and the grape name usually appears on the label.

ALSO LOOK for regional Burgundy wine, such as Bourgogne Blanc or Bourgogne Rouge.

MOST PREMIER CRU wines give you the name of the vineyard on the label, but others are simply called Premier Cru, which is a blend of different cru vineyards.

THE AVERAGE yield for a Village wine in Burgundy is 360 gallons per acre. For the Grand Cru wines it is 290 gallons per acre, a noticeably higher concentration, which produces a more flavorful wine.

OAK AND VINE CLASSIFICATIONS
(A GENERAL RULE)

Village wine: 25% new oak
Premier Cru: 40–70% new oak
Grand Cru: 80–100% new oak

## THE STORY OF KIR

*The apéritif Kir has been popular from time to time. It is a mixture of white wine and crème de cassis (made from black currants). It was the favorite drink of the former mayor of Dijon, Canon Kir, who originally mixed in the sweet cassis to balance the high acidity of the local white wine made from the Aligoté grape.*

## How are the wines of Burgundy classified?

The type of soil and the angle and direction of the slope are the primary factors determining quality. Here are the levels of quality:

**Village wine:** Bears the name of a specific village. Cost: $.

**Premier Cru:** From a specific vineyard with special characteristics, within one of the named villages. Usually a Premier Cru wine will list on the label the village first and the vineyard second. Cost: $$.

**Grand Cru:** From a specific vineyard that possesses the best soil and slope in the area and meets or exceeds all other requirements. In most areas of Burgundy, the village doesn't appear on the label—only the Grand Cru vineyard name is used. Cost: $$$$.

## A NOTE ON THE USE OF WOOD

*Each wine region in the world has its own way of producing wines. Wine was always fermented and aged in wood—until the introduction of cement tanks, glass-lined tanks, and, most recently, stainless-steel tanks. Despite these technological improvements, many winemakers prefer to use the more traditional methods. For example, some of the wines from the firm of Louis Jadot are fermented in wood as follows:*

*One-third of the wine is fermented in new wood*

*One-third of the wine is fermented in year-old wood*

*One-third of the wine is fermented in older wood*

*Jadot's philosophy is that the better the vintage, the newer the wood: younger wood imparts more flavor and tannin, which might overpower wines of lesser vintage. Thus, younger woods are generally reserved for aging the better vintages.*

# CHABLIS

Chablis is the northernmost area in Burgundy, and it produces only white wine.

ALL FRENCH Chablis is made of 100% Chardonnay grapes.

## Isn't Chablis just a general term for white wine?

The name "Chablis" suffers from the same misinterpretation and overuse as does the name "Burgundy." Because the French didn't take the necessary precautions to protect the use of the name, "Chablis" is now randomly applied to many ordinary bulk wines from other countries. Chablis has come to be associated with some very undistinguished wines, but this is not the case with French Chablis. In fact, the French take their Chablis very seriously. There are special classification and quality levels for Chablis.

THERE ARE more than 250 grape growers in Chablis, but only a handful age their wine in wood.

## What are the different quality levels of Chablis?

**Petit Chablis:** The most ordinary Chablis; rarely seen in the United States.

**Chablis:** A wine that comes from grapes grown anywhere in the Chablis district, also known as a Village wine.

**Chablis Premier Cru:** A very good quality of Chablis that comes from specific high-quality vineyards.

**Chablis Grand Cru:** The highest classification of Chablis, and the most expensive because of its limited production. There are only seven vineyards in Chablis entitled to be called Grand Cru.

OF THESE quality levels, the best value is a Chablis Premier Cru.

THERE ARE only 245 acres planted in Chablis Grand Cru vineyards.

CHABLIS VILLAGE $

CHABLIS PREMIER CRU $$

CHABLIS GRAND CRU $$$$

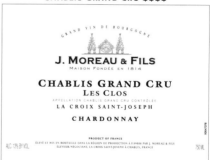

THE WINTER temperatures in some parts of Chablis can match those of Norway.

If you're interested in buying only the best Chablis, here are the seven Grands Crus and the most important Premier Cru vineyards:

THE SEVEN GRAND CRU VINEYARDS OF CHABLIS

| | |
|---|---|
| Blanchots | Preuses |
| Bougros | Valmur |
| Grenouilles | Vaudésir |
| Les Clos | |

SOME OF THE TOP PREMIER CRU VINEYARDS OF CHABLIS

| | |
|---|---|
| Côte de Vaulorent | Montmains |
| Fourchaume | Monts de Milieu |
| Lechet | Vaillon |
| Montée de Tonnerre | |

## How should I buy Chablis?

The two major aspects to look for in Chablis are the shipper and the vintage. Here is a list of the most important shippers of Chablis to the United States:

| | |
|---|---|
| A. REGNARD & FILS | JOSEPH DROUHIN |
| ALBERT PIC & FILS | LA CHABLISIENNE |
| DOMAINE LAROCHE | LOUIS JADOT |
| FRANÇOIS RAVENEAU | LOUIS MICHEL |
| GUY ROBIN | RENÉ DAUVISSAT |
| J. MOREAU & FILS | ROBERT VOCORET |
| JEAN DAUVISSAT | SIMMONET-FEBVRE |
| | WILLIAM FÈVRE |

## When should I drink my Chablis?

*Chablis:* within two years of the vintage
*Premier Cru:* between two and four years of the vintage
*Grand Cru:* between three and eight years of the vintage

### BEST BETS FOR RECENT VINTAGES OF CHABLIS

2005* 2006* 2007 2008* 2009* 2010* 2011*

*Note: * signifies exceptional vintage*

## CÔTE DE BEAUNE

This is one of the two major areas of the Côte d'Or. The wines produced here are some of the finest examples of dry white Chardonnay produced in the world and are considered a benchmark for winemakers everywhere.

The three most important white wine–producing villages of the Côte de Beaune are Meursault, Puligny-Montrachet, and Chassagne-Montrachet. All three produce their white wine from the same grape—100 percent Chardonnay.

## CÔTE DE BEAUNE

*Here is a list of my favorite white wine–producing villages and vineyards in the Côte de Beaune.*

| VILLAGE | PREMIER CRU VINEYARDS | GRAND CRU VINEYARDS |
|---|---|---|
| *Aloxe-Corton* | | *Corton-Charlemagne* |
| | | *Charlemagne* |
| *Beaune* | *Clos des Mouches* | *None* |
| *Meursault* | *Blagny* | |
| | *Les Charmes* | |
| | *Les Genevrières* | |
| | *La Goutte d'Or* | |
| | *Les Perrières* | *None* |
| | *Poruzots* | |
| *Puligny-Montrachet* | *Clavoillons* | |
| | *Les Caillerets* | *Bâtard-Montrachet\** |
| | *Les Champs Gain* | |
| | *Les Combettes* | *Montrachet\** |
| | *Les Folatières* | *Bienvenue-Bâtard-Montrachet* |
| | *Les Pucelles* | *Chevalier-Montrachet* |
| | *Les Referts* | |
| *Chassagne-Montrachet* | *Morgeot* | *Bâtard-Montrachet\** |
| | | *Criots-Bâtard-Montrachet* |
| | *Les Ruchottes* | *Montrachet\** |

*\* The vineyards of Montrachet and Bâtard-Montrachet overlap between the villages of Puligny-Montrachet and Chassagne-Montrachet.*

THE LARGEST Grand Cru, in terms of production, is Corton-Charlemagne, which represents more than 50% of all white Grand Cru wines.

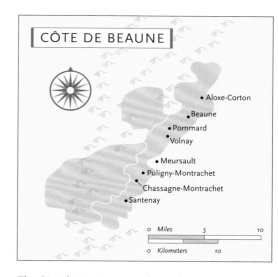

The Côte de Nuit is primarily a red wine–producing region but the villages of Vougeot and Musigny make some exceptional white wines.

| VILLAGE $ | PREMIER CRU $$ | GRAND CRU $$$ |
|---|---|---|
|  |  |  |

*"The difference between the Village wine, Puligny-Montrachet, and the Grand Cru Montrachet is not in the type of wood used in aging or how long the wine is aged in wood. The primary difference is in the location of the vineyards, i.e., the soil and the slope of the land."*

—ROBERT DROUHIN

## What makes each Burgundy wine different?

In Burgundy, one of the most important factors in making a good wine is soil. The quality of the soil is the main reason why there are three levels and price points between a Village, a Premier Cru, and a Grand Cru wine. Another major factor that differentiates each wine is the vinification procedure the winemaker uses—the recipe. It's the same as if you were to compare the chefs at three different restaurants: They may start out with the same ingredients, but it's what they do with those ingredients that matters.

### BEST BETS FOR CÔTE DE BEAUNE WHITE

2002* 2005* 2006* 2007* 2008* 2009* 2010* 2011

*Note: \* signifies exceptional vintage*

## CÔTE CHÂLONNAISE

The Côte Châlonnaise is the least known of the major wine districts of Burgundy. Although the Châlonnaise produces such red wines as Givry and Mercurey (see Class Four, "The Red Wines of Burgundy and the Rhône Valley"), it also produces some very good white wines that not many people are familiar with, which means value for you. I'm referring to the wines of Montagny and Rully. These wines are of the highest quality produced in the area, similar to the white wines of the Côte d'Or but less costly.

Look for the wines of Antonin Rodet, Faiveley, Louis Latour, Moillard, Olivier Leflaive, and Jacques Dury.

# MÂCONNAIS

The southernmost white wine–producing area in Burgundy, the Mâconnais has a climate warmer than that of the Côte d'Or and Chablis. Mâcon wines are, in general, pleasant, light, uncomplicated, reliable, and a great value.

## What are the different quality levels of Mâconnais wines?

From basic to best:

**1. MÂCON BLANC**

**2. MÂCON SUPÉRIEUR**

**3. MÂCON-VILLAGES**

**4. ST-VÉRAN**

**5. POUILLY-VINZELLES**

**6. POUILLY-FUISSÉ**

Of all Mâcon wines, Pouilly-Fuissé is unquestionably one of the most popular. It is among the highest-quality Mâconnais wines, fashionable to drink in the United States long before most Americans discovered the splendors of wine. As wine consumption increased in America, Pouilly-Fuissé and other famous areas such as Pommard, Nuits-St-Georges, and Chablis became synonymous with the best wines of France and could always be found on any restaurant's wine list.

In my opinion, Mâcon-Villages is the best value. Why pay more for Pouilly-Fuissé—sometimes three times as much—when a simple Mâcon will do just as nicely?

**BEST BETS FOR RECENT VINTAGES OF MÂCON WHITE**

2008*   2009**   2010*   2011

*Note: \* signifies exceptional vintage*

*\*\* signifies extraordinary vintage*

MORE THAN four-fifths of the wines from the Mâconnais are white.

THERE IS a village named Chardonnay in the Mâconnais area, where the grape's name is said to have originated.

*Joseph Drouhin®*

POUILLY-FUISSÉ

APPELLATION CONTROLÉE

MIS EN BOUTEILLE PAR JOSEPH DROUHIN NÉGOCIANT ÉLEVEUR A BEAUNE, CÔTE - D'OR, FRANCE, AUX CELLIERS DES ROIS DE FRANCE ET DES DUCS DE BOURGOGNE

ALC. 13.0% BY VOL.

SINCE MÂCON wines are usually not aged in oak, they are ready to drink as soon as they are released.

IF YOU'RE taking a client out on a limited expense account, a safe wine to order is Mâcon. If the sky's the limit, go for the Meursault!

DOMAINE LEFLAIVE'S wines are named for characters and places in a local medieval tale. The Chevalier of Puligny-Montrachet, lonely for his son who was off fighting in the Crusades, amused himself in the ravinelike vineyards (Les Combettes) with a local maiden (Pucelle), only to welcome the arrival of another son (Bâtard-Montrachet) nine months later.

ESTATE-BOTTLED wine: The wine is made, produced, and bottled by the owner of the vineyard.

# OVERVIEW

Now that you're familiar with the many different white wines of Burgundy:

## How do you choose the right one for you?

First look for the vintage year. With Burgundy, it's especially important to buy a good year. After that, your choice becomes a matter of taste and cost. If price is no object, aren't you lucky?

Also, after some trial and error, you may find that you prefer the wines of one shipper over another. Here are some of the shippers to look for when buying white Burgundy:

BOUCHARD PÈRE & FILS
CHANSON
JOSEPH DROUHIN
LABOURÉ-ROI
LOUIS JADOT

LOUIS LATOUR
OLIVIER LEFLAIVE FRÈRES
PROSPER MAUFOUX
ROPITEAU FRÈRES

Although 80 percent of Burgundy wines are sold through shippers, some fine estate-bottled wines are available in limited quantities in the United States. The better ones include:

CHÂTEAU FUISSÉ (POUILLY-FUISSÉ)
DOMAINE BACHELET-RAMONET (CHASSAGNE-MONTRACHET)
DOMAINE BOILLOT (MEURSAULT)
DOMAINE BONNEAU DU MARTRAY (CORTON-CHARLEMAGNE)
DOMAINE COCHE-DURY (MEURSAULT, PULIGNY-MONTRACHET)
DOMAINE DES COMTES LAFON (MEURSAULT)
DOMAINE ÉTIENNE SAUZET (PULIGNY-MONTRACHET)
DOMAINE LUCIEN LE MOINE (CORTON-CHARLEMAGNE)
DOMAINE LEFLAIVE (MEURSAULT, PULIGNY-MONTRACHET)
DOMAINE MATROT (MEURSAULT)
DOMAINE PHILIP COLIN (CHASSAGNE-MONTRACHET)
DOMAINE VINCENT GIRARDIN (CHASSAGNE-MONTRACHET)

## Forty years later in white Burgundy

If you are looking for pure unoaked Chardonnay at its best, then the crisp flavorful Chablis region of France will satisfy your needs. Over the last forty years these wines have gotten only better. After overcoming serious frosts in the late fifties through improved methods of frost protection, the region has increased its vineyard acreage from 4,000 acres to 12,000 acres without losing its quality. Great news for the consumer.

The white wines of the Mâconnais and Châlonnaise represent some of the great value wines made from 100 percent Chardonnay, yet most are usually priced under $20 a bottle.

One of the big changes, especially in Mâcon, is the inclusion of the grape variety on the label. With increased competition from the new-world Chardonnay producers, the French government has finally realized that Americans and other countries buy wines by the grape variety.

The great white wines of the Côte d'Or have achieved greatness in the last forty years. For me these are the best white wines in the world! With a new generation of winemakers who have studied around the world, there is more control in the vineyards and in the cellars, plantings of new clones, and picking lower yields. Chaptalization, the once prevalent addition of sugar to the fermenting juice to increase the alcohol content, is rarely used today. The wines today have a better natural balance.

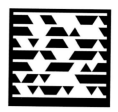

ONLINE STORE
http://bit.ly/foGF0p

*Links at the end of class lead you to Sherry-Lehmann's online store, where you can buy many of Kevin's recommended wines for the region you just studied.*

**FOR FURTHER READING**

I recommend *Burgundy* by Anthony Hanson; *Burgundy* by Robert M. Parker Jr.; *The Wines of Burgundy* and *Côte d'Or* by Clive Coates, M.W.; and *Making Sense of Burgundy* by Matt Kramer.

## WINE AND FOOD

*When you choose a white Burgundy wine, you have a whole gamut of wonderful food possibilities. Let's say that you decide upon a wine from the Mâconnais area: very reasonably priced, Mâconnais wines are suitable for picnics, as well as for more formal dinners. Or, you might select one of the fuller-bodied Côte de Beaune wines, or, if you prefer, an all-purpose Chablis that can even stand up to a hearty steak. Here are some tempting combinations offered by the winemakers.*

ROBERT DROUHIN: *With a young Chablis or St-Véran, Mr. Drouhin enjoys shellfish. "Fine Côte d'Or wines match well with any fish or light white meat such as veal or sweetbreads. But please, no red meat."*

CHRISTIAN MOREAU: *"A basic Village Chablis is good as an apéritif and with hors d'oeuvres and salads. A great Premier Cru or Grand Cru Chablis needs something more special, such as lobster. It's an especially beautiful match if the wine has been aged a few years."*

PIERRE HENRY GAGEY *(Louis Jadot): "My favorite food combination with white Burgundy wine is, without doubt, homard grillé Breton (blue lobster). Only harmonious, powerful, and delicate wines are able to go with the subtle, thin flesh and very fine taste of the Breton lobster."*

*Mr. Gagey says Chablis is a great match for oysters, snails, and shellfish, but a "Grand Cru Chablis should be had with trout."*

*On white wines of the Côte de Beaune,*

*Mr. Gagey gets a bit more specific: "With Village wines, which should be had at the beginning of the meal, try a light fish or quenelles (light dumplings). Premier Cru and Grand Cru wines can stand up to heavier fish and shellfish such as lobster—but with a wine such as Corton-Charlemagne, smoked Scottish salmon is a tasty choice."*

*Mr. Gagey's parting words on the subject: "Never with meat."*

LOUIS LATOUR: *"With Corton-Charlemagne, filet of sole in a light Florentine sauce. Otherwise, the Chardonnays of Burgundy complement roast chicken, seafood, and light-flavored goat cheese particularly well." Mr. Latour believes that one should have Chablis with oysters and fish.*

# Class One:
# The White Wines of France

Welcome to the first tasting in the book. This tasting will start with a lighter-styled Riesling from Alsace and end with a sweet Sauternes from Bordeaux. Remember to use the 60-second wine expert worksheet (page 23) when tasting these wines. Pay attention to the balance of fruit and acid, and note that some high-acid wines will taste better with food, especially shellfish.

## THE WINES

### Understanding Riesling

**One Riesling, tasted alone**

    1. Alsace Riesling

### Understanding Melon and Sauvignon Blanc

**Two wines from the Loire Valley compared**

    2. Muscadet
    3. Pouilly-Fumé

3.

1.

## Understanding Sauvignon Blanc and Sémillon

### *One Bordeaux, tasted alone*

4. Château from Graves or Pessac-Leognan

## Understanding Chardonnay

### *Four wines from Burgundy compared*

5. Unoaked Mâcon-Villages
6. Oaked Chablis Premier Cru
7. Village wine, such as Meursault
8. Premier Cru, such as Puligny-Montrachet Les Folitières

## Understanding Gewürztraminer

### *One Alsace wine, tasted alone*

9. Gewürztraminer

## Understanding Sémillon

### *One Sauternes, tasted alone*

10. Bordeaux, Château from Sauternes

4.

5.

9.

8.

6.

7.

*Please note that labels are suggestions for wineries and producers to look for. For more examples, see pages 34, 37, 39, 41, 46, 47, and 50.*

# Questions for Class One:
# The White Wines of France

REFER TO PAGE

1. Match grape variety with wine region. . . . . . . . . . . . . . . . . . . . . . . . . . . . . . . . . . . . . . . . . . . . . . . . . .31

    a. Riesling                        \_\_\_Champagne

    b. Sauvignon Blanc         \_\_\_Loire Valley

    c. Chardonnay             \_\_\_Alsace

    d. Sémillon                  \_\_\_Burgundy

    e. Gewürztraminer         \_\_\_Bordeaux

    f. Grenache                 \_\_\_Côtes du Rhône

    g. Pinot Noir

    h. Cabernet Sauvignon

    i. Chenin Blanc

    j. Syrah

    k. Merlot

2. When were the Appellation d'Origine Contrôlée (AOC) laws first established? . . . . . . . . . . . . . . . . . . . . . .32

3. How many acres are there in a hectare? . . . . . . . . . . . . . . . . . . . . . . . . . . . . . . . . . . . . . . . . . . . . . . . . .32

4. How many gallons are there in a hectoliter? . . . . . . . . . . . . . . . . . . . . . . . . . . . . . . . . . . . . . . . . . . . . . .32

5. What is one difference in style between a Riesling from Alsace and a Riesling from Germany? . . . . . . . .33

6. What is the most planted grape in Alsace? . . . . . . . . . . . . . . . . . . . . . . . . . . . . . . . . . . . . . . . . . . . . . . . .33

7. Name two important shippers of Alsace wine. . . . . . . . . . . . . . . . . . . . . . . . . . . . . . . . . . . . . . . . . . . . . .34

8. What is the grape variety for the wines Sancerre and Pouilly-Fumé? . . . . . . . . . . . . . . . . . . . . . . . . . . . . 36

9. What is the grape variety for the wine Vouvray? . . . . . . . . . . . . . . . . . . . . . . . . . . . . . . . . . . . . . . . . . . . .36

# The White Wines of California

# The Wines of Washington, Oregon, and New York

AMERICAN WINE AND WINEMAKING • THE WHITE WINES OF CALIFORNIA •

WASHINGTON STATE • OREGON • NEW YORK • ROUNDING OUT THE TOP TWELVE

WINE-PRODUCING STATES

VIDEO
http://bit.ly/hp4ari

PRONUNCIATIONS
http://bit.ly/zSs4AY

LEIF ERIKSSON, upon discovering North America, named it Vineland. In fact, there are more species of native grape in North America than on any other continent.

**PAST AND PRESENT**

U.S. consumption of wine:
1970: 267 million gallons
2012: 856 million gallons
An increase of almost 600 million gallons!

THE FRENCH Huguenots established colonies in Jacksonville, Florida, in 1562 and produced wine using the wild Scuppernong grape. Evidence indicates that there was a flourishing wine industry in 1609 at the site of the early Jamestown settlements. In 2004 an old wine cellar was discovered in Jamestown with an empty bottle dating back to the seventeenth century.

EARLY GERMAN immigrants imported Riesling grapes and called their finished wine Hock; the French called their wine Burgundy or Bordeaux; and the Italians borrowed the name "Chianti" for theirs.

# American Wine and Winemaking

ACCORDING TO GALLUP, wine drinking has jumped by more than a third in the United States over the last twenty years, with about 30 percent of Americans drinking at least one glass of wine a week. Americans prefer domestic wines: more than three-quarters of all wines consumed by Americans are produced in the United States. Meanwhile, the number of American wineries has doubled in the last two decades—to close to 6,000—and, for the first time in American history, all fifty states produce wine.

Because American wines are so dominant in the U.S. market, it makes sense to pause here and take a detailed look at winemaking in the United States. While we often think of the wine industry as "young" in America, in fact its roots go back some 400 years.

## What happened in the early days of winemaking in the United States?

A short time after arriving in America, the Pilgrims and early pioneers, accustomed to drinking wine with meals, were delighted to find grapevines growing wild. These thrifty, self-reliant colonists thought they had found in this species (*Vitis labrusca*, primarily) a means of producing their own wine, which would end their dependency on costly wine from Europe. They cultivated the existing local grapevines, harvested the grapes, and made their first American wine. The new vintage possessed an entirely different (and disappointing) flavor compared to wine made from European grapes. Cuttings were ordered from Europe of the *Vitis vinifera* vine, which had for centuries produced the finest wines in the world. Soon ships arrived bearing the tender cuttings, and the colonists, having paid scarce, hard-earned money for these new vines, planted and tended them with great care. They were eager to taste their first wine made from European grapes grown in American soil.

Despite their efforts, few of the European vines thrived. Many died, and those that survived produced few grapes, whose meager yield resulted in very poor-quality wine. Early settlers blamed the cold climate, but today we know that their European vines lacked immunity to the New World's plant diseases and pests. For the next 200 years every attempt at establishing varieties of vinifera—either intact or through crossbreeding with native vines—failed.

Left with no choice, growers throughout the Northeast and Midwest returned to planting *Vitis labrusca,* North America's vine, and a small wine industry managed to survive.

European wine remained the preferred—though high-priced—choice. The failures of these early attempts to establish a wine industry in the United States, along with the high cost of imported wines, resulted in decreasing demand for wine. Gradually, American tastes changed and wine served at mealtime was reserved for special occasions; beer and whiskey had taken over wine's traditional place in American homes.

---

The major varieties of wine produced in the United States are made from these species:

**American:** *Vitis labrusca,* such as the Concord, Catawba, and Delaware; and *Vitis rotundifolia,* commonly called Scuppernong

**European:** *Vitis vinifera,* such as Riesling, Sauvignon Blanc, Chardonnay, Pinot Noir, Merlot, Cabernet Sauvignon, Zinfandel, and Syrah

**Hybrids:** A cross between vinifera and a native American species, such as Seyval Blanc, Vidal Blanc, Baco Noir, or Chancellor

---

*VITIS LABRUSCA,* the "slip-skinned" grape, is native to both the Northeast and the Midwest and produces a unique flavor. It is used in making grape juice—the bottled kind you'll find on supermarket shelves. Wine produced from labrusca grapes tastes, well, more "grapey" (also described as "foxy") than that from European wines.

## When I think of American wines I think of California. How and when did wine arrive in the West?

Wine production in the West began with the Spanish. As the Spanish settlers began pushing northward from Mexico, the Catholic Church followed, and a great era of mission building began. Early missions were more than just churches; they were entire communities conceived as self-sufficient fortifications protecting Spanish colonial interests throughout the Southwest and along the Pacific Coast. Besides growing their own food and making their own clothing, those early settlers also made their own wine, produced primarily for use in the Church. The demand for wine led Padre Junípero Serra to bring *Vitis vinifera* vines—brought to Mexico by the Spaniards—from Mexico to California in 1769. These vines took root, thriving in California due to its moderate climate. The first true California wine industry had been established, albeit on a small scale.

Two events occurred in the mid-1800s that resulted in an explosive growth of quality wine production. The first was the California Gold Rush in 1849, which brought immigrants from Europe and the East Coast along with their

THE EARLY missionaries established wineries in the southern parts of California. The first commercial winery was established in what we know today as Los Angeles.

THE GRAPE variety the missionaries used to make their sacramental wine was actually called the Mission grape. Unfortunately, it did not have the potential to produce a great wine.

IN 1861, First Lady Mary Todd Lincoln served American wines in the White House.

WHEN ROBERT Louis Stevenson honeymooned in the Napa Valley in 1880, he described the efforts of local vintners to match soil and climate with the best possible varietals. "One corner of land after another . . . this is a failure, that is better, this is best. So bit by bit, they grope about for their Clos de Vougeot and Lafite . . . and the wine is bottled poetry."

### WELCH'S GRAPE JUICE

Welch's grape juice has been around since the late 1800s. It was originally produced by staunch Prohibitionists and labeled "Dr. Welch's Unfermented Wine." In 1892 it was renamed "Welch's Grape Juice" and was successfully launched at the Columbian Exposition in Chicago in 1893.

winemaking traditions. They cultivated the vines and were soon producing good-quality commercial wine.

The second critical event occurred in 1861, when the governor of California, understanding the importance of viticulture to the state's growing economy, commissioned Count Agoston Haraszthy to select and import classic *Vitis vinifera* cuttings—such as Riesling, Zinfandel, Cabernet Sauvignon, and Chardonnay—from Europe. The count traveled to Europe, returning with more than 100,000 carefully selected vines. Not only did these grape varieties thrive in California's climate, they also produced good-quality wine! Serious California winemaking began in earnest.

## So, the rest, as they say, is history?

Not at all. In 1863, while California wines were flourishing, European vineyards were in trouble. Phylloxera—an aphid pest native to the East Coast that is very destructive to grape crops—began attacking European vineyards. This infestation, which arrived in Europe on cuttings from native American vines exported for experimental purposes, proved devastating. Over the next two decades, the phylloxera blight destroyed thousands of acres of European vines, severely diminishing European wine production just as demand was rapidly growing.

Since California was now virtually the only area in the world producing wine made from European grapes, demand for its wines skyrocketed. This helped develop, almost overnight, two huge markets for California wine. The first market clamored for good, inexpensive, yet drinkable wine produced on a mass scale. The second market sought higher-quality wines. California growers responded to both demands, and by 1876 California was producing more than 2.3 million gallons of wine per year, some of remarkable quality. California was, for the moment, the new center of global winemaking.

Unfortunately, in that same year, phylloxera arrived in California and began attacking its vineyards. Once it got there, it spread as rapidly as it had in Europe. With thousands of vines dying, the California wine industry faced financial ruin. To this day, the phylloxera blight remains one of the most destructive crop epidemics of all time.

Luckily, other states had continued producing wine made from labrusca vines, and American wine production didn't grind to a complete halt. Meanwhile, after years of research, European winemakers finally found a defense against the pernicious phylloxera aphid. They were the first to successfully graft *Vitis vinifera* vines onto the rootstock of labrusca vines (which were immune to the phylloxera), rescuing their wine industry.

Americans followed, and the California wine industry not only recovered but began producing better-quality wines than ever before. By the late 1800s, California wines were winning medals in international competition, gaining the respect and admiration of the world. And it took only 300 years!

## Prohibition: Yet Another Setback

In 1920, the Eighteenth Amendment to the United States Constitution created yet another setback for the American wine industry. The National Prohibition Act, also known as the Volstead Act, prohibited the manufacture, sale, transportation, importation, exportation, delivery, or possession of intoxicating liquors for beverage purposes. Prohibition, which continued for thirteen years, nearly destroyed what had become a thriving and national industry.

One of the loopholes in the Volstead Act allowed for the manufacture and sale of sacramental wine, medicinal wines for sale by pharmacists with a doctor's prescription, and medicinal wine tonics (fortified wines) sold without prescription. Perhaps more important, Prohibition allowed anyone to produce up to 200 gallons yearly of fruit juice or cider. The fruit juice, which was sometimes made into concentrate, was ideal for making wine. People would buy grape concentrate from California and have it shipped to the East Coast. The top of the container was stamped in big, bold letters: CAUTION: DO NOT ADD SUGAR OR YEAST OR ELSE FERMENTATION WILL TAKE PLACE! Some of this yield found its way to bootleggers throughout America who did just that. But not for long, because the government stepped in and banned the sale of grape juice, preventing illegal wine production. Vineyards stopped being planted, and the American wine industry came to a halt.

Fortified wine, or medicinal wine tonic—containing about 20 percent alcohol, which makes it more like a distilled spirit than regular wine—was still available and became America's number-one wine. American wine was soon popular more for its effect than its taste; in fact, the word "wino" came into use during the Depression from the name given to those unfortunate souls who turned to fortified wine to forget their troubles.

Prohibition came to an end in 1933, but its impact would be felt for decades. By its end, Americans had lost interest in quality wine. During

FORTY DIFFERENT American wineries won medals at the 1900 Paris Exposition, including those from California, New Jersey, New York, Ohio, and Virginia.

IN 1920 there were more than 700 wineries in California. By the end of Prohibition there were 160.

*"Once, during Prohibition, I was forced to live for days on nothing but food and water."*
—W. C. FIELDS

SOME OF THE dilemmas facing winemakers after Prohibition:
Locate on the East Coast or the West Coast?
Make sweet wine or dry wine?
Make high-alcohol wine or low-alcohol wine?
Make inexpensive bulk wine or premium wine?

BEST-SELLING wineries, from 1933 to 1968, were Almaden, Gallo, and Paul Masson.

IN 1933, more than 60% of wine sold in the United States contained more than 20% alcohol.

SOME EXAMPLES of fortified wine may be familiar to consumers today. The list includes Thunderbird and Wild Irish Rose.

THE BEST-KNOWN wineries of California in the 1960s and 1970s:

| | |
|---|---|
| Almaden | Charles Krug |
| Beaulieu | Louis Martini |
| Beringer | Mirassou |
| Buena Vista | Parducci |
| Concannon | Paul Masson |
| Hanzell | Sebastiani |
| Inglenook | Simi |
| Korbel | Wente |

Prohibition, thousands of acres of valuable grapes around the country had been plowed under. Wineries nationwide shut down and the winemaking industry dwindled to a handful of survivors, mostly in California and New York. Many growers on the East Coast returned to producing grape juice—the ideal use for the American labrusca grape. From 1933 to 1968, grape growers and winemakers had little more than personal incentive to produce any wine of quality. Jug wines, which got their name from the containers in which they were bottled, were inexpensive, nondescript, and mass produced. A few wineries, notably in California, were producing some good wines, but the majority of American wines produced during this period were ordinary.

Although Prohibition was devastating to the majority of American wine producers, some endured by making sacramental wines. Beringer, Beaulieu, and the Christian Brothers are a few of the wineries that managed to survive this dry time. Since these wineries didn't have to interrupt production during Prohibition, they had a jump on those that had to start all over.

The federal government, in repealing Prohibition, empowered states to legislate the sale and transportation of alcohol. Some states handed control to counties and, occasionally, even municipalities—a tradition that continues today, varying from state to state and often from county to county.

## The Renaissance of American Wine

I can't say when, exactly, the American wine renaissance began, but let's start in 1968, when, for the first time since Prohibition, table wines—wines with alcohol content between 7 and 14 percent—outsold fortified wines, which have an alcohol content between 17 and 22 percent. Although American wines were improving, consumers still believed the best wines were made in Europe, especially France.

In the midsixties and early seventies, a small group of dedicated California winemakers began concentrating on making high-quality wine to equal Europe's best. Their early wines demonstrated potential and began attracting the attention of astute wine writers and wine enthusiasts around the country.

As they continued to improve their product, these same winemakers began to realize that they had to find a way to differentiate their quality wines from California's mass-produced wines—which had such generic names as Burgundy, Chablis, or Chianti—and to ally their wines, at least in the minds of wine buyers and consumers, with European wines. Their solution was brilliant: they chose to label their best wines by varietal.

Varietal designation calls the wine by the name of the predominant grape used to produce it: Chardonnay, Cabernet Sauvignon, Pinot Noir, etc. The savvy consumer learned that a wine labeled "Chardonnay" would have the general characteristics of any wine made from that grape. This made wine buying easier for both wine buyers and sellers.

Varietal labeling quickly spread throughout the industry and became so successful that, in the eighties, varietal designation became an American industry standard, forcing the federal government to revise its labeling regulations.

Today, varietal labeling is the norm for the highest-quality American wines, has been adopted by many other countries, and has helped bring worldwide attention to California wine. While California still produces 90 percent of American wine, its success has inspired winemakers in other areas of the United States to refocus on producing high-quality wines.

## Where exactly do they make these quality American wines?

To buy American wines intelligently means having knowledge about and familiarity with each state whose wine you're interested in buying, as well as the regions within the state. Some states—or even regions within a state—may specialize in white wine, others in red; and there are even regions that specialize in wine made from a specific grape variety. Therefore, it is helpful to know the defined grape-growing areas within each state or region, the American Viticultural Areas (AVAs).

An AVA, or American Viticultural Area, is a specific grape-growing area within a state or a region recognized by and registered with the federal government. AVA designation began in the 1980s and is a system styled after the European regional system. In France, Bordeaux and Burgundy are strictly enforced regional appellations (marked "Appellation d'Origine Contrôlée," or "AOC"); in Italy, Tuscany and Piedmont are recognized as zones (marked "Denominazione di Origine Controllata," or "DOC").

The Napa Valley, for example, is a defined viticultural area in the state of California. Columbia Valley is an AVA located in Washington State; both Oregon's Willamette Valley and New York's Finger Lakes district are similarly identified.

Vintners are discovering, as their European counterparts did years ago, which grapes grow best in which particular soils and climatic conditions.

IN THE early 1970s, Chenin Blanc was the best-selling white wine and Zinfandel the best-selling red.

THREE MAJOR grapes consumed by Americans are:
1. Chardonnay
2. Cabernet Sauvignon
3. Merlot

THERE ARE more than 200 viticultural areas in the United States, 108 of which are located in California.

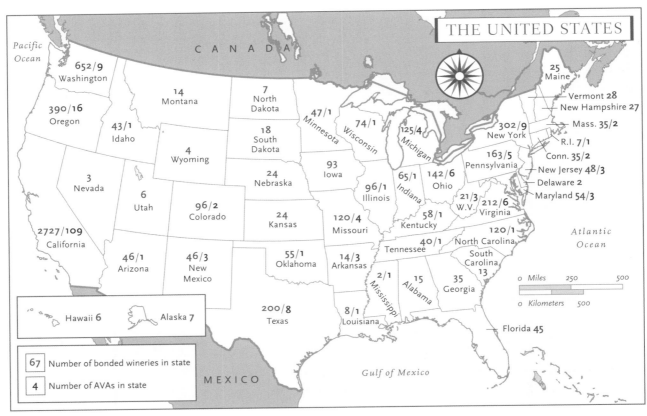

THE UNITED STATES

Pacific Ocean

CANADA

652/9 Washington

390/16 Oregon

14 Montana

7 North Dakota

47/1 Minnesota

74/1 Wisconsin

125/4 Michigan

25 Maine

Vermont 28

New Hampshire 27

Mass. 35/2

302/9 New York

R.I. 7/1

43/1 Idaho

4 Wyoming

18 South Dakota

93 Iowa

65/1 Illinois

142/6 Ohio

163/5 Pennsylvania

Conn. 35/2

New Jersey 48/3

3 Nevada

6 Utah

24 Nebraska

96/1 Indiana

21/3 W.V.

212/6 Virginia

Delaware 2

Maryland 54/3

2727/109 California

96/2 Colorado

24 Kansas

120/4 Missouri

58/1 Kentucky

120/1 North Carolina

Atlantic Ocean

46/1 Arizona

46/3 New Mexico

55/1 Oklahoma

14/3 Arkansas

40/1 Tennessee

13 South Carolina

2/1 Mississippi

15 Alabama

35 Georgia

o Miles    250    500

o Kilometers    500

Hawaii 6    Alaska 7

200/8 Texas

8/1 Louisiana

MEXICO

Gulf of Mexico

Florida 45

67 | Number of bonded wineries in state

4 | Number of AVAs in state

I believe the AVA concept is important to wine buying and will continue to be so as individual AVAs become known for certain grape varieties or wine styles. If an AVA is listed on the label, at least 85 percent of the grapes must come from that region.

For example, let's look at the Napa Valley, which is probably the best-known AVA in the United States, renowned for its Cabernet Sauvignon. Within Napa, there is a smaller inner district called Carneros, which has a cooler climate. Since Chardonnay and Pinot Noir need a cooler growing season to mature properly, these grape varieties are especially suited to that AVA. In New York, the Finger Lakes region is noted for Riesling. And those of you who have seen the movie *Sideways* know that Santa Barbara is a great place for Pinot Noir.

Although not necessarily a guarantee of quality, an AVA designation identifies a specific area well known and established for its wine. It is a point of reference for winemakers and consumers. A wine can be better understood by

**PAST AND PRESENT**

In 2013, there were more than 6,300 wineries in the United States, up from fewer than 500 in 1970. Ninety-nine percent are small and family owned.

its provenance, or where it came from. The more knowledge you have about a wine's origin by region and grape, the easier it is to buy even unknown brands with confidence. As you learn more about the characteristics of major grapes and styles of wine—and which you prefer—you'll be able to identify the AVAs that produce wines you're most likely to enjoy.

## Is that all I need to know?

There is more: an even higher quality of wine is now given a "proprietary" name.

The most recent worldwide trend is to ignore all existing standards by giving the highest-quality wines a proprietary name. A proprietary name helps high-end wineries differentiate their best wines from other wines from the same AVA, from similar varietals, and even from their own other offerings. In the United States, many of these proprietary wines fall under the category called Meritage (see page 168). Some examples of American proprietary wines are Dominus, Opus One, and Rubicon.

Federal laws governing standards and labels are another reason select wineries are increasingly using proprietary names. Federal law mandates, for example, that if a label lists a varietal, at least 75 percent of the grapes used to make the wine must be of that varietal.

Imagine a talented, innovative winemaker in the Columbia Valley region of Washington State. This winemaker is determined to produce an outstanding, full-bodied Bordeaux-style wine consisting of 60 percent Cabernet Sauvignon blended with several other grapes. Our ambitious winemaker has invested considerable time and labor to produce a really great wine: a wine suitable for aging that will be ready to drink in five years—but will be even better in ten.

After five years, our winemaker tastes the fruits of his labor and voilà! It is delicious, with all the promise of a truly outstanding wine. But how does he distinguish this wine; how can he attract buyers willing to pay a premium price for an unknown wine? He can't label it "Cabernet Sauvignon," because less than 75 percent of the grapes used are of that type. For this reason, many producers of fine wine are beginning to use proprietary names. It's indicative of the healthy state of the American wine industry as well. More and more winemakers are turning out better and better wines, and the very best is yet to come!

1. California (3.6 million tons of grapes crushed for wine)
2. Washington (366,000 tons)
3. New York (176,000 tons)
4. Pennsylvania (82,000 tons)
5. Oregon (40,000 tons)

WINERIES IN the United States are opening at the rate of 300 per year.

**THE TOP TEN STATES IN WINE CONSUMPTION PER CAPITA**

Washington, DC (6.7 gallons)
New Hampshire (4.9)
Vermont (4.3)
Massachusetts (4.2)
Nevada (3.8)
New Jersey (3.7)
Delaware (3.6)
Connecticut (3.6)
California (3.5)
Rhode Island (3.5)

IF YOU like to drink, move to New Hampshire. They are number one in beer and distilled spirits and number two in wine consumption per capita!

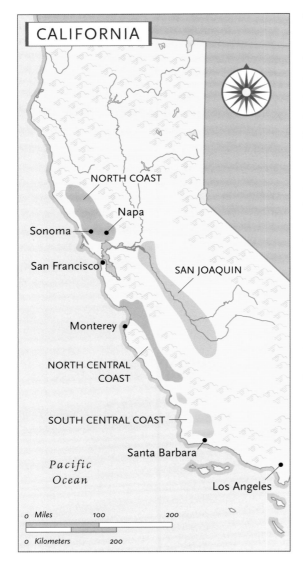

CALIFORNIA

NORTH COAST

Napa

Sonoma

San Francisco

SAN JOAQUIN

Monterey

NORTH CENTRAL
COAST

SOUTH CENTRAL COAST

Santa Barbara

*Pacific
Ocean*

Los Angeles

| 0 Miles | 100 | 200 |
| 0 Kilometers | 200 | |

CALIFORNIA WINES dominate American wine consumption, equaling 61% of all sales in the United States.

THERE ARE more than 60,000 wine labels registered in California.

**PAST AND PRESENT**

1970: 240 wineries
2012: 2,727 wineries

# THE WINES OF CALIFORNIA

No wine-growing area in the world has come so far so quickly as California. It seems ironic, because Americans historically have not been very interested in wine. But from the moment Americans first became "wine conscious," winemakers in California rose to the challenge. Forty years ago we were asking if California wines were entitled to be compared to European wines. Now California wines are available worldwide: exports have increased dramatically in recent years to countries such as Japan, Germany, and England. California produces more than 90 percent of U.S. wine. If the state were a nation, it would be the third leading wine producer in the world!

## AN INTRODUCTION TO CALIFORNIA WINES

### What are the main viticultural areas of California?

The map on this page should help familiarize you with the wine-making regions. It's easier to remember them if you divide them into four groups:

   ***North Coast:*** Napa County, Sonoma County, Mendocino County, Lake County *(Best wines: Cabernet Sauvignon, Zinfandel, Sauvignon Blanc, Chardonnay, Merlot)*
   ***North Central Coast:*** Monterey County, Santa Clara County, Livermore County *(Best wines: Chardonnay, Syrah, Grenache, Viognier, Marsanne, Roussane)*
   ***South Central Coast:*** San Luis Obispo County, Santa Barbara County *(Best wines: Sauvignon Blanc, Chardonnay, Pinot Noir, Syrah)*
   ***San Joaquin Valley:*** Known for jug wines, see page 69

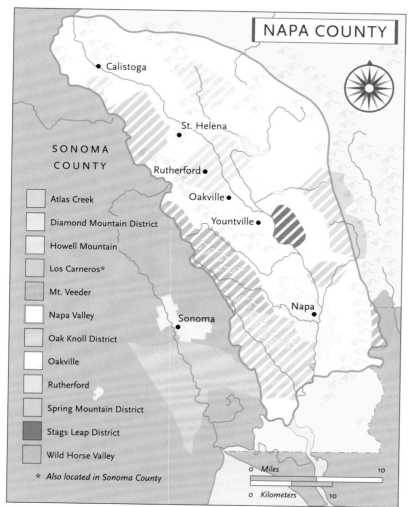

## NAPA COUNTY

- Calistoga
- St. Helena
- Rutherford
- Oakville
- Yountville
- Napa

SONOMA COUNTY

- Sonoma

| | Atlas Creek |
| | Diamond Mountain District |
| | Howell Mountain |
| | Los Carneros* |
| | Mt. Veeder |
| | Napa Valley |
| | Oak Knoll District |
| | Oakville |
| | Rutherford |
| | Spring Mountain District |
| | Stags Leap District |
| | Wild Horse Valley |

\* Also located in Sonoma County

0 Miles 10
0 Kilometers 10

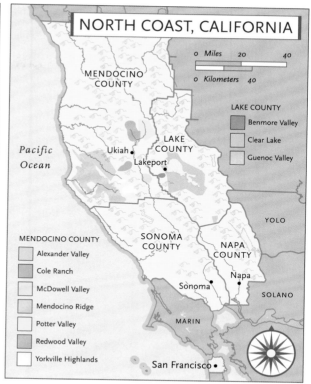

## NORTH COAST, CALIFORNIA

0 Miles 20 40
0 Kilometers 40

MENDOCINO COUNTY

Pacific Ocean

LAKE COUNTY
- Ukiah
- Lakeport

SONOMA COUNTY

NAPA COUNTY
- Napa
- Sonoma

YOLO

SOLANO

MARIN

- San Francisco

LAKE COUNTY
| | Benmore Valley |
| | Clear Lake |
| | Guenoc Valley |

MENDOCINO COUNTY
| | Alexander Valley |
| | Cole Ranch |
| | McDowell Valley |
| | Mendocino Ridge |
| | Potter Valley |
| | Redwood Valley |
| | Yorkville Highlands |

THERE ARE more than 535,000 acres of vineyards in California.

ACRES OF wine grapes planted in Napa: 44,398

### PAST AND PRESENT

1970: 27 wineries in Napa
2012: 400+ wineries in Napa

### TOP GRAPES PLANTED IN NAPA

1. Cabernet Sauvignon (18,887 acres)
2. Merlot (5,902 acres)
3. Chardonnay (6,972 acres)

1838: First wine grapes planted in Napa.

Although you may be most familiar with the names Napa and Sonoma, less than 10 percent of all California wine comes from these two regions combined. Even so, Napa alone accounts for over 30 percent of dollar sales of California wines. In fact, the bulk of California wine is from the San Joaquin Valley, where mostly jug wines are produced. This region accounts for 58 percent of the wine grapes planted. Maybe that doesn't seem too exciting—that the production of jug wine dominates California winemaking history—but Americans are not atypical in their preferences for this type of wine. In France, for example, AOC wines account for only 35 percent of all French wines, while the rest are everyday table wines.

ACRES OF wine grapes planted in Sonoma: 55,575

AS OF 2012, there were 269 wineries in Sonoma.

## TOP GRAPES PLANTED IN SONOMA

1. Chardonnay (14,814 acres)
2. Cabernet Sauvignon (11,335 acres)
3. Pinot Noir (11,644 acres)

LAST YEAR, more than 20 million people visited California wine-growing areas. Vineyards and wineries are the second-most popular California tourist destinations after Disneyland!

## BIGGER THAN HOLLYWOOD

Wine is California's most valuable finished agricultural product, with a $52 billion economic impact. The film industry: $30 billion.

## HOLLYWOOD AND VINE

Many movie actors, directors, and producers have invested in vineyards and wineries throughout California, including Francis Ford Coppola.

ROBERT MONDAVI was a great promoter for the California wine industry. "He was able to prove to the public what the people within the industry already knew—that California could produce world-class wines," said Eric Wente.

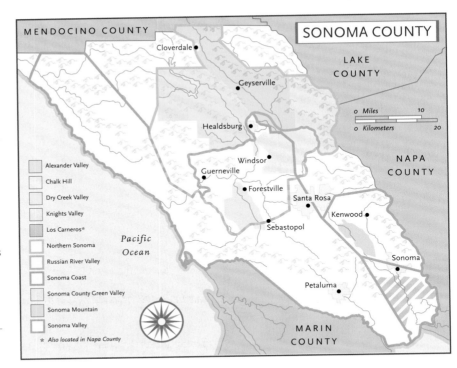

## When did California begin to make better-quality wines?

As early as the 1940s, Frank Schoonmaker, an importer and writer and one of the first American wine experts, convinced some California winery owners to market their best wines using varietal labels.

Robert Mondavi may be one of the best examples of a winemaker who concentrated solely on varietal wine production. In 1966, Mondavi left his family's Charles Krug Winery and started the Robert Mondavi Winery. His role was important to the evolution of varietal labeling of California wines. He was among the first major winemakers to make the total switch that led to higher-quality winemaking.

## A NOTE ON JUG WINES

*The phrase "jug wine" refers to simple, uncomplicated, everyday drinking wine. You're probably familiar with these types of wine: they're sometimes labeled with a generic name, such as Chablis or Burgundy. Inexpensive and well made, these wines were originally bottled in jugs, rather than in conventional wine bottles, hence the name "jug wine." They are very popular and account for the largest volume of California wine sold in the United States.*

*Ernest and Julio Gallo, who began their winery in 1933, are the major producers of jug wines in California. In fact, many people credit the Gallo brothers with converting American drinking habits from spirits to wine. Several other wineries also produce jug wines, among them Almaden, Paul Masson, and Taylor California Cellars.*

*In my opinion, the best-made jug wines in the world are from California. They maintain both consistency and quality from year to year.*

## How did California become a world-class producer in just forty years?

There are many reasons for California's winemaking success, including:

**Location**: Napa and Sonoma counties, two of the major quality-wine regions, are both less than a two-hour drive from San Francisco. The proximity of these regions to the city encourages both residents and tourists to visit the wineries in the two counties, most of which offer wine tastings and sell their wines in their own shops.

**Weather**: Abundant sunshine, warm daytime temperatures, cool evenings, and a long growing season all add up to good conditions for growing many grape varieties. California is certainly subject to sudden changes in weather, but a fickle climate is not a major worry.

**The University of California at Davis and Fresno State University**: Both schools have been the training grounds for many young California winemakers, and their curricula concentrate on the scientific study of wine, viticulture, and, most important, technology. Their research, focused on soil, different strains of yeast, hybridization, temperature-controlled fermentation, and other viticultural techniques, has revolutionized the wine industry worldwide.

THE MAJORITY of California wines retail from $9 to $20.

EXAMPLES OF new winery technology include:
Heat exchanges
Reverse osmosis
Bladder presses

CLONAL SELECTION, wind machines, drip irrigation, biodynamic vineyards, and mechanical harvesting are some new techniques in vineyard management.

THE UNIVERSITY of California at Davis graduated only five students from its oenology department in 1966. Today it has a waiting list of students from all over the world.

EARLY CALIFORNIA winemakers sent their children to study oenology at Geisenheim (Germany) or Bordeaux (France). Today, many European winemakers send their children to the University of California at Davis and to Fresno State University.

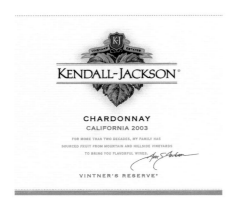

KENDALL-JACKSON

CHARDONNAY
CALIFORNIA 2003

FOR MORE THAN TWO DECADES, MY FAMILY HAS
SOURCED FRUIT FROM MOUNTAIN AND HILLSIDE VINEYARDS
TO BRING YOU FLAVORFUL WINES.

VINTNER'S RESERVE*

SO YOU want to buy a vineyard in California? Today, one acre in the Napa Valley costs between $150,000 to $250,000 unplanted, and it takes an additional $20,000 per acre to plant. This per-acre investment sees no return for three to five years. To this, add the cost of building the winery, buying the equipment, and hiring the winemaker.

### RECORD PRICE

IN 1970 the average price per acre in Napa was $2,000–$4,000.

IN 2002, film director Francis Ford Coppola, owner of Niebaum-Coppola Wine Estate, paid a record price of $350,000 an acre for vineyard land in Napa.

### CREATIVE FINANCING

Overheard at a restaurant in Yountville, Napa Valley: "How do you make a small fortune in the wine business?" "Start with a large fortune and buy a winery."

IN 2011, a Hong Kong investment company paid $40 million for a small (12-acre) Cabernet Sauvignon vineyard in Napa Valley.

***Money and Marketing Strategy***: This cannot be overemphasized. Marketing may not make the wine, but it certainly helps sell it. As more and more winemakers concentrated on making the best wine they could, American consumers responded with appreciation. They were willing to buy—and pay—more as quality improved. In order to keep up with consumer expectations, winemakers realized that they needed more research, development, and—most important—working capital. The wine industry turned to investors, both corporate and individual.

Since 1967, when the now defunct National Distillers bought Almaden, multinational corporations have recognized the profit potential of large-scale winemaking and have aggressively entered the wine business. They've brought huge financial resources and expertise in advertising and promotion that have helped advance American wines domestically and internationally. Other early corporate participants included Pillsbury and Coca-Cola.

On the other side of the investor scale are the individual investor/growers drawn to the business by their love of wine and their desire to live the winemaking "lifestyle." These individuals are more focused on producing quality wines.

Both corporate and individual investors had, by the 1990s, helped California fine-tune its wine industry, which today produces not only delicious and reliable wines in great quantity but also truly outstanding wines, many with investment potential.

## EARLY PIONEERS

*Some of the pioneers of the back-to-the-land movement:*

| "FARMER" | WINERY | ORIGINAL PROFESSION |
|---|---|---|
| Robert Travers | Mayacamas | Investment banker |
| David Stare | Dry Creek | Civil engineer |
| Tom Jordan | Jordan | Geologist |
| James Barrett | Chateau Montelena | Attorney |
| Tom Burgess | Burgess | Air Force pilot |
| Jess Jackson | Kendall-Jackson | Attorney |
| Warren Winiarski | Stag's Leap | College professor |
| Brooks Firestone | Firestone | Take a guess! |

## What's meant by "style"? How are different styles of California wine actually created?

"Style" refers to the characteristics of the grapes and wine. It is the trademark of the individual winemaker—an artist who tries different techniques to explore the fullest potential of the grapes.

Most winemakers will tell you that 95 percent of winemaking is in the quality of the grapes they begin with. The other 5 percent can be traced to the "personal touch" of the winemaker. Here are just a few of the hundreds of decisions a winemaker must make when developing his or her style of wine:

- When should the grapes be harvested?

- Should the juice be fermented in stainless-steel tanks or oak barrels? How long should it be fermented? At what temperature?

- Should the wine be aged at all? How long? If so, should it be aged in oak? What kind of oak—American, French?

- What varieties of grapes should be blended, and in what proportion?

- How long should the wine be aged in the bottle before it is sold?

The list goes on. Because there are so many variables in winemaking, producers can create many styles of wine from the same grape variety—so you can choose the style that suits your taste. With the relative freedom of winemaking in the United States, the style of California wines continues to be diversity.

## Why is California wine so confusing?

The renaissance of the California wine industry began only about forty years ago. Within that short period of time, some 1,700 new wineries have been established in California. Today, there are more than 2,300 wineries in California, most of them making more than one wine, and the price differences are reflected in the styles (you can get a Cabernet Sauvignon wine in any price range from Two Buck Chuck at $1.99 to Harlan Estate at more than $500 a bottle—so how do you choose?). The constant changes in the wine industry through experimentation keep California winemaking in a state of flux.

IN CALIFORNIA many winemakers move around from one winery to another, just as good chefs move from one restaurant to the next. This is not uncommon. They may choose to carry and use the same "recipe" from place to place, if it is particularly successful, and sometimes they will experiment and create new styles.

I'VE MENTIONED stainless-steel fermentation tanks before, so I'll give a description, in case you need one. These tanks are temperature controlled, allowing winemakers to control the temperature at which the wine ferments. For example, a winemaker could ferment wines at a low temperature to retain fruitiness and delicacy, while preventing browning and oxidation.

*"There is more potential for style variation in California than Europe because of the greater generosity of the fruit."*
—WARREN WINIARSKI, *founder, Stag's Leap Wine Cellars, Napa Valley*

AMBASSADOR ZELLERBACH, who created Hanzell Winery, was one of the first California winemakers to use small French oak aging barrels because he wanted to re-create a Burgundian style.

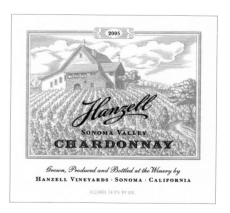

## NUMBER OF BONDED WINERIES IN CALIFORNIA

| Year | Wineries |
| --- | --- |
| 1970 | 240 |
| 1975 | 330 |
| 1980 | 508 |
| 1983 | 641 |
| 1985 | 712 |
| 1990 | 807 |
| 1995 | 944 |
| 2000 | 1,450 |
| 2011 | 2,628 |
| 2012 | 2,727 |

Source: The Wine Institute

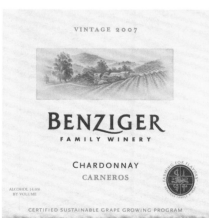

## American wineries selected by *Wine Spectator* for the California Wine Experience

L'Angevin
A. P. Vin
John Anthony
Araujo
Archery Summit
Argyle
David Arthur
Au Bon Climat
L'Aventure
Bacio Divino
Barnett
Beaulieu
Bennett Lane
Bergström
Beringer
Betz Family
Big Basin
Black Kite
Bond
Bonny Doon
Bounty Hunter
Buccella
David Bruce
Buehler
Cadence
Calera
Carter
Caymus
Cayuse
Chalk Hill
Chalone
Chappellet
Chateau St. Jean
Chateau Ste. Michelle
Chehalem
Chimney Rock
Clos du Bois
Col Solare
Columbia Crest
Continuum
Cornerstone

Côte Bonneville
Robert Craig
Darioush
Dark Horse
Delectus
DeLille
Diamond Creek
Dolce
Domaine Drouhin
Domaine Alfred
Domaine Carneros
Domaine Chandon
Domaine Serene
Dominus Estate
Donum Estate
Duckhorn
DuMOL
Dunn
Merry Edwards
El Molino
Elk Cove
Emeritus
Eroica—Ste. Michelle/
 Dr. Loosen
Etude
Far Niente
Gary Farrell
Ferrari-Carano
Gloria Ferrer
Fisher
Flora Springs
Foley Estate
Robert Foley
Foursight
Foxen
Freestone
Gemstone
Girard
Goldeneye
Gorman
Grgich Hills Estate

Groth
Hall
Hanzell
Harlan
Heitz
Hess Collection
Hewitt
Hidden Ridge
Paul Hobbs
Honig
Iron Horse
J Vineyards & Winery
Jericho Canyon
Justin
Kamen Estate
Kapcsándy Family
Keller Estate
Kathryn Kennedy
Tor Kenward Family
Kistler
Kosta Browne
Kutch
Ladera
Lagier Meredith
Lail
Lang & Reed
Cliff Lede
Lewis
Londer
Long Shadows
Loring
Luna
MacRostie
Marston Family
Martinelli
McPrice Meyers
Merus
Peter Michael
Michael Mondavi
Robert Mondavi
Morgan

| | | |
|---|---|---|
| Mount Eden | Ridge | Spring Valley |
| Mumm Napa | Rocca Family | Stag's Leap |
| Neiman | Rochioli | Staglin Family |
| Neyers | Owen Roe | D. R. Stephens |
| Nickel & Nickel | Roederer Estate | Sterling |
| Northstar | Rosenblum | Rodney Strong |
| Novy Family | Stephen Ross | Orin Swift |
| Opus One | Rubicon Estate | Switchback Ridge |
| Outpost | Rutherford Hill | Tablas Creek |
| Pahlmeyer | St. Clement | Robert Talbott |
| Paloma | Sanford | Talley |
| Papapietro Perry | Sbragia Family | Testarossa |
| Paradigm | Schrader | Treana |
| Fess Parker | Schramsberg | Trefethen |
| Patz & Hall | Sebastiani | Truchard |
| Penner-Ash | Seghesio Family | Turnbull |
| Joseph Phelps | Selene | Versant |
| Pine Ridge | Shafer | Viader |
| PlumpJack | Shea | Vision |
| Pride Mountain | Siduri | WillaKenzie |
| Provenance | Silver Oak | Robert Young Estate |
| Quintessa | W. H. Smith | Zepaltas |
| Ramey | Snowden | |
| Martin Ray | Sonoma-Loeb | |
| Realm | Souverain | |
| Revana | Spottswoode | |

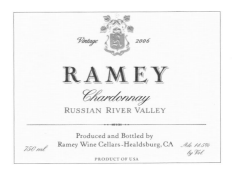

## What about the prices of California varietal wines?

You can't necessarily equate quality with price. Some excellent varietal wines that are produced in California are well within the budget of the average consumer. On the other hand, some varietals (primarily Chardonnay and Cabernet Sauvignon) may be quite expensive.

As in any market, it is mainly supply and demand that determines price. However, new wineries are affected by start-up costs, which sometimes are reflected in the price of the wine. Older, established wineries, which long ago amortized their investments, are able to keep their prices low when the supply/demand ratio calls for it. Remember, when you're buying California wine, price doesn't always reflect quality.

VINTAGE OF A LIFETIME
In 2012 California had its largest wine grape crop in history—over 4 million tons—and great quality is expected of this vintage.

## How do I choose a good California wine?

One of the reasons California produces such a wide variety of wine is that it has so many different climates. Some are as cool as Burgundy, Champagne, and the Rhein, while others are as warm as the Rhône Valley, Portugal, and the southern regions of Italy and Spain. If that's not diverse enough, these wine-growing areas have inner districts with "microclimates," or climates within climates. One of the microclimates (which are among the designated AVAs) in Sonoma County, for example, is the Russian River Valley.

To better understand this concept, let's take a close look at the Rudd label.

**State:**
California
**County:**
Sonoma
**Viticultural Area (AVA):**
Russian River Valley
**Vineyard:**
Bacigalupi
**Winery:**
Rudd

California labels tell you everything you need to know about the wine—and more. Here are some quick tips you can use when you scan the shelves at your favorite retailer. The label shown above will serve as an example.

The most important piece of information on the label is the producer's name. In this case, the producer is Rudd.

If the grape variety is on the label, a minimum of 75 percent of the wine must be derived from that grape variety. This label shows that the wine is made from the Chardonnay grape.

If the wine bears a vintage date, 95 percent of the grapes must have been harvested that year.

If the wine is designated "California," then 100 percent of the grapes must have been grown in California.

If the label designates a certain federally recognized viticultural area (AVA), such as the Russian River Valley (as on our sample label above), then at least 85 percent of the grapes used to make that wine must have been grown in that location.

The alcohol content is given in percentages. Usually, the higher the percentage of alcohol, the "fuller" the wine will be.

"Produced and bottled by" means that at least 75 percent of the wine was fermented by the winery named on the label.

Some wineries tell you the exact varietal content of the wine, and/or the sugar content of the grapes when they were picked, and/or the amount of residual sugar (to let you know how sweet or dry the wine is).

## How is California winemaking different from the European technique?

Many students ask me this, and I can only tell them I'm glad I learned all about the wines of France, Italy, Germany, Spain, and the rest of Europe before I tackled California. European winemaking has established traditions that have remained essentially unchanged for hundreds of years. These practices involve the ways grapes are grown and harvested, and in some cases include winemaking and aging procedures.

In California, there are few traditions, and winemakers are able to take full advantage of modern technology. Furthermore, there is freedom to experiment and create new products. Some of the experimenting the California winemakers do, such as combining different grape varieties to make new styles of wine, is prohibited by some European wine-control laws. Californians thus have greater opportunity to try many new ideas.

Another way in which California winemaking is different from European is that many California wineries carry an entire line of wine. Many of the larger ones produce more than twenty different labels. In Bordeaux, most châteaux produce only one or two wines.

In addition to modern technology and experimentation, you can't ignore the fundamentals of wine-growing: California's rainfall, weather patterns, and soils are very different from those of Europe. The greater abundance of sunshine in California can result in wines with greater alcohol content, ranging on average from 13.5 percent to 14.5 percent, compared to 12 percent to 13 percent in Europe. This higher alcohol content changes the balance and taste of the wines.

THE LEGAL limit for the alcohol content of table wine is 7–13.9%, with a 1.5% allowance either way, so long as the allowance doesn't go beyond the legal limit. If the alcohol content of a table wine exceeds 14%, the label must show that. Sparkling wines may be 10–13.9%, with the 1.5% allowance.

I'M SURE you'll recognize the names of some of the early European winemakers:

**Finland**
Gustave Niebaum (Inglenook): 1879

**France**
Paul Masson: 1852
Étienne Thée and Charles LeFranc (Almaden): 1852
Pierre Mirassou: 1854
Georges de Latour (Beaulieu): 1900

**Germany**
Beringer Brothers: 1876
Carl Wente: 1883

**Ireland**
James Concannon: 1883

**Italy**
Giuseppe and Pietro Simi: 1876
John Foppiano: 1895
Samuele Sebastiani: 1904
Louis Martini: 1922
Adolph Parducci: 1932

*"You are never going to stylize the California wines the same way that European wines have been stylized, because we have more freedom to experiment. I value my freedom to make the style of wine I want more than the security of the AOC laws. Laws discourage experimentation."*
—LOUIS MARTINI

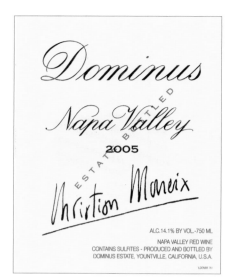

## EUROWINEMAKING IN CALIFORNIA

*Many well-known and highly respected European winemakers have invested in California vineyards to make their own wine. There are more than forty-five California wineries owned by European, Canadian, or Japanese companies. For example:*

- *One of the most influential joint ventures matched Baron Philippe de Rothschild, then the owner of Château Mouton-Rothschild in Bordeaux, and Robert Mondavi, of the Napa Valley, to produce a wine called Opus One*
- *The owners of Château Pétrus in Bordeaux, the Moueix family, have vineyards in California. Their wine is a Bordeaux-style blend called Dominus.*
- *Moët & Chandon, which is part of Moët-Hennessy, owns Domaine Chandon in the Napa Valley*

*Other European wineries with operations in California:*
- *Roederer has grapes planted in Mendocino County and produces Roederer Estate*
- *Mumm produces a sparkling wine called Mumm Cuvée Napa*
- *Taittinger has its own sparkling wine called Domaine Carneros*
- *The Spanish sparkling-wine house Codorníu owns a winery called Artesa; and Freixenet owns land in Sonoma County and produces a wine called Gloria Ferrer*
- *The Torres family of Spain owns a winery called Marimar Torres Estate in Sonoma County*
- *Frenchman Robert Skalli (Fortant de France) owns more than 6,000 acres in the Napa Valley and the winery St. Supery*
- *Tuscan wine producer Piero Antinori owns Atlas Peak winery in Napa*

## What happened when phylloxera returned to the vineyards of California in the 1980s?

In the 1980s the plant louse phylloxera destroyed a good part of the vineyards of California, costing more than $1 billion in new plantings. Now this may sound strange, but it proved that good can come from bad. So what's the good news?

This time, vineyard owners didn't have to wait to discover a solution; they already knew what they would have to do to replace the dead vines—replant with a different rootstock that they knew was resistant to phylloxera. So while the short-term effects were terribly expensive, the long-term effect should be better-quality wine. Why is this?

In the early days of California grape-growing, little thought was given to where a specific grape would grow best. Many Chardonnays were planted in climates that were much too warm, and Cabernet Sauvignons were planted in climates that were much too cold. With the onset of phylloxera, winery owners had a chance to rectify their errors; when replanting, they matched the climate and soil with the best grape variety. Grape growers also had the opportunity to plant different grape clones. But the biggest change was in the planting density of the vines themselves. Traditional spacing used by most wineries was somewhere between 400 and 500 vines per acre. Today with the new replanting, it is not uncommon to have more than a thousand vines per acre. Many vineyards have planted more than 2,000 per acre.

The bottom line is that if you like California wines now, you'll love them more with time. The quality is already better and the costs are lower—making it a win-win situation for everyone.

# THE WHITE WINES OF CALIFORNIA

### What is the major white-grape variety grown in California?

The most important white-wine grape grown in California is Chardonnay. This green-skinned (*Vitis vinifera*) grape is considered by many the finest white-grape variety in the world. It is responsible for all the great French white Burgundies, such as Meursault, Chablis, and Puligny-Montrachet. In California, it has been the most successful white grape, yielding a wine of tremendous character and magnificent flavor. The wines are often aged in small oak barrels, increasing their complexity. In the vineyard, yields are fairly low and the grapes command high prices. Chardonnay is always dry, and benefits from aging more than any other American white wine. Superior examples can keep and develop well in the bottle for five years or longer.

### Why do some Chardonnays cost more than other varietals?

In addition to everything we've mentioned before, the best wineries age these wines in wood, sometimes for more than a year. French oak barrels have doubled in price over the last five years, averaging $800 per barrel. Add to this the cost of the grapes and the length of time before the wine is actually sold, and you can see why the best of the California Chardonnays cost more than $25.

THE TWO leading white wines planted in California in 2012:
1. Chardonnay (92,791 acres)
2. Sauvignon Blanc (15,248 acres)

SOME 800 different California Chardonnays are available to the consumer.

CALIFORNIA HAS more Chardonnay planted than any country in the world!

THERE ARE more than 24 different varieties of white-wine grapes grown in California.

IN THE 2009 vintage, Kistler Vineyards produced six Chardonnays from six specific vineyards!

ONE-THIRD of all grapes grown in Sonoma are Chardonnay.

## What makes one Chardonnay different from another?

Put it this way: There are many brands of ice cream on the market. They use similar ingredients, but there is only one Ben & Jerry's. The same is true for wine. Among the many things to consider: Is a wine aged in wood or stainless steel? If wood, what type of oak? Was it barrel fermentation? Does the wine undergo a malolactic fermentation? How long does it remain in the barrel (part of the style of the winemaker)? Where do the grapes come from?

The major regions for California Chardonnay are Carneros, Napa, Santa Barbara, and Sonoma.

## Kevin Zraly's Favorite Chardonnays

| | |
|---|---|
| **ACACIA** | **LANDMARK** |
| **ARROWOOD** | **MARCASSIN** |
| **AU BON CLIMAT** | **MARTINELLI** |
| **BERINGER** | **PAUL HOBBS** |
| **BREWER-CLIFTON** | **PETER MICHAEL** |
| **CAKEBREAD** | **PHELPS** |
| **CHALK HILL** | **RAMEY** |
| **CHATEAU MONTELENA** | **ROBERT MONDAVI** |
| **CHATEAU ST. JEAN** | **RUDD WINERY** |
| **DIATOM** | **SAINTSBURY** |
| **DUTTON GOLDFIELD** | **SBRAGIA FAMILY** |
| **FERRARI-CARANO** | **SILVERADO** |
| **GRGICH HILLS** | **TALBOTT** |
| **KISTLER** | **TESTAROSSA** |
| **KONGSGAARD** | |

### BEST BETS FOR CALIFORNIA CHARDONNAY

*Carneros* 2002\* 2003 2004\* 2006 2007\* 2008 2009\* 2010 2011

*Napa* 2002\* 2004 2005 2006 2007\* 2008\* 2009\* 2010 2011

*Sonoma* 2002\*\* 2003 2004\*\* 2005\*\* 2006 2007\*\* 2008\* 2009\* 2010 2011

*Santa Barbara* 2002\* 2004 2005 2007\* 2008 2009\* 2010 2011

*Note: \* signifies exceptional vintage \*\*signifies extraordinary vintage*

## What are the other major California white-wine grapes?

**Sauvignon Blanc**: Sometimes labeled "Fumé Blanc." This is one of the grapes used in making the dry white wines of the Graves region of Bordeaux, and the white wines of Sancerre and Pouilly-Fumé in the Loire Valley of France, as well as New Zealand. California Sauvignon Blanc makes one of the best dry white wines in the world. It is sometimes aged in small oak barrels and occasionally blended with the Sémillon grape.

**Chenin Blanc**: This is one of the most widely planted grapes in the Loire Valley. In California, the grape yields a very attractive, soft, light-bodied wine. It is usually made very dry or semisweet; it is a perfect apéritif wine, simple and fruity.

**Viognier**: One of the major white grapes from the Rhône Valley in France, Viognier thrives in warmer and sunny climates, so it's a perfect grape for the weather conditions in certain areas of California. It has a distinct fragrant bouquet. Not as full-bodied as most Chardonnays, nor as light as most Sauvignon Blancs, it's an excellent food wine.

## Kevin Zraly's Favorite Sauvignon Blancs

| | |
|---|---|
| BRANDER | KENWOOD |
| CAYMUS | MATANZAS CREEK |
| CHALK HILL | MASON |
| CHATEAU ST. JEAN | MERRY EDWARDS |
| DRY CREEK | ORIN SWIFT |
| FERRARI-CARANO | QUINTESSA |
| GIRARD | ROBERT MONDAVI |
| GREY STACK | SILVERADO |
| HONIG | SIMI |
| JOSEPH PHELPS | VOGELZANG |

## What have been the trends in wines of California over the last forty years?

To best answer that question, we should go back even farther to see where the trends have been going since before 1970. The 1960s were a decade of expansion and development. The 1970s were a decade of growth, especially in terms of the number of wineries that were established in California and

MALOLACTIC FERMENTATION is a second fermentation that lowers tart malic acids and increases the softer lactic acids, making for a richer-style wine. The result is what many wine tasters refer to as a buttery bouquet.

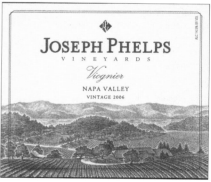

THE 2005 HARVEST was the largest ever in California.

WHY IS SAUVIGNON BLANC often labeled as Fumé Blanc? Robert Mondavi realized that no one was buying Sauvignon Blanc, so he changed its name to Fumé Blanc. Strictly a marketing maneuver—it was still the same wine. Result: sales took off. Mondavi decided not to trademark the name, allowing anyone to use it (and many producers do).

CALIFORNIA IS BEGINNING to have fun with wine brands: Marilyn Merlot, Lewis Race Car Red, Mia's Playground, and Screw Kappa Napa. Expect more to come.

## CALIFORNIA TRENDS THROUGH THE DECADES

*1960s and 1970s:* Jug wines (Chablis, Burgundy)
*1980s:* Varietal wines (Chardonnay, Cabernet Sauvignon)
*1990s:* Varietal location (Cabernet Sauvignon—Napa, Pinot Noir—Santa Barbara)
*2000s:* Specific vineyards for varietals
*2010:* Consistently great wines

## FAMOUS INDIVIDUAL VINEYARDS OF CALIFORNIA

Bacigalupi
Bien Nacido
Dutton Ranch
Durell
Robert Young
Bancroft Ranch
Gravelly Meadow
Hudson
Hyde
Martha's Vineyard
McCrea
S.L.V.
To-Kalon
Beckstoffer
Monte Rosso

the corporations and individuals that became involved. The 1980s and 1990s were the decades of experimentation, in grape-growing as well as in wine-making and marketing techniques.

Over the past twenty years, I have seen the winemakers finally get a chance to step back and fine-tune their wine. Today, they are producing wines that have tremendous structure, finesse, and elegance that many lacked in the early years of the California winemaking renaissance. They are also making wines that can give pleasure when young, and also great wines that I hope I will be around to share with my grandchildren. The benchmark for quality has increased to such a level that the best wineries have gotten better, but more important to the consumer is that even the wines under $20 are better than ever before.

There has been a trend toward wineries specializing in particular grape varieties. Forty years ago, I would have talked about which wineries in California were the best overall. Today, I'm more likely to talk about which winery, AVA, or individual vineyard makes the best Chardonnay, which winery makes the best Sauvignon Blanc.

Chardonnay remains the major white-grape variety by far in California. Sauvignon Blancs/Fumé Blancs have greatly improved, and they're easier to consume young. Although they still don't have the cachet of a Chardonnay, I find them better matched with most foods. However, other white-grape varieties, such as Riesling and Chenin Blanc, aren't meeting with the same success, and they're harder to sell. Still, just to keep it interesting, some winemakers are planting more European varietals, including Viognier and Pinot Gris.

### FOR FURTHER READING

I recommend *The Oxford Companion to the Wines of North America* by Bruce Cass and Jancis Robinson, *Wine Atlas of California* by James Halliday, *Making Sense of California Wine* and *Matt Kramer's New California Wine* by Matt Kramer, *Wine Spectator's California Wine* by James Laube, *American Vintage: The Rise of American Wine* by Paul Lukacs, and *The Wine Atlas of California and the Pacific Northwest* by Bob Thompson. Lovers of gossip will have fun reading *The Far Side of Eden* and *Napa: The Story of an American Eden* by James Conaway.

# THE WINES OF WASHINGTON STATE

I began teaching about the vineyards and wines of Washington State in the early 1970s, just as I was starting out as a wine educator and only a few years after Washington had begun producing its first quality wine. Forty years later, Washington's wine industry has matured considerably and within the state there are some of the best wine regions of the world.

It has taken Americans a while to understand and appreciate the wines of Washington State for many reasons, not the least of which is weather. Ask the average American wine drinker about winemaking in this northwestern U.S. region and one of the most common responses you'll get is, "How do you make great wine in a rainy climate like Seattle's?"

Of course, Washington State is also split into two regions—the east and the west—by the Cascade Mountains, which include two active volcanoes, Mount Rainier and Mount St. Helens. On the eastern side of this mountain range, geologic cataclysms—dramatic lava flows from fifteen million years ago and monstrous floods that took place during the last Ice Age—created soil conditions ideal for growing superior grapes and making high-quality wine. There is an enormous difference between Washington's west-coast maritime climate and its eastern continental climate: sixty inches of annual rainfall along the Pacific coast versus eight inches in eastern Washington where wine grapes thrive in its arid, hot summers. The eastern wine-growing region also has an ideal irrigation system that is partly sourced from the Columbia River, which helps produce perfectly ripe grapes.

Unlike California, Washington's winemaking history is all about the present and future, not about the past, and the recent changes have not been *bam*, but *boom*! Some say, "A new winery opens in Washington every week." After only ten wineries in 1970, there are more than 500 today. It was wheat to grapes, orchards to vineyards, and Rieslings to reds (think Cabernet Sauvignon, Merlot, and Syrah). Still, Washington State remains the number-one American producer of Riesling (4,400 acres), and its Chardonnays, with their balance, great fruit, and lively acidity, are some of the best in the country.

| California | Washington |
|---|---|
| 535,000 acres | 44,000 acres |
| 2,727 wineries | 652 wineries |
| **Oregon** | **New York** |
| 20,400 acres | 37,000 acres |
| 390 wineries | 302 wineries |

WASHINGTON IS the second largest wine-producing state.

THE PACIFIC NORTHWEST wine-growing region includes Washington, Oregon, and Idaho in the United States and British Columbia in Canada.

**PAST AND PRESENT**

1970: 10 wineries
      9 acres
2012: 652 wineries
      44,000 acres

WASHINGTON STATE'S wine production is 50% white, 50% red.

CHATEAU STE. MICHELLE is the world's largest Riesling producer and has recently formed a winemaking partnership with the famous German wine producer Dr. Loosen to produce a new Riesling wine called Eroica.

IN 2012, Washington State had its largest harvest.

## KEVIN ZRALY'S FAVORITE WASHINGTON STATE PRODUCERS

| | |
|---|---|
| Andrew Will | Hogue Cellars |
| Betz Family | Januik |
| Canoe Ridge | L'Ecole No. 41 |
| Cayuse | Leonetti Cellar |
| Chateau | Long Shadows |
| Ste. Michelle | McCrea Cellars |
| Columbia Crest | Pepper Bridge |
| Columbia Winery | Quilceda Creek |
| DiStefano | Seven Hills |
| Doyenne | Woodward Canyon |
| Fidelitas | Winery |
| Gramercy Cellars | |

## What are the major grapes grown in Washington State?

The major white grapes are:

*Chardonnay* (7,654 acres)                  *Sauvignon Blanc* (1,173 acres)

*Riesling* (6,320 acres)                          *Gewürztraminer* (775 acres)

The major red grapes are:

*Cabernet Sauvignon* (10,293 acres)      *Syrah* (3,103 acres)

*Merlot* (8,235 acres)

## What are the wine regions of Washington State?

| AVA (Date AVA established) | Columbia Gorge (2004) |
|---|---|
| *Yakima Valley* (1983) | *Horse Heaven Hills* (2005) |
| *Walla Walla Valley* (1984) | *Wahluke Slope* (2006) |
| *Columbia Valley** (1984) | *Rattlesnake Hills* (2006) |
| *Puget Sound* (1995) | *Snipes Mountain* (2009) |
| *Red Mountain* (2001) | *Lake Chelan* (2009) |

*Largest viticultural area, responsible for 95 percent of wine production.*

### BEST BETS FOR WASHINGTON WINES

2005*   2006*   2007**   2008*   2009*   2010*   2011

*Note: * signifies exceptional vintage   ** signifies extraordinary vintage*

### FOR FURTHER READING

*Washington Wines & Wineries: The Essential Guide* by Paul Gregutt.

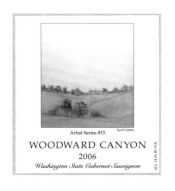

# THE WINES OF OREGON

## The Burgundy of the United States

Although grapes were planted and wine was made as early as 1847, Oregon's modern viticultural era began roughly forty years ago with a handful of intrepid wine pioneers including David Lett (Erie winery), Dick Erath (Erath winery), and Dick Ponzi (Ponzi winery). This new breed of grape growers and winemakers were convinced that the cool-climate varietals such as Pinot Noir, Chardonnay, and Pinot Gris would not only grow in Oregon, but would produce world-class wines as well—and they have! What separated Oregon winemaking from its neighbors in California and Washington was their importation of French clones from Burgundy and Alsace.

Most of the Oregon wineries are small, family-owned, artisanal producers. Their proximity to the city of Portland and Oregon's beautiful coastline make this a "must visit" wine region.

## What are the major grapes grown in Oregon?

> **Pinot Noir** (12,560 acres)
> **Pinot Gris** (2,590 acres)
> **Chardonnay** (950 acres)

## What are the major wine regions in Oregon?

Oregon has sixteen AVAs. Here are the ones you are most likely to find in wine stores:

> **AVA** (Date AVA established)
>
> **Willamette Valley** (1984)
> **Umpqua Valley** (2004)
> **Rogue Valley** (2004)
> **Applegate Valley** (2004)

1970:  5 wineries
       35 acres
2012:  390 wineries
       20,400 acres

COLUMBIA VALLEY and Walla Walla Valley are AVAs whose boundaries encompass parts of Oregon as well as Washington state.

MORE THAN 70% of Oregon wineries are located in the Willamette Valley.

BOTH THE Willamette Valley and Burgundy, France, are located at 45 degrees north latitude.

## Kevin Zraly's Favorite Oregon Wineries

OVER HALF of Oregon's vineyards are planted with Pinot Noir.

OREGON STATE LAW requires that a wine labeled "Pinot Noir" must contain 100% Pinot Noir.

| | |
|---|---|
| ADELSHEIM | EVENING LAND |
| ARCHERY SUMMIT | EYRIE |
| ARGYLE | KEN WRIGHT |
| BEAUX FRÈRES | KING ESTATE |
| BERGSTRÖM | PONZI |
| BETHEL HEIGHTS | REX HILL |
| CHEHALEM | SHEA |
| CRISTOM | SOKOL BLOSSER |
| DOMAINE DROUHIN | SOTER |
| DOMAINE SERENE | ST. INNOCENT |
| ERATH | TUALATIN |

### BEST BETS FOR WINES FROM OREGON

2005* 2006* 2008** 2009 2010* 2011

*Note: \* signifies exceptional vintage   \*\* signifies extraordinary vintage*

### BEFORE *SIDEWAYS*: IN SEARCH OF THE BEST PINOT NOIR

One of the great wine festivals in the United States is the International Pinot Noir Celebration, which has been held in Oregon since 1987.

### FOR FURTHER READING

I recommend *The Oxford Companion to the Wines of North America* by Bruce Cass and Jancis Robinson, *Wines of the Pacific Northwest* by Lisa Shara Hall, and *The Northwest Wine Guide* by Andy Perdue.

THE KING ESTATE in Oregon is the largest producer of Pinot Gris in the United States.

### GET IT RIGHT, DAMMIT!

Willamette Valley is pronounced Wil-AM-it, not Wil-AH-mit.

# THE WINES OF NEW YORK STATE

New York is the third largest wine-producing state in the United States, with nine AVAs. The three premium wine regions in New York are:

**Finger Lakes:** with the largest wine production east of California
**Hudson Valley:** concentrating on premium farm wineries
**Long Island:** New York's red-wine region

NEW YORK'S Hudson Valley is one of America's oldest wine-growing regions. French Huguenots planted the grapevines in the 1600s. The Hudson Valley also boasts the oldest active winery in the United States—Brotherhood, which recorded its first vintage in 1839.

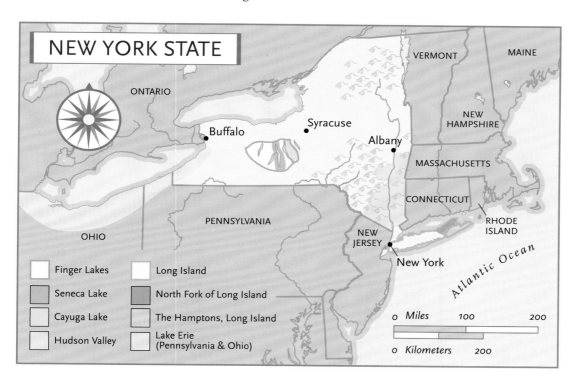

## Which grapes grow in New York State?

There are three main categories:

**Native American:** *Vitis labrusca*
**European:** *Vitis vinifera*
**French-American:** hybrids

THE FIRST winery on Long Island was started in 1973 by Alex and Louisa Hargrave.

THE THREE AVAs on Long Island are the North Fork, the Hamptons, and Long Island.

## NATIVE AMERICAN VARIETIES

The *Vitis labrusca* vines are very popular among grape growers in New York because they are hardy grapes that can withstand cold winters. Among the most familiar grapes of the *Vitis labrusca* family are Concord, Catawba, and Delaware. Until the last decade, these were the grapes that were used to make most New York wines. In describing these wines, words such as "foxy," "grapey," "Welch's," and "Manischewitz" are often used. These words are a sure sign of *Vitis labrusca*.

THE CLIMATE on Long Island has more than 200 days of sunshine and a longer growing season, making it perfect for Merlot- and Bordeaux-style wines.

EXAMPLES OF *Vitis vinifera* grapes are Pinot Grigio, Riesling, Sauvignon Blanc, Chardonnay, Pinot Noir, Merlot, Cabernet Sauvignon, and Syrah.

**PAST AND PRESENT**

There are 302 wineries in New York State, up from fewer than 10 in 1970.

IN THE THREE major regions, the Finger Lakes region has 87 wineries, the Hudson Valley has 26, and Long Island has 56.

FROM 2001 to 2011, 198 wineries have opened in New York State.

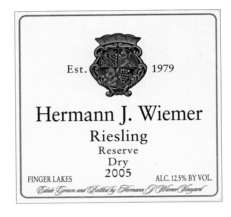

## EUROPEAN VARIETIES

Forty years ago, some New York wineries began to experiment with the traditional European (*Vitis vinifera*) grapes. Dr. Konstantin Frank, a Russian viticulturist skilled in cold-climate grape-growing, came to the United States and catalyzed efforts to grow *Vitis vinifera* in New York. This was unheard of—and laughed at—back then. Other vintners predicted that he'd fail, that it was impossible to grow vinifera in New York's cold and capricious climate.

"What do you mean?" Dr. Frank replied. "I'm from Russia—it's even colder there."

Most people were still skeptical, but Charles Fournier of Gold Seal Vineyards was intrigued enough to give Konstantin Frank a chance to prove his theory. Sure enough, Dr. Frank was successful with the vinifera and has produced some world-class wines, especially his Riesling and Chardonnay. So have many other New York wineries, thanks to the vision and courage of Dr. Frank and Charles Fournier.

## FRENCH-AMERICAN VARIETIES

Some New York and East Coast winemakers have planted French-American hybrid varieties, which combine European taste characteristics with American vine hardiness to withstand the cold winters in the Northeast. French viticulturists originally developed these varieties in the nineteenth century. Seyval Blanc and Vidal are the most prominent white-wine varieties; Baco Noir and Chancellor are the most common reds.

### Forty years later in New York

The most significant developments are taking place on Long Island and in the Finger Lakes region. Both have experienced tremendous growth of new vineyards. Since 1973, grape-growing acreage on Long Island has increased from 100 acres to more than 3,000 acres, with more expansion expected in the future.

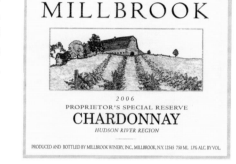

The predominant use of *Vitis vinifera* varieties allows Long Island wineries to compete more effectively in the world market, and Long Island's longer growing season offers greater potential for red grapes.

The Millbrook Winery in the Hudson Valley has shown that this region can produce world-class wines—not only white, but red too, from such grapes as Pinot Noir and Cabernet Franc.

The wines of the Finger Lakes region continue to get better as the winemakers work with grapes that thrive in the cooler climate, including European varieties such as Riesling, Chardonnay, and Pinot Noir.

**WINERIES TO LOOK FOR IN NEW YORK STATE**

*The Finger Lakes*
Anthony Road
Château Lafayette-Reneau
Dr. Konstantin Frank
Fox Run
Glenora
Hermann Wiemer
Heron Hill
Red Newt Cellars
Red Tail Ridge
Standing Stone
Wagner

*The Hudson Valley*
Benmarl
Brotherhood
Clinton Vineyards
Hudson-Chatham Winery
Millbrook

*Long Island*
Bedell
Channing Daughters
Lenz
Macari
Martha Clara
Osprey's Dominion
Palmer
Paumanok
Peconic Bay
Pellegrini
Pindar
Raphael
Schneider
Shinn Estate
Wölffer

THE FINGER LAKES wineries produce 85% of New York's wine.

2010 and 2012 are the best vintages in New York State since 1995.

# ROUNDING OUT THE TOP TWELVE WINE-PRODUCING STATES

### THE TOP 12 STATES IN NUMBER OF BONDED WINERIES

1. California (2727)
2. Washington (652)
3. Oregon (390)
4. New York (302)
5. Virginia (212)
6. Texas (200)
7. Pennsylvania (163)
8. Ohio (142)
9. Michigan (125)
10. (tie) Missouri (120)
10. (tie) North Carolina (120)
12. Illinois (96)

### THE TOP 12 STATES IN GRAPE ACREAGE

1. California (489,000)
2. Washington (35,000)
3. New York (37,000)
4. Oregon (17,000)
5. Michigan (14,200)
6. Pennsylvania (13,600)
7. Texas (3,000)
8. Virginia (2,700)
9. Ohio (1,900)
10. North Carolina (1,800)
11. Missouri (1,700)
12. Illinois (1,083)

*Source: Wine Business Monthly*
*\*includes grapes for wine and table grapes*

Americans are drinking American wine! More than 75 percent of wines consumed in the United States are from this country, and not just from the top four states: California, Washington, Oregon, and New York. When I began studying wine in 1970, two-thirds of the states had no wineries at all. Now with all fifty states producing wine, I want to expand with eight other states to represent the dozen with the most number of wineries.

While there are plenty of wine books written on French, Italian, and Spanish (etc.) wines, there are very few books available on American wines. One of the most exciting trends in the world of wines over the last twenty years has been the remarkable rise in the quality of wine production and the increase in wine consumption in America. These two trends, of course, keep reinforcing each other, so we can continue to expect great things in American winemaking for many years to come.

American wine also has an enormous "fun factor." To me, studying and tasting the wines from around this country is truly exciting! It is a lesson in U.S. geography, history, agriculture, and the passion of American grape growers and winemakers. It thrills me to find undiscovered gems from states such as Virginia, Pennsylvania, and Texas, and enjoy them accompanied with great American cooking.

Wineries in the United States have become major tourist attractions. "Wine trails" have sprung up all across the United States in combination with other historical landmarks in those particular regions. Wine has definitely gone mainstream in America.

Finally our time has arrived. Thanks to the conviction and determination of American producers and the demands of American consumers, I can proudly say that many of the best wines in the world are produced in the United States of America.

# THE WINES OF VIRGINIA

I started off as a history major in college and wrote many papers on the life of Thomas Jefferson. I also started studying wines when I was nineteen years old, and one of the reasons I was attracted to wine was Jefferson's appreciation of wine. Before he became our third president he was the minister to France and in my opinion America's first wine connoisseur, importing some of the great wines from

France and planting his own vineyard in Virginia. It was as challenging back then for Jefferson as it is today in Virginia. Even his buddy George (as in George Washington) was unsuccessful with his vineyard.

Although the number-one grape planted is Chardonnay, Viognier has become the increasingly popular white grape; Norton, a native grape, has a strong following; and beautiful red blends have also succeeded. Northern Virginia has seen the most growth in the last seven to ten years, and has produced tremendous wines. Virginia is one of the fastest growing wine regions outside the big four.

## What are the major grapes grown in Virginia?

**Chardonnay** (362 acres)
**Cabernet Franc** (322 acres)
**Merlot** (301 acres)
**Cabernet Sauvignon** (260 acres)
**Viognier** (201 acres)

**Vidal Bland** (160 acres)
**Petit Verdot** (146 acres)
**Chambourcin** (134 acres)
**Norton** (124 acres)

## What are the major wine regions of Virginia?

Virginia has six AVAs throughout the state.

<u>**AVA** (Date AVA established)</u>

**Northern Neck George Washington Birthplace** (1987)
**North Fork of Roanoke** (1987)

**Monticello** (1984)
**Rocky Knob** (1987)
**Shenandoah Valley** (1987)
**Virginia's Eastern Shore** (1991)

VIRGINIA ranks number five in the U.S. with 201 wineries and 2,700 acres of vines.

**WELL-KNOWN VIRGINIA WINERIES**

AmRhein Wine Cellars
Barboursville Vineyards
Boxwood Winery
Château Morrisette
Fabbiloi Cellars
Horton Vineyards
Jefferson Vineyards
Keswick Vineyards
King Family Vineyards
Rappahannock Cellars
The Winery at La Grange
Trump Winery
White Hall Vineyards

BARBOURSVILLE VINEYARD, located in Orange County, provided two of the wines served at an inauguration ball for President Obama in 2009.

IN 2010, Donald Trump purchased the well-known Kluge Estate, which is now called Trump Winery.

IN 1979, Virginia only had six wineries. Records from the Jamestown colony show that vineyards were planted and wine was made in 1609.

TEXAS is ranked number six in the United States with 193 wineries and 3,000 acres of vines.

IN 2001, Texas had 46 wineries. In 2011, there are 193 wineries.

IN 1986, Llano Estacado Winery won a double gold award at the prestigious San Francisco Fair Wine Competition, putting Texas wine on the world stage.

CABERNET SAUVIGNON, Chardonnay, and Merlot account for 41% of the total state's acreage.

THE FIRST vineyard established in Texas was planted by the missionaries in 1662.

TEXAS'S oldest winery, Val Verde Winery, has been in operation since 1883.

IN 2010, Texas had the largest production of wine in its history.

**WELL-KNOWN TEXAS WINERIES**

Alamosa Wine Cellars
Fall Creek Vineyards
Llano Estacado
Lost Creek Vineyard and Winery
Messina Hof
Spicewood Vineyards

# THE WINES OF TEXAS

In the early 1980s, before I started hearing about the quality of Washington and Oregon wines, the wineries of Texas were approaching me to put their wines on the Windows on the World wine list. Among those Texans were the Aulers from Fall Creek Vineyards and the sales representatives of Llano Estacado. Although one might not think the climatic conditions would produce good wine, I was pleasantly surprised. Learning more, I realized that the wineries of Texas were committed to growing primarily Cabernet Sauvignon and Chardonnay. Recent plantings of Malbec and Viognier point to an interesting future.

The wineries are spread throughout the state within eight American Viticultural Areas, the largest being the Texas Hill Country with over six hundred acres and seventy wineries.

## What are the major grapes grown in Texas?

*Cabernet Sauvignon* (580 acres)      *Muscat Canelli* (110 acres)
*Chardonnay* (360 acres)              *Viognier* (90 acres)
*Merlot* (300 acres)                  *Malbec* (50 acres)

## What are the major wine regions in Texas?

There are eight AVAs in Texas.

**AVA** (Date AVA established)

*Mesilla Valley* (1985)               *Escondido Valley* (1992)
*Bell Mountain* (1986)                *Texas High Plains* (1993)
*Fredericksburg in the                *Texas Davis Mountains* (1998)
   Texas Hill Country* (1989)         *Texoma* (2006)
*Texas Hill Country* (1991)

# THE WINES OF PENNSYLVANIA

Having been born and raised in New York I have spent a lot of time in Pennsylvania, and for many years taught a wine school in Philadelphia. Pennsylvania is a "control state," meaning that all the wines are purchased by the state and sold through their stores. The state of Pennsylvania is one of the largest single buyers of wines in the United States. It is also the fifth largest wine-grape producer in the nation.

Like my own home state of New York, Pennsylvania produces wines from Native American grapes such as Concord and Niagara, vinifera grapes such as Cabernet Sauvignon and Chardonnay, and also hybrids such as Seyval Blanc and Chambourcin.

Eric Miller, the founder of the largest winery (Chaddsford), and I started our wine careers together in a restaurant in upstate New York. His family owned the Benmarl Winery in New York's Hudson Valley, which was the first vineyard I ever experienced. Eric and I are still very close today and he continues to advise me with the planting of my own vineyard.

## What are the major grapes grown in Pennsylvania?

*Concord* (8,000 acres for juice; 1,000 acres for wine)
*Catawba* (183 acres)

*Chambourcin* (135 acres)
*Vidal Blanc* (130 acres)
*Cabernet Sauvignon* (123 acres)

## What are the major wine regions in Pennsylvania?

Pennsylvania has five AVAs.

**AVA** (Date AVA established)
*Lancaster Valley* (1982)
*Lake Erie* (1983)

*Cumberland Valley* (1985)
*Central Delaware Valley* (1987)
*Lehigh Valley* (2008)

PENNSYLVANIA is ranked number seven in the United States with 144 wineries and 13,600 acres of vines.

WILLIAM PENN planted the first vineyard in Pennsylvania in 1683.

PENNSYLVANIA is the site of America's first commercial vineyard—the Pennsylvania Vine Company, established in 1793.

MOST OF Pennsylvania's wineries are concentrated in the warmer, southeastern portion of the state such as York, Bucks, Chester, and Lancaster counties.

IN 1998 there were only 57 bonded wineries in Pennsylvania, compared with 144 today.

**WELL-KNOWN PENNSYLVANIA WINERIES**

Allegro Vineyards
Arrowhead Wine Cellars
Blue Mountain
Chaddsford Winery
J. Maki
Manatawny Creek
Pinnacle Ridge Winery
VaLa Vineyards

OHIO ranks number eight in the United States with 127 wineries and 1,900 acres of vines.

THE HIGHEST concentration of wineries is in the Lake Erie region, all within a 45-minute drive.

THE OLDEST and largest winery in Ohio is Meier's Winery, established in 1856.

THE OHIO Wine Producers Association has organized a special wine trail between Toledo and Cleveland that combines bird-watching and wine!

DURING the turn of the century, dozens of wineries were located on the islands of Lake Erie and thousands of gallons of wine were produced. It became known as the "Lake Erie Grape Belt."

**WELL-KNOWN OHIO WINERIES**

Debonne Vineyards
Ferrante Winery
Harpersfield Winery
Henke Wines
John Christ Winery
Kinkead Ridge Winery
Klingshirn Winery
Meier's Wine Cellars
Valley Vineyards

# THE WINES OF OHIO

At one time around the 1860s Ohio was the largest producer of wine in the United States. Traditionally most of the vineyards were planted with Native American grapes. The first vineyards were planted in 1823 and by 1842 there were twelve hundred acres. The most planted grape during that time was Catawba, and Ohio became famous for its Sparkling Catawba. Unfortunately the majority of the vines died from disease and the wine industry was severely curtailed during Prohibition.

At last count there were over thirty different grapes planted in Ohio, a blend of *Vitis labrusca*, hybrids such as Seyval Blanc and Chambourcin, and more recently *Vitis vinifera* such as Riesling and Cabernet Franc. Through the efforts of the Ohio State Viticultural and Enology programs, the quality of the wines has improved dramatically.

## What are the major grapes grown in Ohio?

*Riesling* (46 acres)                    *Cabernet Franc* (27 acres)

*Pinot Gris/Pinot Grigio* (23 acres)     *Pinot Noir* (15 acres)

## What are the major wine regions in Ohio?

There are six AVAs in Ohio.

**AVA** (Date AVA established)

*Isle St. George* (1982)       *Lake Erie* (1983)

*Loramie Creek* (1982)         *Kanawha River Valley* (1986)

*Grand River Valley* (1983)    *Ohio River Valley* (1987)

# THE WINES OF MISSOURI

Grapes were first planted in Missouri in the early 1800s. At one time Missouri was second in the United States in production, just behind New York. Of course this was before California started making wine. The oldest winery is Stone Hill Winery, established in 1847. Many German immigrants settled in Hermann, Missouri, in 1837 because of its resemblance to the Rhine Valley in Germany and planted vineyards on both sides of the Missouri River.

Today, Missouri grows a combination of *Vitis labrusca* (Concord) as well as French hybrids (Vignoles), but its most important grape is Norton, which produces a pleasant dry-style red wine. Although Norton originated in Virginia, today it is the official grape of Missouri.

## What are the major grapes grown in Missouri?

*Norton* (307 acres)
*Vignoles* (207 acres)
*Chardonel* (190 acres)
*Chambourcin* (154 acres)

*Concord* (139 acres)
*Traminette* (105 acres)
*Vidal Blanc* (117 acres)

## What are the major wine regions in Missouri?

There are four AVAs in Missouri.

**AVA** (Date AVA established)

*Augusta* (1980)
*Ozark Mountain* (1986)

*Hermann* (1987)
*Ozark Highlands* (1987)

MISSOURI ranks number nine in the United States with 116 wineries and 1,700 acres of vines.

AUGUSTA became the first federally recognized AVA in 1980.

HERMANN held its first Weinfest in the fall of 1848, a tradition that continues in today's Octoberfest celebrations.

MOUNT PLEASANT Winery started to export its Vidal Chardonnay, Pink Catawba, Claret, and Norton to China in August 2010.

THE HECK FAMILY, creators of Korbel, began its winemaking career in Missouri.

THE GRAPE VARIETY Norton is sometimes referred to as the grape Cynthiana.

**WELL-KNOWN MISSOURI WINERIES**

Augusta Winery
Blumenhof Winery
Chaumette Vineyards & Winery
Les Bourgeois Winery and Vineyards
Montelle Winery
Mount Pleasant Winery
St. James Winery
Stone Hill Winery

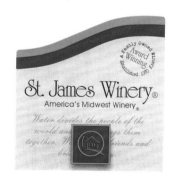

**WELL-KNOWN NORTH CAROLINA WINERIES**

Biltmore Estate Winery
Childress Vineyards
Duplin Wine Cellars
RagApple Lassie Vineyards
RayLen Vineyards
Shelton Vineyards
Westbend Vineyards

# THE WINES OF NORTH CAROLINA

French explorer Giovanni de Verrazano is credited with discovering the Scuppernong grape in the Cape Fear River Valley in 1524. Sir Walter Raleigh, the English aristocrat, was sent to explore the Carolinas in the late 1500s and wrote that the land overflowed with grapes. This was the first grape cultivated in the United States and is to this day the official fruit of North Carolina.

But that was the old North Carolina. The number of wineries has more than quadrupled since 2001 with a new focus on European-style vinifera grapes such as Cabernet Sauvignon, Chardonnay, and Merlot. Most of the vinifera is planted in the northwestern and Piedmont regions of the state, with the most important grape-growing area being the Yadkin Valley. I will never forget being flown there by Charlie and Ed Shelton, owners of Shelton Winery. I was a speaker at the Charlotte Wine and Food Festival, one of the best in the country, and accepted their offer. The winery and wines were spectacular and changed my opinion of the future of North Carolina wines, which is not just about Scuppernong.

## What are the major grapes grown in North Carolina?

*Cabernet Franc* (75 acres)          *Merlot* (90 acres)
*Chardonnay*                         *Scuppernong*
*Cabernet Sauvignon* (150 acres)

## What are the major wine regions in North Carolina?

There are three AVAs in North Carolina.

<u>**AVA**</u> (Date AVA established)          *Swan Creek* (2008)
*Yadkin Valley* (2003)                  *Haw River Valley* (2009)

# THE WINES OF MICHIGAN

Of the 14,200 acres of grapes in the state of Michigan only 2,000 acres are used for the production of wine, and 65 percent of the wine made comes from *Vitis vinifera*, 35 percent are hybrids, and 3 percent are Native American.

Michigan is greatly influenced by its maritime climate. The Leelanau Peninsula, which is home to over 50 percent of Michigan's wineries, benefits from the "lake effect" in many ways. The snow insulates the vines during winter, slowing down the bud break in spring and preventing damaging frost, making the growing season last much longer. Presently the Michigan Grape Council is testing other areas within the state to find the best grape-growing land and to increase production. With this research and modern technology I am expecting to see more quality wines from Michigan.

MICHIGAN ranks number eleven in the United States with 105 wineries and 14,200 acres of vines.

MICHIGAN'S vineyard acreage has grown 60% over the last ten years.

ICE WINE was first produced by Château Grand Traverse in 1983.

THE RIESLING grape is thriving in the cool climate of Michigan and plantings have increased substantially over the last ten years.

## What are the major wine grape varieties grown in Michigan?

**Riesling** (340 acres)

**Chardonnay** (195 acres)

**Vidal Blanc** (145 acres)

**Pinot Noir** (135 acres)

**Pinot Gris** (115 acres)

## What are the major wine regions in Michigan?

Michigan has four AVAs.

**AVA** (Date AVA established)

**Fennville** (1981)

**Lake Michigan Shore** (1983)

**Leelanau Peninsula** (1982)

**Old Mission Peninsula** (1987)

All four regions are located in a 25-mile proximity to Lake Michigan.

**WELL-KNOWN MICHIGAN WINERIES**

Bel Lago Winery
Château Grand Traverse
Château Fontaine
Château de Leelanau
Fenn Valley Vineyards
Forty-Five North Vineyard & Winery
L. Mawby Vineyards
Tabor Hill
Winery at Black Star Farms

# THE WINES OF ILLINOIS

1778: FRENCH settlers in La Ville de Maillet (what is now Peoria) bring the winemaking expertise of their homeland to Illinois. The village features a winepress and an underground wine vault.

1857: EMILE Baxter and Sons open a winery in Nauvoo, along the banks of the Mississippi River. Baxter's Vineyards remains Illinois's oldest operating winery, run by a fifth generation of Baxters.

ONE OF the largest Kosher wine producers, Mogen David Wine, was originally based in Chicago.

## WELL-KNOWN ILLINOIS WINERIES

Alto Vineyards
Baxter's Vineyards
Fox Valley Winery
Galena Cellars
Hickory Ridge Vineyard
Lynfred Winery
Mary Michelle Winery & Vineyard
Owl Creek Vineyard
Spirit Knob Winery and Winery
Vahling Vineyards

Illinois traces its grape-growing history back into the late 1700s. The vines were planted by the French settlers near Peoria. In the 1850s, farmers started planting the Concord grape. Over the past fifteen years, the Illinois wine industry has exploded, growing from just twelve wineries in 1997 to more than ninety today. During this time, the acreage devoted to grape production has grown at a tremendous rate, and today Illinois is consistently among the top twelve wine-producing states. The Illinois wine industry is made up of more than 90 wineries and 450 vineyards across the state.

## What are the major grapes grown in Illinois?

*Chardonel* (85 acres)　　　　*Seyval* (31 acres)
*Vignoles* (63 acres)　　　　*Vidal Blanc* (24 acres)
*Norton* (50 acres)

## What are the major wine regions of Illinois?

There are two AVA in Illinois.

**AVA** (Date AVA established)

*Shawnee Hills* (2006)　　　　*Upper Mississippi River Valley* (2009)

# CALIFORNIA WINE AND FOOD

**MARGRIT BIEVER AND ROBERT MONDAVI:**
*With Chardonnay: oysters, lobster, a more complex fish with beurre blanc, pheasant salad with truffles. With Sauvignon Blanc: traditional white meat or fish course, sautéed or grilled fish (as long as it isn't an oily fish).*

**DAVID STARE** *(Dry Creek): With Chardonnay: fresh boiled Dungeness crab cooked in Zatarain's crab boil, a New Orleans–style boil. Serve this with melted butter and a large loaf of sourdough French bread. With Sauvignon Blanc, "I like fresh salmon cooked in almost any manner. Personally, I like to take a whole fresh salmon or salmon steaks and cook them over the barbecue in an aluminum foil pocket. Place the salmon, onion slices, lemon slices, copious quantities of fresh dill, salt, and pepper on aluminum foil and make a pocket. Cook over the barbecue until barely done. Place the salmon in the oven to keep it warm while you take the juices from the aluminum pocket, reduce the juices, strain, and whisk in some plain yogurt. Enjoy!"*

**WARREN WINIARSKI** *(Stag's Leap Wine Cellars): With Chardonnay: seviche, shellfish, salmon with a light hollandaise sauce.*

**JANET TREFETHEN:** *With Chardonnay: barbecued whole salmon in a sorrel sauce. With White Riesling: sautéed bay scallops with julienne vegetables.*

**RICHARD ARROWOOD:** *With Chardonnay: Sonoma Coast Dungeness crab right from the crab pot, with fennel butter as a dipping sauce.*

**BO BARRETT** *(Chateau Montelena Winery): With Chardonnay: salmon, trout, or abalone, barbecued with olive oil and lemon leaf and slices.*

**JACK CAKEBREAD:** *"With my Cakebread Cellars Napa Valley Chardonnay: bruschetta with wild mushrooms, leek-and-mushroom-stuffed chicken breast, and halibut with caramelized endive and chanterelles."*

**ED SBRAGIA** *(Sbragia Family Vineyards): With Chardonnay: lobster or salmon with lots of butter.*

ONLINE STORE
http://bit.ly/hwobVq

U.S. WINE exports have increased from $0 in 1970 to over $1 billion in 2011.
   The top export markets are:
1. Canada
2. United Kingdom
3. Hong Kong
4. Japan
5. Italy

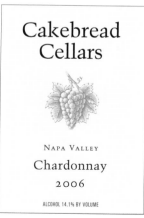

# Class Two:
# The Wine of Washington, Oregon, and New York; The White Wines of California

In the first class, we studied the white wines of France. In Class Two, we'll follow the same wine styles as with France, but this time we'll use American white wines. Try to start with an unoaked, low-alcohol Riesling, which will leave the palate refreshingly light. Then move on to some food-friendly Sauvignon Blancs, and work your way through some great Chardonnays.

## THE WINES

### Understanding American Riesling

#### One Riesling, tasted alone

    1. Finger Lakes, New York, Riesling

### Understanding American Sauvignon Blanc

#### Two Sauvignon Blancs compared

    2. Sonoma County Sauvignon Blanc
    3. Napa Valley Sauvignon Blanc

1.

2.

3.

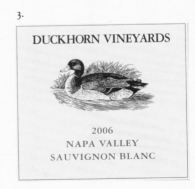

## Understanding American Chardonnay

### *One Chardonnay, tasted alone*

    4. Unoaked California Chardonnay

### *Two Chardonnays compared (blind tastings)*

**5. Blind Tasting 1:**

Unoaked California Chardonnay vs. Heavily Oaked California Chardonnay

*or*

Sonoma Valley Chardonnay vs. Napa Valley Chardonnay

**6. Blind Tasting 2:**

White Burgundy vs. Napa or Sonoma Valley Chardonnay

*or*

New York Chardonnay vs. California Chardonnay

*or*

Australian Chardonnay vs. California Chardonnay

In both blind tastings, to be fair, both wines should be of the same quality, vintages within a year of each other, and in the same price range.

### *Four Chardonnays compared, from four different AVAs*

    7. Sonoma County Chardonnay
    8. Santa Barbara Chardonnay
    9. Monterey Chardonnay
    10. Carneros Chardonnay

### *Aged Chardonnay (over five years old), tasted alone*

    11. Napa, aged Chardonnay

9.

4.

8.

*\*Please note that labels are suggestions for wineries and producers to look for. For more examples, see pages 72–73, 78, 79, 82, 84, and 87.*

# Questions for Class Two: The Wines of Washington, Oregon, and New York; The White Wines of California

# The White Wines of Germany

GRAPE VARIETIES • THE STYLE OF GERMAN WINES •

PRÄDIKATSWEIN LEVELS • UNDERSTANDING GERMAN WINE LABELS • TRENDS

VIDEO
http://bit.ly/g41IGe

PRONUNCIATIONS
http://bit.ly/ySxpo1

**PAST AND PRESENT**

1970: 77,372 hectares
2011: 102,186 hectares

THERE HAS been a 10% increase in German vineyards planted over the last ten years.

FRANCE PRODUCES ten times as much wine as Germany.

IN GERMANY, 100,000 grape growers cultivate nearly 270,000 acres of vines, meaning the average holding per grower is 2.7 acres.

# About German Wines

BEFORE WE BEGIN OUR STUDY of the white wines of Germany, tell me this: Have you memorized the 7 Grands Crus of Chablis, the 32 Grands Crus of the Côte d'Or, and the 391 different wineries of the Napa Valley? I hope you have, so you can begin to memorize the more than 1,400 wine villages and 2,600-plus vineyards of Germany. No problem, right? What's 4,000 simple little names?

Actually, if you were to have studied German wines before 1971, you would have had 30,000 different names to remember. There used to be very small parcels of land owned by an assortment of different people; that's why so many names were involved.

In an effort to make German wines less confusing, the government stepped in and passed a law in 1971. The new ruling stated that a vineyard must encompass at least twelve and a half acres of land. This law cut the list of vineyard names considerably, but it increased the number of owners.

Germany produces only 2 or 3 percent of the world's wines. (Beer, remember, is the national beverage.) And what wines it does produce depends largely on the weather. Why is this? Well, look at where the wines are geographically. Germany is the northernmost country in which vines can grow. And 80 percent of the quality vineyards are located on hilly slopes. Germans can forget about mechanical harvesting.

The following chart should help give you a better idea of the hilly conditions vintners must contend with in order to grow grapes that produce the highest-quality wines in Germany.

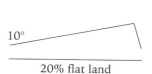

10°
20% flat land

45°
14% hillsides

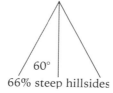

60°
66% steep hillsides

## What are the most important grape varieties?

*Riesling:* This is the most widely planted and the best grape variety produced in Germany. If you don't see the name "Riesling" on the label, then there's probably very little, if any, Riesling grape in the wine. And remember, if the label gives the grape variety, then there must be at least 85 percent of that grape in the wine, according to German law. Of the grapes planted in Germany, 21 percent are Riesling.

*Müller-Thurgau:* A cross between two grapes (Riesling and Chasselas), it accounts for 13.5 percent of Germany's wines.

*Silvaner:* This is another grape variety, and it accounts for 5 percent of Germany's wines.

Ahr
Baden
Franken
Hessische Bergstrasse
Mittelrhein
Nahe
Saale-Unstrut
Sachsen
Württemberg

OF MOSEL wines, 80% are made from the Riesling grape, while 82% of Rheingau wines are made from Riesling.

# What are the main winemaking regions of Germany?

There are thirteen winemaking regions. Do you have to commit them all to memory like the hundreds of other names I've mentioned in the book so far? Absolutely not. Why should you worry about all thirteen when you only need to be familiar with four?

One of the reasons I emphasize these regions above the others is that in the United States you rarely see wine from the other German wine-growing regions. The other reason to look closely at these regions is that they produce the best German wines. They are:

## RHEINHESSEN

## RHEINGAU

## MOSEL
### (UNTIL 2007 KNOWN AS MOSEL-SAAR-RUWER)

### PFALZ
### (UNTIL 1992 KNOWN AS RHEINPFALZ)

LEITZ
WEINGUT

2007
Rüdesheimer
Magdalenenkreuz
Spätlese

RHEINGAU | GERMANY

RIESLING

## What's the style of German wines?

Simply put, it's a balance of sweetness with acidity and low alcohol. Remember the equation:

GERMAN WINES tend to be 8% to 10% alcohol, compared to an average 11% to 13% for French wines.

$$Sugar + Yeast = Alcohol + Carbon\ Dioxide\ (CO_2)$$

Where does the sugar come from? The sun! If you have a good year, and your vines are on a southerly slope, you'll get a lot of sun, and therefore the right sugar content to produce a good wine. Many times, however, the winemakers aren't so fortunate and they don't have enough sun to ripen the grapes. The result: higher acidity and lower alcohol. To compensate for this, some winemakers add sugar to the must (the juice of the grape) before fermentation to increase the amount of alcohol. As mentioned before, this process is called chaptalization. (Chaptalization is not permitted for higher-quality German wines.)

The three basic styles of German wine are:

**Trocken:** dry
**Halbtrocken:** medium-dry
**Fruity:** semidry to very sweet

## What are the ripeness levels of German wine?

As a result of the German law of 1971, there are two main categories, Tafelwein and Qualitätswein.

**Tafelwein:** Literally, "table wine." The lowest designation given to a wine grown in Germany, it never carries the vineyard name. It is rarely seen in the United States.

**Qualitätswein:** Literally, "quality wine," of which there are two types.

1. **Qualitätswein bestimmter Anbaugebiete:** QbA indicates a quality wine that comes from one of the thirteen specified regions.
2. **Prädikatswein:** This is quality wine with distinction—the good stuff. These wines may not be chaptalized.

AS OF the 2007 vintage, Qualitätswein mit Prädikat has been replaced by Prädikatswein.

In ascending order of quality, price, and ripeness at harvest, here are the Prädikatswein levels:

*Kabinett:* Light, semidry wines made from normally ripened grapes.

*Spätlese:* Breaking up the word, *spät* means "late" and *lese* means "picking." Put them together and you have "late picking." That's exactly what this medium-style wine is made of—grapes that were picked after the normal harvest. The extra days of sun give the wine more body and a more intense flavor.

*Auslese:* Translated as "out picked," this means that the grapes are selectively picked out from particularly ripe bunches, which yields a medium-to-fuller-style wine. You probably do the same thing in your own garden if you grow tomatoes: you pick out the especially ripe ones, leaving the others on the vine.

*Beerenauslese:* Breaking the word down, you get *beeren*, or "berries," *aus*, or "out," and *lese*, or "picking." Quite simply (and don't let the bigger names fool you), these are berries (grapes) that are picked out individually. These luscious grapes are used to create the rich dessert wines for which Germany is known. Beerenauslese is usually made only two or three times every ten years.

*Trockenbeerenauslese:* A step above the Beerenauslese, but these grapes are dried (*trocken*), so they're more like raisins. These "raisinated" grapes produce the richest, sweetest, honeylike wine—and the most expensive.

*Eiswein:* A very rare, sweet, concentrated wine made from frozen grapes left on the vine. They're pressed while still frozen. According to Germany's 1971 rules for winemaking, this wine must now be made from grapes that are at least ripe enough to make a Beerenauslese.

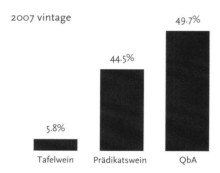

2007 vintage

49.7% — QbA

44.5% — Prädikatswein

5.8% — Tafelwein

FIFTY YEARS AGO, most German wines were dry and very acidic. Even in the finer restaurants, you'd be offered a spoonful of sugar with a German wine to balance the acidity.

## A NOTE ON SÜSSRESERVE

*A common misconception about German wine is that fermentation stops and the remaining residual sugar gives the wine its sweetness naturally. On the contrary, some wines are fermented dry. Many German winemakers hold back a certain percentage of unfermented grape juice from the same vineyards, the same varietal, and the same sweetness level. This Süssreserve contains all the natural sugar and it's added back to the wine after fermentation. The finest estates do not use the Süssreserve method, but rely on stopping the fermentation to achieve their style.*

GIVEN GOOD WEATHER, the longer the grapes remain on the vine, the sweeter they become—but the winemaker takes a risk when he does this because all could be lost in the event of bad weather.

## What's the difference between a $100 Beerenauslese and a $200 Beerenauslese (besides a hundred bucks)?

The major difference is the grapes. The $100 bottle is probably made from Müller-Thurgau grapes or Silvaner, while the $200 bottle is from Riesling. In addition, the region the wine comes from will, in part, determine its quality. Traditionally, the best Beerenauslese and Trockenbeerenauslese come from the Rhein or the Mosel.

Quality is higher in wine when:

- The wine is produced from low yields

- The grapes come from great vineyards

- The wine is produced by great winemakers

- The grapes were grown in a great climate or are from a great vintage

TODAY, MOST German wines, including Beerenauslese and Trockenbeerenauslese, are bottled in spring and early summer. Many no longer receive additional cask or tank maturation, because it has been discovered that this extra barrel aging destroys the fruit.

IN 1921, the first Trockenbeerenauslese was made in the Mosel region.

## THE SPÄTLESE RIDER: THE FIRST LATE-HARVEST WINE

*The story goes that at the vineyards of Schloss Johannisberg, the monks were not allowed to pick the grapes until the Abbot of Fulda gave his permission. During the harvest of 1775, the abbot was away attending a synod. That year the grapes were ripening early and some of them had started to rot on the vine. The monks, becoming concerned, dispatched a rider to ask the abbot's permission to pick the grapes. By the time the rider returned, the monks believed all was lost, but they went ahead with the harvest anyway. To their amazement, the wine was one of the best they had ever tasted. That was the beginning of Spätlese-style wines.*

| | |
|---|---|
| C. von Schubert | Mosel |
| Dr. H. Thanisch | Mosel |
| Dr. Loosen | Mosel |
| Dr. Pauly-Bergweiler | Mosel |
| Egon Müller | Mosel |
| Friedrich-Wilhelm-Gymnasium | Mosel |
| Fritz Haag | Mosel |
| J. J. Prum | Mosel |
| Joh. Jos. Christoffel Erben | Mosel |
| Kesselstatt | Mosel |
| Rheinhold Haart | Mosel |
| S. A. Prum | Mosel |
| Schloss Leiser | Mosel |
| Selbach-Oster | Mosel |
| Keller | Rheinhessen |
| Strub | Rheinhessen |
| Josef Leitz | Rheingau |
| Kessler | Rheingau |
| Robert Weil | Rheingau |
| Schloss Johannisberg | Rheingau |
| Schloss Vollrads | Rheingau |
| Basserman-Jordan | Pfalz |
| Darting | Pfalz |
| Dr. Bürklin Wolf | Pfalz |
| Dr. Deinhard | Pfalz |
| Lingenfelder | Pfalz |
| Muller-Catoir | Pfalz |

ONE QUICK way to tell the difference between a Rhein and a Mosel wine on sight is to look at the bottle. Rhein wine comes in a brown bottle, Mosel in a green bottle.

## When I'm ordering a German wine in a restaurant or shopping at my local retailer, what should I look for?

The first thing I would make sure of is that it comes from one of the four major regions. These regions are the Mosel, Rheinhessen, Rheingau, and Pfalz, which, in my opinion, are the most important quality wine–producing regions in all of Germany.

Next, look to see if the wine is made from the Riesling grape. Anyone who studies and enjoys German wines finds that Riesling shows the best-tasting characteristics. Riesling on the label is a mark of quality.

Also, be aware of the vintage. It's important, especially with German wines, to know if the wine was made in a good year.

Finally, the most important consideration is to buy from a reputable grower or producer.

## What's the difference between Rhein and Mosel wines?

Rhein wines generally have more body than do Mosels. Mosels are usually higher in acidity and lower in alcohol than Rhein wines. Mosels show more autumn fruits like apples, pears, and quince, while Rhein wines show more summer fruits like apricots, peaches, and nectarines.

Some important villages to look for:

*Mosel:* Erden, Piesport, Bernkastel, Graach, Ürzig, Brauneberg, Wehlen
*Pfalz:* Deidesheim, Forst, Wachenheim, Ruppertsberg, Dürkheimer
*Rheingau:* Eltville, Erbach, Rüdesheim, Rauenthal, Hochheim, Johannisberg
*Rheinhessen:* Oppenheim, Nackenheim, Nierstein

## WHOSE VINEYARD IS IT, ANYWAY?

Piesporter Goldtröpfchen—350 owners
Wehlener Sonnenuhr—250 owners
Brauneberger Juffer—180 owners

## Can you take the mystery out of reading German wine labels?

German wine labels give you plenty of information. For example, take a look at the label above.

**Joh. Jos. Christoffel Erben** is the producer.

**Mosel** is the region of the wine's origin. Note that the region is one of the big four we discussed earlier in this chapter.

**2001** is the year the grapes were harvested.

**Ürzig** is the town and **Würzgarten** is the vineyard from which the grapes originate. The Germans add the suffix "er" to make *Ürziger,* just as a person from New York is called a New Yorker.

**Riesling** is the grape variety. Therefore, this wine is at least 85 percent Riesling.

**Auslese** is the ripeness level, in this case from bunches of overripe grapes.

**Qualitätswein mit Prädikat** is the quality level of the wine.

**A.P. Nr. 2 602 041 008 02** is the official testing number—proof that the wine was tasted by a panel of tasters and passed the strict quality standards required by the government.

**Gutsabfüllung** means "estate-bottled."

ALL QUALITÄTSWEIN and Prädikatswein must pass a test by an official laboratory and tasting panel to be given an official number, prior to the wine's release to the trade.

IMPRESS YOUR friends with this kind
of trivia:
**A.P. Nr. 2 602 041 008 02**
  **2** = the government referral office or testing station
  **602** = location code of bottler
  **041** = bottler ID number
  **008** = bottle lot
  **02** = the year the wine was tasted by the board

SINCE THIS wine is a 2001 vintage, the designation is still Qualitätswein mit Prädikat. Starting with the 2007 vintage, this has been changed to Prädikatswein.

THE 2003 harvest was one of the earliest in decades.

## WHAT IS *BOTRYTIS CINEREA?*

*Botrytis cinerea, known as Edelfäule in German, is a mold that (under special conditions) attacks grapes, as was described in the section on Sauternes. I say "special" because this "noble rot" is instrumental in the production of Beerenauslese and Trockenbeerenauslese.*

*Noble rot occurs late in the growing season when the nights are cool and heavy with dew, the mornings have fog, and the days are warm. When noble rot attacks the grapes, they begin to shrivel and the water evaporates, leaving concentrated sugar. (Remember, 86 percent of wine is water.) Grapes affected by this mold may not look very appealing, but don't let looks deceive you: The proof is in the wine.*

THE 2011 VINTAGE in Germany was the warmest in 40 years and the driest in the last 50 years. It was also the earliest harvest on record.

PAST GREAT VINTAGES of Beerenauslese and Trockenbeerenauslese: 1985, 1988, 1989, 1990, 1996.

THE 2010 VINTAGE in Germany was one of the smallest harvests in 30 years.

## What are the recent trends in the white wines of Germany?

Germany is producing higher-quality wines than ever before, and American interest in these wines has increased at the same time.

I feel the lighter-style Trocken (dry), Halbtrocken (medium-dry), Kabinetts, and even Spätleses are wines that can be easily served as an apéritif, or with very light food and also grilled food, and in particular with spicy or Pacific Rim cuisines. If you haven't had a German wine in a long time, the 2001 through 2006 are spectacular vintages that show the greatness of what German white wines are all about.

And the great news is that those hard-to-read Gothic script German wine labels have become more user-friendly—easier to read, with more modern designs.

### BEST BETS FOR RECENT VINTAGES IN GERMANY

2001** 2002* 2003* 2004* 2005**
2006* 2007** 2008* 2009* 2010 2011

*Note: * signifies exceptional vintage        ** signifies extraordinary vintage*

### FOR FURTHER READING

I recommend *Gault-Millau: The Guide to German Wines* by Armin Diel and Joel Payne.

# WINE AND FOOD

ONLINE STORE
http://bit.ly/dKcMXR

RAINER LINGENFELDER *(Weingut Lingenfelder Estate, Pfalz)*: *With Riesling Spätlese Halbtrocken, "We have a tradition of cooking freshwater fish that come from a number of small creeks in the Palatinate Forest, so my personal choice would be trout, either herbed with thyme, basil, parsley, and onion and cooked in wine; or smoked with a bit of horseradish. We find it to be a very versatile wine, a very good match with a whole range of white meat. Pork is traditional in the Palatinate region, as are chicken and goose dishes."*

JOHANNES SELBACH *(Selbach-Oster, Mosel)*: *"What kinds of food do we have with Riesling Spätlese? Anything we like! This may sound funny, but there's a wide variety of food that goes very well with—and this is the key—a fruity, only moderately sweet, well-balanced Riesling Spätlese. Start with mild curries and sesame- or ginger-flavored, not-too-spicy dishes. Or try either gravlax or smoked salmon. You can even have Riesling Spätlese with a green salad in a balsamic vinaigrette, preferably with a touch of raspberry, as long as the dressing is not too vinegary. Many people avoid pairing wine with a salad, but it works beautifully.*

*"For haute cuisine, fresh duck or goose liver lightly sautéed in its own juice, or veal sweetbreads in a rich sauce. Also salads with fresh greens, fresh fruit, and fresh seafood marinated in lime or lemon juice or balsamic vinegar.*

*"With an old, ripe Spätlese: roast venison, dishes with cream sauces, and any white-meat dish stuffed with or accompanied by fruit. It is also delicious with fresh fruit itself or as an apéritif."*

*With Riesling Spätlese Halbtrocken: "This is a food-friendly wine, but the first thing that comes to mind is fresh seafood and fresh fish. Also wonderful with salads with a mild vinaigrette, and with a course that's often difficult to match: cream soups. If we don't know exactly what to drink with a particular food, Spätlese Halbtrocken is usually the safe bet.*

*"It may be too obvious to say foie gras with Eiswein, but it is a classic."*

# Class Three:
# The White Wines of Germany

I've found that German wines are not as well known or as well understood as French or California wines to most Americans. German wines are often dismissed because they seem complicated, and also because they are light-bodied white wines and the best German wines have higher levels of residual sugar. Don't make that mistake. Once you learn the main villages, vineyards, classifications, and a little German pronunciation, you'll find it easy to understand and you'll be able to enjoy the charm and elegance of the great German wines.

## THE WINES

### Understanding a Quality German Wine

#### One wine, tasted alone

    1. Any Qualitätswein from Germany

### Understanding Kabinett

#### Two Kabinetts compared

    2. Mosel Riesling Kabinett
    3. Rheinhessen Riesling Kabinett

1.

3.

## Understanding Spätlese

### Two Spätleses compared

4. Mosel Riesling Spätlese
5. Pfalz Riesling Spätlese

## Understanding Auslese

### Two Ausleses compared

6. Pfalz Riesling Auslese
7. Rheingau Riesling Auslese

## Understanding Tokaji Aszú (see pp. 224–225)

### One Tokaji, tasted alone

8. Tokaji Aszú from Hungary

4.

5.

6.

8.

*Please note that labels are suggestions for wineries and producers to look for. For more examples, see page 110.*

# Questions for Class Three:
# The White Wines of Germany

12. What are the two main categories of Qualitätswein?

13. Name the levels of ripeness of Prädikatswein.

14. What does the word *Spätlese* mean in English?

15. What does the German term *Trocken* say about the style of the wine?

16. What is Eiswein?

17. What is Süssreserve?

18. Match the region to the village.

    a. Rheingau                 \_\_\_Oppenheim

    b. Mosel                    \_\_\_Rüdesheim

    c. Rheinhessen           \_\_\_Bernkastel

    d. Pfalz                     \_\_\_Piesport

                                    \_\_\_Johannisberg

                                    \_\_\_Deidesheim

                                    \_\_\_Nierstein

19. What does the German term *Gutsabfüllung* indicate?

20. What is *Botrytis cinerea* (*Edelfäule*)?

# The Red Wines of Burgundy and the Rhône Valley

THE RED WINES OF BURGUNDY · BEAUJOLAIS ·

CÔTE CHÂLONNAISE · CÔTE D'OR · RHÔNE VALLEY

VIDEO
http://bit.ly/edIIR1

PRONUNCIATIONS
http://bit.ly/yaHV2q

**2,000 YEARS OF EXPERIENCE**

Burgundy's reputation for winemaking
dates as far back as 51 B.C.

# The Red Wines of Burgundy

NOW WE'RE GETTING INTO a whole new experience in wines—the reds. The complexity, nuances, flavors, and length of taste in red wines evoke a sense of excitement for me and my students, and we tend to concentrate more when we taste red wines.

**LAND OF 1,000 NAMES**

There are more than 1,000 names and
more than 110 appellations you must
memorize to become a Burgundy wine
expert.

## What's so different about red wines (beyond their color)?

We're beginning to see more components in the wines—more complexities. In the white wines, we were looking mainly for the acid/fruit balance, but now, in addition, we're looking for other characteristics, such as tannin.

## Why is Burgundy so difficult to understand?

Before we go any further, I must tell you that there are no shortcuts. Burgundy is one of the most difficult subjects in the study of wines. People get confused about Burgundy. They say, "There's so much to know," and "It looks so hard." Yes, there are many vineyards and villages, and they're all important. But there are really only fifteen to twenty-five names you should know if you'd like to understand and speak about Burgundy wines intelligently. Not to worry. I'm going to help you decode all the mysteries of Burgundy: names, regions, and labels.

## What are the main red wine–producing areas of Burgundy?

Côte d'Or {  | Côte de Nuits | Beaujolais |
|---|---|
| Côte de Beaune | Côte Châlonnaise |

## What major grape varieties are used in red Burgundy wines?

The two major grape varieties are Pinot Noir and Gamay. Under Appellation d'Origine Contrôlée laws, all red Burgundies are made from the Pinot Noir grape, except Beaujolais, which is produced from the Gamay grape.

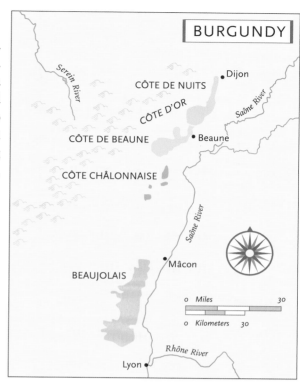

THE CÔTE D'OR is only 30 miles long and half a mile wide.

**BLAME NAPOLEON**

If you're having trouble understanding the wines of Burgundy, you're not alone. After the French Revolution in 1789, all the vineyards were sold off in small parcels. The Napoleonic Code also called for a law of equal inheritance for the children— continuing to fragment the vineyards even further.

## THE MAGNIFICENT AND DIFFICULT PINOT NOIR

*The fame of the Pinot Noir has its origins in Burgundy, France. I have a tremendous amount of respect for the individuals who have chosen to plant Pinot Noir, since it is a difficult grape to make into a great wine. You have to be really passionate and patient when growing this thin-skinned grape. It is susceptible to many different diseases, and too much sunlight (heat) during the growing season will end the chances of making a balanced wine.*

*What you will get from a great Pinot Noir is less tannin, less extraction of color, and less body. The best Pinot Noirs in Burgundy are not about muscle and density but rather elegance and finesse.*

# BEAUJOLAIS

- The wine is made from 100 percent Gamay grapes
- This wine's style is typically light and fruity. It's meant to be consumed young. Beaujolais can be chilled.
- Beaujolais is the best-selling Burgundy in the United States by far, probably because there is so much of it, it's so easy to drink, and it's very affordable
- Most bottles cost between $8 and $20, although the price varies with the quality level

## What are the different quality levels of Beaujolais?

There are three different quality levels of Beaujolais:

*Beaujolais:* This basic Beaujolais accounts for the majority of all Beaujolais produced. Cost: $.

*Beaujolais-Villages:* This comes from certain villages in Beaujolais. There are thirty-five villages that consistently produce better wines. Most Beaujolais-Villages are a blend of wines from these villages, and usually no particular village name is included on the label. Cost: $$.

*Cru:* A cru is actually named for the village that produces this highest quality of Beaujolais. Cost: $$$$.

There are ten crus (villages):

| | |
|---|---|
| BROUILLY | JULIÉNAS |
| CHÉNAS | MORGON |
| CHIROUBLES | MOULIN-À-VENT |
| CÔTE DE BROUILLY | RÉGNIÉ |
| FLEURIE | SAINT-AMOUR |

## What's Beaujolais Nouveau?

Beaujolais Nouveau is even lighter and fruitier in style than your basic Beaujolais and it is best to drink it young. Isn't that true of all Beaujolais wines? Yes, but Nouveau is different. This "new" Beaujolais is picked, fermented, bottled, and available at your local retailer in a matter of weeks. (I don't know what you call that in your business, but I call it good cash flow in mine. It gives the winemaker a virtually instant return.)

There's another purpose behind Beaujolais Nouveau: like a preview of a movie, it offers the wine-consuming public a sample of the quality of the vintage and style that the winemaker will produce in his regular Beaujolais for release the following spring.

Beaujolais Nouveau is meant to be consumed within six months of bottling. So if you're holding a 2000 Beaujolais Nouveau, now is the time to give it to your "friends."

## How long should I keep a Beaujolais?

It depends on the level of quality and the vintage. Beaujolais and Beaujolais-Villages are meant to last between one and three years. Crus can last longer because they are more complex: they have more fruit and tannin. I've tasted Beaujolais crus that were more than ten years old and still in excellent condition. This is the exception, though, not the rule.

## Which shippers/producers should I look for when buying Beaujolais?

BOUCHARD   DROUHIN   DUBOEUF

JADOT   MOMMESSIN

### BEST BETS FOR RECENT VINTAGES OF BEAUJOLAIS

2005*   2008   2009**   2010

*Note: * signifies exceptional vintage   ** signifies extraordinary vintage*

## TO CHILL OR NOT TO CHILL?

*As a young student studying wines in Burgundy, I visited the Beaujolais region, excited and naive. In one of the villages, I stopped at a bistro and ordered a glass of Beaujolais. (A good choice on my part, don't you think?) The waiter brought the glass of Beaujolais and it was chilled, and I thought that these people had not read the right books! Every wine book I'd ever read always said you serve red wines at room temperature and white wines chilled.*

*Obviously, I learned from my experience that when it comes to Beaujolais Nouveau, Beaujolais, and Beaujolais-Villages, it's a good idea to give them a slight chill to bring out the fruit and liveliness (acidity) of the wines. That is why Beaujolais is my favorite red wine to have during the summer.*

*However, to my taste, the Beaujolais crus have more fruit and more tannin and are best served at room temperature.*

GEORGES DUBŒUF
BEAUJOLAIS-VILLAGES NOUVEAU
APPELLATION BEAUJOLAIS VILLAGES CONTRÔLÉE
RED BEAUJOLAIS WINE
ALC 12% BY VOL.   750 ML
MIS EN BOUTEILLES PAR LES VINS GEORGES DUBŒUF
71570 ROMANÈCHE-THORINS FRANCE
PRODUCE OF FRANCE

## BEAUJOLAIS NOUVEAU MADNESS

*The exact date of release is the third Thursday in November, and Beaujolais Nouveau is introduced to the consumer amid great hoopla. Restaurants and retailers all vie to be the first to offer the new Beaujolais to their customers.*

ONE-THIRD of the Beaujolais grapes are used to make Beaujolais Nouveau.

THE FIRST Beaujolais I ever tasted was from the 1969 vintage. The 2009 vintage is the best since 1969.

*"Beaujolais is one of the very few red wines that can be drunk as a white. Beaujolais is my daily drink. And sometimes I blend one-half water to the wine. It is the most refreshing drink in the world."*

—DIDIER MOMMESSIN

OTHER GREAT Beaujolais producers: Daniel Bouland, Guy Breton, Château des Jacques, Thibault Liger-Belair, Dominique Piron, Clos de la Roilette, Domaine Rochette, Domaine des Terres Poréss, and Georges Descombes.

## WINE AND FOOD

*Beaujolais goes well with almost anything—especially light, simple meals and cheeses—nothing overpowering. Generally, try to match your Beaujolais with light food, such as veal, fish, or fowl. Here's what some of the experts say:*

GEORGES DUBOEUF: *"A lot of dishes can be eaten with Beaujolais—what you* choose depends on the appellation and vintage. With charcuteries and pâtés you can serve a young Beaujolais or Beaujolais-Villages. With grilled meat, more generous and fleshy wines, such as Juliénas and Morgon crus, can be served. With meats cooked in a sauce (for example, coq au vin), I would suggest a Moulin-à-Vent cru from a good vintage."

ANDRÉ GAGEY (Louis Jadot): *"Beaujolais with simple meals, light cheeses, grilled meat—everything except sweets."*

DIDIER MOMMESSIN: *"Serve with an extremely strong cheese, such as Roquefort, especially when the wine is young and strong enough for it. Also with white meat and veal."*

# CÔTE CHÂLONNAISE

Now we're getting into classic Pinot Noir wines that offer tremendous value.

You should know three villages from this area:

*Mercurey:* 95 percent red

*Givry:* 90 percent red

*Rully:* 50 percent red

Mercurey is the most important, producing wines of high quality. Because they are not well known in the United States, Mercurey wines are often a very good buy.

## Which shippers/producers should I look for when buying wines from the Côte Châlonnaise?

| MERCUREY | CHÂTEAU DE CHAMIREY |
| | DOMAINE DE SUREMAIN |
| | FAIVELEY |
| | MICHEL JUILLOT |
| GIVRY | CHOFFLET-VALDENAIRE |
| | DOMAINE JABLOT |
| | DOMAINE THENARD |
| | LOUIS LATOUR |
| RULLY | ANTONIN RODET |

# CÔTE D'OR

Here is the heart of Burgundy. The Côte d'Or (pronounced "coat door") means "golden slope." This region gets its name from the color of the foliage on the hillside, which in autumn is literally golden, as well as the income it brings to the winemakers. The area is very small and its best wines are among the priciest in the world. If you are looking for a $7.99 everyday bottle of wine, this is not the place that will produce it.

## What's the best way to understand the wines of the Côte d'Or?

First, you need to know that these wines are distinguished by quality levels—generic, Village, Premier Cru vineyards, and Grand Cru vineyards. Let's look at the quality levels with the double pyramid shown below. As you can see, not much Grand Cru wine is produced, but it is the highest quality and extremely expensive. Generic wine, on the other hand, is more readily available. Although much is produced, very few generic wines can be classified as outstanding.

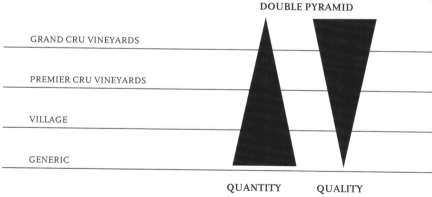

**DOUBLE PYRAMID**

GRAND CRU VINEYARDS

PREMIER CRU VINEYARDS

VILLAGE

GENERIC

QUANTITY    QUALITY

The Côte d'Or is divided into two regions:

*Côte de Beaune:* Red and white wines (70 percent red and 30 percent white).

*Côte de Nuits:* 95 percent red wines; the highest-quality red Burgundy wines come from this region.

Another way to understand the wines of the Côte d'Or is to become familiar with the most important villages, Grand Cru vineyards, and some of the Premier Cru vineyards.

GENERIC WINES are labeled simply "Burgundy" or "Bourgogne." A higher level of generic wines will be labeled "Côte de Beaune Villages" or "Côte de Nuits Villages," being a blend of different Village wines.

THERE ARE 32 Grand Cru vineyards:
8 white
24 red
24 from the Côte de Nuits
8 from the Côte de Beaune

Fixin
Marsannay
Monthélie
Pernand-Vergelesses
Santenay
Savigny-lés-Beaune

BY FAR the most-produced red Grand Cru is Corton, representing about 25% of all Grand Cru red wines.

THERE ARE more than 500 Premier Cru vineyards in Burgundy.

THE FOUR smallest French appellations are located in the Côte de Nuits:
Griotte Chambertin (2.63 acres)
La Grande Rue (1.65 acres)
La Romanée Conti (1.63 acres)
La Romanée (0.85 acres acres)

CHAMBERTIN CLOS DE BÈZE was the favorite wine of Napoleon, who is reported to have said: "Nothing makes the future look so rosy as to contemplate it through a glass of Chambertin." Obviously, he ran out of Chambertin at Waterloo!

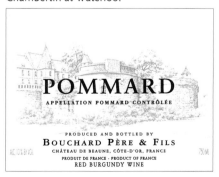

## THE IMPORTANCE OF SOIL TO BURGUNDY WINES

*If you talk to any producers of Burgundy wines, they'll tell you the most important element in making their quality wines is the soil in which the grapes are grown. This, together with the slope of the land and the climatic conditions, determines whether the wine is a Village wine, a Premier Cru, or a Grand Cru. This concept of soil, slope, and climatic conditions is known as terroir.*

*During one of my trips to Burgundy, it rained for five straight days. On the sixth day I saw the workers at the bottom of the slopes with their pails and shovels, collecting the soil that had run down the hillside and returning it to the vineyard. This goes to show the importance of the soil to Burgundy wines.*

## Côte de Beaune—Red

| MOST IMPORTANT VILLAGES | MY FAVORITE PREMIER CRU VINEYARDS | GRAND CRU VINEYARDS |
|---|---|---|
| Aloxe-Corton | Chaillots | Corton |
| | Fournières | Corton Bressandes |
| | | Corton Clos du Roi |
| | | Corton Maréchaude |
| | | Corton Renardes |
| Beaune | Bressandes | None |
| | Clos des Mouches | |
| | Fèves | |
| | Grèves | |
| | Marconnets | |
| Pommard | Épenots | None |
| | Rugiens | |
| Volnay | Caillerets | None |
| | Clos des Chênes | |
| | Santenots | |
| | Taillepieds | |

# Côte de Nuits—Red

Finally, we reach the Côte de Nuits. If you're going to spend any time studying your geography, do it now. The majority of Grand Cru vineyards are located in this area.

| MOST IMPORTANT VILLAGES | MY FAVORITE PREMIER CRU VINEYARDS | GRAND CRU VINEYARDS |
|---|---|---|
| Chambolle-Musigny | Charmes | Bonnes Mares (partial) |
| | Les Amoureuses | Musigny |
| Flagey-Échézeaux | | Échézeaux |
| | | Grands-Échézeaux |
| Gevrey-Chambertin | Aux Combottes | Chambertin |
| | Clos St-Jacques | Chambertin Clos de Bèze |
| | Les Cazetiers | Chapelle-Chambertin |
| | | Charmes-Chambertin |
| | | Griotte-Chambertin |
| | | Latricières-Chambertin |
| | | Mazis-Chambertin |
| | | Mazoyères-Chambertin |
| | | Ruchottes-Chambertin |
| Morey-St-Denis | Clos des Ormes | Bonnes Mares (partial) |
| | Les Genevrières | Clos de la Roche |
| | Ruchots | Clos des Lambrays |
| | | Clos de Tart |
| | | Clos St-Denis |
| Nuits-St-Georges | Les St-Georges | None |
| | Porets | |
| | Vaucrains | |
| Vosne-Romanée | Beaux-Monts | La Grande-Rue |
| | | La Romanée |
| | | La Tâche |
| | | Malconsorts |
| | | Richebourg |
| | | Romanée-Conti |
| | | Romanée-St-Vivant |
| Vougeot | | Clos de Vougeot |

### SLEEPY HOLLOW

There is a village in Westchester County, New York, called Sleepy Hollow. It was originally called North Tarrytown, but the locals, trying to capitalize on "The Legend of Sleepy Hollow" for tourism, changed its name.

And so it is with some villages in Burgundy. Starting in the 1800s, they have added the name of their most famous vineyard to the name of the village. For example, the village of Gevrey became Gevrey-Chambertin, and the village of Puligny became Puligny-Montrachet. Can you figure out the others?

### THE NEWEST GRAND CRU

La Grande-Rue, a vineyard tucked between the Grands Crus La Tâche and Romanée-Conti in Vosne-Romanée, was itself elevated to the Grand Cru level, bringing the number of Grands Crus in the Côte d'Or to 32.

MANY WINE writers and lovers of Burgundy use the word "seductive" to describe the taste of Pinot Noir.

HAS THIS ever happened to you? In a restaurant, you order a Village wine—Gevrey Chambertin, for example—and by mistake the waiter brings you a Grand Cru Le Chambertin. What would you do?

**$**
Village Only = Village Wine

**$$**
Village + Vineyard
(Clos Saint-Jacques) = Premier Cru

**$$$$**
Vineyard Only
(Le Chambertin) = Grand Cru

**IT'S THE LAW!**

Beginning with the 1990 vintage, all Grand Cru Burgundies must include the words "Grand Cru" on the label.

## Why are we bothering with all this geography? Must we learn the names of all the villages and vineyards?

I thought you'd never ask. First of all, the geography is important because it helps make you a smart buyer. If you're familiar with the most important villages and vineyards, you're more likely to make an educated purchase.

You really don't have to memorize all the villages and vineyards. I'll let you in on a little secret of how to choose a Burgundy wine and tell at a glance if it's a Village wine, a Premier Cru, or a Grand Cru—usually the label will tip you off in the manner illustrated here.

This is the method I use to teach Burgundy wine. Ask yourself the following:

**Where is the wine from?** France

**What type of wine is it?** Burgundy

**Which region is it from?** Côte d'Or

**Which area?** Côte de Nuits

**Which village is the wine from?** Chambolle-Musigny

**Does the label give more details?** Yes, it tells you that the wine is from a vineyard called Musigny, which is one of the thirty-two Grand Cru vineyards.

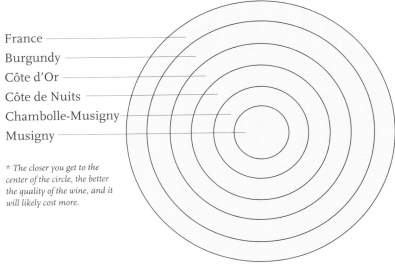

France
Burgundy
Côte d'Or
Côte de Nuits
Chambolle-Musigny
Musigny

*\* The closer you get to the center of the circle, the better the quality of the wine, and it will likely cost more.*

## Forty years later in Burgundy

The red wines of Burgundy still remain the benchmark for Pinot Noir throughout the world. Over the last forty years, the great wines of Burgundy have gotten only better (and more expensive!), and the good wines have become more consistent and of higher quality. Better clonal selection, vineyard management, and a new generation of winemakers will continue to give pleasure for decades to come. Both the shippers' (*négociants'*) wines and the estate-bottled producers are making the best wines that Burgundy has ever known.

IN THE 1960S, Burgundy wines were fermented and vatted for up to three weeks. Today's Burgundy wines are usually fermented and vatted for six to twelve days.

## Why are the well-known great Burgundies so expensive?

The answer is simple: supply and demand. The Burgundy growers and shippers of the Côte d'Or have a problem all businesspeople would envy—not enough supply to meet the demand. It has been this way for years, and it will continue because Burgundy is a small region that produces a limited amount of wine. The Bordeaux wine region produces three times as much wine as Burgundy does.

### BURGUNDY WINE HARVEST

*(average number of cases over a five-year period for red and white)*

| | |
|---|---|
| Regional appellations | 2,136,674 |
| Beaujolais | 11,503,617 |
| Côte Châlonnaise | 357,539 |
| Côte d'Or (Côte de Nuits) | 511,594 |
| Côte d'Or (Côte de Beaune) | 1,391,168 |
| Chablis | 755,188 |
| Mâconnais | 2,136,674 |
| Other appellations | 339,710 |
| Total Burgundy harvest | 19,132,164 cases |

### BEST BETS FOR RECENT VINTAGES OF CÔTE D'OR

1999\*  2002\*  2003\*  2005\*\*  2006  2007  2008\*  2009\*
2010  2011

*Note: \* signifies exceptional vintage   \*\* signifies extraordinary vintage*

1970s: 15% Domaine-bottled Burgundy
2011: 60% Domaine-bottled Burgundy

IF YOU DON'T want to be disappointed by the Burgundy wine you select, make sure you know your vintages. Also, due to the delicacy of the Pinot Noir grape, red Burgundies require proper storage, so make sure you buy from a merchant who handles Burgundy wines with care.

HOW IMPORTANT is the producer? Clos de Vougeot is the single largest Grand Cru vineyard in Burgundy, totaling 125 acres, with more than 80 different owners. Each owner makes his own winemaking decisions, such as when to pick the grapes, the style of fermentation, and how long to age the wine in oak. Obviously, all Clos de Vougeot is not created equal.

# Who are the most important shippers to look for when buying red Burgundy wine?

**BOUCHARD PÈRE ET FILS**
**CHANSON**
**JAFFELIN**
**JOSEPH DROUHIN**

**LABOURÉ-ROI**
**LOUIS JADOT**
**LOUIS LATOUR**

Some fine estate-bottled wines are available in limited quantities in the United States. Look for the following:

**DOMAINE ARMAND ROUSSEAU**
**DOMAINE CLERGET**
**DOMAINE COMTE DE VOGÜE**
**DOMAINE DANIEL RION**
**DOMAINE DE LA ROMANÉE-CONTI**
**DOMAINE DUJAC**
**DOMAINE FAIVELEY**
**DOMAINE GEORGES ROUMIER**
**DOMAINE GROFFIER**
**DOMAINE HENRI GOUGES**
**DOMAINE HENRI LAMARCHE**
**DOMAINE JAYER**
**DOMAINE JEAN GRIVOT**

**DOMAINE LEROY**
**DOMAINE LOUIS TRAPET**
**DOMAINE MÉO CAMUZET**
**DOMAINE MONGEARD-**
**MUGNERET**
**DOMAINE PARENT**
**DOMAINE PIERRE DAMOY**
**DOMAINE POTEL**
**DOMAINE POUSSE D'OR**
**DOMAINE PRINCE DE MÉRODE**
**DOMAINE TOLLOT-BEAUT**
**DOMAINE VINCENT GIRARDIN**
**MAISON FAIVELEY**

## FOR FURTHER READING

I recommend *The Wines of Burgundy* by Clive Coates, M.W.; *Burgundy* by Anthony Hanson; *Making Sense of Burgundy* by Matt Kramer; *The Great Domaines of Burgundy* by Remington Norman; and *Burgundy* by Robert M. Parker Jr.

# WINE AND FOOD

*To get the most flavor from both the wine and the food, some of Burgundy's famous wine-makers offer these suggestions:*

ROBERT DROUHIN: *"In my opinion, white wine is never a good accompaniment to red meat, but a light red Burgundy can match a fish course (not shellfish). Otherwise, for light red Burgundies, white meat—not too many spices; partridge, pheasant, and rabbit. For heavier-style wines, lamb and steak are good choices." Personally, Mr.*

*Drouhin does not enjoy red Burgundies with cheese—especially goat cheese.*

PIERRE HENRY GAGEY *(Louis Jadot): "With red Beaujolais wines, such as Moulin-à-Vent Château des Jacques, for example, a piece of pork like an andouillette from Fleury is beautiful. A Gamay, more fruity and fleshy than Pinot Noir, goes perfectly with this typical meal from our terroir. My favorite food combination with a red Burgundy wine*

*is poulet de bresse demi d'oeil. The very thin flesh of this truffle-filled chicken and the elegance and delicacy from the great Pinot Noir, which come from the best terroir, go together beautifully."*

LOUIS LATOUR: *"With Château Corton Grancey, filet of duck in a red-wine sauce. Otherwise, Pinot Noir is good with roast chicken, venison, and beef. Mature wines are a perfect combination for our local cheeses, Chambertin and Citeaux."*

# THE RHÔNE VALLEY

As a sommelier, I was often asked to recommend a big, robust red Burgundy wine to complement a rack of lamb or filet mignon. To the customers' surprise, I didn't recommend a Burgundy at all. The best bet is a Rhône wine, which is typically a bigger and fuller wine than one from Burgundy, and usually has a higher alcoholic content. The reason for these characteristics is quite simple. It all goes back to location and geography.

## Where's the Rhône Valley?

The Rhône Valley is in southeastern France, south of the Burgundy region, where the climate is hot and the conditions are sunny. The extra sun gives the grapes more sugar, which, as we have discussed, boosts the level of alcohol. The soil is full of rocks that retain the intense summer heat during both day and night.

Winemakers of the Rhône Valley are required by law to make sure their wines have a specified amount of alcohol. For example, the minimum alcoholic content required by the AOC is 10.5 percent for Côtes du Rhône and 12.5 percent for Châteauneuf-du-Pape.

## What are the different quality levels of the Rhône Valley?

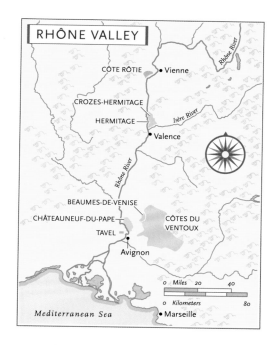

|  | % of production |
|---|---|
| 1. Côtes du Rhône ($) | 58% |
| 2. Côtes du Rhône Villages ($$) | 8% |
| 3. Côtes du Rhône Crus (specific regions) ($$$$) | 10% |
|    Northern Rhône |  |
|    Southern Rhône |  |
| 4. Other appellations | 24% |

OF ALL the wines made in the Rhône Valley, 91% are red, 6% are rosé, and 3% are white.

SOME OF the oldest vineyards in France are in the Rhône Valley. Hermitage, for example, has been in existence for more than 2,000 years.

CÔTES DU RHÔNE wine can be produced from grapes grown in either or both the northern and southern Rhône regions. More than 90% of all Côtes du Rhône wines come from the southern region.

LEADING ACREAGE of Grenache/Garnacha:
France (96,000 hectares)
Spain (83,000 hectares)
California (7,700 hectares)
Australia (4,000 hectares)

TWO OTHER important red grapes in the
   Rhône Valley are:
Cinsault
Mourvèdre

### THE 13 CRUS OF THE RHÔNE VALLEY

**North**
Château-Grillet (white)
Condrieu (white)
Cornas
Côte-Rôtie
Crozes-Hermitage
Hermitage
St-Joseph
St-Peray

**South**
Châteauneuf-du-Pape
Gigondas
Lirac
Tavel (rosé)
Vacqueyras

## What are the winemaking regions in the Rhône Valley?

The region is divided into two distinct areas: northern and southern Rhône. The most famous red wines that come from the northern region are:

CROZES-HERMITAGE (3,000+ ACRES)       HERMITAGE (324 ACRES)
CÔTE RÔTIE (555 ACRES)

The most famous red wines from the southern region are:

CHÂTEAUNEUF-DU-PAPE (7,822 ACRES)
GIGONDAS (3,036 ACRES)

Two distinct microclimates distinguish the north from the south. It is important for you to understand that these areas make distinctly different wines because of:

- Soil
- Location
- Different grape varieties used in making the wines of each area

## What are the main red-grape varieties grown in the Rhône Valley?

The two major grape varieties in the Rhône Valley are:

GRENACHE          SYRAH

## Which wines are made from these grapes?

The Côte Rôtie, Hermitage, and Crozes-Hermitage from the north are made primarily from the Syrah grape. These are the biggest and fullest wines from that region.

For Châteauneuf-du-Pape, as many as thirteen different grape varieties may be included in the blend. But the best producers use a greater percentage of Grenache and Syrah in the blend.

## What's Tavel?

It's a rosé—an unusually dry rosé, which distinguishes it from most others. It's made primarily from the Grenache grape, although nine grape varieties can be used in the blend. When you come right down to it, Tavel is just like a red wine, with all the red-wine components but less color. How do they make a rosé wine with red-wine characteristics but less color? It's all in the vatting process.

## What's the difference between "short-vatted" and "long-vatted" wines?

When a wine is "short-vatted," the skins are allowed to ferment with the must (grape juice) for a short period of time—only long enough to impart that rosé color. It's just the opposite when a winemaker is producing red Rhône wines, such as Châteauneuf-du-Pape or Hermitage. The grape skins are allowed to ferment longer with the must, giving a rich, ruby color to the wine.

## What's the difference between a $25 bottle of Châteauneuf-du-Pape and a $75 bottle of Châteauneuf-du-Pape?

A winemaker is permitted to use thirteen different grapes for his Châteauneuf-du-Pape recipe, as I mentioned earlier. It's only logical, then, that the winemaker who uses a lot of the best grapes (which is equivalent to cooking with the finest ingredients) will produce the best-tasting—and the most expensive—wine.

For example, a $25 bottle of Châteauneuf-du-Pape may contain only 20 percent of top-quality grapes (Grenache, Mourvèdre, Syrah, and Cinsault) and 80 percent of lesser-quality grapes; a $75 bottle may contain 90 percent of the top-quality grapes and 10 percent of others.

### BEST BETS FOR RED RHÔNE VALLEY WINES

*North* 1995  1996  1997  1998  1999*  2000  2001
2003*  2004  2005*  2006*  2007  2009**  2010**  2011*
*South* 1995  1998*  1999  2000*  2001*  2003*
2004*  2005*  2006*  2007**  2008  2009*  2010**  2011

*Note: * signifies exceptional vintage*

*** signifies extraordinary vintage*

## How do I buy a red Rhône wine?

You should first decide if you prefer a light Côtes du Rhône wine or a bigger, more flavorful one, such as an Hermitage. Then you must consider the vintage and the producer. Two of the oldest and best-known firms are M. Chapoutier and Paul Jaboulet Aîné. Also look for the producers Guigal, Chave, Clos St. John, Beaucastel, Jean-Luc Colombo, Domaine du Vieux Télégraphe, Alain Graillot, Clos des Papes, Roger Sabon & Fils, Mont Redon, Le Vieux Donjon, Domaine du Pégau, and Château Rayas.

TRIVIA QUESTION: What are the 13 grapes allowed in Châteauneuf-du-Pape?

| | |
|---|---|
| Grenache | Muscardin |
| Syrah | Vaccarèse |
| Mourvèdre | Picardin |
| Cinsault | Clairette |
| Picpoul | Roussanne |
| Terret | Bourboulenc |
| Counoise | |

The first four grapes represent 92% of the grapes used, with Grenache by far the most.

CHÂTEAUNEUF-DU-PAPE means "new castle of the Pope," so named for the palace in the Rhône city of Avignon in which Pope Clément V (the first French pope) resided in the fourteenth century.

RHÔNE VALLEY vintages can be tricky: a good year in the north may be a bad year in the south, and vice versa.

### OLDER GREAT VINTAGES

*North:* 1983, 1985, 1988, 1989, 1990, 1991
*South:* 1985, 1988, 1989, 1990

A SIMPLE Côtes du Rhône is similar to a Beaujolais—except the Côtes du Rhône has more body and alcohol. A Beaujolais, by AOC standards, must contain a minimum of 9% alcohol; a Côtes du Rhône, 10.5%.

THERE IS no official classification for Rhône Valley wines.

SUNSHINE QUOTIENT

| Region | Hours per Year |
|---|---|
| Burgundy | 2,000 |
| Bordeaux | 2,050 |
| Châteauneuf-du-Pape | 2,750 |

THE MEDIEVAL papal coat of arms appears on some Châteauneuf-du-Pape bottles. Only owners of vineyards are permitted to use this coat of arms on the label.

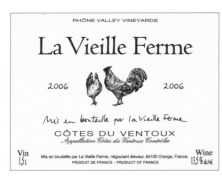

A GOOD VALUE is Côtes du Ventoux. One of the most widely available wines to look for in this category is La Vieille Ferme.

## When should I drink my Rhône wine?

**Tavel:** within two years

**Côtes du Rhône:** within three years

**Crozes-Hermitage:** within five years

**Châteauneuf-du-Pape:** after five years, but higher-quality Châteauneuf-du-Pape is better after ten years

**Hermitage:** seven to eight years, but best after fifteen, in a great year

RHÔNE VALLEY HARVEST

*(average number of cases over a five-year period)*

| | |
|---|---|
| Côtes du Rhône regional appellation | 20.4 million |
| Northern and southern Crus | 4.3 million |
| Côtes du Rhône-Villages appellation | 3.6 million |
| Total Rhône Valley harvest | 28.3 million cases |

## Forty years later in the Rhône Valley

Forty years ago the Rhône Valley wines were overshadowed by the red wines of Burgundy and Bordeaux. Today they are all equals except that the best quality value of the three is the Rhône. The region has also been blessed with great weather (think great vintages) over the last ten years, especially in the south. This all makes for superb wines at a reasonable cost.

### THE RED RHÔNE VALLEY ROUNDUP

**NORTHERN WINES** *Côte Rôtie • Hermitage • Crozes-Hermitage • St-Joseph • Cornas*

**GRAPE** *Syrah*

**SOUTHERN WINES** *Châteauneuf-du-Pape • Tavel • Côtes du Rhône • Côtes du Rhône-Villages • Côtes du Ventoux • Gigondas*

**MAJOR GRAPES** *Grenache • Syrah • Cinsault • Mourvèdre*

# WINE AND FOOD

JEAN PIERRE AND FRANÇOIS PERRIN (Château de Beaucastel and La Vieille Ferme): "The white wines of Château de Beaucastel can be drunk either very young—in the first three or four years—or should be kept for ten years or more. The combination of white meat with truffles and mushrooms is an exquisite possibility.

"Red Rhône wines achieve their perfection from ten years and beyond, and are best when combined with game and other meats with a strong flavor.

"A good dinner could be wild mushroom soup and truffles with a white Beaucastel and stew of wild hare á la royale (with foie gras and truffles) served with a red Château de Beaucastel."

MICHEL CHAPOUTIER: With a Côtes du Rhône wine, he recommends poultry, light meats, and cheese. Côte Rôtie goes well with white meats and small game. Châteauneuf-du-Pape complements the ripest of cheese, the richest venison, and the most lavish civet of wild boar. An Hermitage is suitable with beef, game, and any full-flavored cheese. Tavel rosé is excellent with white meat and poultry.

FRÉDÉRIC JABOULET: "My granddad drinks a bottle of Côtes du Rhône a day and he's in his eighties. It's good for youth. It goes with everything except old fish," he jokes.

More specifically, Mr. Jaboulet says, "Hermitage is good with wild boar and mushrooms. A Crozes Hermitage, particularly our Domaine de Thalabert, complements venison or roast rabbit in a cream sauce, but you have to be very careful with the sauce and the weight of the wine.

"Beef ribs and rice go well with a Côtes du Rhône, as does a game bird like roast quail. Tavel, slightly chilled, is refreshing with a summer salad. Muscat de Beaumes-de-Venise, of course, is a beautiful match with foie gras."

ONLINE STORE
http://bit.ly/fMK13Q

HERMITAGE IS the best and the longest-lived of the Rhône wines. In a great vintage, Hermitage wines can last for 50 years.

U.S. IMPORTS of Rhône wines have risen more than 200% in the last five years.

THE TWO most famous white wines of the Rhône Valley are called Condrieu and Château Grillet. Both are made from the grape variety called Viognier.

THERE IS a white Châteauneuf-du-Pape and a white Hermitage, but only a few thousand cases are produced each year.

**FOR FURTHER READING**

I recommend *The Wines of the Rhône Valley* by Robert M. Parker Jr.

FOR THOSE who prefer sweet wines, try Beaumes-de-Venise, made from the Muscat grape.

# Class Four:
# The Red Wines of Burgundy and the Rhône Valley

The three most important things to know about Burgundy wine, ranked in order of importance, are: the producer, the vintage, and the classification system. Each of these differences becomes more evident after tasting each flight.

Some of my favorite wines come from the Rhône Valley. From the simple, medium-bodied Côtes du Rhône; to the spicy Crozes-Hermitage; to the big, voluptuous, high-alcohol Châteauneuf-du-Papes, these are some of the greatest wines in the world and still represent one of the best values in all winedom. If I ever add another wine class to the school and to the book, it would be devoted to wines made from the Grenache and Syrah grape varieties, and leading the way would be the wines of the Rhône Valley.

## THE WINES

### Understanding the Côte d'Or

#### Two Beaujolais wines compared

1. Beaujolais Villages
2. Beaujolais Cru

#### One wine, tasted alone

3. A wine from Côte Châlonnaise

**Two Côte de Beaune wines compared**

4. Village wine
5. Premier Cru wine

**Two Côte de Nuits wines compared**

6. Village wine
7. Premier Cru

# Understanding the Côtes du Rhône

**Three Côtes du Rhône wines compared**

8. Côtes du Rhône
9. Crozes-Hermitage
10. Châteauneuf-du-Pape

4.

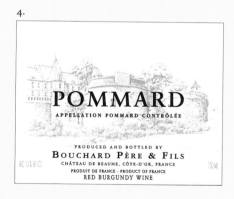

5.

9.

10.

*Please note that labels are suggestions for wineries and producers to look for. For more examples, see pages 123, 124, 126, 127, 130, and 133.*

# Questions for Class Four: The Red Wines of Burgundy and the Rhône Valley

CLASS FIVE

# The Red Wines of Bordeaux

APPELLATIONS · GRAPE VARIETIES · QUALITY LEVELS ·

THE GREAT RED WINES OF BORDEAUX · MÉDOC · GRAVES ·

POMEROL · ST-ÉMILION · CHOOSING A RED BORDEAUX

VIDEO
http://bit.ly/fıldng

PRONUNCIATIONS
http://bit.ly/woXLmM

THE ENGLISH word "claret" refers to dry red wines from Bordeaux.

THE BORDEAUX region produces 60–70 million cases (720–840 million bottles) of wine for each vintage.

MIS EN BOUTEILLE AU CHATEAU

CHATEAU
LES ORMES DE PEZ

SAINT-ESTÈPHE

1995

13.0%Vol        APPELLATION SAINT-ESTÈPHE CONTRÔLÉE        750ml

A. CAZES, PROPRIETAIRE A SAINT ESTEPHE (FRANCE)

PRODUCE OF FRANCE

BORDEAUX IS much larger in acreage than Burgundy.

OF ALL the AOC wines of France, 27% come from the Bordeaux region.

IN DOLLAR value, the United States is the second-largest importer of Bordeaux wines.

IN 2011, 85% of Bordeaux wine was red.

UNTIL 1970, Bordeaux regularly produced more white wine than red.

# The Red Wines of Bordeaux

THIS PROVINCE OF FRANCE is rich with excitement and history, and the best part is that the wines speak for themselves. You'll find this region much easier to learn about than Burgundy. For one thing, the plots of land are bigger, and they're owned by fewer landholders. And, as the wine-loving English author Samuel Johnson once said, "He who aspires to be a serious wine drinker must drink claret." That is, the dry red table wine known as Bordeaux.

Some fifty-seven wine regions in Bordeaux produce high-quality wines that are allowed to carry the AOC designation on the label. Of these fifty-seven places, four stand out in my mind for red wine:

*Médoc:* 40,199 acres (produces only red wines)

*Pomerol:* 1,846 acres (produces only red wines)

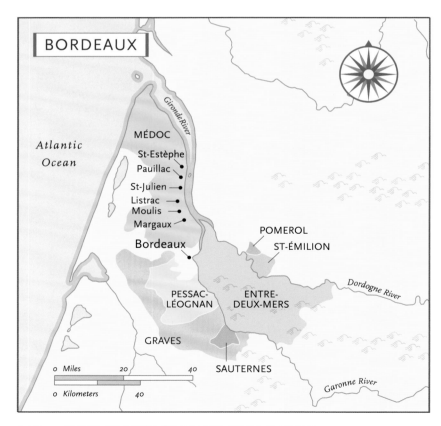

***Graves/Pessac-Léognan:*** 9,855 acres (produces both red and dry white wines)

***St-Émilion:*** 23,384 acres (produces only red wines)

In the Médoc, there are seven important inner appellations you should be familiar with:

**HAUT MÉDOC     ST-ESTÈPHE     PAUILLAC     ST-JULIEN**

**MARGAUX     MOULIS     LISTRAC**

## Which grape varieties are grown in Bordeaux?

The three major grapes are:

*Merlot*

*Cabernet Sauvignon*

*Cabernet Franc*

Unlike Burgundy, where the winemaker must use 100 percent Pinot Noir to make most red wines (100 percent Gamay for Beaujolais), in Bordeaux the red wines are almost always made from a blend of grapes.

## What are the different quality levels of Bordeaux wine?

***Bordeaux:*** This is the lowest level of AOC wine in Bordeaux—wines that are nice, inexpensive, and consistent "drinking" wines. These are sometimes known as "proprietary" wines—wines known by what you could almost call a brand name, such as Mouton-Cadet, rather than by the particular region or vineyard. These are usually the least expensive AOC wines in Bordeaux. Cost: $.

***Region:*** Regional wines come from one of the fifty-seven different regions. Only grapes and wines made in those areas can be called by their regional names: Pauillac and St-Émilion, for example. These wines are more expensive than those labeled simply "Bordeaux." Cost: $$.

***Region + Château:*** Château wines are the products of individual vineyards. There are more than 7,000 châteaux in Bordeaux. As far back as 1855, Bordeaux officially classified the quality levels of some of its châteaux. Hundreds have been officially recognized for their quality. In the Médoc, for example, the 61 highest-level châteaux are called Grand Cru Classé. There are also 247 châteaux in the Médoc that are entitled to be called Cru Bourgeois, a step below Grand Cru Classé. Other areas, such as St-Émilion and Graves, have their own classification systems. Cost: $$–$$$$.

THE GRAVES region produces 60% red wine, 40% white wine.

IN 1987, a communal appellation was established to create a higher-level appellation in the northern Graves region. It's called Pessac-Léognan (for both reds and whites).

TAKE A LOOK at the map on page 142. As a general rule of thumb, red wines from the villages and regions on the left bank of the rivers primarily use the Cabernet Sauvignon grape and on the right bank they use Merlot.

IN ALL of Bordeaux, there are some 172,000 acres of Merlot, 72,000 acres of Cabernet Sauvignon, and 33,000 acres of Cabernet Franc.

TWO OTHER grapes that are sometimes used in the blending of Bordeaux wines are Petit Verdot and Malbec.

PROPRIETARY WINES you may be familiar with:

| | |
|---|---|
| Baron Philippe | Michel Lynch |
| Lacour Pavillon | Mouton-Cadet |
| Lauretan | |

THE MAJOR shippers of regional wines from Bordeaux are:

Baron Philippe de Rothschild
Barton & Guestier (B & G)
Borie-Manoux
Cordier
Dourthe Kressmann
Dulong
Eschenauer
Ets J-P Moueix
Sichel
Yvon Mau

WINES PRICED between $8 and $25 represent 80% of the total production of Bordeaux.

THE TYPICAL Médoc blend can vary from 60% to 80% Cabernet Sauvignon, 25% to 40% Merlot, and 10% to 20% Cabernet Franc.

| BORDEAUX (PROPRIETARY) APPELLATION BORDEAUX CONTRÔLÉE | REGIONAL APPELLATION PAUILLAC CONTRÔLÉE | CHÂTEAU APPELLATION PAUILLAC CONTRÔLÉE WITH CHÂTEAU NAME |
|---|---|---|
|  |  |  |

All three of these wines are owned by the same family, the Rothschilds, who also own Château Mouton-Rothschild.

IF YOU see a château on the label, French law dictates that the château really exists and is the château of that winemaker. What you see is what you get.

ACCORDING TO French law, a château is a house attached to a vineyard having a specific number of acres, as well as having winemaking and storage facilities on the property. A wine may not be called a château wine unless it meets these criteria. The terms *domaine, clos,* and *cru* are also used.

Here are the major red Bordeaux classifications:

*Médoc* (Grands Crus Classé): 1855; sixty-one châteaux
*Médoc* (Crus Bourgeois): 1920, revised 1932, 1978, and 2003; 247 châteaux
*Graves* (Grands Crus Classé): 1959; twelve châteaux
*Pomerol:* No official classification
*St-Émilion:* 1955, revised 1996, revised 2006; fifteen Premiers Grands Crus Classé and forty-six Grands Crus Classé

## What is a château?

When most people think of a château, they picture a grandiose home filled with Persian rugs and valuable antiques and surrounded by rolling hills of vineyards. Well, I'm sorry to shatter your dreams (and the dictionary's definition), but most châteaux are not like that at all. Yes, a château could be a mansion on a large estate, but it could also be a modest home with a two-car garage.

Château wines are usually considered the best-quality wines from Bordeaux. They are the most expensive wines; some examples of the best known of the Grand Cru Classé command the highest wine prices in the world!

Let's take a closer look at the châteaux. One fact I've learned from my years of teaching wine is that no one wants to memorize the names of thousands of châteaux, so I'll shorten the list by starting with the most important classification in Bordeaux.

# THE GREAT RED WINES OF BORDEAUX

## MÉDOC: GRAND CRU CLASSÉ, 1855; 61 CHÂTEAUX

### When and how were the château wines classified?

More than 150 years ago in the Médoc region of Bordeaux, a wine classification was established. Brokers from the wine industry were asked by Napoleon III to select the best wines to represent France in the International Exposition of 1855. The top Médoc wines were ranked according to price, which at that time was directly related to quality. (After all, don't we class everything, from cars to restaurants?) According to this new system, the top four (now five, see sidebar on page 147) vineyards—or *crus*—produced "first-growth" wines; the next fourteen best vineyards, second-growth; and so on until you reach the fifth-growth producers. The brokers agreed, provided the classification would never become official. Voilà! Refer to the chart on page 147 for the Official Classification of 1855.

### Is there an easier way to understand the 1855 classification?

I've always found the 1855 classification to be a little cumbersome, so one day I sat down and drew up my own chart. I separated the classification into growths (first, second, third, etc.) and then I listed the communes (Pauillac, Margaux, St-Julien, etc.) and set down the number of distinctive vineyards in each one. My chart shows which communes of Bordeaux have the most first growths—all the way down to fifth growths. It also shows which commune corners the market on all growths. Since I was inspired to figure this out during baseball's World Series, I call my chart a box score of the 1855 classification.

A quick glance at my box score gives you some instant facts that may guide you when you want to buy a Bordeaux wine from Médoc.

Tallying the score, Pauillac has three of the five first growths and twelve fifth growths. Margaux practically clean-sweeps the third growths. In fact, Margaux is the overall winner, because it has the greatest number of classed vineyards in all of Médoc. Margaux is also the only area to have a château rated in each category. St-Julien has no first or fifth growths, but is very strong in the second and fourth.

THE GRAND CRU Classé châteaux represent less than 5% of the total volume of Bordeaux.

## KEVIN ZRALY'S BOX SCORE OF THE 1855 CLASSIFICATION

| Commune | 1st | 2nd | 3rd | 4th | 5th | Total |
|---|---|---|---|---|---|---|
| Margaux | 1 | 5 | 10 | 3 | 2 | 21 |
| Pauillac | 3 | 2 | 0 | 1 | 12 | 18 |
| St-Julien | 0 | 5 | 2 | 4 | 0 | 11 |
| St-Estèphe | 0 | 2 | 1 | 1 | 1 | 5 |
| Haut-Médoc | 0 | 0 | 1 | 1 | 3 | 5 |
| Graves | 1 | 0 | 0 | 0 | 0 | 1 |
| Total Châteaux | 5 | 14 | 14 | 10 | 18 | 61 |

GRAND CRU CLASSÉ

CHATEAU LA LAGUNE
HAUT·MÉDOC
APPELLATION HAUT·MÉDOC CONTROLÉE
1995
SOCIÉTÉ CIVILE AGRICOLE DU CHATEAU LA LAGUNE
PROPRIÉTAIRE A LUDON (GIRONDE) FRANCE

PRODUCE OF FRANCE
MIS EN BOUTEILLE AU CHATEAU

GRAND VIN
DE
CHATEAU LATOUR
PREMIER GRAND CRU CLASSÉ
PAUILLAC
1993
12.5 % Vol.                    750 ml
DÉPOSE    APPELLATION PAUILLAC CONTRÔLÉE
STE. CIVILE DU VIGNOBLE DE CHATEAU LATOUR, PROPRIÉTAIRE A PAUILLAC (GIRONDE)· LG 93

Château
Prieuré-Lichine
GRAND CRU CLASSÉ
1996

MARGAUX
APPELLATION MARGAUX CONTROLÉE
MIS EN BOUTEILLE AU CHATEAU
S.A. CHATEAU PRIEURÉ-LICHINE PROPRIÉTAIRE A CANTENAC · FRANCE
12.5% vol.    Cette bouteille porte le    N°L2 249072  750ml e

1990
CHATEAU DUCRU-BEAUCAILLOU
GRAND CRU CLASSÉ DE MÉDOC EN 1855

SAINT-JULIEN
12.5%Vol.                         750 ml
L. 90 DB    APPELLATION SAINT-JULIEN CONTRÔLÉE
JEAN-EUGÈNE BORIE. PROPRIÉTAIRE A SAINT-JULIEN-BEYCHEVELLE (GIRONDE)   PRODUCE OF FRANCE

MIS EN BOUTEILLE AU CHÂTEAU
CHATEAU MARGAUX
GRAND VIN

1995
PREMIER GRAND CRU CLASSÉ
MARGAUX
12.5%vol.                     75 cl
APPELLATION MARGAUX CONTRÔLÉE
SCA CHATEAU MARGAUX PROPRIÉTAIRE A MARGAUX - FRANCE

GRAND VIN

CHATEAU
LYNCH · BAGES
GRAND CRU CLASSÉ
PAUILLAC
APPELLATION PAUILLAC CONTRÔLÉE
1995   A. CAZES Propriétaire à PAUILLAC (Gironde)   12% vol.   500 d

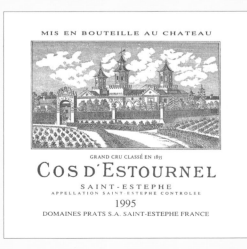

MIS EN BOUTEILLE AU CHATEAU

GRAND CRU CLASSÉ EN 1855
COS D'ESTOURNEL
SAINT-ESTEPHE
APPELLATION SAINT-ESTEPHE CONTROLEE
1995
DOMAINES PRATS S.A. SAINT-ESTEPHE FRANCE

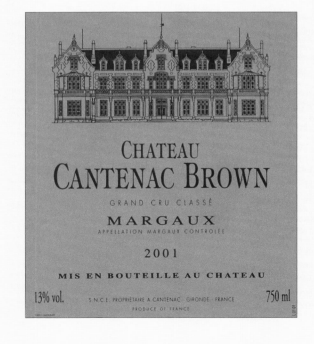

CHATEAU
CANTENAC BROWN
GRAND CRU CLASSÉ
MARGAUX
APPELLATION MARGAUX CONTROLÉE
2001
MIS EN BOUTEILLE AU CHATEAU
13% vol.    S.N.C.E. PROPRIÉTAIRE A CANTENAC - GIRONDE - FRANCE    750 ml
PRODUCE OF FRANCE

# The Official (1855) Classification of the Great Red Wines of Bordeaux

## THE MÉDOC

### FIRST GROWTHS—PREMIERS CRUS (5)

| Vineyard | AOC |
|---|---|
| Château Lafite-Rothschild | Pauillac |
| Château Latour | Pauillac |
| Château Margaux | Margaux |
| Château Haut-Brion | Pessac-Léognan (Graves) |
| Château Mouton-Rothschild | Pauillac |

### SECOND GROWTHS—DEUXIÈMES CRUS (14)

| Vineyard | AOC |
|---|---|
| Château Rausan-Ségla | Margaux |
| Château Rausan Gassies | Margaux |
| Château Léoville-Las-Cases | St-Julien |
| Château Léoville-Poyferré | St-Julien |
| Château Léoville-Barton | St-Julien |
| Château Durfort-Vivens | Margaux |
| Château Lascombes | Margaux |
| Château Gruaud-Larose | St-Julien |
| Château Brane-Cantenac | Margaux |
| Château Pichon-Longueville-Baron | Pauillac |
| Château Pichon-Longueville-Lalande | Pauillac |
| Château Ducru-Beaucaillou | St-Julien |
| Château Cos d'Estournel | St-Estèphe |
| Château Montrose | St-Estèphe |

### THIRD GROWTHS—TROISIÈMES CRUS (14)

| Vineyard | AOC |
|---|---|
| Château Giscours | Margaux |
| Château Kirwan | Margaux |
| Château d'Issan | Margaux |
| Château Lagrange | St-Julien |
| Château Langoa-Barton | St-Julien |
| Château Malescot-St-Exupéry | Margaux |
| Château Cantenac-Brown | Margaux |
| Château Palmer | Margaux |
| Château La Lagune | Haut-Médoc |
| Château Desmirail | Margaux |
| Château Calon-Ségur | St-Estèphe |
| Château Ferrière | Margaux |
| Château d'Alesme (formerly Marquis d'Alesme) | Margaux |
| Château Boyd-Cantenac | Margaux |

### FOURTH GROWTHS—QUATRIÈMES CRUS (10)

| Vineyard | AOC |
|---|---|
| Château St-Pierre | St-Julien |
| Château Branaire-Ducru | St-Julien |
| Château Talbot | St-Julien |
| Château Duhart-Milon-Rothschild | Pauillac |
| Château Pouget | Margaux |
| Château La Tour-Carnet | Haut-Médoc |
| Château Lafon-Rochet | St-Estèphe |
| Château Beychevelle | St-Julien |
| Château Prieuré-Lichine | Margaux |
| Château Marquis de Terme | Margaux |

### FIFTH GROWTHS—CINQUIÈMES CRUS (18)

| Vineyard | AOC |
|---|---|
| Château Pontet-Canet | Pauillac |
| Château Batailley | Pauillac |
| Château Grand-Puy-Lacoste | Pauillac |
| Château Grand-Puy-Ducasse | Pauillac |
| Château Haut-Batailley | Pauillac |
| Château Lynch-Bages | Pauillac |
| Château Lynch-Moussas | Pauillac |
| Château Dauzac | Haut-Médoc |
| Château d'Armailhac (called Château Mouton-Baron-Philippe from 1956 to 1988) | Pauillac |
| Château du Tertre | Margaux |
| Château Haut-Bages-Libéral | Pauillac |
| Château Pédesclaux | Pauillac |
| Château Belgrave | Haut-Médoc |
| Château Camensac | Haut-Médoc |
| Château Cos Labory | St-Estèphe |
| Château Clerc-Milon-Rothschild | Pauillac |
| Château Croizet Bages | Pauillac |
| Château Cantemerle | Haut-Médoc |

ON THE 1945 Mouton-Rothschild bottle there is a big V that stands for "victory" and the end of World War II. Since 1924, and every year since 1945, Philippe de Rothschild asked a different artist to design his labels, a tradition continued by the Baroness Philippine, his daughter. Some of the most famous artists in the world have agreed to have their work grace the Mouton label, including:

Jean Cocteau—1947
Salvador Dalí—1958
Henry Moore—1964
Joan Miró—1969
Marc Chagall—1970
Pablo Picasso—1973
Robert Motherwell—1974
Andy Warhol—1975
John Huston—1982
Saul Steinberg—1983
Keith Haring—1988
Francis Bacon—1990
Setsuko—1991
Antoni Tàpies—1995
Gu Gan—1996
Robert Wilson—2001
HRH Charles, Prince of Wales—2004
Giuseppe Penone—2005
Xu Lei—2008

## HAVE THERE EVER BEEN ANY CHANGES IN THE 1855 CLASSIFICATION?

*Yes, but only once, in 1973. Château Mouton-Rothschild was elevated from a second-growth to a first-growth vineyard. There's a little story behind that.*

## EXCEPTION TO THE RULE . . .

*In 1920, when the Baron Philippe de Rothschild took over the family vineyard, he couldn't accept the fact that back in 1855 his château had been rated a second growth. He thought it should have been classed a first growth from the beginning—and he fought to get to the top for some fifty years. While the baron's wine was classified as a second growth, his motto was:*

> *First, I cannot be.*
> *Second, I do not deign to be.*
> *Mouton, I am.*

*When his wine was elevated to a first growth in 1973, Rothschild replaced the motto with a new one:*

> *First, I am.*
> *Second, I was.*
> *But Mouton does not change.*

**PABLO PICASSO, 1973**

## Is the 1855 classification still in use today?

Every wine person knows about the 1855 classification, but much has changed over the last century and a half. Some vineyards have doubled or tripled their production by buying up their neighbors' land, which is permitted by law. Obviously the châteaux have seen many changes of ownership. And, like all businesses, Bordeaux has seen good times and bad times.

A case in point was in the early 1970s, when Bordeaux wines were having a difficult time financially, even at the highest level. At Château Margaux, the well-known first-growth vineyard, the quality of the wine fell off from its traditional excellence for a while when the family that owned the château wasn't putting enough money and time into the vineyard. In 1977, Château Margaux was sold to a Greek-French family (named Mentzelopoulos) for $16 million, and since then the quality of the wine has risen even beyond its first-growth standards.

Château Gloria, in the commune of St-Julien, is an example of a vineyard that didn't exist at the time of the 1855 classification. The late mayor of St-Julien, Henri Martin, bought many parcels of second-growth vineyards. As a result, he produced top-quality wine that is not included in the 1855 classification.

It's also important to consider the techniques used to make wine today. They're a lot different from those used in 1855. Once again, the outcome is better wine. As you can see, some of the châteaux listed in the 1855 classification deserve a lesser ranking, while others deserve a better one.

That said, I believe, even after its 150th anniversary, in most cases it is still a very valid classification in terms of quality and price.

## MÉDOC CRU BOURGEOIS: 1920, REVISED 1932, 1978, AND 2003; 247 CHÂTEAUX

### What does Cru Bourgeois mean?

The Crus Bourgeois of the Médoc are châteaux that were originally classified in 1920, and not in the 1855 classification. In 1932 there were 444 properties listed, but by 1962 there were only 94 members. Today there are 247. The latest classification of Crus Bourgeois of the Médoc and Haut-Médoc was in 2003. Because of the high quality of the 2000, 2003, 2005, and 2009 vintages, some of the best values in wine today are in the Cru Bourgeois classification.

The following is a partial list of Crus Bourgeois to look for:

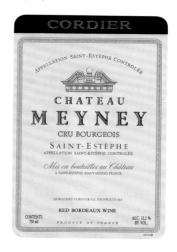

THE CRU BOURGEOIS Château Larose-Trintaudon is the largest vineyard in the Médoc area, making nearly 100,000 cases of wine per year.

CHÂTEAU CHASSE-SPLEEN
CHÂTEAU COUFRAN
CHÂTEAU D'ANGLUDET
CHÂTEAU DE LAMARQUE
CHÂTEAU DE PEZ
CHÂTEAU FOURCAS-HOSTEN
CHÂTEAU GREYSAC
CHÂTEAU HAUT-MARBUZET
CHÂTEAU LABÉGORCE-ZÉDÉ
CHÂTEAU LA CARDONNE
CHÂTEAU LAROSE-TRINTAUDON
CHÂTEAU MARBUZET

CHÂTEAU MEYNEY
CHÂTEAU MONBRISON
CHÂTEAU LES ORMES-DE-PEZ
CHÂTEAU LES ORMES-SORBET
CHÂTEAU PATACHE D'AUX
CHÂTEAU PHÉLAN-SÉGUR
CHÂTEAU PIBRAN
CHÂTEAU PONTENSAC
CHÂTEAU POUJEAUX
CHÂTEAU SIRAN
CHÂTEAU SOCIANDO-MALLET
CHÂTEAU VIEUX ROBIN

Grapes are the source of the latest trend to hit the skin-care world. Guests at an exclusive hotel in the vineyards of Château Smith-Haut-Lafitte can enjoy treatments featuring grapevine extracts, crushed grape seeds, and grapeseed oil. For example, pampering includes a crushed Cabernet body scrub made from grapeseed oil, Bordeaux honey, and ten concentrated plant extracts.

THE RED wines of Pomerol tend to be softer, fruitier, and ready to drink sooner than the Médoc wines.

THE MAJOR grape used to produce wine in the Pomerol region is Merlot. Very little Cabernet Sauvignon is used in these wines.

IT TAKES Château Pétrus one year to make as much wine as Gallo makes in six minutes.

THE VINEYARD at Château Pétrus makes one of the most expensive wines of Bordeaux. It's planted with 95% Merlot.

# GRAVES: 1959 GRANDS CRUS CLASSÉS; 12 CHÂTEAUX

The most famous château—we have already seen it in the 1855 classification—is Château Haut-Brion. Other good red Graves classified in 1959 as Grands Crus Classés are:

**CHÂTEAU BOUSCAUT**
**CHÂTEAU CARBONNIEUX**
**DOMAINE DE CHEVALIER**
**CHÂTEAU DE FIEUZAL**
**CHÂTEAU HAUT-BAILLY**
**CHÂTEAU LA MISSION-HAUT-BRION**
**CHÂTEAU LA TOUR-MARTILLAC**
**CHÂTEAU MALARTIC-LAGRAVIÈRE**
**CHÂTEAU OLIVIER**
**CHÂTEAU PAPE-CLÉMENT**
**CHÂTEAU SMITH-HAUT-LAFITTE**

# POMEROL: NO OFFICIAL CLASSIFICATION

This is the smallest of the top red-wine districts in Bordeaux. Pomerol produces only 15 percent as much wine as St-Émilion; as a result, Pomerol wines are relatively scarce. And if you do find them, they'll be expensive. Although no official classification exists, here's a list of some of the finest Pomerols on the market:

**CHÂTEAU BEAUREGARD**
**CHÂTEAU BOURGNEUF**
**CHÂTEAU CLINET**
**CHÂTEAU GAZIN**
**CHÂTEAU LA CONSEILLANTE**
**CHÂTEAU LAFLEUR**
**CHÂTEAU LA FLEUR-PÉTRUS**
**CHÂTEAU LA POINTE**
**CHÂTEAU LATOUR-À-POMEROL**
**CHÂTEAU L'ÉGLISE CLINET**
**CHÂTEAU LE PIN**
**CHÂTEAU L'ÉVANGILE**
**CHÂTEAU NÉNIN**
**CHÂTEAU PETIT-VILLAGE**
**CHÂTEAU PÉTRUS**
**CHÂTEAU PLINCE**
**CHÂTEAU TROTANOY**
**VIEUX CHÂTEAU-CERTAN**

# ST-ÉMILION: 1955, REVISED 1996, REVISED 2006, revised 2009\*; 15 PREMIERS GRANDS CRUS CLASSÉS AND 46 CHÂTEAUX GRANDS CRUS CLASSÉS

This area produces about two-thirds as much wine as the entire Médoc, and St-Émilion is one of the most beautiful villages in France (in my opinion). The wines of St-Émilion were finally classified officially in 1955, one century after the Médoc classification. There are fifteen first growths comparable to the Cru Classé wines of the Médoc.

## THE FIFTEEN FIRST GROWTHS OF ST-ÉMILION (PREMIERS GRANDS CRUS CLASSÉS)

CHÂTEAU ANGÉLUS

CHÂTEAU AUSONE

CHÂTEAU BEAU-SÉJOUR-BÉCOT

CHÂTEAU BEAUSÉJOUR-DUFFAU-LAGARROSSE

CHÂTEAU BELAIR

CHÂTEAU CANON

CHÂTEAU CHEVAL BLANC

CHÂTEAU FIGEAC

CHÂTEAU CLOS FOURTET

CHÂTEAU LA GAFFELIÈRE

CHÂTEAU MAGDELAINE

CHÂTEAU PAVIE

CHÂTEAU PAVIE MARQUIN

CHÂTEAU TROPLONG MONDOT

CHÂTEAU TROTTEVIEILLE

Important Grands Crus Classés and other St-Émilion wines available in the United States:

CHÂTEAU CANON-LA-GAFFELIÈRE

CHÂTEAU DASSAULT

CHÂTEAU FAUGÈRES

CHÂTEAU GRAND-MAYNE

CHÂTEAU HAUT-CORBIN

CLOS DES JACOBINS

CHÂTEAU LA TOUR-FIGEAC

CHÂTEAU MONBOUSQUET

CHÂTEAU TERTRE ROTEBOEUF

CHÂTEAU TRIMOULET

CHÂTEAU TROTANOY

### GRAPE VARIETIES OF ST-ÉMILION

| | |
|---|---|
| Merlot | 70% |
| Cabernet Franc | 25% |
| Cabernet Sauvignon | 5% |

SOME OTHER appellations to look for in Bordeaux red wines:
Château Côtes de Blaye
Château Côtes de Bourg
Château Fronsac

*Lawsuits were filed in early 2013 to overturn the official ranking of 2009. Stay tuned.*

THE 1999 VINTAGE was the largest harvest ever in Bordeaux.

ABOUT VINTAGES, Alexis Lichine, a noted wine expert, once said: "Great vintages take time to mature. Lesser wines mature faster than the greater ones. . . . Patience is needed for great vintages, hence the usefulness and enjoyment of lesser vintages." He summed up: "Often vintages which have a poorer rating—if young—will give a greater enjoyment than a better-rated vintage—if young."

DRINK YOUR lighter vintages such as 2001 and 2004 Bordeaux while you wait patiently for your great vintages such as 2000, 2003, and 2005 to mature.

THE EARLIEST harvest since 1893 was 2003.

THE 2003 VINTAGE suffered summer heat waves, fierce storms, and hail, reducing production to the lowest since 1991.

WITH THE great vintages of 2000, 2003, 2005, and 2009, this was considered by many to be the best decade for wine in the history of Bordeaux.

Now that you know all the greatest red-wine regions of Bordeaux, let me take you a step further and show you some of the best vintages.

## BORDEAUX VINTAGES

### "LEFT BANK"
### MÉDOC/ST-JULIEN/MARGAUX/ PAUILLAC/ST-ESTÈPHE/GRAVES

| GOOD VINTAGES | GREAT VINTAGES | OLDER GREAT VINTAGES |
|---|---|---|
| 1994 | 1990 | 1982 |
| 1997 | 1995 | 1985 |
| 1998 | 1996 | 1986 |
| 1999 | 2000 | 1989 |
| 2001 | 2003 | |
| 2002 | 2005 | |
| 2004 | 2009 | |
| 2006 | 2010 | |
| 2007 | | |
| 2008 | | |
| 2011 | | |
| 2012 | | |

### "RIGHT BANK"
### ST-ÉMILION/POMEROL

| GOOD VINTAGES | GREAT VINTAGES | OLDER GREAT VINTAGES |
|---|---|---|
| 1995 | 1990 | 1982 |
| 1996 | 1998 | 1989 |
| 1997 | 2000 | |
| 1999 | 2001 | |
| 2002 | 2005 | |
| 2003 | 2009 | |
| 2004 | 2010 | |
| 2006 | | |
| 2007 | | |
| 2008 | | |
| 2011 | | |
| 2012 | | |

## How do I buy—and drink—a red Bordeaux?

One of the biggest misconceptions about Bordeaux wines is that they are all very expensive. In reality, there are thousands of Bordeaux wines at all different price ranges.

First and foremost, ask yourself if you want to drink the wine now, or if you want to age it. A great château Bordeaux in a great vintage needs a *minimum* of ten years to age. Going down a level, a Cru Bourgeois or a second label of a great château in a great vintage needs a minimum of five years to age. A regional wine may be consumed within two or three years of the vintage year, while a wine labeled simply "Appellation Bordeaux Contrôlée" is ready to drink as soon as it's released.

The next step is to be sure the vintage is correct for what you want. If you're looking for a wine you want to age, you must look for a great vintage. If you want a wine that's ready to drink now and you want a greater château, you should choose a lesser vintage. If you want a wine that's ready to drink now and you want a great vintage, you should look for a lesser château.

In addition, remember that Bordeaux wines are a blend of grapes. Ask yourself if you're looking for a Merlot-style Bordeaux, such as St-Émilion or Pomerol, or if you're looking for a Cabernet style, such as Médoc or Graves, remembering that the Merlot is more accessible and easier to drink when young.

## What separates a $20 red Bordeaux from a $300 red Bordeaux?

- The place the grapes are grown
- The age of the vines (usually the older the vine, the better the wine)
- The yield of the vine (lower yield means higher quality)
- The winemaking technique (for example, how long the wine is aged in wood)
- The vintage

### ON DRINKING THE WINES OF BORDEAUX

*"The French drink their Bordeaux wines too young, afraid that the Socialist government will take them away.*

*"The English drink their Bordeaux wines very old, because they like to take their friends down to their wine cellars with the cobwebs and dust to show off their old bottles.*

*"And the Americans drink their Bordeaux wines exactly when they are ready to be drunk, because they don't know any better."*

—Author Unknown

### THE MAGICAL 20

In November 2011, Robert Parker conducted a Bordeaux Wine Tasting at WineFuture in Hong Kong. "I have chosen estates that produce wines of first-growth quality . . . and because they are undervalued and very smart acquisitions."

The following Châteaux were selected by Mr. Parker: Château Cos d'Estournel, Château Pontet-Canet, Château Pichon Lalande, Château Léoville Poyferré, Château Léoville-Las-Cases, Château Palmer, Château Malescot St. Exupéry, Château Pape-Clément, Château Haut-Bailly, Château Angélus, Château Trotanoy, Château La Conseillante, Château Pichon Baron, Château Lynch-Bages, Château Smith-Haut-Lafitte, Château La Fleur-Pétrus, Château Clos Fourtet, Château Rausan-Ségla, Château Brane-Cantenac, and Château Le Gay.

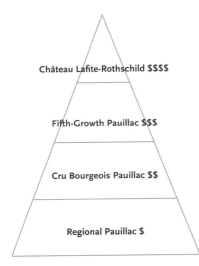

Château Lafite-Rothschild $$$$

Fifth-Growth Pauillac $$$

Cru Bourgeois Pauillac $$

Regional Pauillac $

THE FIRST GROWTHS Château Margaux, Château Latour, Château Lafite-Rothschild, and Château Mouton Rothschild use less than 40% of the crop for their wines. The rest goes into their second labels.

## Is it necessary to pay a tremendous sum of money to get a great-tasting red Bordeaux wine?

It's nice if you have it to spend, but sometimes you don't. The best way to get the most for your money is to use what I call the reverse pyramid method. For example: Let's say you like Château Lafite-Rothschild, which is at the top of the pyramid at left, but you can't afford it. What do you do? Look at the region. It's from Pauillac. You have a choice: You can go back to the 1855 classification and look for a fifth-growth wine from Pauillac that gives a flavor of the region at a lesser price, though not necessarily one-fifth the price of a first growth. Still too pricey? Drop a level further on the inverted pyramid and go for a Cru Bourgeois from Pauillac. Your other option is to buy a regional wine labeled "Pauillac."

I didn't memorize the 6,000 châteaux myself. When I go to my neighborhood retailer, I find a château I've never heard of. If it's from Pauillac, from a good vintage, and it's $20 to $25, I buy it. My chances are good. Everything in wine is hedging your bets.

Another way to avoid skyrocketing Bordeaux châteaux prices is to take the time to look for their second-label wines. These wines are from the youngest parts of the vineyard and are lighter in style and quicker to mature and are much less expensive than the château wine.

| CHÂTEAU | SECOND-LABEL WINES |
| --- | --- |
| Château Haut-Brion | Château Bahans Haut-Brion |
| Château Lafite-Rothschild | Château Carruades de Lafite |
| Château Latour | Château Les Forts de Latour |
| Château Léoville-Barton | La Réserve de Léoville-Barton |
| Château Léoville-Las-Cases | Clos du Marquis |
| Château Lynch-Bages | Château Haut Bages-Averous |
| Château Margaux | Pavillon Rouge du Château Margaux |
| Château Mouton-Rothschild | Petit Mouton |
| Château Palmer | Réserve du Général |
| Château Pichon Lalande | Réserve de la Comtesse |
| Château Pichon-Longueville | Les Tourelles de Longueville |

## Forty years later in Bordeaux

The most dramatic change in the wine world over the last forty years has been the worldwide demand for the best châteaux of Bordeaux. In 1985, the most important market for Bordeaux was the United Kingdom. In the eighties and nineties, interest in Bordeaux was with the Americans and Japanese. Today, Asia has become the new and growing market. There has been strong growth in Hong Kong, South Korea, and China. All of this means higher prices for the best of Bordeaux.

For me it is the end of an era. My first "eureka" moment that wine would become my number-one passion was with a twenty-year-old Bordeaux that cost less than $25. It was a lot of money for a college student but it was worth it. I doubt many young people today can afford the $2,000 price tag for a 2005 Château Latour that probably won't be ready to drink for twenty years! The great châteaux have become wines of prestige and entitlement reserved for the wealthy.

That said, there are still some excellent values for us common folk, from the other 7,000 châteaux. Since 1970, the top châteaux high-quality standard has filtered down to the rest of Bordeaux and as a region they are making the best wines ever in the history of Bordeaux, especially in regions like Médoc, St-Émilion, Graves, Côtes de Boug, and Côtes de Blaye.

**FOR FURTHER READING**

I recommend *Grands Vins* by Clive Coates, M.W.; *The Bordeaux Atlas and Encyclopedia of Chateaux* by Hubrecht Duijker and Michael Broadbent; and *Bordeaux* by Robert M. Parker Jr.

ONLINE STORE
http://bit.ly/hgs1gj

WHILE NAPOLEON BONAPARTE preferred the Burgundy Chambertin, the late president Richard Nixon's favorite wine was Château Margaux. Nixon always had a bottle of his favorite vintage waiting at his table from the cellar of the famous "21" Club in New York.

HAD YOU dined at the Four Seasons restaurant in New York when it first opened in 1959, you could have had a 1918 Château Lafite-Rothschild for $18, or a 1934 Château Latour for $16. Or if those wines were a bit beyond your budget, you could have had a 1945 Château Cos d'Estournel for $9.50.

## WINE AND FOOD

**Denise Lurton-Moulle** (*Château La Louvière, Château Bonnet*): With *Château La Louvière Rouge: roast leg of lamb or grilled duck breast.*

**Jean-Michel Cazes** (*Château Lynch-Bages, Château Haut-Bages-Averous, Château Les Ormes-de-Pez*): "*For Bordeaux red, simple and classic is best! Red meat, such as beef and particularly lamb, as we love it in* Pauillac. *If you can grill the meat on vine cuttings, you are in heaven.*"

**Jacques and Fiona Thienpont** (*Château Le Pin*): *Sunday lunches at Le Pin include lots of local oysters with chilled white Bordeaux followed by thick entrecôte steaks on the barbecue with shallots and a selection of the family's Pomerols, Margaux, or Côtes de France red Bordeaux.*

**Antony Perrin** (*Château Carbonnieux*): With red Bordeaux: *magret de canard* (duck breast) with *wild mushrooms, or* pintade aux raisins (*guinea hen with grapes*).

**Christian Moueix** (*Château Pétrus*): *With red Bordeaux, especially Pomerol wine: lamb is a must.*

# Class Five:
# The Red Wines of Bordeaux

We now enter the second half of the wine-tasting course and the ideal opportunity to showcase my favorite red wines: those of Bordeaux. Bordeaux has more than 7,000 châteaux, which makes narrowing down to just ten wines very difficult.

The three major grapes cultivated in Bordeaux are Merlot, Cabernet Sauvignon, and Cabernet Franc. Merlot is the most widely planted with almost twice as many vines planted as Cabernet Sauvignon, and three times the number of vines as Cabernet Franc.

Bordeaux wines have a reputation of being expensive and requiring long aging. This is not entirely true: 80 percent of all Bordeaux wines retail between $8 and $25 and most of those can be consumed when you buy them or within two years of purchase. In class, we taste wines that cost from $10 to over $100.

## THE WINES

### Understanding Bordeaux

#### *Four wines, tasted together*

1. Appellation Bordeaux Controlée
2. Appellation Margaux Controlée
3. Château: Cru Bourgeois
4. Château: Grand Cru Classé

1.

2.

4.

## Understanding Second Labels

### Two wines, from the same producer, tasted together

5. Second-label Château wine
6. First-label Château wine

## Understanding the Hierarchy of Bordeaux

### Three wines, tasted together, each wine from the same vintage

7. Château: Cru Bourgeois:
8. Château: Third, Fourth, or Fifth Growth
9. Château: Second Growth

## Understanding the Aging Process

### One wine, tasted alone

10. Aged Bordeaux (at least 10 years old)

6.

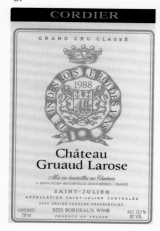

7.

10.

*Please note that labels are suggestions for wineries and producers to look for. For more examples, see pages 143, 145, 147, 149, 150, 151, and 153.*

## Questions for Class Five:
## The Red Wines of Bordeaux

12. How many châteaux were classified in the official classification of the Mèdoc? . . . . . . . . . . . . . . . . . . . . . .144

13. What percentage does the Grand Cru Classé Châteaux represent of the total . . . . . . . . . . . . . . . . . . . . . . . 145
    volume of Bordeaux?

14. Name one château from each of the five growths: . . . . . . . . . . . . . . . . . . . . . . . . . . . . . . . . . . . . . . . . . . . . . . . . 147

    1st _____

    2nd _____

    3rd _____

    4th _____

    5th _____

15. In what year were the wines of Graves first classified? . . . . . . . . . . . . . . . . . . . . . . . . . . . . . . . . . . . . . . . . .150

16. In what year were the wines of St-Émilion first classified? . . . . . . . . . . . . . . . . . . . . . . . . . . . . . . . . . . . . . . .151

17. What is the primary red grape used in the production of St-Émilion wine? . . . . . . . . . . . . . . . . . . . . . . . .151

18. Name three great recent vintages from the "left bank" of Bordeaux. . . . . . . . . . . . . . . . . . . . . . . . . . . . . 152

19. Name three great recent vintages from the "right bank" of Bordeaux. . . . . . . . . . . . . . . . . . . . . . . . . . . . 152

20. Name two second-label wines of classified châteaux. . . . . . . . . . . . . . . . . . . . . . . . . . . . . . . . . . . . . . . . . . . . 154

# The Red Wines of California

RED VS. WHITE • MAJOR RED GRAPES OF CALIFORNIA •

RED-GRAPE BOOM • MERITAGE • STYLES • TRENDS

VIDEO
http://bit.ly/h54Lq5

PRONUNCIATIONS
http://bit.ly/AC7q4k

CALIFORNIA

NORTH COAST

Napa

Sonoma

San Francisco

SAN JOAQUIN

Monterey

NORTH CENTRAL
COAST

SOUTH CENTRAL COAST

Santa Barbara

*Pacific
Ocean*

Los Angeles

o  Miles          100              200

o  Kilometers        200

# More about California Wines

SINCE WE'VE ALREADY covered the history and geography of California in Class Two, it might be a good idea to go back and review the main viticultural areas of California wine country on page 66 before you continue with the red wines of California. Then, consider the following question that inevitably comes up in my class at the Windows on the World Wine School.

## Are Americans drinking more white wine or red?

The chart below shows you the trend of wine consumption in the United States over the last almost forty years. When I first began studying wines in 1970, people were more interested in red wine than white. From the mid-1970s, when I started teaching, into the mid-1990s, my students showed a definite preference for white wine. Fortunately for me (since I am a red-wine drinker), the pendulum is surely swinging back to more red-wine drinkers.

## Why this change?

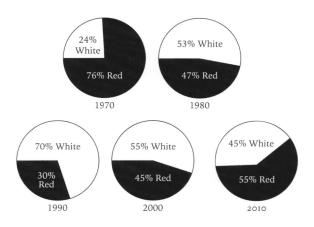

*red versus white—consumption in the United States*

162 • KEVIN ZRALY'S COMPLETE WINE COURSE

Looking back at the American obsession with health and fitness in the 1970s and 1980s, we see many people switching from meat and potatoes to fish and vegetables—a lighter diet that called more for white wine than red. "Chardonnay" became the new buzzword that replaced the call for "a glass of white wine." Bars that never used to stock wine—nothing decent, anyway—began to carry an assortment of fine wines by the glass, with Chardonnay, by far, the best-selling wine. Today, steak is back and the new buzzwords are Cabernet Sauvignon, Merlot, and Pinot Noir.

Another major reason for the dramatic upturn in red-wine consumption is the power of the media. Television popularized the so-called French Paradox (see box below).

Finally, perhaps the most important reason that red-wine consumption has increased in the United States is that California is producing a much better quality red wine than ever before. One of the reasons for improved quality is the replanting of vines over the last twenty years due to the phylloxera problem (see page 76). Some analysts thought the replanting would be financially devastating to the California wine industry, but in reality it may have been a blessing in disguise, especially with regard to quality.

The opportunity to replant allowed vineyard owners to increase their red-grape production. It enabled California grape growers to utilize the knowledge they had gained over the years with regard to soil, climate, microclimate, trellising, and other viticultural practices.

Bottom line: California reds are already some of the greatest in the world, with more and better to come.

**ACREAGE IN CALIFORNIA (2012)**

Currently there are 286,208 acres in red grapes and 175,815 in white grapes planted in California.

ACCORDING TO the U.S. Dietary Guidelines:

    5 oz. wine = 100 calories
    12 oz. beer = 150 calories
    1.5 oz. distilled spirits = 100 calories

THERE ARE more than 30 wine grape varieties planted in California.

**CALIFORNIA RED GRAPES IN 2012**

| Varietal | Acreage |
| --- | --- |
| Cabernet | 75,804 |
| Zinfandel | 47,869 |
| Merlot | 44,849 |

FROM 1991 TO 2011, sales of red wine in the United States grew by more than 125%.

## THE FRENCH PARADOX

*In the early 1990s, the TV series 60 Minutes twice aired a report on a phenomenon known as the French Paradox—the fact that the French have a lower rate of heart disease than Americans, despite a diet that's higher in fat. Since the one thing the American diet lacks, in comparison to the French diet, is red wine, some researchers were looking for a link between the consumption of red wine and a decreased rate of heart disease. Not surprisingly, in the year following this report, Americans increased their purchases of red wines by 39 percent.*

WINE IS fat-free and contains no cholesterol.

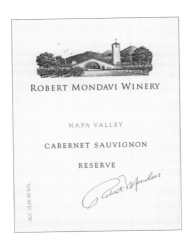

## What are the major red grapes in California?

There are five major red grapes grown in California.

**Cabernet Sauvignon:** Considered the most successful red grape in California, it yields some of the greatest red wines in the world. Cabernet Sauvignon is the predominant variety used in the finest red Bordeaux wines, such as Château Lafite-Rothschild and Château Latour. Almost all California Cabernets are dry, and depending upon the producer and vintage, they range in style from light and ready to drink, to extremely full-bodied and long-lived. California Cabernet has become the benchmark for some of the best California wines.

My favorite California Cabernet Sauvignons are:

| | |
|---|---|
| ARROWOOD | JOSEPH PHELPS |
| BEAULIEU PRIVATE RESERVE | LA JOTA |
| BERINGER PRIVATE RESERVE | LAUREL GLEN |
| CAKEBREAD | MONDAVI RESERVE |
| CAYMUS | OPUS ONE |
| CHAPPELLET | PAUL HOBBS |
| CHATEAU MONTELENA | PINE RIDGE |
| CHATEAU ST. JEAN, CINQ CÉPAGES | PRIDE MOUNTAIN |
| CLOS DU VAL | RIDGE MONTE BELLO |
| DALLA VALLE | SBRAGIA FAMILY VINEYARDS |
| DIAMOND CREEK | SCHRADER |
| DUCKHORN | SHAFER HILLSIDE SELECT |
| DUNN HOWELL MOUNTAIN | SILVER OAK |
| GALLO OF SONOMA ESTATE | SPOTTSWOODE |
| GROTH RESERVE | STAGLIN |
| HEITZ | STAG'S LEAP CASK |
| HESS COLLECTION | TREFETHEN |
| JORDAN | WHITEHALL LANE |

### BEST BETS FOR CABERNET SAUVIGNON (NAPA VALLEY)

1994*  1995*  1996*  1997*  1999*  2001**  2002**
2003  2004  2005*  2006**  2007**  2008**
2009**  2010**  2011  2012*

*Note: \* signifies exceptional vintage   \*\* signifies extraordinary vintage*

*Pinot Noir:* Known as the "headache" grape because of its fragile quality, Pinot Noir is temperamental, high maintenance, expensive, and difficult to grow and make into wine. The great grape of the Burgundy region of France—responsible for such famous wines as Pommard, Nuits-St-Georges, and Gevrey-Chambertin—is also one of the principal grapes in French Champagne. In California, many years of experimentation in finding the right location to plant the Pinot Noir and to perfect the fermentation techniques have elevated some of the Pinot Noirs to the status of great wines. Pinot Noir is usually less tannic than Cabernet and matures more quickly, generally in two to five years. Because of the extra expense involved in growing this grape, the best examples of Pinot Noirs from California may cost more than other varietals. The three top counties for Pinot Noir are Sonoma (11,000 acres), Monterey (6,204 acres), and Santa Barbara (3,401 acres).

My favorite California Pinot Noirs are:

| | |
|---|---|
| ACACIA | MARCASSIN |
| ARTESA | MELVILLE |
| AU BON CLIMAT | MERRY EDWARDS |
| BREWER-CLIFTON | MORGAN |
| BYRON | PAPAPIETRO-PERRY |
| CALERA | PATZ & HALL |
| DEHLINGER | PAUL HOBBS |
| ETUDE | PISONI |
| FLOWERS | ROBERT SINSKEY |
| FOXEN | SAINTSBURY |
| GARY FARRELL | SANFORD |
| GOLDENEYE | SEA SMOKE |
| J. ROCHIOLI | SIDURI |
| KOSTA BROWNE | TALLEY |
| LITTORAI | WILLIAMS SELYEM |

### BEST BETS FOR PINOT NOIR

*Sonoma* 2007* 2008 2009** 2010* 2011 2012*
*Carneros* 2008* 2009* 2010** 2011 2012*
*Santa Barbara* 2008 2009* 2010** 2011 2012*
*Monterey* 2008* 2009** 2010* 2011 2012*

Note: * signifies exceptional vintage    ** signifies extraordinary vintage

Napa really is red-wine country, with 33,784 acres in red grapes versus 10,614 in whites. Leading the red grapes are Cabernet Sauvignon, with 18,887 acres, and Merlot, with 5,902 acres.

SONOMA has the most wineries and acreage for Pinot Noir in California.

ONE AUTHOR, trying to sum up the difference between a Pinot Noir and a Cabernet Sauvignon, said, "Pinot is James Joyce, while Cabernet is Dickens. Both sell well, but one is easier to understand."

COMMON PINOT NOIR aromas:
Red berries    Red cherry
Leather    Tobacco (older)

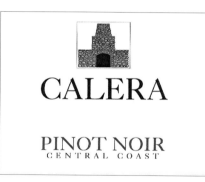

SOUTHERN CALIFORNIA—especially the Santa Barbara area, as the characters in the movie *Sideways* could tell you—has become one of the prime locations for Pinot Noir production, with plantings up by more than 200% in the past decade. In fact, Pinot Noir sales overall have increased at least 20% since the film was released in 2004.

CARNEROS, MONTEREY, Sonoma, and Santa Barbara are great places to grow Pinot Noir because of their cooler climate. Sonoma has the most acres and wineries for Pinot Noir in California.

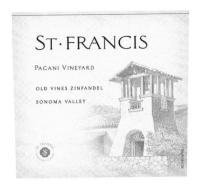

## OLD VINES

There are some Zinfandel vines that are over 150 years old and still producing wine in California.

RECENT DNA studies have concluded that Zinfandel is the same grape as the Primitivo in Italy.

WHITE ZINFANDEL, at 35 million cases sold, far outsells red Zinfandel.

SOME ZINFANDELS have more than 16% alcohol.

## WHICH ROSENBLUM IS IT?

Rosenblum makes over 20 different Zinfandels a year.

## MERLOT MADNESS

There were only two acres of Merlot planted in all of California in 1960. Today there are close to 50,000!

COMMON MERLOT aromas:

| | |
|---|---|
| Blackberry | Chocolate |
| Cassis | Coffee |
| Cherry | Oak |

*Zinfandel:* The surprise grape of California, Zinfandel was used to make "generic" or "jug" wines in the early years of California winemaking. Over the past thirty years, however, it has developed into one of the best red varietal grapes. The only problem in choosing a Zinfandel wine is that so many different styles are made. Depending on the producer, the wines can range from a big, rich, ripe, high-alcohol, spicy, smoky, concentrated, intensely flavored style with substantial tannin, to a very light, fruity wine. And let's not forget white Zinfandel!

My favorite Zinfandels are:

| | |
|---|---|
| **BEDROCK** | **RAFANELLI** |
| **CARLISLE** | **RAVENSWOOD** |
| **CLINE** | **RIDGE** |
| **DRY CREEK WINERY** | **ROSENBLUM** |
| **FIFE** | **ROSHAMBO** |
| **HARTFORD FAMILY** | **SBRAGIA** |
| **J. ROCHIOLI** | **SEGHESIO** |
| **MARTINELLI** | **SIGNORELLO** |
| **MAZZOCCO** | **ST. FRANCIS** |
| **MERRY EDWARDS** | **TURLEY** |

### BEST BETS FOR ZINFANDEL (NORTH COAST)

2003* 2005 2006* 2007 2008* 2009*
2010* 2011 2012*

*Note: \* signifies exceptional vintage*

*Merlot:* For many years Merlot was thought of as a grape only to be blended with Cabernet Sauvignon, because Merlot's tannins are softer and its texture is more supple. Merlot has now achieved its own identity as a super-premium varietal. Of red-grape varietals in California, Merlot has seen the fastest rate of new plantings over the last twenty years. It produces a soft, round wine that generally does not need the same aging as a Cabernet Sauvignon. It is a top seller at restaurants, where its early maturation and compatibility with food make it a frequent choice by consumers.

My favorite North Coast Merlots are:

| | |
|---|---|
| **BERINGER HOWELL MOUNTAIN** | **MATANZAS CREEK** |
| **CHIMNEY ROCK** | **NEWTON** |
| **CLOS DU BOIS** | **PALAMO** |
| **DUCKHORN** | **PINE RIDGE** |
| **FRANCISCAN** | **PRIDE** |
| **HAVENS** | **PROVENANCE** |
| **LEWIS CELLARS** | **SHAFER** |
| **LUNA** | **ST. FRANCIS** |
| **MARKHAM** | **WHITEHALL LANE** |

**BEST BETS FOR MERLOT (NORTH COAST)**

2002* 2004* 2005* 2007* 2008 2009** 2010 2011 2012*

*Note: \* signifies exceptional vintage    \*\* signifies extraordinary vintage*

*Syrah:* The up-and-coming red grape in California is definitely Syrah. I don't know why it's taken so long, since Syrah has always been one of the major grapes of the Rhône Valley in France, making some of the best and most long-lived wines in the world. Further, the sales of Australian Syrah (which they call Shiraz) have been phenomenal in the United States. Americans like the spicy, robust flavor of this grape. It's a perfect grape for California because it thrives in sunny, warm weather.

My favorite Syrahs are:

| | | |
|---|---|---|
| **ALBAN** | **JUSTIN** | **QUPE** |
| **BONNY DOON** | **LAGIER MEREDITH** | **SINE QUA NON** |
| **CAKEBREAD** | **LEWIS** | **TABLAS CREEK** |
| **CLOS DU BOIS** | **NEYERS** | **VIADER** |
| **DUMOL** | **OJAI** | **WILD HORSE** |
| **EDMUNDS ST. JOHN** | **PAX** | **ZACA MESA** |
| **FESS PARKER** | **PEAY** | |
| **FOXEN** | **PHELPS** | |

SAN LUIS OBISPO and Sonoma counties have the most acreage of Syrah grapes in California.

**BEST BETS FOR SYRAH**

***South Central Coast*** 2006* 2007** 2008** 2009**
2010** 2011 2012

***North Coast*** 2004** 2006** 2007** 2008* 2009**
2010* 2011 2012*

*Note: \* signifies exceptional vintage    \*\* signifies extraordinary vintage*

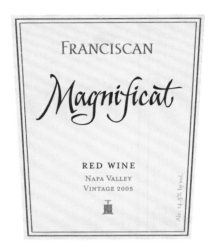

SOME EXAMPLES of Meritage wines of California:
Cain Five
Dominus (Christian Moueix)
Insignia (Phelps Vineyards)
Magnificat (Franciscan)
Opus One (Mondavi/Rothschild)
Trefethen Halo

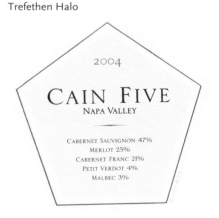

# RED-GRAPE BOOM

Look at the chart below to see how many acres of the major red grapes were planted in California in 1970, and how those numbers have increased. Rapid expansion has been the characteristic of the California wine industry!

TOTAL BEARING ACREAGE OF RED-WINE GRAPES PLANTED

GRAPE-BY-GRAPE COMPARISON

| GRAPE | 1970 | 1980 | 1990 | 2013 |
|---|---|---|---|---|
| Cabernet Sauvignon | 3,200 | 21,800 | 24,100 | 75,804 |
| Zinfandel | 19,200 | 27,700 | 28,000 | 47,869 |
| Merlot | 100 | 2,600 | 4,000 | 44,849 |
| Pinot Noir | 2,100 | 9,200 | 8,600 | 36,988 |
| Syrah | | | 400 | 18,825 |

## What are Meritage wines?

Meritage (which rhymes with *heritage*) is the name for red and white wines made in America from a blend of the classic Bordeaux wine-grape varieties. This category was created because many winemakers felt stifled by the required minimum amount (75 percent) of a grape that must go into a bottle for it to be named for that variety. Some winemakers knew they could make a better wine with a blend of, say, 60 percent of the major grape and 40 percent of secondary grapes. This blending of grapes allows producers of Meritage wines the same freedom that Bordeaux winemakers have in making their wines.

For red wine, the varieties include Cabernet Sauvignon, Merlot, Cabernet Franc, Petit Verdot, and Malbec. For white wine, the varieties include Sauvignon Blanc and Sémillon.

## When I buy a Cabernet, Zinfandel, Merlot, Pinot Noir, Syrah, or Meritage wine, how do I know which style I'm getting? Is the style of the wine indicated on the label?

Unless you just happen to be familiar with a particular vineyard's wine, you're stuck with trial-and-error tastings. You're one step ahead, though, just by knowing that you'll find drastically different styles from the same grape variety.

With some 2,300 wineries in California and more than half of them

## OPUS ONE

*Amid grand hoopla in the wine world, Robert Mondavi and the late Baron Philippe de Rothschild released Opus One. "It isn't Mouton and it isn't Mondavi," said Robert Mondavi. Opus One is a Bordeaux-style blend made from Cabernet Sauvignon, Merlot, and Cabernet Franc grapes grown in the Napa Valley. It was originally produced at the Robert Mondavi Winery in the Napa Valley, but is now produced across Highway 29 in its own spectacular winery.*

producing red wines, it is virtually impossible to keep up with the ever-changing styles that are being produced. One of the recent improvements in labeling is that more wineries are adding important information to the back label indicating when the wine is ready to drink, if it should be aged, and many even offer food suggestions.

To avoid any unpleasant surprises, I can't emphasize enough the importance of an educated wine retailer. One of the strongest recommendations I give—especially to a new wine drinker—is to find the right retailer, one who understands wine and your taste.

## Do California red wines age well?

Absolutely, especially from the best wineries that produce Cabernet Sauvignon and Zinfandel. I have been fortunate to taste some early examples of Cabernet Sauvignon going back to the 1930s, 1940s, and 1950s, which for the most part were drinking well—some of them were outstanding—proving to me the longevity of certain Cabernets. Zinfandels and Cabernet Sauvignons from the best wineries in great vintages will need a minimum of five years before you drink them, and they will get better over the next ten years. That's at least fifteen years of great enjoyment.

ONE OF the most memorable tastings I have ever attended in my career was for the 50-anniversary of Beaulieu's Private Reserve wine. Over a two-day period, we tasted every vintage from 1936 to 1986 with winemaker André Tchelistcheff. I think everyone who attended the tasting was amazed and awed by how well many of these vintages aged.

**GREAT CALIFORNIA ROSÉS**

Bonny Doon Vin Gris de Cigare
Etude Pinot Noir Rosé
Frog's Leap La Grenouille
Rouganté
SoloRosa

**NAPA VALLEY PAST AND PRESENT**

1970: $2,000–$4,000 (cost per acre)
2011: $150,000–$350,000+ (cost per acre)

**FROM THE MOVIE SIDEWAYS**
Maya: You know, can I ask you a personal
question, Miles?
Miles: Sure.
Maya: Why are you so into Pinot?
Miles: (laughs softly)
Maya: I mean, it's like a thing with you.
Miles: (continues laughing softly)
Miles: Uh, I don't know, I don't know.
Um, it's a hard grape to know, as you
know. Right? It's uh, it's thin-skinned,
temperamental, ripens early. It's you know,
it's not a survivor like Cabernet, which can
just grown anywhere and uh, thrive even
when it's neglected.

However, one of the things I have noticed in the last ten years, tasting not only as many California wines as I have, but also tasting so many European wines, is that California wines seem to be more accessible when young, as opposed to, say, a Bordeaux. I believe this is one of the reasons California wines sell so well in the United States, especially in restaurants.

## What have been the trends in the red wines of California over the last forty years?

One trend has been the association of a specific grape variety with a region (AVA) and further with individual vineyards. Cabernet Sauvignon and Merlot are Napa Valley, Pinot Noir is Carneros, Sonoma, Santa Barbara, Monterey, and Anderson Valley. Syrah is best in the South Central Coast (San Luis Obispo).

Though California winemakers have settled down, they have not given up experimentation altogether, if you consider the many new grape varieties coming out of California these days. I expect to see more wines made with grapes such as the Mourvèdre, Grenache, Barbera, and especially Syrah, continuing the trend toward diversity in California red wines.

I personally have an issue with the change in alcohol levels over the past forty years, especially in the red wines. Many winemakers are producing wines with over 15 percent alcohol, which for my own taste changes the balance as the elegance and varietal characteristics are replaced with overpowering alcohols. The reality is that most wines around the world have increased in alcohol content, but not to the extent that they have in California.

**FOR FURTHER READING**

I recommend *Wine Atlas of California* by James Halliday, *Making Sense of California Wine* and *Matt Kramer's New California Wine* by Matt Kramer, *Wine Spectator's California Wine* by James Laube, and *The Wine Atlas of California and the Pacific Northwest* by Bob Thompson.

# WINE AND FOOD

**MARGRIT BIEVER AND ROBERT MONDAVI:** *With Cabernet Sauvignon: lamb, or wild game such as grouse and caribou. With Pinot Noir: pork loin, milder game such as domestic pheasant, and coq au vin.*

**TOM JORDAN:** *"Roast lamb is wonderful with the flavor and complexity of Cabernet Sauvignon. The wine also pairs nicely with sliced breast of duck, and grilled squab with wild mushrooms. For a cheese course with mature Cabernet, milder cheeses such as young goat cheeses, St. André and Taleggio, are best so the subtle flavors of the wine can be enjoyed."*

**MARGARET AND DAN DUCKHORN:** *"With a young Merlot, we recommend lamb shanks with crispy polenta, or grilled duck with wild rice in Port sauce. One of our favorites is barbecued leg of lamb with a mild, spicy, fruit-based sauce. With older Merlots at the end of the meal, we like to serve Cambazzola cheese and warm walnuts."*

**JANET TREFETHEN:** *With Cabernet Sauvignon: prime cut of well-aged grilled beef; also—believe it or not— with chocolate and chocolate-chip cookies. With Pinot Noir: roasted quail stuffed with peeled kiwi fruit in a Madeira sauce. Also with pork tenderloin in a fruity sauce.*

**PAUL DRAPER** *(Ridge Vineyards):* *With Zinfandel: a well-made risotto of Petaluma duck. With aged Cabernet Sauvignon: Moroccan lamb with figs.*

**WARREN WINIARSKI** *(Stag's Leap Wine Cellars):* *With Cabernet Sauvignon: lamb or veal with a light sauce.*

**JOSH JENSEN** *(Calera Wine Co.):* *"Pinot Noir is so versatile, but I like it best with fowl of all sorts—chicken, turkey, duck, pheasant, and quail, preferably roasted or mesquite grilled. It's also great with fish such as salmon, tuna, and snapper."*

**RICHARD ARROWOOD:** *With Cabernet Sauvignon: Sonoma County spring lamb or lamb chops prepared in a rosemary herb sauce.*

**DAVID STARE** *(Dry Creek Vineyard):* *"My favorite food combination with Zinfandel is marinated, butterflied leg of lamb. Have the butcher butterfly the leg, then place it in a plastic bag. Pour in half a bottle of Dry Creek Zinfandel, a cup of olive oil, six mashed garlic cloves, salt and pepper to taste. Marinate for several hours or overnight in the refrigerator. Barbecue until medium rare. While the lamb is cooking, take the marinade, reduce it, and whisk in several pats of butter for thickness. Yummy!"*

**BO BARRETT** *(Chateau Montelena Winery):* *With Cabernet Sauvignon: a good rib eye, barbecued with a teriyaki-soy-ginger-sesame marinade; venison or even roast beef prepared with olive oil and tapenade with rosemary, or even lamb. But when it comes to a good Cabernet Sauvignon, Bo is happy to enjoy a glass with "nothing at all—just a good book."*

**PATRICK CAMPBELL** *(owner/winemaker, Laurel Glen Vineyard):* *"With Cabernet Sauvignon, try a rich risotto topped with wild mushrooms."*

**JACK CAKEBREAD:** *"I enjoy my 1994 Cakebread Cellars Napa Valley Cabernet Sauvignon with farm-raised salmon with a crispy potato crust or an herb-crusted Napa Valley rack of lamb, with mashed potatoes and a red-wine sauce."*

**ED SBRAGIA** *(winemaker, Sbragia Family Vineyards):* *"I like my Cabernet Sauvignon with rack of lamb, beef, or rare duck."*

**TOM MACKEY** *(winemaker, St. Francis Merlot):* *With St. Francis Merlot Sonoma County: Dungeness crab cakes, rack of lamb, pork roast, or tortellini. With St. Francis Merlot Reserve: hearty minestrone or lentil soup, venison, or filet mignon, or even a Caesar salad.*

# Class Six:
# The Red Wines of California, Oregon, and Washington

This is the sixth class and you've tasted more than fifty wines. You've ingested a tremendous amount of information—and wine!—over the last five classes. In Class Two we covered the vital information of California and the rest of the United States. In this class I hope you'll learn more about tasting, and further identify your own preferences on wine styles.

Pour the first six wines at the same time so that you can clearly see the difference in color between the Pinot Noirs, Zinfandels, and Merlots. I hope that after you taste these first six wines, you will be able to choose the grape variety that best suits your personality: your "eureka" moment.

## THE WINES

### Understanding American Pinot Noir

***Two Pinot Noirs, from the same vintage***

1. Carneros Pinot Noir
2. Oregon Pinot Noir

### Understanding California Zinfandel

***Two Zinfandels, from the same vintage***

3. Sonoma Zinfandel
4. Napa Zinfandel

4.

3.

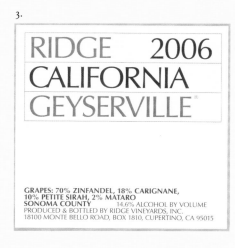

GRAPES: 70% ZINFANDEL, 18% CARIGNANE, 10% PETITE SIRAH, 2% MATARO
SONOMA COUNTY        14.6% ALCOHOL BY VOLUME
PRODUCED & BOTTLED BY RIDGE VINEYARDS, INC.
18100 MONTE BELLO ROAD, BOX 1810, CUPERTINO, CA 95015

1.

## Understanding American Merlot

### Two Merlots compared, from the same vintage

5. Washington State Merlot
6. Napa Merlot

## Understanding California Cabernet Sauvignon

### One wine, tasted alone (medium style and medium price)

7. Napa Valley Cabernet Sauvignon

### Three California Cabernet Sauvignons compared (blind tasting)

8, 9, 10. For example, three different vintages; three different price ranges; or three different California wine regions

### One aged Cabernet Sauvignon (over 8 years old), tasted alone

11. Napa Valley Cabernet Sauvignon

11.

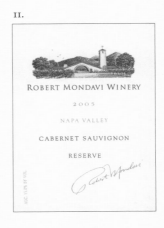

6.

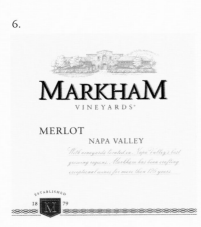

8.

*Please note that labels are suggestions for wineries and producers to look for. For more examples, see pages 164, 165, 166, 167 and 169.*

# Questions for Class Six:
# The Red Wines of California

# The Wines of Spain and Italy

SPAIN • RIOJA • RIBERA DEL DUERO • PENEDÈS • PRIORAT

ITALY • TUSCANY • PIEDMONT • VENETO

VIDEO
http://bit.ly/e22O3T

PRONUNCIATIONS
http://bit.ly/yo976b

SOLE AGENTS. CLASSICAL WINES-SEATTLE, WA

# PASANAU®

*La Morera de Montsant*
RED WINE
**PRIORAT**
DENOMINACIÓ D'ORIGEN QUALIFICADA

ESTATE-BOTTLED
*Elaborador, embotellador: Pasanau Germans s.l.*

| ALC/ VOL. 14% | R.E. núm. 29.004.00 CAT *Product of Spain* | 750ML |

ALTHOUGH THERE are nearly 800 different wineries in Spain, about 80% of their production comes from a handful of companies.

---

# The Wines of Spain

SPAIN IS THE WORLD's third largest producer of wine behind Italy and France. With 2.7 million acres of land planted, Spain has more acreage dedicated to grapevines than any other country in the world.

Despite thousands of years of grape growing and winemaking history, Spain has undergone a radical change over the last forty years. Since joining the European Union in 1986, Spain has benefited from the infusion of capital for its vineyards and wineries. Modern technology, with its stainless steel fermentors and new vineyard trellis systems, has helped create outstanding wines from all of Spain's diverse wine regions. To offset a dry climate and frequent droughts, especially in the center and south of the country, irrigation was made legal in 1996 for grapevines, which has increased both the quality and volume of Spain's wine production.

## What are the major grape varieties planted in Spain?

There are hundreds of grape varieties grown in Spain. Here are the ones you most likely find in the wine store or restaurant:

| NATIVE TO SPAIN | | INTERNATIONAL | |
|---|---|---|---|
| *White* | *Red* | *White* | *Red* |
| Albariño | Tempranillo | Chardonnay | Cabernet |
| Verdejo | (Tinto Fino) | Sauvignon Blanc | Sauvignon |
| Macabeo (Viura) | Garnacha | | Merlot |
| Cariñena | Monastrell | | Syrah |

THERE ARE more than 600 grape varieties planted in Spain.

## What are the major wine regions of Spain?

Spain first established Denominación de Origen (DO) laws in 1970 and revised them in 1982. There were twenty-five DOs in 1982, and today Spain has sixty-nine DO regions and two DOC regions. Similar to the AOC laws of France, Spain's DO laws control a region's boundaries, grape varieties, wine-making practices, yield per acre, and most important, the aging of the wine before it can be released.

My favorite wine regions of Spain with the most important grapes include the following:

**Rioja:** Tempranillo
**Ribera del Duero:** Tinto Fino
**Penedès:** Macabeo, Cabernet Sauvignon, Cariñena, Garnacha
**Priorat:** Garnacha, Cariñena
**Rueda:** Verdejo
**Rías Baixas:** Albariño
**Sherry (Jerez):** Palomino

YOU WILL find the word *cosecha*, which means "harvest" or "vintage" in Spanish, on some labels. It can also indicate a wine that has little barrel aging, and is often used by producers for their "modern-style" wines.

DOC IS the highest level of quality wine in Spain. As of 2009 there are only two that qualify: Rioja and Priorat.

We'll put aside the region of Jerez for now, since you will become a Sherry expert in a later chapter. Let's begin with Rioja, which is located in northern Spain near the French border. In fact, it's less than a five-hour (200-mile) drive to Rioja from Bordeaux, which has influenced the style of Rioja winemaking since the 1800s.

During the 1870s the phylloxera blight, traveling from north to south, arrived in Bordeaux and nearly destroyed the wine industry there. Many of Bordeaux's winemakers and owners chose to relocate to Rioja, where the blight had yet to appear and whose climate and growing conditions were similar to that of Bordeaux. As they established their own wineries and vineyards, they influenced how Rioja wine was made. This influence is still apparent in today's Rioja wines.

# RIOJA

Despite a surge in diverse and interesting wines from elsewhere in Spain, Rioja still reigns as the principal red wine–producing region. Rioja offers both quality and quantity and sits comfortably alongside the world's greatest wine-producing regions. In 1985, Rioja had roughly 100,000 acres planted in grapes; in 2009, there were more than 150,000 acres. One of the biggest recent changes in Rioja has been the rejuvenation of its vineyards: 41 percent of all its vines have been planted over the last ten years. Since 1993 the amount of red grapes planted has doubled and now accounts for 90 percent of total grape production.

Rioja continues to innovate within its traditional style and offers consumers a tremendous range of quality at price points appealing to both novices and collectors.

## What are the primary red grapes used in Rioja wines?

**TEMPRANILLO**             **GARNACHA**

**THE NEW RIOJA**

A new style of wine is emerging in Rioja. It is a contemporary wine that is bigger and more concentrated. Wineries of this style include Allende, Remelluri, Palacios, Remondo, and Remirez de Ganuza.

THE BEST wine museum I have ever visited is located at Bodegas Dinastia Vivanco in Briones, Rioja. The museum is divided into six areas dedicated to the history and origins of wine. If you go, plan on spending the day—it is that good!

GRENACHE IS the French spelling of Garnacha, a Spanish grape, which was brought to France from Spain during the time of the popes of Avignon, some of whom were Spanish.

YOU WILL occasionally find the word *joven* on a wine label. It indicates that the wine is unoaked or slightly oaked and should be drunk "young."

## Why are Rioja wines so easy to understand?

All you need to know when buying a Rioja wine is the style (level) and the reputation of the Rioja winemaker/shipper. The grape varieties are not found on the wine labels, and there's no classification to be memorized. The three major levels of Rioja wines are:

*Crianza:* Released after two years of aging, with a minimum of one year in oak barrels. Cost: $.

*Reserva:* Released after three years of aging, with a minimum of one year in oak barrels. Cost: $$.

*Gran Reserva:* Released after five to seven years of aging, with a minimum of two years in oak barrels. Cost: $$$.

CRIANZA

RESERVA

GRAN RESERVA

## How would I know which Rioja wine to buy?

Aside from going with your preferred style and the reputation of the wine-maker/shipper, you may also be familiar with a Rioja wine by its proprietary name. The following are some bodegas to look for, along with some of their better-known proprietary names. Also, three of the best U.S. importers for Spanish wine are Steve Metzler (Classical Wines), Jorge Ordoñez (Fine Estates from Spain), and Eric Solomon (European Cellars).

**Baron de Ley**
**Bodegas Bretón**
**Bodegas Dinastía Vivanco**
**Bodegas Lan**
**Bodegas Montecillo**
**Bodegas Muga—Muga Reserva, Prado Enea, Torre Muga**
**Bodegas Remírez de Ganuza**

VINOS DE PAGOS means that the wine comes from a single estate.

SPANISH WINERIES are sometimes called *bodegas.*

THE BODEGA Marqués de Cáceres is owned by a Spaniard who also owns Château Camensac, a fifth-growth Bordeaux.

IN 2011, THERE were over 500 bodegas in Rioja.

FINCA MEANS "farm."

MARQUÉS DE MURRIETA was the first commercial bodega in Rioja, established in 1852.

SOME OF THE TOP Rioja winemakers say that the 2001 and 2004 vintages are the best they have ever tasted.

**BODEGAS RIOJANAS—MONTE REAL, VIÑA ALBINA**

**BODEGAS RODA**

**BODEGAS TOBÍA**

**CUNE—IMPERIAL, VIÑA REAL**

**CONTINO**

**EL COTO**

**FINCA ALLENDE**

**FINCA VALPIEDRA**

**LA RIOJA ALTA—VIÑA ALBERDI, VIÑA ARDANZA**

**LÓPEZ DE HEREDÍA**

**MARQUÉS DE CÁCERES**

**MARQUÉS DE MURRIETA**

**MARQUÉS DE RISCAL**

**MARTÍNEZ BUJANDA—CONDE DE VALDEMAR**

**PALACIOS REMONDO**

**REMELLURI**

**SEÑORIO DE SAN VICENTE**

**YSIOS**

**BEST BETS FOR RIOJA**

1994* 1995* 2001** 2004** 2005**
2009* 2010** 2011* 2012

Note: *signifies exceptional vintage  ** signifies extraordinary vintage

# RIBERA DEL DUERO

When I wrote the original edition of this book, I did not include the Ribera del Duero region. Back then most of the region's wines were made at cooperatives except, arguably, that of the most famous winery of Spain, Bodegas Vega Sicilia, which has been making wine since the 1860s. But one wine does not a region make.

In the early 1980s another wine, Pesquera, received great reviews from the wine press, setting the tone for astounding growth and helping stimulate quality wine production in the region. Today there are over 270 wineries there, covering nearly 50,000 acres and a new generation of quality winemakers is emerging.

## AALTO

*One of the newest wineries in Ribera del Duero, Aalto, released its first vintage in 1999. It was created by the former legendary winemaker at Vega Sicilia, Mariano Garcia, and his business partner, Javier Zaccagnini. They presently are making two wines, Aalto and Aalto PS. Judging by the reviews both wines have received, they need to be added to your wine cellar!*

## What are the major red grapes used in Ribera del Duero?

| | |
|---|---|
| TINTO FINO (AKA TEMPRANILLO) | MALBEC |
| CABERNET SAUVIGNON | GARNACHA |
| MERLOT | |

### BEST BETS FOR RIBERA DEL DUERO

1996*   2001**   2004**   2005**   2009*   2010**   2011   2012

Note: *signifies exceptional vintage   ** signifies extraordinary vintage

# PENEDÈS

Located just outside of Barcelona, the Penedès region produces the famous sparkling wine called Cava, protected under its own DO. The two best-known names of Spanish sparkling wine in the United States are Codorníu and Freixenet, two of the biggest producers of bottle-fermented sparkling wine in the world. One of the best features of these wines is their reasonable price for a traditional-method sparkling wine.

In addition to Cava, the Penedès region is known for high-quality table wine. The major producer is the Torres family, whose name is synonymous with quality. Their most famous wine, Gran Coronas Black Label, is made with 100 percent Cabernet Sauvignon, and is rare and expensive. But the Torres family also produces a full range of fine Spanish wines in all price categories.

KEVIN ZRALY'S FAVORITE
RIBERA DEL DUERO PRODUCERS

Aalto
Abadía Retuerta
Alejandro Fernandez
Arzuaga
Bodegas Emilio Moro
Bodegas Felix Callejo
Bodegas Los Astrales
Condado de Haza
Dominio de Pingus
García Figuero
Hacienda Monasterio
Montecastro
Pago de los Capellanes
Pesquera
Vega Sicilia
Viña Mayor

KEVIN ZRALY'S FAVORITE
PENEDÈS PRODUCERS

Albet i Noya
Jean Leon
Marques de Monistrol
Torres (Mas La Plana)

PRIORAT WINES must have a minimum of 13.5% alcohol.

MOST VINEYARDS are so steep in Priorat that mechanical equipment is difficult to maneuver, so mules are used instead (just like the old days!).

**PRIORAT PAST AND PRESENT**

1995: 16 wineries
2011: 82 wineries

THE PRIORAT vineyards are located at an altitude of 1,000 to 3,000 feet.

## What grapes are used in Penedès?

| FOR CAVA | FOR RED | FOR WHITE |
|---|---|---|
| Macabeo | Tempranillo | Chardonnay |
| Parellada | Cabernet Sauvignon | Parellada |
| Xarel-lo | Garnacha | Macabeo |
| Chardonnay | Merlot | Riesling |
| | | Gewürztraminer |

# PRIORAT

This region, located a few hours south of the Penedès region, epitomizes the renaissance of Spanish wines. The Carthusian monks farmed the vineyards for over 800 years until the early 1800s, when the government auctioned off their land to local farmers. In the late 1800s, phylloxera blight forced most farmers to stop planting grapes, and many began to cultivate hazelnuts and almonds. By 1910 most wine was made in cooperatives and, up until twenty-five years ago, Priorat was mostly known for sacramental wine.

In the late 1980s some of the most well-known Spanish wine producers, including René Barbier and Alvaro Palacios, started to revive the old Carthusian vineyards. Today Priorat produces some of the best red wine in Spain. In fact, the Spanish government has awarded Priorat the highest status of DOC. Only two regions in Spain have this rating (the other is Rioja). Because of extremely low yields and demand, it is difficult to find an inexpensive Priorat. The best easily sell for over $100 a bottle.

## ALVARO PALACIOS

*Alvaro Palacios is one of Spain's wine mavericks. Starting at his family's winery in Rioja, he has expanded into the Priorat and Bierzo regions—two regions that he helped revitalize. His Priorat wine, L'Ermita, is one of the most expensive and highly rated wines in Spain. For better value, try the Finca Dofí and, for the best value, Les Terrasses.*

## What are the grapes used in making red Priorat wines?

**Native to Spain:** Garnacha (Grenache), Cariñena (Carignan)
**International:** Cabernet Sauvignon, Merlot, Syrah

### BEST BETS FOR PRIORAT

2001** 2004** 2005** 2006* 2007* 2008
2009* 2010 2011 2012

*Note: \*signifies exceptional vintage  \*\* signifies extraordinary vintage*

# WHITE WINES OF SPAIN

*Rueda:* Located in north-central Spain, Rueda wines have been well known for centuries. Up until the 1970s, Ruedas were fortified wines whose major grape was Palomino. They were similar to Sherry in style.

The "modern" style of Rueda white wine is dry, fruity, and fresh. It is made from Verdejo, Viura, and occasionally Sauvignon Blanc grapes.

*Rías Baixas:* Rías Baixas is located in the northwestern part of Spain in the region of Galicia. Like Rueda, Rías Baixas began to make outstanding white wines in the 1980s. Over 90 percent of the wine is made from the Albariño grape.

**FOR FURTHER READING**

I recommend *The New Spain* by John Radford, *The New and Classical Wines of Spain* by Jeremy Watson, *The Wine Region of Rioja* by Ana Fabiano, *Peñín Guide to Spanish Wine* edited by Jose Penin and produced by Grupo Penin (annual), and *Rioja and Northwest Spain* by Jesus Barquin, Luis Gutierrez, and Victor de la Serna.

Alvaro Palacios
Clos Daphne
Clos de L'Obac
Clos Erasmus
Clos Martinet
Clos Mogador
Mas Igneus
Mas La Mola
Pasanau
Vall Llach

FOR THE PRIORAT TOURIST: Remnants of the priory called Scala Dei ("God's Stairway") and a museum devoted to its history are open to the public.

OTHER WINE-PRODUCING
AREAS OF SPAIN

Bierzo
Castilla-La Mancha
Jumilla
Navarra
Toro

ITALY PRODUCES 50% white wines and 50% red.

# The Red Wines of Italy

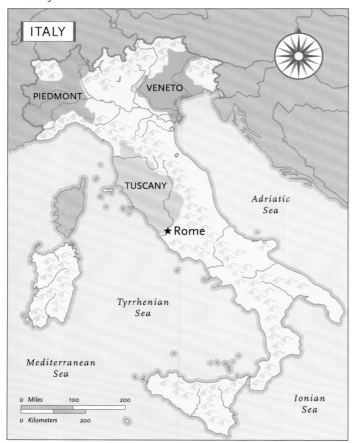

ITALY

PIEDMONT

VENETO

TUSCANY

★Rome

*Adriatic Sea*

*Tyrrhenian Sea*

*Mediterranean Sea*

*Ionian Sea*

o Miles   100   200

o Kilometers   200

**TOP THREE REGIONS IN PRODUCTION OF ITALIAN WINES**

| | |
|---|---|
| 1. Veneto | 17.7% |
| 2. Piedmont | 17.1% |
| 3. Tuscany | 10.7% |

MANY WINE producers in Italy are now making wines from Cabernet Sauvignon, Merlot, and Chardonnay.

ITALY HAS BEEN THE WORLD'S largest producer of wine since 2011. It has been producing wine for more than 3,000 years, and the vines grow everywhere. As one retailer of fine Italian wine once told me, "There is no country. Italy is one vast vineyard from north to south."

Italian wines are good for any occasion—from quaffing to serious tasting. Some of my favorite wines are Italian. In fact, 25 percent of my personal wine cellar is stocked with them.

There are more than 2,000 different wine labels, if you care to memorize them; twenty regions; and ninety-six provinces. But don't worry. If you want to know the basics of Italian wines, concentrate on the three regions listed below, and you'll be well on your way to having Italy in the palm of your hand.

**TUSCANY     PIEDMONT     VENETO**

## What are the major red-grape varieties in Italy?

There are over 2,000 varieties of grapes planted throughout Italy. In Tuscany, the major red-grape variety is Sangiovese, in Piedmont it is Nebbiolo, and in Veneto, it is Corvina.

## How are Italian wines controlled?

The Denominazione di Origine Controllata (abbreviated DOC), the Italian equivalent of the French AOC, defines where wine is produced and how it can be labeled. Italy's DOC laws went into effect in 1963.

During the 1980s, the Italian agricultural ministry took quality control one step further than the regular DOC, by adding the higher-ranking DOCG. The G stands for *Garantita*, meaning that tasting-control boards absolutely guarantee the stylistic authenticity of a wine.

A third classification, Indicazione Geografica Tipica (IGT), indicates that a wine does not meet the requirements for a DOC designation, but many wines are at a higher level than table wine with a DOC designation.

As of 2011, the wines from Tuscany and Piedmont that qualified for the DOCG were:

| TUSCANY | PIEDMONT |
|---|---|
| Brunello di Montalcino | Acqui or Brachetto d'Acqui |
| Carmignano | Alta Langa |
| Chianti | Barbera d'Asti |
| Chianti Classico | Barbera del Monteferrato Superiore |
| Elba Aleatico Passito | Barbaresco |
| Montecucco Sangiovese | Barolo |
| Morellino di Scansano | Dolcetta Diano d'Alba |
| Vernaccia di San Gimignano | Dolcetto di Dogliani Superiore |
| Vino Nobile di Montepulciano | Dolcetto di Ovada Superiore |
| | Erbaluce di Caluso |
| | Gattinara |
| | Gavi or Cortese di Gavi |
| | Ghemme |
| | Moscato d'Asti/Asti |
| | Roero |
| | Ruche di Castagnole Monferrato |

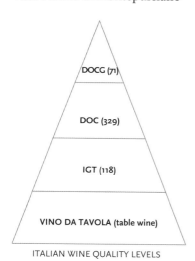

ITALIAN WINE QUALITY LEVELS

(Pyramid labels, top to bottom: DOCG (71); DOC (329); IGT (118); VINO DA TAVOLA (table wine))

## DOC LAWS

### The DOC governs:

*The geographical limits of each region*

*The grape varieties that can be used*

*The percentage of each grape used*

*The maximum amount of wine that can be produced per acre*

*The minimum alcohol content of the wine*

*The aging requirements, such as how long a wine should spend in wood or bottle, for certain wines*

### A SELECTION OF DOCG WINES FROM OTHER REGIONS

Aglianico del Vulture Superiore
Aglianico de Taburno
Albana di Romagna
Amarone della Valpolicella
Bardolino Superiore
Castelli di Jesi Verdicchio Riserva
Cerasuolo di Vittoria
Cesanese del Piglio
Colli Asolani Prosecco
Colli Bolognesi Classico Pignoletto
Colli Euganei Fior d'Arancio
Colli Orientali del Friuli Picolit
Conegliano Valdobbiadene-Prosecco
Conero
Fiano di Avellino
Franciacorta
Frascati Superiore
Greco di Tufo
Lison
Montepulciano d'Abruzzo Colline
    Teramane
Oltrepo Pavese Metodo Classico
Piave Malanotte
Ramandolo
Recioto della Valpolicella
Recioto di Gambellara
Recioto di Soave
Sagrantino di Montefalco
Scanzo
Sforzato di Valtellina
Soave Superiore
Taurasi
Torgiano Riserva Montefalco
Valtellina Superiore
Verdicchio del Castelli di Jesi
    Classico Riserva
Verdicchio di Matelica Riserva
Vermentino di Gallura
Vernaccia di Serrapetrona

THERE ARE more than 300 DOC wines accounting for 20% of Italy's total wine production.

OF ALL Italian DOC wines, 60% are red. ONLY ONE-fifth of all Chianti is Chianti Classico Riserva.

| WINERIES | | ACRES |
|---|---|---|
| 964 | CHIANTI CLASSICO | 18,000 |
| 72 | VINO NOBILE DI MONTEPULCIANO | 2,982 |
| 208 | BRUNELLO DE MONTALCINO | 5,189 |

# TUSCANY—THE HOME OF CHIANTI

## What are the different levels of Chianti?

*Chianti:* The first level. Cost: $.
*Chianti Classico:* From the inner historic district of Chianti. Cost: $$.
*Chianti Classico Riserva:* From a Classico area, and must be aged for a minimum of two years, three months. Cost: $$$$.

## How should I buy Chianti?

First of all, find the style of Chianti you like best. There is a considerable variation in Chianti styles. Second, always buy from a shipper or producer whom you know—one with a good, reliable reputation.

Some quality Chianti producers are:

| | |
|---|---|
| ANTINORI | FONTODI |
| BADIA A COLTIBUONO | FRESCOBALDI |
| BROLIO | MELINI |
| CAPANNELLE | MONSANTO |
| CASTELLO BANFI | NOZZOLE |
| CASTELLO DI AMA | RICASOLI |
| CASTELLO DI BOSSI | RUFFINO |

## Which grapes are used in Chianti?

According to updated DOCG requirements, winemakers are required to use at least 80 percent Sangiovese to produce Chianti. The DOCG also encourages the use of other grapes by allowing an unprecedented 20 percent nontraditional grapes (Cabernet Sauvignon, Merlot, Syrah, etc.). These changes, along with better winemaking techniques and better vineyard development, have all contributed greatly to improving Chianti's image over the last twenty-five years. A separate DOCG has been established for Chianti Classico, and many producers of this wine now use 100 percent Sangiovese.

## Which other high-quality wines come from Tuscany?

Five of the greatest Tuscan red wines are Brunello di Montalcino, Vino Nobile di Montepulciano, Carmignano, Bolgheri, and Maremma. All of these wines are made with the Sangiovese grape. If you purchase the Brunello, keep in mind that it probably needs more aging (five to ten years) before it reaches peak drinkability. There are more than 150 producers of Brunello.

My favorite producers of Brunello di Montalcino are:

| | |
|---|---|
| ALTESINO | GAJA |
| BARBI | LA FUGA |
| CAPANNA | LA PODERINA |
| CAPARZO | LISINI |
| CARPINETO | MARCHESI DE FRESCOBALDI |
| CASTELGIOCONDO | POGGIO ANTICO |
| CASTELLO BANFI | POGGIO IL CASTELLARE |
| COL D'ORCIA | SOLDERA |
| CONSTANTI | UCCELLIERA |

Those of Vino Nobile di Montepulciano are:

| | |
|---|---|
| AVIGNONESI | ICARIO |
| BINDELLA | LA BRACCESCA |
| BOSCARELLI | POGGIO ALLA SALA |
| DEI | POLIZIANO |
| FASSATI | SALCHETO |
| FATTORIA DEL CERRO | |

For Carmignano, look for:

| | |
|---|---|
| ARTIMINO | VILLA CAPEZZANA |
| POGGIOLO | |

### BEST BETS FOR WINES FROM TUSCANY

1997** 1999** 2004** 2005* 2006** 2007** 2008*
2009 2010* 2011 2012

*Note: \* signifies exceptional vintage  \*\* signifies extraordinary vintage*

### BRUNELLO IS CHANGING

Beginning with the 1995 vintage, Brunellos are required to be aged in oak for a minimum of two years instead of the previous three. The result? A fruitier, more accessible wine.

BRUNELLO DI MONTALCINO, because of its limited supply, is sometimes very expensive. For one of the best values in Tuscan red wine, look for Rosso di Montalcino.

IN 2008 THE winemakers of Brunello voted to maintain 100% Sangiovese for their wines and not to blend with other grape varieties.

# PIEDMONT—THE BIG REDS

Some of the finest red wines in the world are produced in Piedmont. Two of the best DOCG wines to come from this region in northwest Italy are Barolo and Barbaresco.

The major grapes of Piedmont are:

**DOLCETTO    BARBERA    NEBBIOLO**

Barolo and Barbaresco, the "heavyweight" wines from Piedmont, are made from the Nebbiolo variety. These wines have the fullest style and a high alcohol content. Be careful when you try to match young vintages of these wines with your dinner; they may overpower the food.

My favorite producers of Piedmont wines are:

| | |
|---|---|
| **A. CONTERNO** | **LA SPINETTA** |
| **ANTONIO VALLANA** | **LUCIANO SANDRONE** |
| **BARBERA D'ASTI** | **MARCARINI** |
| **BARBERA DEL MONFERRATO SUPERIORE** | **MARCHESI DI BAROLO** |
| **B. GIACOSA** | **MARCHESI DI GRESY** |
| **CERETTO** | **M. CHIARLO** |
| **CONTERNO FANTINO** | **PAOLO SCAVINO BORGOGNO** |
| **DOLCETTO DI DIANO D'ALBA** | **PIO CESARE** |
| **DOLCETTO DI OVADA SUPERIORE** | **PRODUTTORI DEL BARBARESCO** |
| **DOMENICO CLERICO** | **PRUNOTTO** |
| **ERBALUCE DI CALUSO** | **RENATO RATTI** |
| **FONTANAFREDDA** | **ROBERTO VOERZIO** |
| **GAJA** | **RUCHE DI CASTAGNOLE MONFERRATO** |
| **GATTINARA** | **VIETTI** |
| **G. CONTERNO** | |

### BEST BETS FOR WINES FROM PIEDMONT

1990*    1996**    1997*    1999*    2000**    2001**    2004**
2005*    2006*    2007*    2008*    2009*    2010    2011    2012

*Note: * signifies exceptional vintage    ** signifies extraordinary vintage*

## BAROLO VERSUS BARBARESCO

| BAROLO<br>(MORE THAN 8 MILLION BOTTLES) | BARBARESCO<br>(NEARLY 3 MILLION BOTTLES) |
|---|---|
| Nebbiolo grape | Nebbiolo grape |
| Minimum 12.5% alcohol | Minimum 12.5% alcohol |
| More complex flavor, more body | Lighter; sometimes less body than Barolo, but fine and elegant |
| Must be aged at least three years (one in wood) | Requires two years of aging (one in wood) |
| "Riserva" = five years of aging | "Riserva" = four years of aging |

THE BIGGEST difference between the AOC of France and the DOC of Italy is that the DOC mandates aging requirements.

IN ONE of the biggest changes in the DOCG regulations, the wines of Barolo now have to be aged in wood for only one year, and the minimum alcohol has been changed to 12.5%. Before 1999, Barolo had a mandatory two years of wood aging and 13% minimum alcohol.

ANOTHER GREAT Piedmont wine is called Gattinara. Look for the Antoniolo Reservas.

THE PRODUCTION of Barolo and Barbaresco at 11 million bottles a year is equivalent to that of only a medium-size California winery!

*BRICCO* = hillside vineyard

**TOP THREE RED GRAPES OF PIEDMONT**

Barbera (41,000 acres)
Dolcetto (16,000 acres)
Nebbiolo (9,000 acres)

THE MOST planted white varietal is Moscato with 25,000 acres.

# VENETO—THE HOME OF AMARONE

This is one of Italy's largest wine-producing regions. Even if you don't recognize the name immediately, I'm sure you've had Veronese wines at one time or another, like Valpolicella, Bardolino, and Soave. All three are very consistent, easy to drink, and ready to be consumed whenever you buy them. They don't fit into the category of a Brunello di Montalcino or a Barolo, but they're very good table wines and they're within everyone's budget. The best and most improved of the three is Valpolicella. Look for Valpolicella Superiore made by the *ripasso* method.

*RIPASSO:* The adding back of grape skins from Amarone wine to Valpolicella, giving it extra alcohol and more flavor.

Easy-to-find Veneto producers are:

**ALLEGRINI**          **QUINTARELLI**
**ANSELMI**            **SANTA SOFIA**
**BOLLA**              **ZENATO**
**FOLONARI**

THE NAME "Amarone" derives from *amar*, meaning "bitter," and *one* (pronounced "oh-nay"), meaning "big."

*CLASSICO*: All the vineyards are in the historical part of the region.

*SUPERIORE*: Higher levels of alcohol and longer aging.

## What's Amarone?

Amarone is a type of Valpolicella wine made by a special process in the Veneto region. Only the ripest grapes (Corvina, Rondinella, and Molinara) from the top of each bunch are used. After picking, they're left to "raisinate" (dry and shrivel) on straw mats. Does this sound familiar to you? It should, because this is similar to the process used to make German Trockenbeerenauslese and French Sauternes. One difference is that with Amarone, the winemaker ferments most of the sugar, bringing the alcohol content to 14 to 16 percent.

My favorite producers of Amarone are:

**ALLEGRINI**          **QUINTARELLI**
**BERTANI**            **TEDESCHI**
**MASI**               **TOMMASI**
**NICOLIS**            **ZENATO**

### BEST BETS FOR AMARONE

1990*   1993   1995*   1996   1997*   1998   2000*   2001   2002*
2003*   2004   2005   2006   2008*   2009   2010

*Note: \* signifies exceptional vintage*

## HOW ITALIAN WINES ARE NAMED

*Winemaking regions have different ways of naming their wines. In California, you look for the grape variety on the label. In Bordeaux, most often you will see the name of a château. But in Italy, there are three different ways that wine is named: by grape variety, by village or district, or simply by a proprietary name. See the examples below.*

| GRAPE VARIETY | VILLAGE OR DISTRICT | PROPRIETARY |
|---|---|---|
| Barbera | Chianti | Tignanello |
| Nebbiolo | Barolo | Sassicaia |
| Pinot Grigio | Barbaresco | Ornellaia |
| Sangiovese | Montalcino | Summus |

## Forty years later in Italy

Forty years ago most Italian wine was made to be consumed in Italy, and not for the export market. To the Italians, wine was an everyday thing like salt and pepper on their table to enhance the taste of their food.

But since then, winemaking has become more of a business, and the Italian winemakers' philosophy has changed considerably from making casual-drinking wines to much better-made wines that are also much more marketable around the world. They've accomplished this by using modern technology, modern vinification procedures, and updated vineyard management as a basis for experimentation.

Another area of major experimentation is with nontraditional grape varieties such as Cabernet Sauvignon and Merlot. As a result, the biggest news in the whole wine industry over the last forty years is the change in Italian wines. When I talk about experimentation, you must remember that this isn't California we're talking about, but Italy, with thousands of years of traditions that are being changed. In Italy, the producers have had to unlearn and relearn winemaking techniques in order to make better wines for the export market.

The prices of Italian wines have also increased tremendously over the last twenty-five years—not good news for consumers. Some of the wines from Italy have become among the most expensive in the world. That's not to say they're not worth it, but the pricing situation isn't the same as it was forty years ago.

IN ITALY, vineyards aren't classified as they are in Bordeaux and Burgundy. There are neither Grands Crus nor Premiers Crus.

AN INTERESTING observation in Italy: bottled water and beer consumption are both increasing, while wine consumption is decreasing.

ONE OF the newest trends in Italy is single-vineyard labeling.

THE 800,000 hectares of vineyards in Italy are owned by more than one million growers.

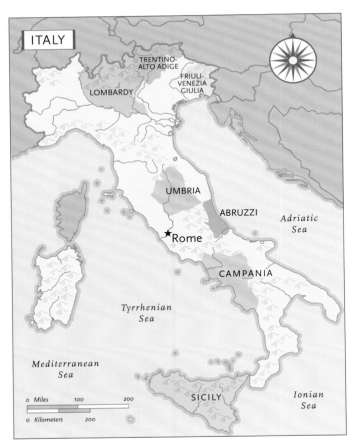

ITALY

TRENTINO-
ALTO ADIGE

LOMBARDY

FRIULI-
VENEZIA
GIULIA

UMBRIA

ABRUZZI   *Adriatic
Sea*

★Rome

CAMPANIA

*Tyrrhenian
Sea*

*Mediterranean
Sea*

o Miles    100      200

o Kilometers   200

SICILY   *Ionian
Sea*

IN THE last 10 years, Italians have become more weight- and health-conscious, so they're changing their eating habits. As a result, the leisurely four-hour lunch and siesta is a thing of the past. Yes, all good things must come to an end.

MY ITALIAN-WINE friends sometimes refer to Veneto as Tri-Veneto, which includes Trentino, Alto-Adige, and Friuli. Some of the best white wines of Italy come from those regions.

# A Quick Guide to Other Important Regions

I SOMETIMES WISH THAT it was possible for my book to cover every one of the world's wine regions, especially when it comes to a country like Italy. Of course, that would defeat the purpose of a "simple" guide to wine. But in Italy, where all twenty regions produce good to great wine, it is important that you have a quick look at the less well known regions along with a brief guide to the wines to look for.

### ABRUZZI
*Grapes:* Montepulciano
*Best Wine:* Montepulciano d'Abruzzo
*Favorite Producers:* Elio Monti, Emidio Pepe, La Valentina, Masciarelli

### FRIULI-VENEZIA GIULIA
*Grapes:* Pinot Bianco, Pinot Grigio, Chardonnay, Sauvignon Blanc
*Favorite Producers:* Bastianich, Jermann, Livio Felluga, Marco Felluga, Mario Schiopetto, Vie di Romans

### TRENTINO-ALTO ADIGE
*Grapes:* White—Pinot Bianco, Pinot Grigio, Chardonnay, Sauvignon, Gewürztraminer
Red—Cabernet Franc, Cabernet Sauvignon, Lagrein, Merlot
*Favorite Producers:* Alois Lageder, Cantina di Terlano, Colterenzio, Ferrari, Foradori, H. Lun, Rotaliano, Teroldego, Tiefenbrunner, Tramin

### LOMBARDY
*Grapes:* Nebbiolo, Trebbiano
*Wines:* Franciacorta (Sparkling), Lugana, Valtellina (Grumello, Sassella, Inferno, Valgella)
*Favorite Producers: Sparkling*—Bellavista, Ca' del Bosco
*Valtellina*—Conti Sertoli, Fay, Nino Negri, Rainoldi

### UMBRIA

**Grapes:** Trebbiano, Sagrantino, Sangiovese

**Wines:** Orvieto, Sagrantino di Montefalco, Torgiano Rosso Riserva

**Favorite Producers:** Arnaldo Caprai, Lungarotti, Paolo Bea

### CAMPANIA

**Grapes:** Aglianico, Fiano, Greco, Sangiovese

**Best Wines:** Greco di Tufo, Fiano di Avellino, Taurasi

**Favorite Producers:** Feudi di San Gregorio, Mastroberardino, Molettiera, Montevetrano, Mustilli, Villa Matilde

### SICILY

**Grapes: White**—Catarratto, Chardonnay, Grecanico, Inzolia, Malvasia, Moscato

**Red**—Cabernet Sauvignon, Merlot, Nero d'Avola (Calabrese), Syrah

**Best Wines:** Marsala, Moscato di Pantelleria, Nero d'Avola

**Favorite Producers:** De Bartoli, Duca di Salaparuta (Duca Enrico), Gulfi, Morgante, Palari, Planeta, Rapitalà, Regaleali (Rosso del Conte), Santa Anastasia

## Italian Whites

I am often asked why I don't teach a class on Italian white wines. The answer is quite simple. Take a look at the most popular white wines: Soave, Frascati, and Pinot Grigio, among others. Most of them retail for less than $15. The Italians traditionally do not put the same effort into making their white wines as they do their reds—in terms of style or complexity—and they are the first to admit it.

Plantings of international white varieties such as Chardonnay and Sauvignon Blanc, along with some of the better indigenous grapes, have recently elevated the quality of Italian white wines.

PINOT GRIGIO is a white-grape variety that is also found in Alsace, France, where it is called Pinot Gris. It is also grown with success in Oregon and California.

FOR GREAT Italian whites, try Gavi from Piedmont, and wines from the Friuli region.

**FOR FURTHER READING**

I recommend *The Simon & Schuster Pocket Guide to Italian Wines* and *Wine Atlas of Italy* by Burton Anderson, *Vino Italiano* by Joseph Bastianich and David Lynch, *Italian Wine* by Victor Hazan, and *Italian Wines for Dummies* by Mary Ewing Mulligan and Ed McCarthy.

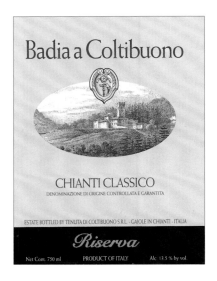

"Piedmontese wines show better with food than in a tasting."

—ANGELO GAJA

"When you're having Italian wines, you must not taste the wine alone. You must have them with food."

—GIUSEPPE COLLA of Prunotto

# WINE AND FOOD

*In Italy, the wine is made to go with the food. No meal is served without wine. Take it from the experts.*

*The following food-and-wine suggestions are based on what some of the Italian wine producers enjoy having with their wine. You don't have to take their word for it. Get yourself a bottle of wine, a tasty dish, and* mangia!

AMBROGIO FOLONARI *(Ruffino):* "Chianti with prosciutto, chicken, pasta, and of course pizza." *When it comes to a Chianti Classico Riserva, Dr. Folonari says,* "Pair it with a hearty prime-rib dinner or a steak."

EZIO RIVELLA *(Castello Banfi):* "A Chianti is good with all meat dishes, but I save the Brunello for 'stronger' dishes, such as steak, wild boar, pheasant, and other game, as well as Pecorino Toscano cheese."

ANGELO GAJA: "Barbaresco with meat and veal, and also with mature cheeses that are 'not too strong,' such as Emmenthaler and Fontina." *Mr. Gaja advises against Parmesan and goat cheese when you have a Barbaresco. And if you're having a Barolo, Mr. Gaja's favorite is roast lamb.*

GIUSEPPE COLLA *(Prunotto):* "I enjoy light-style Dolcetto with all first courses and all white meat—chicken and veal especially." *He prefers not to have Dolcetto with fish.* "The wine doesn't stand up well to spicy sauce, but it's great with tomato sauce and pasta."

RENATO RATTI: *Mr. Ratti once told me that both Barbera and Dolcetto are good with chicken and lighter foods. However, Barolo and Barbaresco need to be served with heavier dishes to match their own body. Mr. Ratti also suggests: a roast in its natural sauce or, better yet,* brasato al Barolo—*braised in Barolo; meat cooked with wine; pheasant, duck, wild rabbit; and cheeses. For a special dish, try* risotto al Barolo *(rice cooked with Barolo wine). And when serving wine with dessert, Mr. Ratti recommends* "strawberries or peaches with Dolcetto wine." *The dryness in the wine, contrasted with the natural sweetness of the fruit, makes for a taste sensation!*

LORENZA DE'MEDICI *(Badia a Coltibuono): Since Tuscan cooking is very simple, she recommends* "an assortment of simple foods." *She prefers herbs to heavy sauces. With young Chianti, she suggests* "roast chicken, squab, or pasta with meat sauce." *To complement an older Chianti, she recommends a wide pasta with meat braised in Chianti, pheasant or other game, wild boar, or roast beef.*

PIERO ANTINORI: "I enjoy Chianti with the grilled foods for which Tuscany is famous, especially its* bistecca alla Fiorentina *[steak]." He suggests poultry and even hamburgers as other tasty possibilities. With Chianti Classico Riserva, Mr. Antinori enjoys having the best of the vintages with wild boar and fine aged Parmesan cheese.* "The wine is a perfect match for roast beef, roast turkey, lamb, or veal."

# Class Seven:
# The Red Wines of Spain and Italy

I look forward to this tasting since many of my students know something about French or American wines but very little about Spanish or Italian wines. This is a class of discovery: finding new wine styles made from indigenous grapes such as Tempranillo, Nebbiolo, and Sangiovese.

## THE WINES

### Understanding Wines from Rioja

#### *Three wines compared*

1. Crianza
2. Reserva
3. Gran Reserva

### Understanding Wines from Italy

#### *Three wines compared, all from Tuscany*

4. Chianti Classico Riserva
5. Vino Nobile di Montelpulciano
6. Brunello di Montalcino

#### *Three wines compared, all from Piedmont*

7. Barbera
8. Barbaresco
9. Barolo

#### *One wine from Veneto, tasted alone*

10. Amarone

1.

8.

10.

*Please note that labels are suggestions for wineries and producers to look for. For more examples, see pages 181–183, 185, 187, 188, 189, 190, 192, 194, and 195.*

# Questions for Class Seven: The Wines of Spain and Italy

# Champagne, Sherry, and Port

CHAMPAGNE · MÉTHODE CHAMPENOISE · STYLES OF CHAMPAGNE ·

OPENING CHAMPAGNE · CHAMPAGNE GLASSES ·

SPARKLING WINE · SHERRY · PORT

VIDEO
http://bit.ly/ht4Nx6

PRONUNCIATIONS
http://bit.ly/AflXDB

CHAMPAGNE · SHERRY · PORT

Atlantic Ocean

Paris

CHAMPAGNE

FRANCE

Oporto

DOURO

Madrid

PORTUGAL

SPAIN

Mediterranean
Sea

Lisbon

0 Miles 100 200 300

0 Kilometers 300

SHERRY
DISTRICT

# Champagne, Sparkling Wines, and Fortified Wines

NOW WE'RE BEGINNING our last class—the last chapter on the wine itself. This is where the course ends—on a happy note, I might add. What better way to celebrate than with Champagne?

Why do I group together Champagne, Sherry, and Port? Because as diverse as these wines are, the way the consumer will buy them is through the reputation and reliability of the shipper. Since these are all blended wines, the shipper is responsible for all phases of the production—you concern yourself with the house style. In Champagne, for example, Moët & Chandon is a well-known house; in Port, the house of Sandeman; and in Sherry, the house of Pedro Domecq.

## CHAMPAGNE

### What's Champagne?

Everyone knows that Champagne is a sparkling bubbly that everyone drinks on New Year's Eve. It's more than that. Champagne is a region in France—the country's northernmost wine-making region, to be exact—and it's an hour and a half northeast of Paris.

Why do I stress its northern location? Because this affects the taste of the wines. In the Champagne region, the grapes are picked with higher acidity than in most other regions, which is one of the reasons for Champagne's distinct taste.

The Champagne region is divided into four main areas:

**VALLEY OF THE MARNE**      **CÔTE DES BLANCS**
**MOUNTAIN OF REIMS**        **CÔTE DES BAR**

Three grapes can be used to produce Champagne:

*Pinot Noir:* accounts for 38 percent of all grapes planted
*Pinot Meunier:* accounts for 35 percent of all grapes planted
*Chardonnay:* accounts for 27 percent of all grapes planted

In France, only sparkling wines that come from the region of Champagne may be called Champagne. Some American producers have borrowed the name "Champagne" to put on the label of their sparkling wines. These cannot and should not be compared with Champagne from France.

## What are the three major types of Champagne?

*Nonvintage/multiple vintage:* A blend of two or more harvests, 60 to 80 percent base wine from current harvest and 20 to 40 percent wine from previous vintages

*Vintage:* From a single vintage

*"Prestige" cuvée:* From a single vintage with longer aging requirements

## Why is there such a tremendous price difference between nonvintage and "prestige" cuvée Champagnes?

"Prestige" Champagnes usually meet the following requirements to be designated as such:

• Made from the best grapes of the highest-rated villages

• Made from the first pressing of the grapes

• Spent more time aging in the bottle than nonvintage Champagnes

• Made only in vintage years

• Made in small quantity, and the demand is high. Price is dictated largely by supply and demand.

THE CHAMPAGNE region has 43,680 acres of vineyards.

THERE ARE OVER 20,000 growers who sell mostly to the 250 *négociants* (shippers).

**THE NERVOUS SYSTEM OF WINE**

Acidity in Champagne not only gives freshness to the wines, but is also important to their longevity, and it stimulates the palate before lunch or dinner.

THE BALANCE of the fruit and acidity, together with the bubbles ($CO_2$), is what makes good Champagne.

NONVINTAGE Champagne is more typical of the house style than vintage Champagne.

VINTAGE CHAMPAGNE must contain 100% of that vintage year's harvest.

MORE THAN 80% of the Champagnes produced are not vintage dated. This means they are blends of several years' wines.

## Is every year a vintage year?

No, but more recently, 1995\*\*, 1996\*\*, 1998, 1999, 2000, 2002\*\*, 2004\*\*, 2005, and 2008 were (\* signifies exceptional vintage, \*\* signifies extraordinary vintage). Note: These were vintage years for most Champagne houses. "Vintage" in Champagne is different from other wine regions, because each house makes its own determination on whether or not to declare a vintage year.

## How is Champagne made?

Champagne is made by a process called *Méthode Champenoise*. When a similar method is used outside Champagne, it is called *Méthode Traditionnelle* or Classic Method or *Método Tradicional*, etc. The use of the expression *Méthode Champenoise* is not allowed in the European Union outside of Champagne.

# MÉTHODE CHAMPENOISE

*Harvest:* Harvest usually takes place in late September or early October.

*Pressing the grapes:* Only two pressings of the grapes are permitted. Prestige cuvée Champagnes are usually made exclusively from the first pressing. The second pressing, called the *taille,* is generally blended with the cuvée to make vintage and nonvintage Champagnes.

*Fermentation:* All Champagnes undergo a first fermentation when the grape juice is converted into wine. Remember the formula: Sugar + Yeast = Alcohol + $CO_2$. The carbon dioxide dissipates. The first fermentation takes two to three weeks and produces still wines.

*Blending:* The most important step in Champagne production is the blending of the still wines. Each of these still wines is made from a single grape variety from a single village of origin. The winemaker has to make many decisions here. Three of the most important ones are:

1. Which grapes to blend—how much Chardonnay, Pinot Noir, and Pinot Meunier?

2. From which vineyards should the grapes come?

3. Which years or vintages should be blended? Should the blend be made from only the wines of the harvest, or should several vintages be blended together?

**Liqueur de Tirage:** After the blending process, the winemaker adds Liqueur de Tirage (a blend of sugar and yeast), which will begin the wine's second fermentation. At this point, the wine is placed in its permanent bottle with a temporary bottle cap.

**Second Fermentation:** During this fermentation, the carbon dioxide stays in the bottle. This is where the bubbles come from. The second fermentation also leaves natural sediments in the bottle. Now the problems begin. How do you get rid of the sediments without losing the carbon dioxide? Go on to the next steps.

**Aging:** The amount of time the wine spends aging on its sediments is one of the most important factors in determining the quality of the wine.

**Riddling:** The wine bottles are now placed in A-frame racks, necks down. The *remueur*, or riddler, goes through the racks of Champagne bottles and gives each bottle a slight turn while gradually tipping the bottle further downward. After six to eight weeks, the bottle stands almost completely upside down, with the sediments resting in the neck of the bottle.

**Dégorgement:** The top of the bottle is dipped into a brine solution to freeze it, and then the temporary bottle cap is removed and out fly the frozen sediments, propelled by the carbon dioxide.

**Dosage:** A combination of wine and cane sugar is added to the bottle after dégorgement. At this point, the winemaker can determine whether he wants a sweeter or a drier Champagne.

**Recorking:** The wine is recorked with a real cork instead of a bottle cap.

## DOSAGE

*The dosage determines whether the wine will be dry, sweet, or any style in between. The following shows you the guidelines the winemaker uses when he adds the dosage.*

**Brut:** Dry

**Extra dry:** Semidry

**Sec:** Semisweet

**Demi-sec:** Sweet

---

COMMON CHAMPAGNE AROMAS:

Apple — Yeast (bread dough)

Toast — Hazelnuts/walnuts

Citrus

---

**WOMEN AND CHAMPAGNE**

Women, particularly ones attached to royal courts, deserve much of the credit for Champagne's international fame. Madame de Pompadour said that Champagne was the only drink that left a woman still beautiful after drinking it. Madame de Parabère once said that Champagne was the only wine to give brilliance to the eyes without flushing the face.

IT IS RUMORED that Marilyn Monroe once took a bath in 350 bottles of Champagne. Her biographer George Barris said that she drank and breathed Champagne "as if it were oxygen."

WHEN A London reporter asked Madame Lilly Bollinger when she drank Champagne, Madame Bollinger replied: "I drink it when I'm happy and when I'm sad. Sometimes I drink it when I'm alone. When I have company I consider it obligatory. I trifle with it if I'm not hungry and drink it when I am. Otherwise I never touch it—unless I'm thirsty."

"R.D." ON a Champagne wine label means that the wine was recently disgorged (dégorgement).

UNTIL AROUND 1850, all Champagne was sweet.

OCCASIONALLY A Champagne will be labeled "extra brut," which is drier still than brut.

BRUT AND EXTRA DRY are the wines to serve as apéritifs, or throughout the meal. Sec and demi-sec are the wines to serve with desserts and wedding cake!

## What accounts for the different styles of Champagne?

Going back to the three grapes we talked about that are used to make Champagne, the general rule is: The more white grapes in the blend, the lighter the style of the Champagne. And the more red grapes in the blend, the fuller the style of the Champagne.

Also, some producers ferment their wines in wood. Bollinger ferments some, and Krug ferments all its wines this way. This gives the Champagne fuller body and bouquet than those fermented in stainless steel.

## How do I buy a good Champagne?

First, determine the style you prefer, whether full-bodied or light-bodied, a dry brut or a sweet demi-sec. Then make sure you buy your Champagne from a reliable shipper/producer. Each producer takes pride in its distinctive house style and strives for a consistent blend, year after year. The following are some brands in national distribution to look for. While it is difficult to be precise, the designations generally conform to the style of the houses.

LIGHT, DELICATE

A. Charbaut et Fils
Jacquesson
Lanson

LIGHT TO MEDIUM

Billecart-Salmon
Deutz
G. H. Mumm
Laurent-Perrier
Nicolas Feuillatte
Perrier-Jouët
Pommery
Ruinart Père & Fils
Taittinger

MEDIUM

Charles Heidsieck
Moët & Chandon
Piper-Heidsieck
Pol Roger
Salon

MEDIUM TO FULL

Henriot
Louis Roederer

FULL, RICH

A. Gratien
Bollinger
Krug
Veuve Clicquot

## When is Champagne ready to drink?

As soon as you buy it. Champagne is something you can drink right away. Nonvintage Champagnes are meant to be drunk within two to three years, and vintage and prestige cuvée Champagnes can be kept longer, about ten to fifteen years. So if you're still saving that Dom Pérignon that you received for your tenth wedding anniversary fifteen years ago, don't wait any longer. Open it!

## What's the correct way to open a bottle of Champagne?

Before we sip Champagne in class, I always take a few moments to show everyone how to open a bottle of Champagne properly. I do this for a good reason. Opening a bottle of Champagne can be dangerous, and I'm not kidding. If you know the pounds per square inch that are under pressure in the bottle, you know what I'm talking about.

### OPENING CHAMPAGNE CORRECTLY

1. It is especially important that the bottle be well chilled before you open it.

2. Cut the foil around the top of the bottle.

3. Place your hand on top of the cork, never removing your hand until the cork is pulled out completely. (I know this may seem a bit awkward, but it's very important.)

4. Undo the wire. Either leave it on the cork or take it off carefully.

5. Carefully put a cloth napkin over the top of the cork; if the cork pops, it will go safely into the napkin.

6. Remove the cork gently, slowly turning the bottle in one direction and the cork in another. The idea behind opening a bottle is to ease the cork out gently rather than cracking the bottle open with a loud pop and letting it foam. That may be a lot of fun, but it does nothing for the Champagne. When you pop off the cork, you allow the carbon dioxide to escape. That carbon dioxide is what gives Champagne its sparkle. If you open a bottle of Champagne in the way I've just described, it can be opened hours before your guests arrive with no loss of carbon dioxide.

IN 2010, DIVERS found around 150 champagne bottles in an almost two-hundred-year-old shipwreck. Among the bottles (believed to be the oldest in the world) were Veuve Clicquot, Juglar (now Jaquesson), and Hiedsieck. Some of the bottles were still drinkable!

*"It's not a Burgundy; it's not a Bordeaux; it's a white wine; it's a sparkling wine that should be kept no longer than two to three years. It should be consumed young."*
—CLAUDE TAITTINGER

**THE TOP FIVE CHAMPAGNE HOUSES IN SHIPMENTS TO THE UNITED STATES IN 2011**

1. Moët & Chandon
2. Veuve Clicquot
3. Perrier-Jouët
4. Piper Heidsieck
5. Nicolas Feuillatte

CHAMPAGNE HOUSES market about two-thirds of Champagne's wines, but they own less than 10% of the vineyards.

THE PRESSURE in a bottle of Champagne is close to 90 pounds per square inch (or "six atmospheres," or roughly three times the pressure in an automobile tire). Champagne is put into heavy bottles to hold the pressurized wine. This is another reason why Champagne is more expensive than ordinary wine.

**MILLENNIUM MADNESS**

In 1999, a record 327 million bottles of Champagne were sold.

AS BEAUTIFUL as Helen was, the resulting glass was admittedly wide and shallow.

TO EVALUATE Champagne, look at the bubbles. The better wines have smaller bubbles and more of them. Also, with a good Champagne, the bubbles last longer. Bubbles are an integral part of the wines of Champagne. They create texture and mouthfeel.

HOW MANY bubbles are in a bottle of Champagne? According to scientist Bill Lembeck, 49 million per bottle!

**CHAMPAGNE BOTTLE SIZES**

| | |
|---|---|
| Magnum | 2 bottles |
| Jeroboam | 4 bottles |
| Rehoboam | 6 bottles |
| Methuselah | 8 bottles |
| Salmanazar | 12 bottles |
| Balthazar | 16 bottles |
| Nebuchadnezzar | 20 bottles |

**GOING GREEN**

New Champagne bottles have been designed to be lighter by 7% and more environmentally friendly. Two big changes: the bottles will be slimmer and the punt at the bottom will be deeper and wider.

## Which glasses should Champagne be served in?

No matter which Champagne you decide to serve, you should serve it in the proper glass. There's a little story behind the Champagne glass, dating back to Greek mythology. The first *coupe,* a footed glass with a shallow cup that widens toward the rim, was said to be molded from the breast of Helen of Troy. The Greeks believed that wine drinking was a sensual experience, and it was only fitting that the most beautiful woman take part in shaping the chalice.

Centuries later, Marie Antoinette, Queen of France, decided it was time to create a new Champagne glass. She had coupes molded to her own breasts, which changed the shape of the glass entirely, since Marie Antoinette was, shall we say, a bit more well endowed than Helen of Troy.

The glasses shown to the left are the ones commonly used today—the flute and the tulip-shaped glass. Champagne does not lose its bubbles as

## WINE AND FOOD

*Champagne is one of the most versatile wines that you can drink with a number of foods, from apéritif to dessert. Here are some Champagne-and-food combinations that experts suggest:*

CLAUDE TAITTINGER: *Mr. Taittinger's general rule is: "Never with sweets." Instead, he suggests "a Comtes de Champagne Blanc de Blancs drunk with seafood, caviar, or pâté of pheasant." Another note from Mr. Taittinger: he doesn't serve Champagne with cheese because, he says, "The bubbles do not go well." He prefers red wine with cheese.*

CHRISTIAN POL ROGER: *With brut nonvintage: light hors d'oeuvres, mousse of pike. With vintage: pheasant, lobster, other seafood. With rosé: a strawberry dessert.*

quickly in these glasses as it did in the old-fashioned model, and these shapes also enhance the smell and aromas of the wine in the glass.

## What's the difference between Champagne and sparkling wine?

As I've already mentioned, Champagne is the wine that comes from the Champagne region of France. In my opinion, it is the best sparkling wine in the world, because the region has the ideal combination of elements conducive to excellent sparkling winemaking. The soil is fine chalk, the grapes are the best grown anywhere for sparkling wine, and the location is perfect. This combination of soil, climate, and grapes is reflected in the wine.

Sparkling wine, on the other hand, is produced in many areas, and the quality varies from wine to wine. The Spanish produce the popular Codorníu and Freixenet—both excellent values and good sparkling wines, known as *cavas*. The German version is called *Sekt*. Italy has *Spumante*, which means "sparkling" and, from Veneto, the fast-growing Prosecco.

New York State and California are the two main producers of sparkling wine in this country. New York is known for Great Western, Taylor, and Gold Seal. California produces many fine sparkling wines, such as Domaine Chandon, Korbel, Piper-Sonoma, Schramsberg, Mumm Cuvée Napa, Roederer Estate, Domaine Carneros, Iron Horse, Scharffenberger, and "J," by Jordan Winery. Many of the larger California wineries also market their own sparkling wines.

DOMAINE CHANDON is owned by the Moët-Hennessy Group, which is responsible for the production of Dom Pérignon in France. In fact, the same winemaker is flown into California to help make the blend for the Domaine Chandon.

ABOUT 20% OF the sparkling wines made in the United States are made by *Méthode Champenoise*.

PROSECCO SALES went up 35% in the U.S. in the last 3 years.

PROSECCO WAS originally the name of the grape and, in 2008, Prosecco became the name of the region. The best Prosecco is designated DOCG. The style is medium weight, aromatic, fresh, fruit, and a "welcome wine." It has high acidity, elegance, balance, and low alcohol (11.5–12%).

PIPER-HEIDSIECK has sold the Piper-Sonoma and its vineyards to Jordan Winery. Jordan now produces the wines for Piper-Sonoma.

## Is there a difference between the way Champagne and sparkling wines are made?

Sometimes. All authentic Champagnes and many fine sparkling wines are produced by *Méthode Champenoise,* described earlier in this chapter, and which, as you now know, is laborious, intensive, and very expensive. If you see a bottle of sparkling wine for $8.99, you can bet that the wine was not made by this process. The inexpensive sparkling wines are made by other methods. For example, in one method the secondary fermentation takes place in large tanks. Sometimes these tanks are big enough to produce 100,000 bottles of sparkling wine.

# SHERRY

The two greatest fortified wines in the world are Port and Sherry. These wines have much in common, although the end result is two very different styles.

## What exactly is fortified wine?

Fortified wine is made when a neutral grape brandy is added to wine to raise the wine's alcohol content. What sets Port apart from Sherry is when the winemaker adds the neutral brandy. It's added to Port during fermentation. The extra alcohol kills that yeast and stops the fermentation, which is why Port is relatively sweet. For Sherry, on the other hand, the brandy is added after fermentation.

## Where is Sherry made?

Sherry is produced in sunny southwestern Spain, in Andalusia. An area within three towns makes up the Sherry triangle. They are:

**JEREZ DE LA FRONTERA**

**PUERTO DE SANTA MARÍA**

**SANLÚCAR DE BARRAMEDA**

## Which grapes are used to make Sherry?

There are two main varieties:

*Palomino:* this shouldn't be too difficult for horse lovers to remember
*Pedro Ximénez:* named after Peter Siemons, who brought the grape from Germany to Sherry

## What are the different types of Sherry?

*Manzanilla:* dry
*Fino:* dry
*Amontillado:* dry to medium-dry
*Oloroso:* dry to medium-dry
*Cream:* sweet

ANOTHER FORTIFIED wine is Madeira. Although it is not as popular as it once was, Madeira wine was probably the first wine imported into America. It was favored by the colonists, including George Washington, and was served to toast the Declaration of Independence.

TWO OTHER famous fortified wines are Marsala (from Italy) and Vermouth (from Italy and France).

THE NEUTRAL grape brandy, when added to the wine, raises the alcohol content to 15% to 20%.

FOR YOU HISTORIANS, Puerto de Santa María is where Christopher Columbus's ships were built and where all the arrangements were made with Queen Isabella for his journey of discovery.

THE PALOMINO grape accounts for 90% of the planted vineyards in Sherry.

## What are the unique processes that characterize Sherry production?

Controlled oxidation and fractional blending. Normally a winemaker guards against letting any air into the wine during the winemaking process. But that's exactly what makes Sherry—the air that oxidizes the wine. The winemaker places the wine in barrels and stores it in a bodega.

## What's a bodega?

In Sherry, a "bodega" is an aboveground structure used to store wine. Why do you think winemakers would want to store the wine above ground? For the air. Sherry is an oxidized wine. They fill the barrels approximately two-thirds full, instead of all the way, and they leave the bung (cork) loosely in the barrel to let the air in.

### THE ANGEL'S SHARE

*When Sherry is made, winemakers let air into the barrels, and some wine evaporates in the process. Each year they lose a minimum of 3 percent of their Sherry to the angels, which translates into thousands of bottles lost through evaporation!*

*Why do you think the people of Sherry are so happy all the time? Besides the excellent sunshine they have, the people breathe in oxygen and Sherry.*

*So much for controlled oxidation. Now for fractional blending. Fractional blending is carried out through the Solera System.*

## What's the Solera System?

The Solera System is an aging and maturing process that takes place through the dynamic and continuous blending of several vintages of Sherry that are stored in rows of barrels. At bottling time, wine is drawn out of these barrels— never more than one-third the content of the barrel—to make room for the new vintage. The purpose of this type of blending is to maintain the "house" style of the Sherry by using the "mother" wine as a base and refreshing it with a portion of the younger wines.

HERE'S ANOTHER abbreviation for you— PX. Do you remember TBA, QbA, AOC, and DOC? If you want to know Sherry, you may have to say "PX," which stands for the Pedro Ximénez grape.

PX IS USED to make Cream Sherry, like Harveys Bristol Cream, among others. Cream Sherry is a blend of PX and Oloroso.

I'M SURE you're familiar with these four top-selling Sherries: Harvey's Bristol Cream, Dry Sack, Tio Pepe, and La Ina.

SHERRY ACCOUNTS for less than 3% of Spanish wine production.

IN TODAY'S Sherry, only American oak is used to age the wine.

SOME SOLERAS can be a blend of 10 to 20 different harvests.

TO CLARIFY the Sherry and rid it of all sediment, beaten egg whites are added to the wine. The sediment attaches itself to the egg whites and drops to the bottom of the barrel. The question always comes up: "What do they do with the yolks?" Did you ever hear of flan? That's the pudding-like dessert made from all the yolks. In Sherry country, this dessert is called *tocino de cielo*, which translated means "the fat of the angels."

OF THE SHERRY consumed in Spain, 90% is Fino and Manzanilla. As one winemaker said, "We ship the sweet and drink the dry."

## How do I buy Sherry?

Your best guide is the producer. It's the producer, after all, who buys the grapes and does the blending. Ten producers account for 60 percent of the export market. The top Sherry producers are:

| | |
|---|---|
| **CROFT** | **OSBORNE** |
| **EMILIO LUSTAU** | **PEDRO DOMECQ** |
| **GONZÁLEZ BYASS** | **SANDEMAN** |
| **HARVEYS** | **SAVORY AND JAMES** |
| **HIDALGO** | **WILLIAMS & HUMBERT** |

## How long does a bottle of Sherry last once it's been opened?

Sherry will last longer than a regular table wine because of its higher alcoholic content, which acts as a preservative. But once Sherry is opened, it will begin to lose its freshness. To drink Sherry at its best, you should consume the bottle within two weeks of opening it and keep the opened bottle refrigerated. Manzanilla and Fino Sherry should be treated as white wines and consumed within a day or two.

**FOR FURTHER READING**

I recommend *Sherry* by Julian Jeffs.

### WINE AND FOOD

MAURICIO GONZÁLEZ: *He believes that Fino should always be served well chilled. He enjoys having Fino as an apéritif with Spanish tapas (hors d'oeuvres), but he also likes to complement practically any fish meal with the wine. Some of his suggestions: clams, shellfish, lobster, prawns, langoustines, fish soup, or a light fish such as salmon.*

JOSÉ IGNACIO DOMECQ: *He suggests that very old and rare Sherry should be served with cheese. Fino and Manzanilla can be served as an apéritif or with light grilled or fried fish, or even smoked salmon. "You get the taste of the smoke better than if you have it with a white wine." Amontillado is not to be consumed like a Fino. It should be served with light cheese, chorizo (sausage), ham, or shish kebab. It is a perfect complement to turtle soup or a consommé. According to Mr. Domecq, dry Oloroso is known as a sporty drink in Spain—something to drink before hunting, riding, or sailing on a chilly morning. With Cream Sherry, Mr. Domecq recommends cookies, pastries, and cakes. Pedro Ximénez, however, is better as a topping for vanilla ice cream or a dessert wine before coffee and brandy.*

# PORT

Port comes from the Douro region in northern Portugal. In fact, in recent years, to avoid the misuse of the name "Port" in other countries, the true Port wine from Portugal has been renamed "Porto" (for the name of Oporto, the port city from which it's shipped).

Just a reminder: neutral grape brandy is added to Port during fermentation, which stops the fermentation and leaves behind up to 9 to 11 percent residual sugar. This is why Port is on the sweet side.

## What are the two types of Port?

**Cask-aged Port:** This includes *Ruby Port*, which is dark and fruity, blended from young nonvintage wines (cost: $); *Tawny Port*, which is lighter and more delicate, blended from many vintages (cost: $$); *Aged Tawny*, which is aged in casks—sometimes up to forty years and longer (cost: $$–$$$); and *Colheita*, which is from a single vintage but wood-aged a minimum of seven years (cost: $$–$$$$).

**Bottle-aged Port:** These wines include *Late Bottled Vintage (LBV)*, which is made from a single vintage, bottled four to six years after the harvest, and similar in style to vintage Port, but lighter, ready to drink on release, with no decanting needed (cost: $$$); *Vintage Character*, which is similar in style to LBV, but is made from a blend of vintages from the better years (cost: $$); *Quinta*, which is from a single vineyard (cost: $$$/$$$$); and *Vintage Port*, which is aged two years in wood and will mature in the bottle over time (cost: $$$$).

PORT WINE has been shipped to England since the 1670s. During the 1800s, to help preserve the Port for the long trip, shippers fortified it with brandy, resulting in Port as we know it today.

PORT IS usually 20% alcohol. Sherry, by comparison, is usually around 18%.

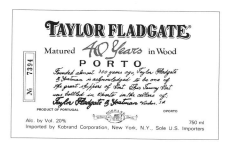

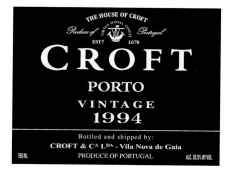

IN A TYPICAL YEAR, 60% of the Port is Tawny and Ruby; 30% is Vintage Character; 7% is Aged Tawny; and 3% is Vintage Port.

## WOOD PORT VERSUS VINTAGE PORT

*The biggest difference between cask-aged Port (such as Ruby and Tawny) and bottle-aged Port is this: the cask-aged Port is ready to drink as soon as it is bottled and it will not improve with age. Bottle-aged Port, on the other hand, gets better as it matures in the bottle. A great Vintage Port will be ready to drink fifteen to thirty years after the vintage date, depending upon the quality of the vintage.*

THE FIRST Vintage Port was recorded in 1765.

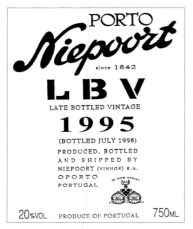

THE BRITISH are known to be Port lovers. Traditionally, upon the birth of a child, parents buy bottles of Port to put away for the baby until its 21st birthday, not only the age of maturity of a child, but also that of a fine Port.

*"The 1994 vintage is the greatest for Port since the legendary 1945."*
—JAMES SUCKLING, Vintage Port

## How do I buy Port?

Once again, as with Sherry, Port's grape variety should not dictate your choice. Find the style and the blend you prefer, but even more important, look for the most reliable producers. Of the Port available in the United States, the most important producers are:

| | |
|---|---|
| A. A. FERREIRA | NIEPOORT & CO., LTD. |
| C. DA SILVA | QUINTA DO NOVAL |
| CHURCHILL | QUINTO DO VESUVIO |
| COCKBURN | RAMOS PINTO |
| CROFT | ROBERTSON'S |
| DOW | SANDEMAN |
| FONSECA | TAYLOR FLADGATE |
| HARVEYS OF BRISTOL | W. & J. GRAHAM |
| | WARRE'S & CO. |

## Should vintage Port be decanted?

Yes, because you are likely to find sediment in the bottle. By making it a practice to decant vintage Port, your enjoyment of it will be enhanced.

## How long will Port last once it's been opened?

Port has a tendency to last longer than ordinary table wine because of its higher alcohol content. But if you want to drink Port at its prime, drink the contents of the open bottle within one week.

## Is every year a vintage year for Port?

No, it varies from shipper to shipper. And in some years, no vintage Port is made at all. For example, in 1994, 1997, 2000, and 2003, four of the recent vintages for Port, most producers declared a vintage. On the other hand, in 1990 and 1993, Port, in general, was not considered vintage quality.

### BEST BETS FOR VINTAGES OF PORT

1963\*  1970\*\*  1977\*  1983\*  1985  1991\*  1992  1994\*\*
1997\*  2000\*  2003\*  2004  2005  2007\*  2008  2009\*  2010

*Note: \* signifies exceptional vintage   \*\* signifies extraordinary vintage*

**FOR FURTHER READING**

I recommend *The Port Companion* by Godfrey Spence and *Vintage Port: The Wine Spectator's Ultimate Guide* by James Suckling.

# Class Eight:
# Final Exam Champagne and Port

This is our eighth and last class. It's your graduation class and there's no better way to celebrate than by beginning with Champagne and ending with Port. Enjoy tasting your way through the sparkling wines of Spain and the United States before moving on to French Champagnes. End the tasting by comparing the three different quality levels of Port: Ruby, Tawny, and, finally, Vintage Port.

## THE WINES

### Understanding Champagnes and Sparkling Wines

**One wine, tasted alone**

    1. Cava Brut (Spain)

*Two wines compared*

    2. Sparkling wine from Anderson Valley
    3. Sparkling wine from Napa Valley

*Three wines compared (blind tastings)*

    4. French Champagne
    5. French Champagne
    6. Sparkling wine from Italy, the U.S., or Spain

### Understanding Port

*Three Port wines compared*

    7. Ruby Port
    8. Tawny Port: 10 Years Old
    9. Vintage Port

4.

5.

7.

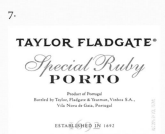

8.

*Please note that labels are suggestions for wineries and producers to look for. For more examples, see pages 206 and 214.*

# Questions for Class Eight: Champagne, Sherry, and Port

# Austria, Hungary, Greece, Australia, New Zealand, South Africa, Canada, Chile, and Argentina

PRONUNCIATION
http://bit.ly/voqk73

AUSTRIA PRODUCES 70% white wine.

VIENNA, ONE of the world's most beautiful cities, is also classified as an Austrian wine region and is the only major city in the world to be named a wine region.

SIXTY PERCENT of all Austrian wines are produced in Lower Austria.

**VIENNA DAY TRIP**

Visit the village of Klosterneuburg on the Danube River to see a monastery that dates from A.D. 1114. While you are in Klosterneuburg, be sure to taste the Grüner Veltliner of Donauland. The oldest school of enology by the same name, formed in 1860, is also worth a visit.

# The Wines of Austria

WHILE AUSTRIAN GRAPE GROWING and winemaking date back to the fourth century B.C., it is only in the past twenty-five years that Austria has been recognized for producing quality wines. Today, Austria produces some of the most elegant and best-tasting white wines—both dry and sweet—in Europe. The Grüner Veltliner and Riesling grapes produce wines that are perfect with food and are one reason for the recent success of Austrian wines in the United States. Both chefs and sommeliers agree that these wines work well with nearly any dish on their menus, from fish and poultry to most meat dishes. And Austrian wines hold their own when paired with Asian spices, too.

## What are the wine regions of Austria?

Austria contains four wine regions: Lower Austria (Niederösterreich), Vienna (Wien), Burgenland, and Styria (Steiermark), all located along Austria's eastern borders. The northern wine regions, which include Lower Austria and Vienna, are defined by the Danube River and the fertile valley that surrounds it.

The two most important regions and their wine districts are:

**LOWER AUSTRIA (WHITE WINES):** Wachau, Kamptal, Kremstal, Donauland
**BURGENLAND (RED AND DESSERT WINES):** Neusiedlersee, Mittelburgenland, Neusiedlersee-Hügelland

## What are the major grapes grown in Austria?

The main white varieties are:

**GRÜNER VELTLINER**   **SAUVIGNON BLANC**
**RIESLING**   **CHARDONNAY**

The main red varieties are:

**BLAUFRÄNKISCH**   **PINOT NOIR**
**ST. LAURENT**

## What are the Wine Laws of Austria?

Austria follows largely the same criteria used in other European countries, specifically Germany, with regard to wine labeling, but maintains stricter control. Base quality levels are determined by the ripeness of the grapes and the sugar content of the fermenting grape juice or must.

The three major quality levels are:

**TAFELWEIN**    **QUALITÄTSWEIN**    **PRÄDIKATSWEIN**

The Austrian wine board tastes and performs a chemical analysis on Qualitätswein and higher levels of wine, giving consumers a guarantee of taste, style, and quality. If a wine lists a specific grape it must contain at least 85 percent of that grape. If a wine has a vintage on the label it must contain a minimum of 85 percent of that vintage. If a wine region is listed, all of the wine (100 percent) must come from that region.

## What is the style of Austrian wines?

As with the wines of Germany, Austria's neighbor to the north, most Austrian wines are white. But unlike German wines, most of Austria's wines are dry, with higher alcohol and more body, resembling the wines of Alsace. Gradation of ripeness is the amount of residual sugar left in the wine after fermentation. It ranges in Austria from the very dry Trocken to the very sweet Trockenbeerenauslese.

GRÜNER VELTLINER accounts for more than one-third of Austrian grape plantings.

IN STYRIA Chardonnay is called Morillon.

**THE BEST OF TWO**

The Zweigelt grape is a cross between Blaufränkisch and St. Laurent.

ANOTHER NAME for Blaufränkisch is Lemberger.

TRY BLAUFRÄNKISCH blended with Cabernet Sauvignon.

TWO-THIRDS of Austrian wine is Qualitätswein.

**ONLY IN THE WACHAU REGION**

**Steinfeder:** maximum alcohol 10.7%
**Federspiel:** maximum alcohol 11.9%
**Smaragd:** minimum alcohol 11.3%

## AUSBRUCH

One of the great dessert wines of the world is Ausbruch, which comes from the village of Rust in Burgenland and has a history that goes back as far as 1617. On a par with a great French Sauternes, German Beeren-auslese, and Hungarian Tokaji, it is made with botrytized grapes and, as with Tokaji, Furmint is its predominate grape variety.

## THE WINEGLASS

Even if you haven't yet tasted one of Austria's great white wines, you probably have used a wineglass produced in Austria by Riedel. In the 1960s the Riedel family's glassworks, one of the most famous in the world, began creating wineglasses specifically shaped to enhance the aroma, bouquet, and taste of individual grape varieties. They also own another top wineglass producer, Spiegelau.

SMARAGD: a term found on wine labels in the Wachau area made from the highest quality grapes and vinified dry.

## Gradations of Ripeness

| DRY | SWEET TO VERY SWEET |
|---|---|
| Trocken | Tafelwein |
| Halbtrocken | Landwein |
| Lieblich | Qualitätswein |
| | Kabinett |
| | Prädikatswein |
| | Spätlese |
| | Auslese |
| | Eiswein |
| | Beerenauslese |
| | Ausbruch |
| | Trockenbeerenauslese |

## Kevin Zraly's Favorite Austrian Wine Producers

| | |
|---|---|
| ALZINGER | KRACHER |
| BRÜNDLMAYER | NIGL |
| F. X. PICHLER | RUDY PICHLER |
| HIRSCH | PRAGER |
| HIRTZBERGER | SCHLOSS GOBELSBURG |
| KNOLL | |

### BEST BETS FOR AUSTRIAN WINES

2006** 2007* 2008** 2009* 2010*

Note: * signifies exceptional vintage ** signifies extraordinary vintage

## FOR FURTHER READING

*The Wines of Austria* by Philipp Blom and *The Ultimate Austrian Wine Guide* by Peter Moser.

# The Wines of Hungary

HUNGARY'S WINE INDUSTRY has thrived culturally and economically for nearly 1,000 years and can be traced back as far as the Roman Empire. Tokaji, its most famous and revered wine, has been produced continuously since the sixteenth century. The reputation of Hungarian wine suffered a major decline from 1949 to 1989 under Communist rule, during which time wine production, controlled by a state monopoly, shifted to bulk wine with little regard to maintaining or improving existing quality wines.

Since the end of Communism in 1989, Hungary's emphasis has shifted back to quality wines, an effort partially funded by capital from Italian, French, and German winemakers. Today, modern winemaking equipment; new vineyard techniques; and the introduction of Sauvignon Blanc, Chardonnay, and Pinot Gris grapes have helped rebuild Hungary's nearly devastated quality wine industry. The famous vineyards of Tokaj were the first to receive attention, but investment has expanded throughout Hungary, which is once again producing some excellent wines.

## What are the major grapes of Hungary?

|  | NATIVE TO HUNGARY | INTERNATIONAL |
|---|---|---|
| **White** | Furmint | Sauvignon Blanc |
|  | Hárslevelü | Chardonnay |
|  | Olaszrizling | Pinot Gris  (Szürkebarát) |
| **Red** | Kadarka | Cabernet Sauvignon |
|  | Kékfrankos | Merlot |
|  | Portugieser | Pinot Noir |

A GRAPE BY ANY OTHER NAME...

The Hungarian language can be difficult for anyone, especially after a glass of wine! Here is a list to help you understand the style of the wine behind the name.

| *Hungarian name* | *AKA* |
|---|---|
| Tramini | Gewürztraminer |
| Szürkebarát | Pinot Gris |
| Zöld Veltlini | Grüner Veltliner |
| Kékfrankos | Blaufränkisch |

## What are the major wine regions of Hungary?

There are twenty-two wine regions in Hungary, seven of which I think you should know. The seven regions, including Tokaj, the most famous and prestigious, along with their most important grapes, are:

**BADACSONY (OLASZRIZLING)**

**EGER (KÉKFRANKOS, PINOT NOIR)**

**SOMOLÓ (FURMINT)**

**SOPRON (KÉKFRANKOS)**

**SZEKSZÁRD (KADARKA, MERLOT, CABERNET SAUVIGNON)**

**TOKAJ (FURMINT, HÁRSLEVELÜ)**

**VILLÁNY-SIKLÓS (CABERNET SAUVIGNON, KÉKFRANKOS)**

**WHAT'S THE CORRECT SPELLING?**

Tokay: English version for Tokaji
Tokaj: The name of the village
Tokaji: From the region

THE LARGEST lake in Europe, Lake Balaton, is located in Hungary near Badacsony.

BOTRYTIS CINEREA, also called noble rot, is a special mold that punctures the skin of a grape allowing water to dissipate, which leaves a higher than normal concentration of sugar and acid.

## Tokaji Aszú: "The Wine of Kings and King of Wines"

My first taste of the Hungarian sweet wine Tokaji Aszú is one of my fondest wine memories. I was mesmerized by its smell and taste and determined to find out how this "liquid gold" was made.

Tokaji Aszú comes from Tokaj, which is located in Hungary's northeastern corner and is one of the oldest wine regions in the world. *Tokaji* means "from the region of Tokaj (the village)" and *Aszú* refers to the dried, shriveled, and botrytized grapes used in its making. Tokaji Aszú is one of the world's greatest sweet wines and is on a par with French Sauternes and German Trockenbeerenauslese.

Tokaji Aszú is usually a blend of four grapes native to Hungary, with the primary grape used Furmint. Throughout the fall harvest season, the grapes affected by the *Botrytis cinerea* mold—or aszú—are picked from the bunch, lightly crushed, and made into an aszú paste. The unaffected grapes are harvested and fermented into a base wine. The aszú paste is collected in baskets called *puttonyos*, then blended into the base wine according to the desired sweetness. Sweetness is measured in puttonyos, or number of baskets of aszú paste added to the base wine, and you will see the word "Puttonyos" on the label of all Tokaji Aszú. The more *Botrytis*-affected grapes (paste) that are added to the base wine, the sweeter the wine. There are four levels of Puttonyos wine:

**3 PUTTONYOS:** 60 grams of sugar per liter
**4 PUTTONYOS:** 90 grams of sugar per liter
**5 PUTTONYOS:** 120 grams of sugar per liter
**6 PUTTONYOS:** 150 grams of sugar per liter

The sweetest of the Tokaj wines are called "Essencia" (or sometimes "Eszencia"). The Tokaji "Aszú Essencia" contains 180 grams of sugar. Tokaji Essencia can have over 800 grams per liter of sugar. It is one of the most unique wines in the world.

## Kevin Zraly's Favorite Tokaji Producers

**CHATEAU PAJZOS**
**DISZNÓKŐ**
**HÉTSZŐLŐ**
**OREMUS**
**ROYAL TOKAJI WINE COMPANY**
**SZEPSY**

**BEST BETS FOR TOKAY ASZÚ**

2000\*   2002   2003   2005\*   2006\*   2009   2010

*Note: \*signifies exceptional vintage*

**FOR FURTHER READING**
I recommend *Wine Guide Hungary* by Gabriella Rohaly and Gabor Meszaros.

THE WORLD'S first vineyard classification was for the region of Tokaj in 1700.

THE TRADITIONAL squat Tokay Aszú bottles contain 500 milliliters versus the normal 750 milliliters.

SZAMORODNI IS another style of wine made in Tokaj. It ranges from semidry to semisweet but has fewer grams of sugar than three Puttonyos.

A FRENCH Sauternes has 90 grams of sugar.

A GERMAN Trockenbeerenauslese has 150 grams of sugar.

DUE TO THE high concentration of sugar, it may take years for Essencia to finish fermentation, and then having an alcohol content of only 2–5%.

LIBATION: from the Greek *leibein*, to pour
SYMPOSIUM: from the Greek *symposion*, to drink together
ENOLOGY: from the Greek *oinos*, wine, and *logos*, reason or speech

*"No thing more excellent or more valuable than wine was ever granted mankind by God."*

—PLATO

*"The wine urges me on, the bewitching wine, which sets even a wise man to singing and laughing gently and rouses him up to dance and brings forth words which were better unspoken."*

—HOMER

THERE ARE over 3,000 islands in Greece and only 63 of them are inhabited.

MEDITERRANEAN CLIMATE: hot summers; a short, mild winter; and long autumns.

*"The peoples of the Mediterranean began to emerge from barbarism when they learnt to cultivate the olive and the vine."*

—THUCYDIDES

# The Wines of Greece

AS A HISTORY MAJOR in college, I was fascinated by ancient Greece. I'm sure that coming across wine references in the works of Aristotle, Homer, Plato, and other ancient Greeks, as well as learning about Dionysus, the god of wine, celebration, and fertility, influenced my decision to study wine.

Wine has played an important role in Greek culture and lifestyle since at least as far back as the seventh century B.C. Wine has also always been one of the most traded commodities throughout Greece and the Mediterranean countries.

Prior to 1985, most Greek wines were somewhat ordinary and were exported by large bulk-wine producers to service mainly Greek communities abroad. Over the last twenty-five years, the Greek wine industry has been concentrating on making quality wines. Since Greece entered the European

Union in 1981, there has been a tremendous investment in winemaking technology and in Greek vineyards. European Union subsidies, together with the winemakers' commitments, have helped finance the building of state-of-the-art wineries throughout Greece.

## What are the main wine grapes in Greece?

The three major white grapes are:
**ASSYRTIKO** (A-SEER-tee-ko)
**MOSCHOFILERO** (Mos-ko-FEE-le-ro)
**RODITIS** (Ro-DEE-tees)

The two major red grapes are:
**AGIORGITIKO** (Ah-your-YEE-ti-ko)
**XINOMAVRO** (Ksee-NO-mav-ro)

## What are the best wine-growing regions of Greece?

*Macedonia (Northern Greece)*
    Amyndeo
    Naoussa
*Peloponnese (Southern Greece)*
    Mantinia
    Nemea
    Patras
*The Islands*
Aegean Sea islands
    Samos
    Santorini
    Rhodes
**Crete**

ANOTHER WELL-KNOWN grape, found in Patras, is Mavrodaphne.

HISTORIANS HAVE established that wine production in the Peloponnese region began over 7,000 years ago.

*"Shall we not pass a law that, in the first place, no children under eighteen may touch wine at all, teaching that it is wrong to pour fire upon fire either in body or in soul . . . and thus guarding against the excitable disposition of the young? And next, we shall rule that the young man under thirty may take wine in moderation, but that he must entirely abstain from intoxication and heavy drinking. But when a man has reached the age of forty, he may join in the convivial gatherings and invoke Dionysus, above all other gods, inviting his presence at the rite (which is also the recreation) of the elders, which he bestowed on mankind as a medicine potent against the crabbedness of Old Age, that thereby we men may renew your youth, and that, through forgetfulness of care, the temper of our souls may lose its hardness and become softer and more ductile . . ."*

— Plato

ATTICA, ANOTHER wine region in Greece, is known for Retsina and Savatiano. It is also where Dionysus gave wine to the Greeks and the home of some of the most exciting experimentation today.

**THE EARLY GREEK WINE PRODUCERS**

| | |
|---|---|
| Achaia Clauss | 1861 |
| Boutari | 1879 |
| Kourtakis | 1895 |

## What is the style of Greek wine?

To understand the difficulty in describing a typical Greek wine, one simply has to look at a map of Greece with its islands, mountains, and proximity to the Aegean and Ionian seas of the Mediterranean. Greece is the third most mountainous country of Europe, and most of the vineyards are found on the slopes of mountains or on remote islands, with a typical vineyard being smaller in size than one hectare (2.471 acres).

While some of Greece's climate is considered Mediterranean, the mountain regions enjoy a more typically Continental climate with lots of sunshine, mild winters, dry summers, and cool evenings. Some Greek vineyards are picked in August, while others are not harvested until October. The volcanic soils on some of the islands make a very different style of wine depending on whether the vineyards are on flatlands or on steep mountain slopes.

There is a tremendous diversity in the wine regions of Greece. The next ten years will be the defining time for the "New Greece" wines.

### RETSINA

*In 2008, I met at Nemea in the Peloponnese with winemakers from all the main wine regions of Greece. Together we tasted over fifty wines from the major white and red grapes. It was a fascinating tasting of Greece's indigenous grapes such as Moschofilero and Agiorgitiko. The last wine we tasted, Retsina, has been the most famous wine of Greece for thousands of years. One of my friends describes its pungent aroma as an "acquired taste" (think turpentine).*

*Retsina is made by adding pine resin to wine as a flavoring agent. In ancient times pine resin was used on amphorae to create an airtight seal in order to keep the wine from oxidizing during storage. Resin would sometimes leak into the wine, and eventually the Greeks became used to the pine flavor.*

*I really think that my Greek winemaker friends wanted to remind me that Retsina, though important, is a wine of the past. The future belongs to the quality wines we had just tasted.*

## How are the wines of Greece regulated?

Many of the better wines fall under the Greek governmental categories of OPAP (Wines of Appellation of Origin of Superior Quality, which are mostly dry) and OPE (Wines of Appellation of Controlled Origin, which are only sweet). Both designations indicate wines that come from viticultural areas that have been defined since 1971. Nemea is an example of an OPAP wine and Muscat of Patras is an example of an OPE wine.

There is also a designation roughly equivalent of France's Vin de Table, called Epitrapezios Oenos (EO), that does not include an appellation of origin and may be a blend of wines from many different regions.

LOOK FOR the red stripe at the top of the bottle for an OPAP wine and a blue stripe for an OPE wine.

## Kevin Zraly's Favorite Greek Producers

| | |
|---|---|
| ALPHA ESTATE | OENOFOROS |
| DRIOPI | PAVLIDIS |
| GAIA ESTATE | SAMOS COOPERATIVE |
| GEROVASSILIOU | SEMELI |
| KIR YIANNI | SIGALAS |
| MANOUSSAKIS | SKOURAS |
| MERCOURI | TSELEPOS |

### BEST BETS FOR WINES FROM GREECE

2005   2007   2008*   2009   2010

*Note: * signifies exceptional vintage*

### FOR FURTHER READING

*The Wines of Greece* by Konstantinos Lazarakis and *The Illustrated Greek Wine Book* by Nico Manessis.

# The Wines of Australia

THE WINE INDUSTRY is not new to Australia: wine, mostly fortified, was produced as early as the late 1700s. Many of Australia's leading wine companies were established more than 175 years ago. Lindemans, Penfolds, Orlando (whose main brand is Jacob's Creek), Henschke, and Seppelt are just a few of the companies that were founded during the nineteenth century. They are now among Australia's largest or most prestigious firms, and continue to produce excellent wines.

In the sixties, Australia was better known for its kangaroos and surfing than for its wine. Today it is the sixth largest producer of wine in the world. The change toward quality varietal wines began in the seventies and has continued with tremendous speed and drive. From 1988 to 2008, exports of Australian wines increased 98.2 percent, and in 2008 exports exceeded $3 billion.

## What are the main grape varieties of Australia?

| RED | WHITE |
| --- | --- |
| Shiraz (25%) | Chardonnay (19%) |
| Cabernet Sauvignon (16%) | Sémillon (4%) |

## What are the main wine regions of Australia?

There are over sixty-four wine-growing regions in Australia, which are called Geographical Indications. Do you need to know them all? Probably not, but to begin your Australian wine journey, you should be familiar with the best districts in four of Australia's six states and what they are known for. They are:

**SOUTH AUSTRALIA**
  *Adelaide Hills:* Chardonnay, Sauvignon Blanc
  *Clare Valley:* Riesling
  *Coonawarra:* Cabernet Sauvignon
  *Barossa Valley:* Shiraz, Grenache
  *McLaren Vale:* Shiraz, Grenache

**NEW SOUTH WALES**
  *Hunter Valley:* Sémillon

**VICTORIA**
  *Yarra Valley:* Chardonnay, Pinot Noir

**WESTERN AUSTRALIA**
  *Margaret River:* Cabernet Sauvignon, Chardonnay, Sauvignon Blanc/Sémillon

**TWO OTHER REGIONS OF AUSTRALIA**

**Tasmania**, known for sparkling wines
**Rutherglen**, known for fortified wines

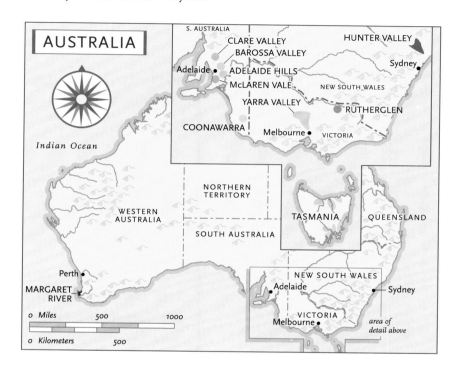

## What are the wine laws of Australia?

The Australian wine industry's Label Integrity Program (LIP) took effect with the 1990 vintage. Although the LIP does not govern as many aspects of wine production as France's AOC laws, the LIP does regulate and oversee vintage, varietal, and Geographical Indication claims. To conform to LIP and other regulations set by the Australian Food Standards Code, Australian wine labels must provide a great deal of information.

FORTY-THREE PERCENT of Australian wines are produced in South Australia. South Australia is one of the few wine regions in the world that has never been affected by phylloxera, so many growers still plant using the vines' own rootstock.

CABERNET SAUVIGNON vine cuttings from Château Haut-Brion in Bordeaux were planted near Melbourne in the 1830s. In 1832, James Busby brought Syrah cuttings from the Chapoutier vineyards in the Rhône Valley, France, which he planted in the Hunter Valley.

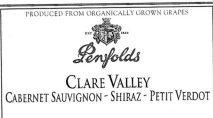

OVER 75% of Australian wine is now bottled with a screw cap.

SOME OF the oldest Shiraz (Syrah) grape vines in the world, many of which are over 100 years old, are found in Australia.

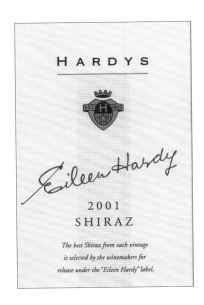

Take a look at the label on the left. One of most important pieces of information is the producer's name. In this case, the producer is Penfolds. In a blend listing the varieties, as in the example of this wine label, the percentages of each varietal must be shown, with the first grape listed having the highest percentage. If the label specifies a particular wine-growing district—Clare Valley in our example—at least 85 percent of the wine must originate there. If a vintage is given, 95 percent of the wine must be of that vintage.

## WHAT IS IN A NAME?

*Australia and most other wine countries have been conforming to a 1994 European Union Wine Agreement that states, in part, that countries must end the use of borrowed generic names such as "Burgundy," "Champagne," "Port," and "Sherry." The most famous wine of Australia has arguably been Penfolds Grange Hermitage. In order to conform to the Wine Agreement, Penfolds dropped the word "Hermitage," which is a wine produced in France's Rhône Valley, and shortened the name of their wine to "Grange." Even with its "new" name, Penfolds Grange remains one of the greatest wines of Australia.*

## THE JIMMY WATSON MEMORIAL TROPHY
### *The Competitive Aussie*

*Australians speak as much about rugby as they do about wine. Walking into an Australian winery is sometimes like walking into a college gymnasium: there are trophy cases with all the awards that their wines have won. The most coveted wine award was established in 1962 after an Australian wine lover named Jimmy Watson. It is awarded to the best one-year-old red wine each year. It is interesting to note that the first fifteen awards were given to wines that were labeled "Burgundy type" or "Claret type." It wasn't until 1976 that a wine labeled as a varietal won the trophy.*

## Kevin Zraly's Top Australian Wine Producers and Some Favorite Wines

- CAPE MENTELLE (CABERNET SAUVIGNON)
- CLARENDON HILLS (HICKINBOTHAM GRENACHE)
- CULLEN WINES (DIANA MADELINE)
- D'ARENBERG (THE DEAD ARM SHIRAZ)
- DE BORTOLI (NOBLE ONE)
- GRANT BURGE (MESHACH SHIRAZ)
- HARDY'S (CHATEAU REYNELLA CELLAR NO. ONE SHIRAZ)
- HENSCHKE (CYRIL CABERNET SAUVIGNON, HILL OF GRACE)
- KATNOOK (ODYSSEY CABERNET SAUVIGNON)
- LEEUWIN ESTATE (ART SERIES CHARDONNAY OR CABERNET SAUVIGNON)
- MOLLYDOOKER SHIRAZ (VELVET GLOVE)
- MOUNT MARY (QUINTET)
- PENFOLDS (GRANGE, BIN 707 CABERNET SAUVIGNON)
- PETALUMA (ADELAIDE HILLS SHIRAZ)
- PETER LEHMANN (RESERVE RIESLING OR SEMILLON)
- SHAW & SMITH (M3 VINEYARD ADELAIDE HILLS CHARDONNAY)
- TAHBILK (ERIC STEVENS PURBRICK SHIRAZ OR CABERNET SAUVIGNON)
- TORBRECK VINTNERS (RUN RIG)
- TURKEY FLAT (BAROSSA VALLEY SHIRAZ)
- TWO HANDS SHIRAZ (BELLA'S GARDEN)
- VASSE FELIX (MARGARET RIVER CHARDONNAY AND SÉMILLON)
- VOYAGER (MARGARET RIVER SAUVIGNON BLANC/SÉMILLON)
- WIRRA WIRRA (RSW SHIRAZ AND ANGELUS CABERNET SAUVIGNON)
- WOLF BLASS (BLACK LABEL SHIRAZ)
- YALUMBA (THE MENZIES COONAWARRA CABERNET SAUVIGNON)
- YERING STATION (SHIRAZ VIOGNIER)

### BEST BETS FOR WINES FROM AUSTRALIA (BAROSSA, MCLAREN VALE, COONAWARRA)

2004** 2005** 2006* 2007 2008
2009 2010** 2011 2012

*Note: * signifies exceptional vintage  ** signifies extraordinary vintage*

### FOR FURTHER READING

I recommend *Australian Wine Companion* by James Halliday and www.langtons.com.au/Tools/VintageReport.aspx.

### WHAT A DIFFERENCE A YEAR MAKES

2007 was the earliest harvest ever
2006 was the latest harvest ever

# The Wines of New Zealand

NEW ZEALAND'S NATURALLY BEAUTIFUL coastline, magnificent mountains, rolling hills, and outstanding weather are showcased best in the movie trilogy *The Lord of the Rings*. New Zealand is also the home of bungee jumping, which pretty much describes the vitality and exuberance of its young wine industry. Over the last twenty years the wines and vineyards of New Zealand have grown by leaps and bounds. Today, New Zealand's Sauvignon Blanc and Pinot Noir wines are acknowledged by the international wine community to be world-class.

The frenzy has calmed down somewhat lately, but New Zealand wines are still evolving. With over twenty-five different grape varieties planted, winemakers are just beginning to fully understand the potential of New Zealand's soil and weather. Think of the winemakers and vineyard owners of New Zealand as both first generation and the new kids on the block and you'll have a fairly good idea of the potential this country has to produce even more world-class wines. (Look for Pinot Gris and Syrah over the next few years.) The New Zealand public relations theme, "The best is yet to be discovered," pretty much says it all.

## What are the most planted grapes in New Zealand?

**SAUVIGNON BLANC** (16,758 hectares)

**PINOT NOIR** (4,803 hectares)

**CHARDONNAY** (3,823 hectares)

THE FIRST recorded vintage of New Zealand wine was produced in 1836.

### GOVERNED BY THE SEA

Ninety-five percent of New Zealand's population is within a 30-mile drive to the ocean.

IN 1985 New Zealand listed 100 wineries. There were 643 wineries in 2010.

### RENT A SHEEP

Besides wine, New Zealand is famous for its dairy products and wool. Wineries let sheep graze freely throughout the vineyards during the winter to keep the fields clear of grass and weeds.

NINETY-THREE PERCENT of New Zealand wines are sealed with screw caps.

TWENTY-FIVE YEARS ago Sauvignon Blanc represented less than 4% of New Zealand's total grape crop.

IN 1996 ONLY 1,000 acres of Pinot Noir were planted in New Zealand. In 2010 there were over 11,000 acres planted.

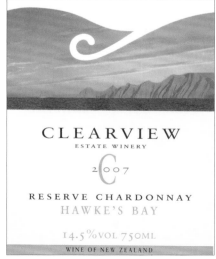

## What are the major wine regions of New Zealand?

There are ten wine regions in New Zealand. The five most important regions, and what they are known for, are:

**NORTH ISLAND**
*Hawke's Bay:* Bordeaux blends, Chardonnay, Syrah
*Gisborne:* Chardonnay
*Martinborough/Wairarapa:* Pinot Noir

**SOUTH ISLAND**
*Central Otago:* Pinot Noir
*Marlborough:* Sauvignon Banc, Pinot Noir

NINETY PERCENT of New Zealand Sauvignon Blanc comes from Marlborough.

THE MOST SOUTHERLY grapes harvested in the world come from Central Otago.

MORE THAN 50% of New Zealand's vineyards are located in Marlborough.

**NEW ZEALAND'S WINE PRODUCTION**

80% white wines
20% red wines

**THE PERFECT SUNRISE**

Because of its proximity to the International Date Line, New Zealand grapes are the first in the world to bask in a new day's sun.

### NEW ZEALAND

Auckland
NORTH ISLAND
*Tasman Sea*
GISBORNE
HAWKE'S BAY
MARLBOROUGH
MARTINBOROUGH/ WAIRARAPA
Wellington
SOUTH ISLAND
*Pacific Ocean*
CENTRAL OTAGO

0 Miles 300
0 Kilometers 300

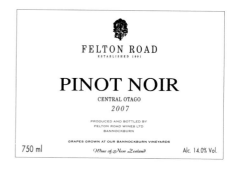

FELTON ROAD
ESTABLISHED 1991

**PINOT NOIR**
CENTRAL OTAGO
*2007*

PRODUCED AND BOTTLED BY
FELTON ROAD WINES LTD
BANNOCKBURN

GRAPES GROWN AT OUR BANNOCKBURN VINEYARDS

750 ml  *Wine of New Zealand*  Alc. 14.0% Vol.

SEVENTY PERCENT of New Zealand vines are ten or fewer years in age.

**TOTAL ACRES OF GRAPES BY YEAR**

| | |
|---|---|
| 1985 | 15,000 acres of grapes |
| 1986 | 11,000 acres of grapes (Vine Pull) |
| 2011 | 60,000 acres of grapes |

## SAUVIGNON BLANC—THE "WILD GRAPE"

*New Zealand touts itself as "the Sauvignon Blanc capital of the world." So what makes this grape so appealing (or unappealing)? It's all about "aromatics," a word that is used a lot in the Marlborough region. The aroma of a New Zealand Sauvignon Blanc is often described by wine writers as pungent, assertive, vibrant, herbaceous, racy, having grapefruit and lime citrus flavors, tropical fruit flavors, or even smelling like cat pee! What's not to like?*

## VINE PULL 1986

*In 1985 there were approximately 15,000 acres of vines planted in New Zealand. The majority of these grapes (Müller Thurgau being the most widely planted) produced large volumes of low-end wines but few wines of quality. In fact, so much wine was produced that there was a huge surplus of unsold wine and the government offered cash to any grower who agreed to uproot a quarter of his vineyard (also know as the Vine Pull). This massive purge of inferior wine grapes led to a resurgence of interest in high-quality wine grapes and to widespread plantings of Sauvignon Blanc, Chardonnay, and Pinot Noir. This marked the New Zealand wine industry's new beginning and a significant shift toward quality wine production.*

## Kevin Zraly's Favorite New Zealand Wineries

| | |
|---|---|
| AMISFIELD | FORREST |
| ATA RANGI | HUNTER'S |
| BABICH | KIM CRAWFORD |
| BRANCOTT (MONTANA) | KUMEU RIVER |
| CARRICK | MATUA VALLEY |
| CHURCH ROAD | MILLS REEF |
| CLEARVIEW | PALLISER |
| CLOUDY BAY | PEREGRINE |
| CRAGGY RANGE | SACRED HILL |
| DOG POINT | SAINT CLAIR |
| DRY RIVER | SERESIN |
| ESK VALLEY | TRINITY HILL |
| FELTON ROAD | VILLA MARIA |

### BEST BETS FOR WINES FROM NEW ZEALAND:
#### NORTH ISLAND (HAWKE'S BAY AND MARTINBOROUGH)

2006* 2007* 2010** 2011 2012

#### SOUTH ISLAND (CENTRAL OTAGO AND MARLBOROUGH)

2008** 2009* 2010* 2011 2012

*Note: * signifies exceptional vintage  ** signifies extraordinary vintage*

**FOR FURTHER READING**

I recommend *Buyer's Guide to New Zealand Wines* by Michael Cooper.

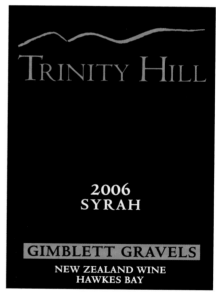

THE YEAR 2008 produced the largest grape crop ever recorded in New Zealand.

# The Wines of South Africa

1970: 270 million liters
      88,770 hectares
2011: 805 million liters
      110,041 hectares

CAPE TOWN was founded in 1652.

THE FIRST South African grape harvest was in 1659.

THERE ARE over 604 wineries in South Africa.

SOUTH AFRICAN soil is among the oldest in the world.

**SOUTH AFRICA WINE PRODUCTION**

Current (2008):    56% white wine
                 44% red wine
Future:            50% white wine
                 50% red wine

FOR THE TOURIST: Most Western Cape wine regions are within a two-hour drive of Cape Town.

SOUTH AFRICA, with the world's oldest wine-growing geology, was settled by the Dutch and by French Huguenots, and has grown grapes and made wine for some 350 years. Until recently, most of its wine was sold domestically or in Europe, and was not available in the United States.

With the democratic election of Nelson Mandela as president in 1994, South Africa's isolation and apartheid officially came to an end, and its wines finally became available to world markets.

There were a few producers making very good wine prior to 1994, but for the most part South African wines were ordinary and production emphasized brandy and fortified wines. These were produced by large cooperatives that based output on a quota system and valued quantity over quality.

Over the last sixteen years, however, South African wines have improved dramatically. Many of them now share center stage with some of the best wines produced in the world. And the best is yet to come, since many of South Africa's vineyards are relatively new—one-third of all vineyards have been

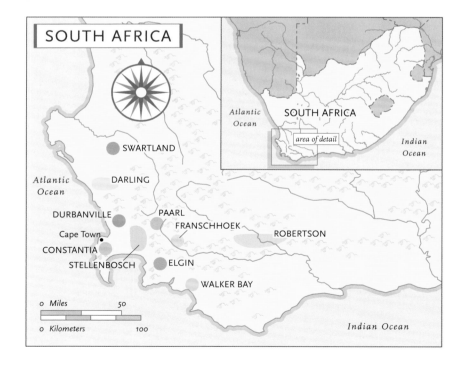

replanted since 1994—and a vine's age plays a decisive role in the quality of the wine produced. Today, the industry calls for quality over quantity, and has one foot firmly planted in the new world of winemaking and the other foot still rooted in the old paradigm of creating uniquely South African styles of wine. The "new" South African winemakers have begun making up for lost time and now produce some of the world's great quality value wines in one of the most beautiful wine regions on earth.

With over 250,000 acres of vineyards, there is a wide diversity of terrain, with four main soil types. Vineyards are found at altitudes from 300 to 1,300 feet. There are cool coastal vineyards and vineyards whose summer days exceed 100 degrees Fahrenheit. Therefore there is no "recipe viticulture"; all wine production is specific to its site. It is a land of contrast, alive with possibilities.

THE JURY IS still out on whether South Africa's benchmark white wine will be Chenin Blanc or Sauvignon Blanc. Historically it has been Chenin Blanc, whose South African vines can be more than one hundred years old. Some producers prefer to age it in oak, others age it unoaked, and several winemakers employ both methods. Personally, I believe that the world's best Chenin Blancs come from either South Africa or from the Loire Valley in France.

## What are the major grapes grown in South Africa?

The major white varieties are:

**CHENIN BLANC**

**SAUVIGNON BLANC**

**CHARDONNAY**

CHENIN BLANC is sometimes labeled as "Steen."

The major red varieties are:

| | |
|---|---|
| **BORDEAUX BLENDS** | **SHIRAZ/SYRAH** |
| **(CABERNET SAUVIGNON,** | **CABERNET SAUVIGNON** |
| **MERLOT, AND CABERNET FRANC)** | **PINOTAGE** |

## What are the main wine regions of South Africa?

South Africa is divided into two main geographic areas: the Western Cape and the Northern Cape. These are further divided into regions, districts, and wards. The most important region is the Coastal Region. Three of the most historically important Wines of Origin (WO) within the Coastal Region, and the grape varietal that each region specializes in, are:

KEVIN ZRALY'S FAVORITE SOUTH AFRICAN CHENIN BLANCS

Cederberg
De Trafford
Groote Post
Iona
Kanu
Rudera

THE WESTERN CAPE produces 97% of all South African wines.

THE CAPE wine lands are the only ones in the world influenced by two oceans, the Atlantic and the Indian.

*Constantia (1652):* Sauvignon Blanc, Muscat

*Stellenbosch (1679):* Chardonnay, Cabernet Sauvignon, Pinotage, Bordeaux blends

*Paarl (1687):* Chardonnay, Syrah, Chenin Blanc

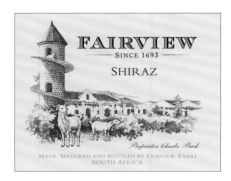

Other important wine areas of South Africa are:

**Darling:** Sauvignon Blanc
**Durbanville:** Sauvignon Blanc, Merlot
**Elgin:** Riesling, Sauvignon Blanc, Pinot Noir
**Franschhoek:** Cabernet Sauvignon, Syrah, Semillon
**Robertson:** Chardonnay, Shiraz
**Swartland:** Shiraz, Pinotage, Rhône style blends
**Walker Bay:** Chardonnay, Pinot Noir

## RETHINKING PINOTAGE

*The first South African wine I ever tasted was made from a grape variety called Pinotage. In 1925 a viticulturist from Stellenbosch University created this grape variety by crossing two grapes, Pinot Noir and Cinsault. Unfortunately, it has never had a single flavor profile. Pinotage can produce an inexpensive, light, somewhat insipid wine smelling of spray paint, acetate, or banana with a very strong, acrid aftertaste; or it can become a big, full-bodied, luscious, and well-balanced wine with tremendous fruit extraction and a long graceful finish that can age for twenty or more years.*

*I have found that the best producers of Pinotage have a similar formula:*

1. *Grapes come from vines at least fifteen years old and planted in cooler climates*
2. *The per-acre crop yield must be low*
3. *The grapes need long skin contact (maceration in open fermentors)*
4. *The wine requires prolonged oak aging (at least two years)*
5. *The Pinotage grape is blended with Cabernet Sauvignon*
6. *The wine needs at least ten years of aging*

*My favorite producers of Pinotage are:*

**FAIRVIEW**            **L'AVENIR**
**KANONKOP**            **SIMONSIG**

## SOUTH AFRICAN DESSERT WINES

*Long before Sauternes from France's Bordeaux region and Germany's Trockenbeer-enauslese were first produced, Hungary (Tokaj) and South Africa (Constantia) produced the two greatest sweet wines in the world. Since the eighteenth century, Constantia has been producing wines using the aromatic and fragrant Muscat grape. The original wine style (of grapes that are dried, not botrytized) is still produced at the wine estate Klein Constantia.*

Other controls set by the WO include vintage dating and varietal labeling. A vintage designation means that 85 percent of the grapes used in its making must be from the stated vintage. A varietal designation means that the wine must contain at least 85 percent of the named grape varietal.

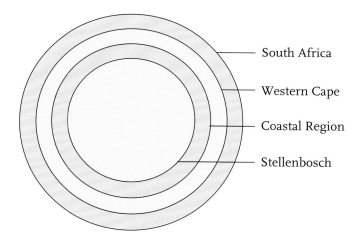

- South Africa
- Western Cape
- Coastal Region
- Stellenbosch

If a wine label states that it is estate bottled, 100 percent of the grapes must be from that estate. If a place of origin is listed on the label, 100 percent of the grapes must come from that region. The two major things not controlled by the WO are the yield per hectare and irrigation.

| | |
|---|---|
| 1652 | The Dutch arrive in Cape Town |
| 1659 | The first wine is produced |
| 1688 | The French Huguenots arrive |
| 1788 | Constantia's sweet wines become legendary |
| 1886 | Phylloxera destroys South African vineyards |
| 1918 | The Cooperative Wine Growers Association (KWV) is established to control the pricing and production of wine throughout South Africa |
| 1918–1995 | The KWV produces mostly brandy and fortified wines |
| 1973 | The Wines of Origin (WO) system is implemented |
| 1990 | Nelson Mandela is released from prison, and trade sanctions end |
| 1994 | Nelson Mandela is elected president |
| 1994 | A new era of South African wine begins |
| 1997 | The KWV is transformed from a cooperative into a group of companies |

FOR SOCCER FANS: The 2010 World Cup was held in South Africa. Do you remember who won?

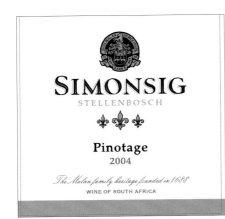

## Kevin Zraly's Favorite South African Wine Producers

### *Stellenbosch*

| | |
|---|---|
| ANWILKA | MORGENSTER |
| DE TOREN | MULDERBOSCH |
| DE TRAFFORD | NEIL ELLIS |
| GLENELLY | RAATS FAMILY |
| JORDAN (AVAILABLE AS JARDIN IN THE UNITED STATES) | RUDERA |
| | RUSTENBERG |
| KANONKOP | SIMONSIG |
| KEN FORRESTER | THELEMA |
| L'AVENIR | VERGELEGEN |
| MEERLUST | VRIESENHOF |
| MORGENHOF | WATERFORD |

### *Paarl*

| | |
|---|---|
| FAIRVIEW | VEENWOUDEN |
| GLEN CARLOU | VILAFONTÉ |
| NEDERBURG | |

### *Franschhoek*

| | |
|---|---|
| BOEKENHOUTSKLOOF | GRAHAM BECK |
| BOSCHENDAL | |

### *Swartland*

SADIE FAMILY

### *Walker Bay*

| | |
|---|---|
| BOUCHARD-FINLAYSON | HAMILTON RUSSELL |

### *Constantia*

| | |
|---|---|
| CONSTANTIA UITSIG | STEENBERG |
| KLEIN CONSTANTIA | |

### *Elgin*

PAUL CLUVER

## FOREIGN INVESTMENT IN SOUTH AFRICAN WINE

**Anwilka:** *Bruno Prats, former owner of Château Cos d'Estournel; and Hubert de Boüard of Château Angélus (Bordeaux, France) with Lowell Jooste of Klein Constantia*

**Glen Carlou:** *Donald Hess (California, Australia, and Argentina)*

**L'Avenir:** *Michel Laroche (Chablis, France)*

**Morgenhof:** *Anne Cointreau-Huchon (France)*

**Morgenster:** *Pierre Lurton, Château Cheval Blanc (Bordeaux, France)*

**Vilafonté:** *Zelma Long (formerly of Simi) and Phil Freese (formerly of Mondavi)*

**Glenelly:** *May de Lencquesaing, Château Pichon-Lalande (Bordeaux, France)*

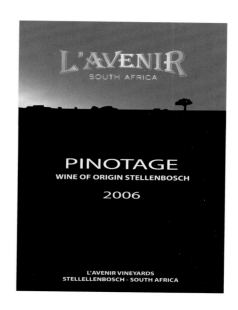

### BEST BETS FOR SOUTH AFRICAN WESTERN CAPE WINES

2006*   2007   2008*   2009**   2010   2011*   2012

*Note: * signifies exceptional vintage*

*** signifies extraordinary vintage*

IN 1685, the Constantia wine estate was established.

# The Wines of Canada

COMMERCIAL WINEMAKING in Canada began in the early 1800s.

THE WINE HISTORY OF CANADA is not that much different from that of my own state, New York: both Canada and New York began winemaking by concentrating on growing the winter-hardy *labrusca* grapes (Concord, Catawba, and Niagara). Like New York, many of Canada's wineries specialized in producing fortified wines. These were often bottled using the borrowed European names "Port" and "Sherry." The first major change in Canadian viticulture occurred during the 1970s, when several small producers began to experiment with French hybrid grapes. Over the last forty years, the best wines of Canada have been made with European *vinifera* grapes.

QUEBEC AND Nova Scotia also grow grapes, primarily hybrids.

## What are the most important grapes grown in Canada?

The major white grapes are:

| | |
|---|---|
| **CHARDONNAY** | **GEWÜRZTRAMINER** |
| **PINOT GRIS** | **VIDAL** |
| **RIESLING** | |

**ONTARIO**

15,074 acres        125 wineries

**BRITISH COLUMBIA**

9,500 acres        193 wineries

The major red grapes are:

| | |
|---|---|
| **PINOT NOIR** | **CABERNET FRANC** |
| **CABERNET SAUVIGNON** | **SYRAH** |
| **MERLOT** | |

## What are the major wine regions of Canada?

Canada has two major wine-producing regions: British Columbia on the Pacific Coast, and Ontario in the eastern Great Lakes region.

*Ontario/Niagara Peninsula:* Chardonnay, Riesling, Pinot Noir, Vidal, Cabernet Franc
*British Columbia/Okanagan Valley:* Chardonnay, Pinot Gris, Merlot, Cabernet Sauvignon, Syrah, Gewürztraminer, Pinot Noir

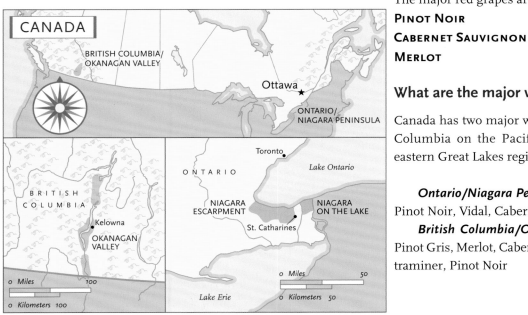

## How are the wines of Canada regulated?

The Vintners Quality Alliance (VQA) was created to regulate the wines of Ontario in 1988 and British Columbia in 1990. A VQA designation stipulates that the wine must be made using 100 percent *vinifera* varieties and controls varietal percentages. If a wine has the grape variety listed on the label it must contain a minimum of 85 percent of that variety. If a designated viticultural area (DVA) is listed, 95 percent must come from that area. If a vineyard is listed, it must be 100 percent from that vineyard. Over one hundred wineries produce VQA wines.

## Kevin Zraly's Favorite Canadian Wineries

CHÂTEAU DES CHARMES          LE CLOS JORDANNE

HENRY OF PELHAM              MISSION HILL

INNISKILLIN                 SUMAC RIDGE

JACKSON-TRIGGS

### BEST BETS FOR WINES FROM CANADA

*Ontario* 2005  2006*  2009  2010*  2011

*British Columbia* 2005  2006  2009  2010  2011

Note: *signifies exceptional vintage

### FOR FURTHER READING

I recommend *The Wine Atlas of Canada, Vintage Canada,* and *Canadian Wine for Dummies,* all by Tony Aspler.

## CANADIAN ICE WINE

*The first great Canadian wine I ever tasted was an ice wine—or Eiswein—made by the Inniskillin Winery. Inniskillin, founded in 1975, was the first new winery founded in Ontario since 1927 and they produced their first ice wine in 1984 after a very cold Canadian winter.*

*To make ice wine, grapes are allowed to freeze on the vine before being picked by hand. The grapes are then carefully pressed while still frozen, yielding a small amount of concentrated juice that is high in sugar and other components. Canadian law dictates that ice wine can be made using only vinifera grapes (usually Riesling) and the French hybrid Vidal. It must also contain at least 125 grams of residual sugar per liter. Most ice wines are expensive and are sold in half bottles.*

CANADA, LIKE the United States, had a period of national prohibition. Canada's prohibition began in 1916 and ended in 1927 (the United States' was from 1920 to 1933).

SIXTY PERCENT of VQA wines are white grapes.

### THE LAKE EFFECT

Many people erroneously think that Canada is too far north and too cold to make great wine. Just like in other cool-climate wine regions such as Germany, most of the best vineyards are planted near water, which tempers the climate. Ontario has Lake Ontario and Lake Erie, and British Columbia has Okanagan Lake.

CANADIANS DAN AYKROYD and Wayne Gretzky both have invested in Canadian wineries.

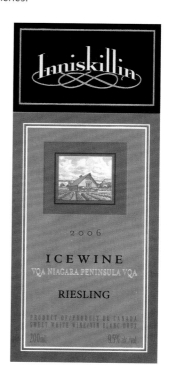

# The Wines of Chile

CHILE

CHILE IS a melting pot of German, French, Spanish, and English.

THE HIGHEST PEAK of the Andes Mountains is called Aconcagua and is over 22,000 feet high.

**TIME LINE IN CHILE**

1551: Spanish plant first grapes

1850s: Wineries such as Cousiño Macul (1856) are established; pre-phylloxera vines imported from Europe

1870s: Chilean wines become more important for export because of the phylloxera epidemic in Europe and the United States

1930s to 1970s: Wines go from quality to ordinary

Mid-1970s: Export market grows

1980s to 1990s: Better-quality wines after big investments in wineries and winemaking equipment

2000 to present: Big investment in vineyards; great world-class wines at reasonable prices.

AFTER A LONG day of tasting Chilean wines, it is a tradition to end with Chile's national drink—a Pisco Sour, a brandy mixed with lemon and/or lime juice, simple syrup, egg white, and a dash of Angostura bitters. The longer the day, the more Pisco you must have!

I WAS IMPRESSED with some of the wineries, and some of the wines I tasted, when I first visited Chile in 1997. It was a country on the verge of producing world-class wine, primarily reds, with the best varietal being Cabernet Sauvignon. In those days I called Chile "a work in progress."

On my 2008–2009 world wine tour I spent ten days in Chile, first as a judge for over 400 wines and then visiting wineries throughout the country. What a difference twelve years can make, and not just in better wines! Chile's infrastructure, especially with its new hotel construction and highways, has transformed this country into a big-time tourist destination.

With over 2,500 miles of Pacific coastline and being, on average, only 109 miles wide, Chile has many different climates, from desertlike conditions in the north to glaciers in the south. In the middle of the country within 150 miles of Santiago, its capital, you will find the perfect Mediterranean climate for growing outstanding wine grapes: warm days, cool nights, and ocean winds.

And one cannot write about Chile without mentioning the majestic snow-capped Andes, which supply all the necessary water through both flood and drip irrigation. The peaks average over 13,000 feet. It is the world's longest mountain range—over 4,000 miles extending into seven countries.

Chile has been making wine since the first grapes were planted there in 1551. The first wine was produced in 1555, and in the mid-1800s, French varietals such as Cabernet Sauvignon and Merlot were imported.

But all this progress came to a grinding halt in 1938 when the government of Chile decreed that no new vineyards could be planted. This law lasted until 1974. The renaissance of the modern wine industry of Chile really only began in the early 1980s. The new technology of stainless-steel fermentors, the old technology of French oak barrels, better vineyard management, and drip irrigation were combined to produce higher-quality wines. Even though Chile is still learning and experimenting in its vineyards and in its winemaking, *its red wines are the best values in the world* in the $15 to $25 range!

## What are the main grape varieties planted in Chile?

The major white grapes are:

**SAUVIGNON BLANC** (30,045 acres)     **CHARDONNAY** (32,326 acres)

The major red grapes are:

**CABERNET SAUVIGNON** (100,641 acres)     **CARMÉNÈRE** (21,811 acres)
**MERLOT** (24,811 acres)     **SYRAH** (14,893)

## What are the major winemaking regions in Chile?

This is a little difficult to answer since you have a country that is so narrow. Maybe the best way is to look at the country in an east-west and north-south division. From the east to the west, you have three different climatic conditions:

**Coastal:** cool climate
**Central Valley:** warm climate
**Andes Mountains:** cool or warm climate

From a north-to-south perspective, the most important regions are:
**Casablanca Valley:** Sauvignon Blanc, Chardonnay, Pinot Noir
**Maipo Valley:** Cabernet Sauvignon
**Rapel Valley/Colchagua:** Cabernet Sauvignon, Merlot, Carménère

MODERN TECHNOLOGY like fermentation in stainless steel vats was introduced to Chile by the Spanish wine family Torres in 1979.

CHILE IS the fourth largest exporter of wine to the United States.

NEW PLANTINGS of Malbec, Carignan, Pinot Noir, and Cinsault will add diversity to Chilean wines over the next ten years.

CABERNET SAUVIGNON accounts for 46% of the total acreage of premium grapes planted in Chile.

THE LARGEST planting of Cabernet Sauvignon in Chile is in the Colchagua Valley.

**OTHER REGIONS OF CHILE**

Aconcagua: Cabernet Sauvignon
Bío Bío: Pinot Noir
Cachapoal: Cabernet Sauvignon
Curicó: Cabernet Sauvignon, Sauvignon Blanc
Limari: Cabernet Sauvignon
Maule: Cabernet Sauvignon
San Antonio: Chardonnay

**THE SEVEN LARGEST WINERIES IN CHILE**

| WINERY | DATE FOUNDED |
| --- | --- |
| San Pedro | 1865 |
| Concha y Toro | 1883 |
| Errazuriz | 1870 |
| Santa Carolina | 1875 |
| Santa Rita | 1880 |
| Undurraga | 1885 |
| Canepa | 1930 |

Some foreign investors in Chile include:

| | |
|---|---|
| Antinori, Italy | Albis |
| Dan Odfjell, Norway | Odfjell Vineyards |
| O. Fournier, Spain | O. Fournier |
| Quintessa, California | Veramonte |
| Torres Winery, Spain | Miguel Torres Winery |

## THE FRENCH CONNECTION (FRENCH INVESTMENT IN CHILE)

| French investor | Chilean winery |
|---|---|
| Baron Philippe de Rothschild | Almaviva |
| Bruno Prats & Paul Pontallier | Aquitania |
| Château Lafite-Rothschild | Los Vascos |
| Château Larose-Trintaudon | Casas del Toqui |
| Grand Marnier | Casa Lapostolle |
| William Fèvre | Fèvre |

## THE TOP FIVE CHILEAN WINE BRANDS IN THE UNITED STATES

Concha y Toro
Walnut Crest
San Pedro
Santa Rita
Santa Carolina

*Source: Impact Databank*

---

## WATCH OUT, ARGENTINA!

In the 2009 Wines of Chile Awards, for which I was one of the nine American judges, we tasted over 400 wines. The Best of Show wine for 2009—Cabernet Sauvignon? No. Carménère? No. It was a Malbec! Odfjell Vineyards's Orzada Orgánico 2006.

---

## RETHINKING CARMÉNÈRE

*Bordeaux winemaking was influential in the early days of Chile's wine industry. That is why Cabernet Sauvignon is the country's number-one red varietal. In the 1850s, Chileans planted other Bordeaux grapes such as Merlot and Cabernet Franc.*

*In 1994, DNA analysis revealed that a substantial amount of grapes that had been produced and sold as Merlot were actually another Bordeaux grape called Carménère.*

*What could have been a marketing disaster turned into a positive new identity for Chile. Carménère is now one of the top varietals in Chile and it is the only country in the world to produce it as a single varietal.*

*When I first visited Chile in 1997, there was a lack of consistency in Carménère from winery to winery; most tasted green and herbaceous. When I revisited Chile in 2009, the quality had changed dramatically. My own tasting experience has shown that to make a great wine from Carménère:*

- *It must be planted in clay-like, well-drained soil*
- *It needs good weather conditions since it is a late-ripening grape. In the early days it was picked too early—the reason for those herbaceous characteristics.*
- *It is better when blended with Cabernet Sauvignon or Syrah*
- *Oak aging is necessary for at least twelve months to integrate the fruit, tannins, and acidity*
- *Older vines make for better Carménère*
- *At the end of the harvest, it is necessary to pull off the Carménère vines' grape leaves and expose the grapes to as much sunlight as possible*
- *Carménère is a thick-skinned grape that has soft, sweet tannins and low acidity. It is wine that you can enjoy young (three to seven years). The best will cost you $20 or more . . . still a great value!*

## What are the wine laws of Chile?

After the restrictive laws of the seventies were repealed, Chile really began opening up its wine industry. In general, the winemakers have a lot of freedom. Wineries adhere to the label requirements of the EU. The wine must contain 85% of the grape variety, vintage, or domaine of origin (D.O.) that appears on the label.

## Kevin Zraly's Favorite Chilean Producers
## (With Some of Their Best Wines)

**ALMAVIVA**
**ANAKENA (ONA)**
**AQUITANIA**
**ARBOLEDA**
**CALITERRA (CENIT)**
**CARMEN (GRANDE VIDURE)**
**CASA LAPOSTOLLE (CUVÉE ALEXANDRE, CLOS APALTA)**
**CASA SILVA**
**CHADWICK**
**CONCHA Y TORO (DON MELCHOR)**
**CONO SUR (OCIO)**
**COUSIÑO MACUL (FINIS TERRAE, ANTIGUAS RESERVAS, LOTA)**
**DE MARTINO**
**ECHEVERRIA**
**EMILIANA ORGÁNICO**
**ERRAZURIZ (DON MAXIMIANO)**
**LEYDA**
**LOS VASCOS (LE DIX DE LOS VASCOS)**
**MATETIC (EQ)**
**MIGUEL TORRES**
**MONTES (ALPHA M, FOLLY)**
**MORANDÉ**
**O. FOURNIER (CENTAURI)**
**ODFJELL**
**SANTA CAROLINA (VIÑA CASABLANCA)**
**SANTA RITA (CASA REAL)**
**SEÑA**
**TARAPACA (RESERVA PRIVADA)**
**UNDURRAGA (ALTAZOR)**
**VALDIVIESO (CABALLO LOCO, ECLAT)**
**VERAMONTE (PRIMUS)**

### BEST BETS FOR CHILE

**Maipo**    2005**  2006*  2007**  2008*  2009  2010  2011  2012
**Casablanca**  2006  2007  2009  2010  2011  2012
**Colchagua**  2005*  2007*  2009  2010  2011  2012

*Note: * signifies exceptional vintage   ** signifies extraordinary vintage*

**KEVIN ZRALY'S CHOICES FOR THE BEST OF CHILE**

Almaviva
Alpha M (Montes)
Antiquas Reservas (Cousiño Macul)
Casa Real (Santa Rita)
Clos Apalta (Casa Lapostolle)
Don Maximiano (Errazuriz)
Don Melchor (Concha y Toro)
Le Dix de Los Vascos
Seña

IN 1995, there were only 12 wineries in Chile. Today there are more than 100.

**JUST A COINCIDENCE?**

The best recent vintages in Chile have occurred in odd years: 1997, 1999, 2001, 2003, 2005, and 2007.

**FOR FURTHER READING**
I recommend *The Wines of Chile* by Peter Richards.

# The Wines of Argentina

M Y WINE STUDENTS are always asking me what country is on the horizon for new wines and wine regions. My answer: Argentina.

There are many reasons for feeling this way. One is great climatic conditions and soil, especially for red wines. Another is the size of Argentina: the second largest country in South America has thousands more acres that can be planted. But the most important reason is tremendous new investment, not only financial but also of world-renowned experts owning their own vineyards and wineries.

Argentina's tradition of making and consuming wine goes back to the colonization by the Spanish in the 1500s. As with many of the great-wine producing countries, it was missionaries (Jesuits, in the case of Argentina) who planted and cultivated vines in Mendoza and to the north in San Juan.

Originally, Argentina never needed to export wine since most of the wine, which was well made and inexpensive, was consumed domestically. But over the last twenty years, much has changed in Argentina. Annual domestic consumption dropped from twenty-four gallons of wine per person a year to eight gallons. In 2001, with the devaluation of the peso, exporting became more profitable. With foreign investment and winemaking consultants already in place, the timing was perfect for Argentina to enter the export market, with the "unique"

### THE FLYING WINEMAKER LANDS IN ARGENTINA!

*The most famous wine consultant in the world, Frenchman Michel Rolland, has invested his winemaking expertise into an estate of five wineries called Clos de los Siete, all located within eyesight of each other. His partners include top winemakers and viticulturists. The* Wine Advocate *wrote of the 2007 vintage that "there may be no finer red wine value in Argentina." The four other wineries involved in the group are Monteviejo, Flechas de los Andes, Cuvelier los Andes, and Diamandes.*

### THE BORDEAUX INVESTMENT CONNECTION
*Monteviejo (Château Le Gay, Pomerol)*
*Cuvelier los Andes (Château Léoville Poyferre, St-Julien)*
*Bodegas Diamandes (Château Malartic-Lagraviere, Pessac-Léognan)*
*Flechas de los Andes (Château Clarke, Listrac; and Château Dassault, St-Émilion)*
*Clos de los Siete (Château le Bon Pasteur, Pomerol)*

grape Malbec giving a wine identity for the country. The quality/price ratio is also one of the best in the world!

With the size of the country and the speed of their winemaking success, look for even more and better wines over the next twenty years.

## What are the main grape varieties of Argentina?

The major white grapes are:

**TORRONTÉS RIOJANO** (20,868 acres)     **CHARDONNAY** (16,254 acres)

The major red grapes are:

**MALBEC** (69,189 acres)     **MERLOT** (17,229 acres)

**CABERNET SAUVIGNON** (43,829 acres)     **TEMPRANILLO** (16,229 acres)

**SYRAH** (32,373 acres)

## What are the main wine regions of Argentina?

**NORTH**
  *Salta:* Torrontés Riojano, Cabernet Sauvignon
  *Cafayate*

**CUYO**
  *Mendoza:* Malbec, Tempranillo, Cabernet Sauvignon
  *Uco Valley*
  *San Juan:* Bonarda, Syrah

**PATAGONIA**
  *Río Negro:* Pinot Noir, Torrontés Riojano
  *Neuquén*

## Kevin Zraly's Favorite Producers of Argentinean Wines

**ACHAVAL FERRER (FINCA MIRADOR)**
**ALTA VISTA (ALTO)**
**BODEGA NORTON (PERDRIEL SINGLE VINEYARD)**
**CATENA ZAPATA (ADRIANNA VINEYARD)**
**CHEVAL DES ANDES**
**CLOS DE LOS SIETE**

MALBEC IS ALSO known as Cot and makes some full-bodied wines in the Cahors region of France.

THE BLENDING grape of Argentina is Barnardo. There are 45,500 acres of Barnardo grown in Argentina, but primarily because of its low tannins it is usually blended with Malbec and Cabernet Sauvignon, and is rarely used as a single variety.

THE REGION OF Mendoza is about the size of Germany.

## FOR THE TOURIST

Take the family to Patagonia, where the most dinosaur fossils in the world are located.

## FOR THE GOURMET

The national dish is beef. Argentineans consume about half a pound of beef per person per day. Also, many of the wineries have exceptional restaurants, from Francis Mallman 1884, to the new Urban at O. Fournier.

ALL ARGENTINEAN varietal wines are 100% of the grape named on the label.

## FOR THE DANCER

Even if you don't know how to tango, you will love watching this sensual dance all over Argentina.

UP AND COMING wine region: Salta.

OVER 70% OF THE 500,000 acres of vineyards planted in Argentina are in Mendoza—about 350,000 acres.

## FOR FURTHER READING

I recommend *Wines of Argentina* by Michel Rolland and Enrique Chrabolowsky.

COBOS (MARCHIORI VINEYARD)
CUVELIER LOS ANDES (GRAND MALBEC)
ENRIQUE FOSTER (MALBEC FIRMADO)
ETCHART
FINCA FLICHMAN
FINCA SOPHENIA
FRANCOIS LURTON (CHACAYES)
KAIKEN
LUCA (NICO BY LUCA)
LUIGI BOSCA (ICONO)
MENDEL (FINCA REMOTA)
O. FOURNIER (ALFA CRUX MALBEC)
SUSANA BALBO
SALENTEIN (PRIMUM MALBEC)
TERRAZAS (MALBEC AFINCADO)
TIKAL (LOCURA)
TRAPICHE
VAL DE FLORES
WEINERT

## FOREIGN INVESTMENT IN ARGENTINA

*With an average price of $30,000 per acre, no wonder so many influential wine personalities and companies have invested in Argentina over the last 10 years.*

| WINERY | COUNTRY | ARGENTINEAN WINERY |
|---|---|---|
| Cordorníu | Spain | Séptima Winery |
| O. Fournier | Spain | O. Fournier |
| Chandon | France | Bodegas Chandon |
| Château Cheval Blanc | France | Cheval des Andes |
| Lurton | France | François Lurton |
| Pernod Ricard | France | Etchart Winery |
| Sogrape Vinhos | Portugal | Finca Flichman |
| Concha y Toro | Chile | Trivento, San Martin |
| Hess | Switzerland | Colomé Winery |
| Paul Hobbs | U.S. | Viña Cobos |

## BEST BETS FOR MENDOZA

2005\* 2006\*\* 2007\* 2008\* 2009\*\* 2010\* 2011\* 2012

*Note: * signifies exceptional vintage  \*\* signifies extraordinary vintage*

# Questions for Wines of the World: Austria, Hungary, Greece, Australia, New Zealand, South Africa, Canada, Chile, and Argentina

## AUSTRALIA REFER TO PAGE

## NEW ZEALAND REFER TO PAGE

## SOUTH AFRICA REFER TO PAGE

## CANADA

## CHILE

## ARGENTINA

# The Greater World of Wine

THE PHYSIOLOGY OF TASTING WINE, WITH WENDY DUBIT • MATCHING WINE AND FOOD,

WITH ANDREA ROBINSON • BEST VALUE LIST • FREQUENTLY ASKED QUESTIONS ABOUT WINE

• WINE RESOURCES • BEST OF THE BEST

PRONUNCIATION
http://bit.ly/zjxlXN

WENDY DUBIT, founder of The Senses
Bureau (www.thesensesbureau.com) and
Vergant Media (www.vergant.com), served
as editor-in-chief of *Friends of Wine* and
*Wine Enthusiast* magazines before starting
a number of media entities ranging from
record labels to television series. She
continues to write and speak on wine, food,
and lifestyle and to lead tastings worldwide, including Wine Workout, which uses
tasting wine as a way to strengthen the
senses, memory, and mind.

# The Physiology of Tasting Wine
## You Smell More Than You Think!

BY KEVIN ZRALY AND WENDY DUBIT

## WINE SMELLING 101

One of the most wonderful things about wine is its ability to bring us to our senses. While all of our senses factor into the enjoyment of wine, none does so powerfully or pleasurably as olfaction, our sense of smell.

Happily, most wine tasters regularly experience what evolving scientific understanding also proves: the importance of smell and its impact on everything from learning and loving to aging and health.

How does our sense of smell work? Why is it so evocative of emotion and so critical to enjoyment?

Our love of wine and fascination with olfaction brought us together to write this chapter. We hope you enjoy it with a good glass of wine, great memories in mind, and more in the making.

## A LETTER FROM KEVIN

I have always been fascinated by the sense of smell. My earliest memories of my grandfather's farm are dominated by the sweet aroma of chamomile tea brewing on the kitchen woodstove. I grew up in a small town not far from New York City in a house surrounded by a forest of clean, fragrant pines. I am convinced their memory led to my building a new house smack in the middle of a pine forest.

I practically lived at the local swimming pool when I was a child, and smelled like chlorine all summer long. Even as an adult, I find the taste and smell of hot buttered popcorn contributes enormously to how much I enjoy a movie. Of course not everything smells like roses or summons sweet memories. We once had a gingko tree planted in our front yard that shed foul, nasty-smelling fruit once a year.

I will never forget the smell of downtown New York following the September 11th terrorist attacks. It lingered for months. I recall an instant a year later, a sudden whiff would catch me by surprise. Ten years later, its mephitic cloud still hovers, a smell indelibly etched in my memory.

I was seduced by the smells of wine—grapes, earth, the wine itself—as a young adult; forty years later I am still in their thrall. The sexy musk of freshly plowed earth, the fragrant balm of fermenting grapes right after harvest, and the lusty bouquet of new Beaujolais still intoxicate. An old red wine with hints of tobacco, mushrooms, and fallen leaves and the damp earth smell of my fifty-five-degree wine cellar still invigorate.

Just as the smell of cooking garlic whets my appetite and the smell of the seashore calms my nerves, the smell of crisp autumn air reminds me that the harvest is in and my favorite time of year has come to its end.

When I was a teenager with skyrocketing hormones, I doused myself in English Leather cologne and, to this day, opening a bottle immediately transports me back to the fun-filled days of youth. I'm not sure why, but I stopped wearing cologne when I began to truly smell wine. Is it coincidence or is it smell?

Smell is critical to the preservation of life and one of our most primitive senses. Yet we humans, having radically reshaped our relationship with the natural world, often take our sense of smell for granted. I continue to examine how smell and taste figure in my life. I hope that you will enjoy exploring the fascinating mysteries of olfaction in this chapter and that it will enrich your daily life and intensify your enjoyment of wine.

## A LETTER FROM WENDY

I've always lived fully attuned to each of the five senses, but it's my nose that I've followed most. Doing so has brought me nearly everywhere I want to be—most notably, to the wine industry.

Implicitly, from as far back as age eight, I linked my sense of smell to my love of learning. If my mind tired during studies, I might peel a tangerine, sit nearer a lilac bush or linden tree. By high school, I used this technique more explicitly, and began blending in color and music for optimal learning and sensory experiences. Concepts and their applications became linked to and triggered by shades and scents of citrus and pine, strands of Vivaldi and Chopin. What I lacked in photographic memory, I could usually compensate for by engaging and summoning my senses.

As a teen, I was invited to the "openings" of my parent's dinner parties, where my dad, who delighted in all things Burgundy and Bordeaux, would offer me a small pour of wine and ask for my olfactory impressions. I'll always remember the evening I discovered a marriage of river rocks, wet leather from the underside of a saddle, hay flecked with wildflowers, and golden apples in a single pour. "Ah," Dad said, nodding in encouragement, "Puligny-Montrachet." And I laughed because the name itself was as delightfully poetic to my ear as the wine had been to my nose and mouth. Even though those youthful days were rich with honest smell—kitchen, backyard, woods, stream, and farm—I'll always remember being most awed by the abundant and complex smells I found in a single glass of wine. A glass of great wine encompasses an entire world of smell, layer upon layer of riches.

Since those early dinner parties, Puligny has become a favorite wine and a symbol of the enduring bond between Dad and me. In fact, the last time I saw Dad was in a hospital—decades after those dinner parties—and I'll always cherish the evening he asked for a glass of Puligny. I was sure he knew that the orderlies wouldn't bring a bottle with his dinner, so I talked to him about the wine. I described its beguiling white Burgundian blend of minerals, acidity, crisp fruit, and toasted oak. I recalled our trips to the Côte de Nuits and the Côte de Beaune, and detailed the particular pleasures of each bottle of wine we'd brought home. As I was talking, my father became increasingly relaxed. By the time I finished he was utterly calm, with a dramatically improved oxygenation level. "Thank you," he said, bowing his head, "I just wanted to hear it in your words."

Wine is both training ground and playground for all five of our senses, our memory, and our intellect. Consequently, our enjoyment and understanding of the full wine-tasting experience improves dramatically if we observe, smell, taste, feel, analyze, and remember more carefully. Good wine demands that we stop and savor each taste to allow its rich, sensuous story to more completely unfold. Every wine deserves the attention of all five senses. But smell, with its ability to evoke memory and feeling, matters most.

## SO, HOW DO WE SMELL?

With each inhalation, we gather essential information about the world around us—its delights, opportunities, and dangers. We can shut our eyes, close our mouths, withdraw our touch, and cover our ears, but the nose, with notable exceptions, is always working, alerting us to potential danger and possible pleasure.

AS PROOF OF the evolutionary importance of smell, 1–2% of our genes are involved in olfaction, approximately the same percent that is involved in the immune system.

Our sense of smell also enhances learning, evokes memory, promotes healing, cements desire, and inspires us to action. It is so important to the preservation and sustenance of life that the instantaneous information it gathers bypasses the thalamus, where other senses are processed, and moves directly to the limbic system. The limbic system controls our emotions, our emotional responses, mood, motivation, and our pain and pleasure sensations, and it is where we analyze olfactory stimuli.

Memory stored in the limbic system uniquely links emotional state with physical sensation, creating our most important and primitive form of learning: working memory. We remember smell differently than we recall sight, sound, taste, or touch because we may respond to smell the same way we respond to emotion: an increased heart rate, enhanced sensitivity, and faster breathing. It is this emotional connection that gives smell the power to stimulate memory so strongly and why a single smell can instantly transport us back to a particular time and place.

In 2004, the Nobel Prize in Medicine was awarded to Columbia University Professor Richard Axel and Fred Hutchinson Cancer Research Center Professor Linda B. Buck for their breakthrough discoveries in olfaction. Axel and Buck discovered a large family of genes in the cells of the epithelium, or

IMPLICIT MEMORIES are perceptual, emotional, sensory, and are often unconsciously encoded and retrieved. Explicit memories are factual, episodic, temporal, and require conscious coding and retrieval. A good wine, well perceived and described, lives on in both forms of memory.

## HOW DO WE SMELL?

*Chemical components—esters, ethers, aldehydes, etc.—of inhaled Puligny swirl upward through the nostrils on currents of air*

*Midway up the nose, millions of olfactory receptor neurons (olfactory epithelia), with their specialized protein receptors, bind the odorants that fit their specific profile*

*Interaction of the specific odor molecules*

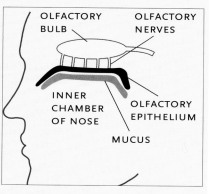

OLFACTORY BULB
OLFACTORY NERVES
INNER CHAMBER OF NOSE
OLFACTORY EPITHELIUM
MUCUS

*matched with the right receptor causes the receptor to change its shape. This change gives rise to an electrical signal that goes first to the olfactory bulb and then to the areas of the brain that convert the electrical signal to the identification of a smell, or group of smells. The brain associates the smell(s) with perception, impressions, emotions, memories, knowledge, and more.*

ALLERGIES, INJURY, illness, and sexual activity are just some of the reasons our noses can become temporarily or permanently clogged or occluded.

A DEVIATED SEPTUM, which can cause problems with proper breathing and nasal discharge, is an abnormal configuration of the cartilage that divides the two sides of the nasal cavity. While definitive treatment may require surgery, it turns out that decongestants, antihistamines, nasal cortisone spray, nasal lavage, and even eating jalapeño peppers and wasabi (which are hot enough to flush a stopped-up nose) can be temporarily helpful.

WHAT ARE OUR wine senses? Hearing (as in corks popping, wine pouring), seeing, smelling, tasting, feeling, and reflecting, to be sure—but also more. Scientists and experts agree that smell accounts for up to 90% of what many perceive as taste and mouthfeel.

SIZE AND SHAPE do matter. Deep, good wineglasses, such as Riedel's lines of stemware, do much to enhance varietal aroma.

THE NOSE KNOWS: Exposure to certain easily recognizable smells while forming memories will link the memory to the smell. So (as Wendy implicitly understood as a young girl) eating tangerines, for example, while studying for a test makes it easier to remember the information by recalling the smell of tangerines while taking the test.

## IT'S A GOOD THING WE HAVE TWO!

*The septum, made up of cartilage, divides the nose into two separate chambers, or nostrils, each with discretely wired epithelium and olfactory bulbs. Each nostril serves a different function and operates at peak capacity at different times. It is rare for both nostrils, even in the healthiest noses, to work at full capacity simultaneously, and people with a deviated septum often report being able to breathe out of only one nostril. Jacobson's Organ author Lyall Watson reports, "A three-hour cycle of alternation between left and right nostrils goes on night and day. At night it contributes to sleep movements." Watson hypothesizes that by day, when we are conscious, right and left nostrils direct information to accordant parts of the brain—the right being the side that perceives, intuits, encodes, and stores implicitly; the left being the side that explicitly analyzes, names, records, and retrieves. "Ideally, we need both. . . . But if a situation is strange and requires action based more on prediction than precedent, you would be better off facing it with a clear left nostril."*

lining, of the upper part of the nose that control production of unique protein receptors, called olfactory receptors. Olfactory receptors specialize in recognizing, then attaching themselves to, thousands of specific molecules of incoming odorants. Once attached, the trapped chemical molecules are converted to electrical signals. These signals are relayed to neurons in the olfactory bulbs (there is one in each nasal cavity) before being carried along the olfactory nerve to the primary olfactory cortex, part of the brain's limbic system, for analysis and response. By the time the electrical signals of smell are directed to the limbic systems the component parts of a smell—wet leather, wildflowers, golden apples, and river rocks—have already been identified and translated into electric signals. The limbic system recombines these components for analysis by scanning its vast memory data bank for related matches. Once analysis is completed, the limbic system triggers an appropriate physiological response. In the case of our Puligny wine, the limbic system might recognize it as a pleasant white wine made from Chardonnay grapes. More experienced wine tasters, with a more highly developed memory data bank, connect our wine to other Puligny wines and recognize it as Puligny. Expert tasters might be able to recall the vineyard, maker, and year. The more we taste, test, and study, the better we become at identification.

The limbic system is the collective name for structures in the human brain involved in emotion, motivation, and emotional association with memory. It plays its role in the formation of memory by integrating emotional states with stored memories of physical sensations—such as smells.

## OLFACTORY PATHWAY OF PULIGNY-MONTRACHET FROM BOTTLE TO BRAIN

We can trace the olfactory pathway of Puligny from bottle to brain, through the following steps:

- We open the bottle, in happy anticipation
- We pour the wine into a proper glass
- We swirl the glass to release the wine's aromas
- We inhale the wine's bouquet deeply and repeatedly
- Chemical components—esters, ethers, aldehydes, etc.—of the Puligny swirl upward through the nostrils on currents of air
- Midway up the nose, millions of olfactory receptor neurons (olfactory epithelia), with their specialized protein receptors, bind the odorants that form the components of the specific wine profile
- Interaction of the specific odor molecules matched with the right receptor causes the receptor to change shape
- This change gives rise to an electrical signal that goes first to the olfactory bulb and then to the areas of the brain that convert the electrical signal to the identification of a smell, or group of smells
- The brain associates the smell(s) with perception, impressions, emotions, memories, knowledge, and more

OLFACTORY BULB

LIMBIC SYSTEM

# HOW DO WE TASTE?

Like smell, taste belongs to our chemical sensing system. Taste is detected by special structures called taste buds, and we have, on average, between five thousand and ten thousand of them, mainly on the tongue but with a few at the back of the throat and on the palate. Taste buds are the only sensory cells that are regularly replaced throughout a person's lifetime, with total regeneration taking place approximately every ten days. Scientists are examining this phenomenon, hoping that they will discover ways to replicate the process, inducing regeneration in damaged sensory and nerve cells.

Clustered within each taste bud are gustatory cells that have small gustatory hairs containing gustatory receptors. The gustatory receptors, like the olfactory receptors, are sensitive to specific types of dissolved chemicals. Everything we eat and drink must be dissolved—usually by the saliva—in order for the gustatory receptors to identify its taste. Once dissolved, the gustatory

FIRST IMPRESSIONS? A well-crafted wine's aroma evolves in the glass and our noses quickly become inured to smell. This is why it's advisable to revisit wine's aroma a few times in any given tasting or flight. Tasters can take a cue from the old perfumer's trick of sniffing their sleeves between the many essences/elixirs they may smell on a given day. In other words, they turn to something completely different—balancing sense with non-sense.

receptors read then translate a food's chemical structure before converting that information to electrical signals. These electrical signals are transmitted, via the facial and glossopharyngeal nerves, through the nose and on to the brain, where they are decoded and identified as a specific taste.

## OUR SALIVATION

Saliva is critical not only to the digestion of food and to the maintenance of oral hygiene, but also to flavor. Saliva dissolves taste stimuli, allowing their chemistry to reach the gustatory receptor cells.

Remember being told to chew your food slowly so that you would enjoy your meal more? It's true. Taking more time to chew food and savor beverages allows more of their chemical components to dissolve and more aromas to be released. This provides more material for the gustatory and olfactory receptors to analyze, sending more complex data to the brain, which enhances perception. Taste and smell intensify.

While the majority of our taste buds are located in the mouth, we also have thousands of additional nerve endings—especially on the moist epithelial surfaces of the mouth, throat, nose, and eyes—that perceive texture, temperature, and assess a variety of factors, which recognize sensations like the prickle of sulfur, the coolness of mint, and the burn of pepper. While humans can detect an estimated 10,000 smells and smell combinations, we can taste just four or five basic flavors—sweet, salty, sour, bitter, and umami (savory). Of these, only sweet, sour, and occasional bitterness are applicable to wine tasting.

The overall word for what we perceive in food and drink through a combination of smelling, tasting, and feeling is flavor, with smell being so predominant of the three that Kevin believes that wine tasting is actually "wine smelling," and some chemists describe wine as "a tasteless liquid that is deeply fragrant." It is flavor that lets us know whether we are eating an apple or a pear, drinking a Puligny-Montrachet or an Australian Chardonnay. Anyone doubting the importance of smell in determining taste is encouraged to hold his or her nose while eating chocolate or cheese, either of which will tend to taste like chalk.

## TASTE PLACE

Though maps, such as the one shown on the next page, typically place concentrated sweet receptors at the tip of the tongue, bitter at the back, and sour at the sides, taste buds are broadly distributed throughout the mouth. In wine

TASTING AND CHEWING increase the rate of salivary flow.

BITTERNESS IN wine arises from a combination of high alcohol and high tannin.

MUCH OF what is commonly described as taste—80–90% or more—is aroma/bouquet as sensed and articulated by our olfactory receptors, and mouthfeel and texture as sensed by surrounding organs.

tasting, it is important to let wine aerate once it reaches your mouth so that it will release more aromas and intensify flavor. This is done by rolling the wine over your tongue and allowing it to linger on the tongue. This process also spreads the wine across a wider array of gustatory receptors, and gives them more time to analyze its taste. You'll discover that a good wine will reveal a first, middle, and lasting impression, which are largely determined by aroma and mouthfeel.

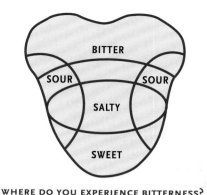

**WHERE DO YOU EXPERIENCE BITTERNESS?**

The back of the tongue
On the sides
In the throat

### Mouthfeel

Mouthfeel is literally how a wine feels in the mouth. These feelings are characterized by sensations that delight, prick, and/or pain our tongue, lips, and cheeks, and that often linger in the mouth after swallowing or spitting. They can range from the piquant tingle of Champagne bubbles to the teeth-tightening astringency of tannin; from the cool expansiveness of menthol/eucalyptus to the heat of a high-alcohol red; and from the cloying sweetness of a low-acid white to the velvet coating of a rich Rhône. The physical feel of wine is also important to mouthfeel, and includes: body, thin to full; weight, light to heavy; and texture, austere, unctuous, silky, and chewy. Each contributes to wine's overall balance. More than just impressions, these qualities can trigger a physical response—drying, puckering, and salivation—which can literally have wines dancing on the tongue and clinging to the teeth.

## SMELL AND TASTE TOGETHER

Recent research presents additional proof that taste seldom works alone (something wine tasters have known for centuries) and provides the first clear scientific evidence that olfaction is uniquely "dual." We often smell by inhaling through both nose and mouth simultaneously, adding to smell's complexity.

There are two paths by which smells can reach the olfactory receptors:

*Orthonasal stimulation:* Odor compounds (smells) reach the olfactory bulb via the "external nares" or nostrils.

*Retronasal stimulation:* Odor compounds reach the olfactory bulb via the "internal nares," located inside the mouth (the respiratory tract at the back of the throat). This is why even if you pinch your nose shut, a strong cheese inhaled through the nose and mouth may still smell. Molecules that stimulate the olfactory receptors float around in your mouth, up through your internal nares, and stimulate the olfactory neurons in the olfactory bulb.

According to an article in the journal *Neuron*, researchers reported that the smell of chocolate stimulated different brain regions when introduced into the olfactory system through the nose (orthonasally) than it did when introduced through the mouth (retronasally). The study suggests that sensing odor through the nose may help indicate the availability of food while identification through the mouth may signify receipt of food.

## OLFACTORY ABILITIES OVER A LIFETIME

Are we born with equal olfactory ability? What accounts for the rise and fall of olfactory abilities over the course of a lifetime, or even over the course of a day?

Experts agree that, except in rare instances of brain disease or damage, we are born with relatively equal ability to perceive smell, although our ability to identify and articulate those smells varies widely. In general, women have the advantage over men in perceiving and identifying smells throughout their life cycle. While it's not known why, it is theorized that because women bear the enormous responsibility of conceiving and raising children, a keen sense of smell evolved as an aid to everything from choosing a mate to caring for a family.

No scientific evidence shows that our olfactory abilities change over the course of a day, although many winemakers and wine professionals believe their senses to be keener and their palates cleaner in the morning. When evaluating wines for my wine class and books, I prefer to taste around 11 a.m. Others prefer tasting wine with a slight edge of hunger, which seems to enhance their alertness. Get to know your own cycles!

SUPER-TASTERS have more than ten thousand taste buds.

**SENSORY OVERLOAD**

Super-tasters can be supersensitive, and they may find wines with tannin and high alcohol too bitter; so Cabernet Sauvignon, for example, may not be to their liking. They may also be put off by any sweetness in wine. Non-tasters are the opposite; they might not be bothered by tannin or high alcohol, and sweet wines would probably be perfectly acceptable.

THIRTY-FIVE PERCENT of women and 15% of men are super-tasters.

### WHO ARE YOU?

*According to Janet Zimmerman, writing in "Science of the Kitchen: Taste and Texture," approximately one-quarter of the population are "super-tasters," one-quarter are "non-tasters," and the remaining half are "tasters." Super-tasters have a significantly higher number of taste buds than tasters, and both groups outnumber non-tasters for taste buds. The averages for the three groups are 96 taste buds per square centimeter for non-tasters, 184 for tasters, and a whopping 425 for super-tasters. Super-tasters tend to taste everything more intensely. Sweets are sweeter, bitters are more bitter, and many foods and beverages, including alcohol, taste and feel unpleasantly strong. Non-tasters are far from picky, and seem less conscious of and therefore less engaged with what they eat and drink. Tasters, the largest and least homogeneous group, vary in their personal preferences but tend to enjoy the widest array of food and drink and relish the act of eating and drinking the most of the three groups.*

Dr. Alan Hirsch of the Smell & Taste Treatment and Research Foundation and experts from the Monell Chemical Senses Center have shed additional light on the evolution and devolution of smell over a lifetime by describing the changes that occur at periods in the life cycle.

**Fetus:** In utero, the fetus acquires its blood supply through the placenta, via which it may receive odorants that help the baby recognize Mom at birth, and which may lead to developing food preferences for what Mom ate or drank.

**Lactation:** Flavors and smells from food and beverage make their way through mother's milk to the infant. As a result, preferences are formed toward sweet and away from bitter. Any wine and spirits the mother consumes while nursing are measurable in the baby.

**Early Childhood:** As a child grows, so does his or her ability to recognize and remember different odors, especially those that are paired with an emotional event. At this point in their development, children usually have a hard time describing smells in words, but they are forming lifelong positive and negative sensory and emotional impressions. For example, smelling roses in the garden with Mom will have a far different impact on the feeling the scent elicits later in life than if a child first smells roses at the funeral of a loved one.

**Elementary School Years:** Boys' and girls' ability to perceive and identify smells continues to develop, becoming more acute, with the ability to distinguish more smells.

**Puberty:** The sense of smell is at its most acute in both men and women, although women surge farther ahead at the onset of menstruation. This heightened sensitivity to smell will persist throughout their fertile years.

**Adulthood:** Women consistently outscore men in their ability to put names to smells in adulthood, and women give higher ratings on pleasure and intensity, lower ratings on unpleasant aromas. Women's sense of smell is particularly acute at ovulation and during pregnancy.

**Midlife:** Men and women slowly begin to lose their acuity of smell between the ages of 35 and 40, though the ability to identify and remember smells can continue to improve over the course of a lifetime.

**Age 65:** By the time they reach age 65, about half the population will experience a decline of, on average, 33 percent in their olfactory abilities. A quarter of the population has no ability to smell after 65.

**Age 80:** A majority of the population will show losses of up to 50 percent in olfactory abilities by age 80.

THE SMELL & TASTE Treatment and Research Foundation published the following lists of the different smells that arouse women and men:

| WOMEN | MEN |
|---|---|
| *Turn-ons* | *Turn-ons* |
| Baby powder | Buns |
| Banana-nut bread | Cinnamon |
| Chocolate | Doughnuts |
| Cucumber | Lavender |
| Good & Plenty candy | Licorice |
| Lavender | Pumpkin pie |
| | |
| *Turn-offs* | *Turn-offs* |
| Charcoal barbecue smoke | None found |
| Cherry | |
| Men's cologne | |

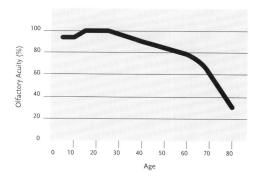

OLFACTORY ACUITY is at its peak in young adulthood.

IMPLICIT LEARNING is largely unconscious. Odors are identified and perceived and associations are made mainly in the background (such as the smell of hot dogs in a baseball stadium). Explicit learning is a conscious process, in which the person is aware of the learning that is taking place (such as at a wine tasting).

IN THE EMPEROR OF SCENT, Chandler Burr uses a particularly pungent Burgundian cheese to illustrate cultural preferences: When they smell the Soumaintrain, "Americans think, 'Good God!' The Japanese think, 'I must now commit suicide.' The French think, 'Where's the bread?'"

ENGLISH WINE writers will occasionally use the word "gooseberries" to describe a wine's aroma, but most Americans are unfamiliar with gooseberries and don't know what they smell like.

# ACCOUNTING FOR SMELL AND TASTE

What accounts for ethnic and cultural differences in smell and taste abilities, perceptions, and preferences? According to Monell Chemical Senses Center anthropologist Claudia Damhuis, while some odor associations/preferences might be innate (e.g., an aversion to the odor of rotten food), the vast majority of them are learned.

## THE WAY WE LEARN

The ability to identify and perceive odors, as well as odor preferences, are learned both implicitly and explicitly through a number of variables including environment, culture, custom, context, and a variety of sociocultural factors.

Among the factors that impact cultural differences in odor preferences are:

- Physiological differences such as the size and presence of glands in different populations
- Differences in hygienic habits
- Acceptability and denial of odors according to cultural norms and etiquette
- Familiarity with specific odors
- The role and function attributed to specific odors
- Cultural differences in food preparations and related olfactory experiences and association
- Precision of language used to express odor perceptions and associations

## THE WAY WE SMELL

*According to Lyall Watson's* Jacobson's Organ and the Remarkable Nature of Smell, *our two square meters of skin come equipped with three million sweat glands. But whereas people of European and African descent have armpits densely packed with apocrine glands, people of Asian origin have far fewer, and some have no armpit glands at all; 90 percent of the population in Japan has no detectable underarm odor. Japanese people who first encountered European traders in the nineteenth century described them as* bata-kusai—"stinks of butter." *Meantime, the French were reveling in their own aromas. Napoléon sent a note to Josephine that read: "I'll be arriving in Paris tomorrow evening. Don't wash."*

## GENERAL PREFERENCES

Across a great variety of ethnicities, odors can be classified into a few general categories of association, which are smells and flavors associated with nature, man, civilization, food and drink, and more.

A worldwide smell survey conducted by *National Geographic* and Monell found universal unpleasantness noted across nine regions for fecal odors, human odors, material in decomposition, and mercaptans (sulfur-containing compounds often added to natural gas as a warning agent). Most odors, however, were rated pleasant, including vegetation, lavender, amyl acetate (banana odor), galaxolide (synthetic musk), and eugenol (synthetic clove oil).

## CULTURAL DIFFERENCES

Physiology, environment, diet, and language all play roles in cultural preference. The Asian reliance on soy rather than dairy products—which carries through even in the smells and flavors of mothers' milk—might account for Asian cultural aversion to strong cheese smells and flavors. Asian-American communities, families, or individuals may or may not exhibit this aversion, depending on the degree to which they retain native food-and-drink customs or adopt local ones.

Other cultural differences might in fact be environmental, as was suggested by a study of the Serer N'Dut of Senegal, who classify their odors in only five categories—scented, milk-fishy, rotten, urinelike, and acidic—or linguistic, as in a cross-cultural French / Vietnamese / American study in which participants' odor categorization did not correlate with their linguistic categorization.

# THINGS THAT CAN AFFECT YOUR SENSE OF SMELL

According to the University of California at San Diego Nasal Dysfunction Clinic, an estimated 1 to 2 percent of the American population suffers from the total loss of the sense of smell.

The primary complaint for the majority of people who seek help for smell loss is that food has lost its flavor. But their lives suffer in other ways, too—from the inability to avoid such dangers as spoiled food and gas leaks to missing out on some of life's greatest and most sensuous pleasures: the sense

*Osme*, the Greek word meaning "odor," is the root of many medical definitions relating to smell, among them:

NORMOSMIA: Normal sense of smell

DYSOSMIA: Any defect or impairment in the sense of smell; a collective term that includes any of the following:

ANOSMIA: Complete loss of the sense of smell

HYPOSMIA: Partial loss of the sense of smell

HYPEROSMIA: Increased ability to smell

PAROSMIA: Distortion of the sense of smell

PHANTOSMIA: Phantom smells and olfactory hallucinations

PRESBYOSMIA: A decrease in the sense of smell, associated with aging

**SMELLING TOO WELL?**

Alan Hirsch of the Smell & Taste Treatment and Research Foundation tells of a woman with Addison's disease whose sense of smell was heightened 1,000%—approaching the olfactory acuity of a bloodhound or cockroach—by the illness. The smells she picked up bothered her immensely. The patient developed agoraphobia (a fear of being in crowds or public places) and was not able to leave her home. Her heightened abilities (or in this case, disabilities) came under control when the disease did.

of smell plays a key role in sexual excitement. And while Americans spend an enormous amount of time and money masking body odors and sexual smells, those smells remain vital to our sense of self and our bonds with others—from the families we are born into to the families we create.

## WHAT CAUSES SMELL AND TASTE DISORDERS?

It is extremely rare to be born with chemosensory disorders. Most smell disorders develop after an injury or illness or in response to irritants or drugs.

An array of injuries, illnesses, and irritants can adversely affect the sense of smell, partially or fully, permanently or temporarily, including head or brain injuries; nose injuries; allergies, colds, and sinusitis; diseases including diabetes, epilepsy, and lupus; and pollutants and toxic chemicals.

Unfortunately, even when an illness is temporary or a chemical irritant is fleeting, damage to nasal plates and passages can be permanent and can impair or destroy the sense of smell. While cells in the olfactory epithelium do regenerate normally, severe damage can eliminate their ability to regenerate.

Treatments that can adversely affect the sense of smell include surgery of the head and neck; dental work; chemotherapy and other cancer treatments; many types of medications; and alcohol.

Some medicines can have a positive impact on the sense of smell and taste. Interestingly, groups of medicines used to treat allergies, sinusitis, infection, and inflammation can open nasal passages and therefore have temporary ameliorative effects on smell and taste. They include antihistamines and decongestants, antibiotics, and nasal douches and lubricants.

Cluster headaches, migraines, and Addison's disease can temporarily heighten (sometimes horrifically) the sense of smell and taste.

## SMELL AND TASTE TESTING AND TREATMENT

There are many interesting ways for professionals and laypeople alike to test the sense of smell. Dr. Richard Doty, founder of Sensonics, Inc., has developed an array of tests that assess chemosensory function. They range from the scratch-and-sniff University of Pennsylvania smell identification test to the smell threshold test, which is often used to identify sensory experts and to screen workers involved with potential hazards. The Smell and Taste Treatment and Research Foundation uses these, as well as hedonic testing, to measure how much subjects like what they smell, and memory testing to see what types of memory (short-term, long-term, implicit, explicit) the smells have been committed to. More information on these and other methods of assessing the olfactory sense can be found by consulting the resources at the end of this chapter.

Because smell can be so important to one's lifestyle, it is not uncommon to find coexisting mood disorders among people with olfactory disorders. Depending on the cause and severity of the smell disorder, treatment ranges from medications such as vitamins, steroids, calcium channel blockers, anticonvulsants, and antidepressants, to surgery. It is important to seek help to identify, assess, treat, and manage these disorders.

For all those who can, we recommend . . . wine tasting!

## TRAINING AND STRENGTHENING

Many animals may have a more highly developed sense of smell than we do. But we humans have brains brilliantly designed to preserve, protect, and enrich all aspects of our lives through smell. In our experience, there is no better way to train and strengthen the senses, memory, and mind than through fully, consciously savoring wine.

The best news? Besides investing in some good bottles, proper storage, and proper glassware, all we need to fully appreciate wine is built in, in the form of our five senses. Wine tasters have known innately for ages what evolving scientific understanding and empiric evidence are only now proving: the power and importance of smell. And while the explicit knowledge of the science of smell is good, it is not always essential to our implicit experience.

That said, to embrace, apply, articulate, and improve on what we already have, let's open a bottle of vino!

## TOWARD A COMMON LANGUAGE OF TASTE AND SMELL

Smell is a relatively inadequate word for our most primitive and powerful sense. It means both the smells that emanate from us (we are what we eat and drink) as well as the smells we perceive. Throughout history, wine tasters have done much to create a common language, and to savor the intersection where

**ONE MAN'S LOSS**

Ben Cohen of Ben & Jerry's is purportedly hyposmic. As often happens with sensory loss, other senses compensate where possible. Might this be why he created Chunky Monkey and so many richly textured ice creams?

SOME YOGA traditions use a neti pot, a kind of nasal douche, for keeping the nose's mucous layer moist and healthy.

ANTIHISTAMINES, while they may clear the nasal passages, also tend to dry them out, so they can be a mixed blessing.

**LANGUAGE OF SMELL**

Finding the language to describe what we smell, and how what we smell affects us, evolves over our lifetime, with women being slightly better at it than men.

DIFFERENT SMELLS of wine come
    from:
The grape
The winemaking
The aging

**SOURCES AND RESOURCES**

Monell Chemical Senses Center,
www.monell.org

National Institutes of Health,
www.nidcd.nih.gov/health/smelltaste

Professional Friends of Wine: A Sensory
User's Manual, www.winepros.org/wine101/
sensory_guide.htm

Sensonics, www.sensonics.com

Sense of Smell Institute,
www.senseofsmell.org

Smell & Taste Treatment and Research
Foundation, www.scienceofsmell.com

The Senses Bureau,
www.thesensesbureau.com

Tim Jacob Smell Research Laboratory,
www.cf.ac.uk/biosi/staff/jacob

University of California San Diego
Nasal Dysfunction Clinic, health.ucsd.edu/
specialties/surgery/otolaryngology/nasal

Wine Aroma Wheel, by Ann Noble, www.
winearomawheel.com

*A Natural History of the Senses* by Diane
Ackerman

*Jacobson's Organ and the Remarkable Nature
of Smell* by Lyall Watson

*Life's a Smelling Success: Using Scent to
Empower Your Memory and Learning* by
Alan Hirsch, M.D.

*The Emperor of Scent: A True Story of
Perfume and Obsession* by Chandler Burr

enlivened and articulated senses meet memory, anticipation, association, and personal preferences throughout history.

Like colors, aroma can be broken down into basic categories which, when combined, yield the rich symphony that is wine. Ann Noble's Wine Aroma Wheel (see resources in the margin for more information) categorizes basic fruit aromas as citrus (grapefruit, lemon), berry (blackberry, raspberry, strawberry, black currant), tree (cherry, apricot, peach, apple), tropical (pineapple, melon, banana), dried (raisin, prune, fig), and others. Likewise, vegetative aromas can be categorized as fresh (stemmy, grassy, green, eucalyptus, mint), canned (asparagus, olive, artichoke), and dried (hay, straw, tea, tobacco). Other aroma categories include nutty, caramelized, woody, earthy, chemical, pungent, floral, and spicy.

Still, no two people are alike in either how they smell or the smells they perceive. It is deeply personal and experiential. Here is our best effort to convey how scent feels and what it means to us.

Wendy says "Puligny" to herself, simply because she loves the word nearly as much as the wine. It serves as a homing signal that brings her to self and center—to a time and a place and a wine she loves, and to the kind of bonds that endure.

Kevin goes out on his porch with a glass of some favorite, special vintage and looks into the night sky. Embodied in every sip is all that he treasures and honors about Windows on the World, and a reason to look up at the stars.

We're hoping and trusting that you'll find wine and spirits like this, and that you'll share words of them with us. In the meantime, here's to your health and happiness, and to savoring wine and life in and with every sense!

# Matching Wine and Food

## BY KEVIN ZRALY AND ANDREA ROBINSON

Y‍ou've tasted your way through eight classes in this book and discovered at least a shopping cart's worth of wines to really enjoy. And for what purpose? Food! The final stop on the wine odyssey—and the whole point of the trip—is the dinner table. Quite simply, wine and food were meant for each other. Just look at the dining habits of the world's best eaters (the French, the Italians, the Spanish): wine is the seasoning that livens up even everyday dishes. Salt and pepper shakers are a fixture of the American table, but in Europe it's the wine bottle.

## WINE-AND-FOOD MATCHING BASICS

First, forget everything you've ever heard about wine-and-food pairing. There's only one rule when it comes to matching wine and food: the best wine to pair with your meal is whatever wine you like. No matter what!

If you know what you want, by all means have it. Worried that your preference of a Chardonnay with a sirloin steak might not seem "right"? Remember, it's your own palate that you have to please.

### What's wine-and-food synergy?

Sounds like a computer game for gourmets, right? If up until now you haven't been the wine-with-dinner type, you're in for a great adventure. Remember, the European tradition of wine with meals was not the result of a shortage of milk or iced tea. Rather, it results from what I call wine-and-food synergy—when the two are paired, both taste better.

How does it work? In the same way that combining certain foods improves their overall taste. For example, you squeeze fresh lemon onto your oysters, or grate Parmesan cheese over spaghetti marinara, because it's the combination of flavors that makes the dish.

ANDREA ROBINSON worked with Kevin at Windows on the World. She is one of only fifteen women in the world to hold the title of Master Sommelier, awarded by the Court of Master Sommeliers. She has written several books on wine and food, and was named Outstanding Wine & Spirits Professional by the James Beard Foundation.

ARE YOU a menu maven or a wine-list junkie? Personally, I look at the wine list first, choose my wine, and then make my meal selection.

CHARDONNAY IS a red wine masquerading as a white wine, which, in my opinion, makes it a perfect match for steak.

**HOW DO I MAKE MY WINE AND FOOD DECISION?**

What kind of wine do I like?
Texture of food (heavy or light)
Preparation (grilled, sautéed, baked, etc.)
Sauce (cream, tomato, wine, etc.)

Apply that idea to wine-and-food pairing; foods and wines have different flavors, textures, and aromas. Matching them can give you a new, more interesting flavor than you would get if you were washing down your dinner with, say, milk (unless you were dining on chocolate-chip cookies). The more flavorful the food, the more flavorful the wine should be.

## Do I have to be a wine expert to choose enjoyable wine-and-food matches?

Why not just use what you already know? Most of us have been tasting and testing the flavors, aromas, and textures of foods since before we got our first teeth, so we're all food experts! As we'll show you, just some basic information about wine and food styles is all you'll need to pick wines that can enhance your meals.

## What about acidity?

Acid acts as a turbocharger for flavor. A high-acid wine is a good choice for dishes with cream or cheese sauces. It enhances and lengthens the flavor of the dish. Watch television's Food Network. The TV chefs are always using lemons and limes—acidic ingredients. Even dishes that aren't "sour" have a touch of an acid ingredient to pump up the flavor. As chef Emeril Lagasse says, "Kick it up a notch!"

## What role does texture play?

There's an obvious difference in the texture or firmness of different foods. Wine also has texture, and there are nuances of flavor in a wine that can make it an adequate, outstanding, or unforgettable selection with the meal. Very full-style wines have a mouth-filling texture and bold, rich flavors that make your palate sit up and take notice. But when it comes to food, these wines tend to overwhelm most delicate dishes (and clash with boldly flavored ones). Remember, we're looking for harmony and balance. A general rule is: The sturdier or fuller in flavor the food, the more full-bodied the wine should be. For foods that are milder the best wines to use would be medium- or light-bodied.

Once you get to know the wines, matching them with food is no mystery. Here are two lists (one for red, one for white) with some suggestions based on the texture of the wines and the foods they can match.

# White Wines

| LIGHT-BODIED WHITES | MEDIUM-BODIED WHITES | FULL-BODIED WHITES |
| --- | --- | --- |
| Alsace Pinot Blanc | Chablis Premier Cru | Chablis Grand Cru |
| Alsace Riesling | Chardonnay* | Chardonnay* |
| Chablis | Gavi | Chassagne- |
| Frascati | Gewürztraminer | Montrachet |
| German Kabinett | Grüner Veltliner | Meursault |
| and Spätlese | Mâcon-Villages | Puligny-Montrachet |
| Muscadet | Montagny | Viognier |
| Orvieto | Pouilly-Fuissé | |
| Pinot Grigio | Pouilly-Fumé | |
| Pinot Gris | Sancerre | |
| Sauvignon Blanc* | Sauvignon Blanc*/ | |
| Soave | Fumé Blanc | |
| Verdicchio | St-Véran | |
| | White Graves | |

MY FAVORITE white wine for picnics is German Riesling Kabinett/Spätlese. On a hot summer day, I can think of no better white wine than a chilled German Riesling. The balance of fruit, acid, and sweetness as well as the lightness (low alcohol) make these wines a perfect match for salads, fruits, and cheese. For those who prefer a drier-style Riesling, try Alsace, Washington State, or the Finger Lakes region of New York.

# Matching Foods

| | | |
| --- | --- | --- |
| Clams | Bass | Duck |
| Flounder | Scallops | Lobster |
| Oysters | Shrimp | Roast chicken |
| Sole | Snapper | Salmon |
| | Veal paillard | Sirloin steak |
| | | Swordfish |
| | | Tuna |

\* Note that starred wines are listed more than once. That's because they can be vinified in a range of styles from light to full texture, depending on the producer. When buying these, if you don't know the style of a particular winery, it's a good idea to ask the restaurant server or wine merchant for help.

# Red Wines

My favorite red wine for picnics is Beaujolais. I'll never forget my first summer in France, sitting outside a bistro in Paris and being served a Beaujolais. A great Beaujolais is the essence of fresh fruit without the tannins, and its higher acidity blends nicely with all picnic fare. For barbecued shrimp in the middle of the summer, I opt for chilled Beaujolais.

My favorite red wine for lunch is Pinot Noir. The light, easy-drinking style of a Pinot Noir will not overpower the usual luncheon fare of soups, salads, and sandwiches.

Pinot Noir is a white wine masquerading as a red wine, which makes it a perfect wine for fish and fowl. Other choices include Chianti Classico and Spanish Riojas (Crianza and Reserva).

Bitterness in wine comes from the combination of high tannin and high alcohol, and these wines are best served with food that is either grilled, charcoaled, or blackened.

| LIGHT-BODIED REDS | MEDIUM-BODIED REDS | FULL-BODIED REDS |
|---|---|---|
| Bardolino | Barbera | Barbaresco |
| Beaujolais | Bordeaux (Crus Bourgeois) | Barolo |
| Beaujolais-Villages | Burgundy Premiers | Bordeaux |
| Bordeaux (proprietary) | and Grands Crus | (great châteaux) |
| Burgundy (Village) | Cabernet Sauvignon* | Cabernet Sauvignon* |
| Pinot Noir* | Chianti Classico Riserva | Châteauneuf-du-Pape |
| Rioja-Crianza | Côtes du Rhône | Hermitage |
| Valpolicella | Crozes-Hermitage | Malbec* |
| | Cru Beaujolais | Merlot* |
| | Dolcetto | Syrah/Shiraz* |
| | Malbec* | Zinfandel* |
| | Merlot* | |
| | Pinot Noir* | |
| | Rioja Reserva and | |
| | Gran Reserva | |
| | Syrah/Shiraz* | |
| | Zinfandel* | |

## Matching Foods

| | | |
|---|---|---|
| Duck | Game birds | Beefsteak (sirloin) |
| Roast chicken | Pork chops | Game meats |
| Salmon | Veal chops | Lamb chops |
| Swordfish | | Leg of lamb |
| Tuna | | |

## COOKING WITH WINE

Try to use the same wine or style that you are going to serve.

*"I cook with wine; sometimes I even add it to food."*
—W. C. Fields

## No-Fault Wine Insurance

Drinking wine with your meals should add enjoyment, not stress, but it happens all too often. You briefly eye the wine list or scan the wine-shop shelf, thinking well, maybe . . . a beer. In the face of so many choices, you end up going with the familiar. But it can be easy to choose a wine to enjoy with your meal.

From endless experimentation at home and in the restaurant, I've come up with a list of "user-friendly" wines that will go nicely with virtually any dish. What these wines have in common is that they are light- to medium-bodied, and they have ample fruit and acidity. The idea here is that you will get a harmonious balance of flavors from both the wine and the food, with neither overwhelming the other. Also, if you want the dish to play center stage, your best bets are wines from this list.

## User-Friendly Wines

| ROSÉ WINES | WHITE WINES | RED WINES |
|---|---|---|
| Virtually any rosé or white Zinfandel | Champagne and sparkling wines | Beaujolais-Villages |
| | German Riesling, Kabinett, and Spätlese | Chianti Classico |
| | Mâcon-Villages | Côtes du Rhône |
| | Pinot Grigio | Merlot |
| | Pouilly-Fumé and Sancerre | Pinot Noir |
| | Sauvignon Blanc/ Fumé Blanc | Rioja Crianza |

These wines work well for what I call "restaurant roulette"—where one diner orders fish, another orders meat, and so on. They can also match well with distinctively spiced ethnic foods that might otherwise clash with a full-flavored wine. And, of course, all these wines are enjoyable to drink on their own.

## Do sauces play a major role when you're matching wine and food?

Yes, because the sauce can change or define the entire taste and texture of a dish. Is the sauce acidic? Heavy? Spicy? Subtly flavored foods let the wine play the starring role. Dishes with bold, spicy ingredients can overpower the flavor nuances and complexity that distinguish a great wine.

**SPICY SAUCES**

Try something with carbon dioxide, such as a Champagne or a sparkling wine.

THE ADDITION of salt to food highlights both the tannins and the alcohol in wine.

YOUNG RED wines with a lot of tannin taste better when paired with foods that have high fat content. The fat softens the tannins.

Let's consider the effect sauces can have on a simple boneless breast of chicken. A very simply prepared chicken paillard might match well with a light-bodied white wine. If you add a rich cream sauce or a cheese sauce, then you might prefer a high-acid, medium-bodied, or even a full-bodied white wine. A red tomato-based sauce, such as a marinara, might call for a light-bodied red wine.

## Wine and Cheese—Friends or Foes?

As in all matters of taste, the topic of wine and food comes with its share of controversy and debate. Where it's especially heated is on the subject of matching wine and cheese.

Wine and cheese are "naturals" for each other. For me, a good cheese and a good wine will enhance the flavors and complexities of both. Also, the protein in cheese will soften the tannins in a red wine.

The key to this match is in carefully selecting the cheese; therein lies the controversy. Some chefs and wine-and-food experts caution that some of the most popular cheeses for eating are the least appropriate for wine because they overpower it—a ripe cheese like Brie is a classic example.

The "keep-it-simple" approach applies again here. I find that the best cheeses for wines are the following: Parmigiano-Reggiano, fresh mozzarella, Pecorino, Taleggio, and Fontina from Italy; Chèvre, Montrachet, Tomme, and Gruyère from France; Dutch Gouda; English or domestic Cheddar; domestic aged or fresh goat cheese and Monterey Jack; and Manchego from Spain.

My favorite wine-and-cheese matches:

**Chèvre/fresh goat cheese**: Sancerre, Sauvignon Blanc

**Manchego**: Rioja, Brunello di Montalcino

**Montrachet, aged (dry) Monterey Jack**: Cabernet Sauvignon, Bordeaux

**Pecorino or Parmigiano-Reggiano**: Chianti Classico Riserva, Brunello di Montalcino, Cabernet Sauvignon, Bordeaux, Barolo, and Amarone

What to drink with Brie? Try Champagne or sparkling wine. And blue cheeses, because of their strong flavor, overpower most wines except—get ready for this—dessert wines! The classic (and truly delicious) matches are Roquefort cheese with French Sauternes, and Stilton cheese with Port.

# SWEET SATISFACTION: WINE WITH DESSERT, WINE AS DESSERT

I remember my first taste of a dessert wine—a Sauternes from France's Bordeaux region. It was magical! Then there are also Port, Sherry, and Beerenauslese, to name a few—all very different wines with one thing in common: sweetness. Hence the name "dessert" wines—their sweetness closes your palate and makes you feel satisfied after a good meal. But with wines like these, dessert is just one part of the wine-and-food story.

"Wine with dessert?" you're thinking. At least in this country, coffee is more common, a glass of brandy or liqueur if you're splurging. But as more and more restaurants add dessert wines to their by-the-glass offerings, perhaps the popularity will grow for these kinds of wine. (Because they're so rich, a full bottle of dessert wine isn't practical unless several people are sharing it. For serving at home, dessert wines in half-bottles are a good alternative.)

I like a dessert wine a few minutes before the dessert itself, to prepare you for what is to come. But you certainly can serve a sweet dessert wine with the course.

Here are some of my favorite wine-and-dessert combinations:

**Asti Spumante**: fresh fruits, biscotti

**Beerenauslese and Late Harvest Riesling**: fruit tarts, crème brûlée, almond cookies

**Madeira**: milk chocolate, nut tarts, crème caramel, coffee- or mocha-flavored desserts

**Muscat Beaumes-de-Venise**: crème brûlée, fresh fruit, fruit sorbets, lemon tart

**Port**: dark chocolate desserts, walnuts, poached pears, Stilton cheese

**Pedro Ximénez Sherry**: vanilla ice cream (with the wine poured over it), raisin-nut cakes, desserts containing figs or dried fruits

**Sauternes**: fruit tarts, poached fruits, crème brûlée, caramel and hazelnut desserts, Roquefort cheese

**Vin Santo**: biscotti (for dipping in the wine)

**Vouvray**: fruit tarts, fresh fruits

Often, I prefer to serve the dessert wine as dessert. That way I can concentrate on savoring the complex and delicious flavors with a clear palate. It's especially convenient at home—all you have to do to serve your guests an exotic dessert is pull a cork! And if you're counting calories, a glass of dessert wine can give you the satisfying sweetness of dessert with a lot less bulk (and zero fat!).

## How much wine should I order for my dinner party?

At a dinner party where several wines will be served, I allow one bottle for every five people, which equals approximately one five-ounce glass per person.

## What's the best wine to serve with hors d'oeuvres for my dinner reception?

Champagne. One of the most versatile wines produced in the world, Champagne has a "magical effect" on guests. Whether served at a wedding or a dinner at home, Champagne remains a symbol of celebration, romance, prosperity, and fun.

**FOR FURTHER READING**

I recommend *Perfect Pairings* by Evan Goldstein and *Great Wine & Food Made Simple* by Andrea Robinson.

12 BOTTLES OF wine = 1 case

**BOTTLE SIZES**

375 ml = 12.7 oz = half-bottle
750 ml = 25.4 oz = full bottle
1.5 liters = 50.8 oz = magnum (two bottles)
3 liters = 101.6 oz = double magnum
  (4 bottles)
6 liters = 203.2 oz = imperial (8 bottles)
9 liters = 304.8 oz = salamanazar
  (12 bottles)

# Best Value List: $30 and Under

IN 2009, I finished a trip around the world to fifteen countries, eighty regions, and 400 wine appellations, and tasted over 6,000 wines. It was an eye-opening experience about the high quality of wines at all price points, which is certainly good news for the consumer. The great wines will always remain expensive and unfortunately will be consumed only by a few. The worldwide recession has actually been beneficial to the pricing of most wines. It has helped change the concept that in order for a wine to be really good it has to cost a lot of money. Today there are hundreds of wines priced under $30 that are equal in quality to wines that I have tasted that cost over $100. Bottom line: this is one of the best times ever for buying a very good bottle of wine at a reasonable price.

There are many great wine values in the world that I would have included in this chapter, but many of them are not available in all markets, and therefore are not listed. *Note: An asterisk indicates that a wine is heavier in body.*

## FRANCE

Although France sometimes has a reputation for very expensive wines (great châteaux of Bordeaux, domaines of Burgundy, etc.) there always have been great values made in France. From Alsace: Rieslings, Pinot Blancs, and Pinot Gris; from the Loire Valley: Muscadet, Sancerre, and Pouilly-Fumé; from Burgundy: Beaujolais, Mâcons, Chablis, and Bourgogne Blanc and Rouge; from the Rhône Valley: Côtes du Rhône and Crozes-Hermitage; from Bordeaux: Petit Château and Cru Bourgeois; and the wines from Provence, Languedoc, and Roussillon areas.

Here are some of my favorite French producers and their value wines:

### Red

"A" d'Aussières Rouge Corbières
Château Cabrières
   Châteauneuf-du-Pape*
Château de Clairefont
Château de Sales
Château Greysac
Château Labat
Château Larose-Trintaudon
Château Le Sartre
Château Malromè
Château Meyney*

Chapelle-St-Arnoux Châteauneuf-
   du-Pape Vieilles Vignes*
Château Cantemerle
Château de Maison Neuve
Château Gloria*
Château Haut du Peyrat
Château La Cardonne
Château Le Bonnat
Château Malmaison
Château Maris La Touge Syrah
Château Phélan Ségur*

TOP VALUE WINE REGIONS

Chianti (Italy)
Côtes du Rhône (France)
Maipo (Chile)
Marlborough (New Zealand)
Mendoza (Argentina)
Rías Baixas (Spain)

Château Picard
Château Segondignac
Château Tour Leognan
Coudoulet de Beaucastel
Domaine Bouchard Pinot Noir
Domaine de Chevalier Rouge Pessac-Leognan
Domaine Michel Poinard Crozes-Hermitage*
Domaine de'Obrieu Côtes du Rhône
   Villages "Cuvée les Antonins"
Georges Duboeuf Beaujolais-Villages
Georges Duboeuf Morgon
   "Cave Jean-Ernest Descombes"
Jaboulet Côtes du Rhône Parallèle 45
Jean-Maurice Raffault Chinon
Joseph Drouhin Pinot Noir
   Côte de Beaune-Villages
Lafite Réserve Spéciale
Le Baron de Brane
Louis Jadot Château des Jacques
   Moulin-à-Vent
Marquis de Calon
Montirius Côtes du Rhône
   "Jardin Secret"
Perrin & Fils Côtes du Rhône
Sarget de Gruaud-Larose
Thiery Germain Saumur-Champigny

Château Puynard
Château Simard*
Château Thébot
Domaine Andrè Brunel Côtes-du-
   Rhone Cuvée Sommelongue
Domaine de Lagrézette Cahors*
Domaine du Vieux
   Télégraphe "Télégramme"
   Chateauneuf-du-Pape
Georges Duboeuf Fleurie
Gerard Bertrand Grand Terroir Tautavel
Guigal Côtes du Rhône
Jaboulet Crozes-Hermitage Les Jalets
J. L. Chave Saint-Joseph "Offerus"
J. Vidal-Fleury Côtes du Rhône
La Baronne Rouge "Montagne d'Alaric"
La Vieille Ferme Côtes du Ventoux
Louis Jadot Château de Bellevue Morgon
Maison Champy Pinot Noir Signature
Marjosse Reserve du Château
Mas de Gourgonnier Les Baux
   de Provence Rouge
Montirius Gigondas Terres des Aînés
Perrin & Fils Côtes du Rhône
   Cairanne Peyre Blanche
Villa Ponciago Fleurie La Réserve
   Beaujolais

## White

Bertranon Bordeaux Blanc
Château de Mercey Mercurey Blanc
Château du Trignon
   Côtes du Rhône Blanc
Château Fuissé (Pouilly-Fuissé)
Château Larrivet-Haut-Brion Blanc
Clarendelle (Bordeaux Blanc)
Domaine des Baumard
   Savenniéres
Domaine du Tunnel Saint Joseph
Domaine Mardon Quincy
   "Très Vieilles Vignes"
Faiveley Bourgogne Blanc
Georges Duboeuf Pouilly-Fuissé
Helfrich Riesling
Hugel & Fils Riesling
Jeanguillon Blanc
Louis Jadot Saint-Véran
Louis Latour Pouilly-Vinzelles
Mâcon-Villages (most producers)
Sauvion Pouilly-Fumé Les Ombelles

Château Bonnet Blanc
Château de Sancerre
Château de Rully Blanc
   "La Pucelle" 1er Cru
Château Graville-Lacoste*
Château Olivier Blanc
Claude Lafond Reuilly
Domaine Delaye Saint-Veran
   "Les Pierres Grises"
Domaine Jean Chartron
   Bourgogne Aligoté
Doisy-Daëne Bordeaux Blanc
Francis Blanchet Pouilly Fumé
   "Cuvée Silice"
Helfrich Gewürztraminer Steinkoltz
Hugel & Fils Gentil
La Croix de Carbonnieux Blanc*
Louis Latour Ardèche Chardonnay
Louis Latour Montagny
Olivier Leflaive Saint-Aubin
Sauvion Sancerre Les Brulis

Simonnet-Febvre Chablis
Trimbach Riesling
William Fèvre Chablis
William Fèvre Chablis "Montmains"

Thierry Germain Saumur
    Blanc Cuvée "Soliterre"
William Fèvre Chablis "Domaine"
Willm Cuvèe Emile Willm Riesling
    Rèserve

### Rosé
Château Miraval Côtes de Provence Rosé "Pink Floyd"

# ITALY

Italy is now making its best wines ever! And great values come from all over. From Tuscany: Chianti Classico Riserva, Rosso di Montalcino, and Rossi di Montepulciano; from Piedmont: Barbaras and Dolcetto; from Veneto: Valpolicella, Soave, and the sparkling wine Prosecco; and from Abruzzi: Montelpulciano d'Abruzzo; from northern Italy the Pinot Grigios and Pinot Biancos; and from Sicily, the Nero d'Avola.

Here are some of my favorite Italian producers and their value wines:

### Red
Aldo Rainoldi Nebbiolo
Allegrini "La Grola"
Allegrini Valpolicella Classico
Antinori Santa Cristina Sangiovese
Avignonesi Vino Nobile di Montepulciano*
Bruno Giacosa Barbera d'Alba
Cascata Monticello Dolcetto d'Asti
Castello Banfi Toscana Centine
Di Majo Norante Sangiovese Terre degli Osci
Francesco Rinaldi Dolcetto d'Alba
Le Chiuse Rosso di Montalcino
Lungarotti Rubesco
Masi "Campofiorin"
Michele Chiarlo Barbera d'Asti
Mocali Rosso di Montalcino
Morgante Nero d'Avola
Poggio il Castellare Rosso di Montalcino
Regaleali (Tasca d'Almerita)
    Rosso Nero d'Avola
Sandrone Nebbiolo  d'Alba Valmaggiore
San Polo "Rubio"
Tenuta dell'Ornellaia Le Volte
Zaccagnini Montepulciano d'Abruzzo Riserva*
Zenato Valpolicella

Aleramo Barbera
Allegrini Palazzo Della Torre
Altesino Rosso di Altesino
Antinori Badia a Passignano
    Chianti Classico
Casal Thaulero Montepulciano d'Abruzzo
Castello Monaci Liante Salice Salentino
Col d'Orcia Rosso di Montalcino
Fattoria di Felsina Chianti
    Classico Riserva
Le Rote Vernaccia di San Gimignano
Manzone Nebbiolo Langhe "Crutin"
Marchesi de Frescobaldi Chianti
    Rúfina Castello di Nipozzano Riserva
Montesotto Chianti Classico
Poggio al Casone La Cattura
Poggio il Castellare Sangiovese
Ruffino Chianti Classico Riserva
Ruffino Chianti Classico "Riserva
    Ducale" (Tan label)
Taurino Salice Salentino
Tolaini "Valdisanti"
Zenato "Ripassa"

### White

Alois Lageder Pinot Grigio
Antinori Chardonnay della
  Sala Bramito del Cervo
Bollini Trentino Pinot Grigio
Botromagno Gravina Bianco
Clelia Romano Fiano di Avellino
  "Colli di Lapio"
La Carraia Orvieto Classico
Le Rote Vernaccia di San Gimignano
Malabaila Roero Arneis
Marco Felluga Collio Pinot Grigio
Mastroberardino Falanghina
Pieropan Soave
Terenzuola Vermentino Colli di Luni

Anselmi Soave
Antinori Vermentino Guado al Tasso
Bolla Soave Classico
Boscaini Pinot Grigio
Cantina Terlano Pinot Bianco
Coppo Gavi "La Rocca"
Eugenio Collavini Pinot Grigio
  "Canlungo"
Maculan "Pino & Toi"
Marchetti Verdicchio dei Castelli
  di Jesi Classico
Paolo Scavino Bianco
Pighin Pinot Grigio
Teruzzi & Puthod "Terre di Tufi"

### Rosé

Antinori Guado al Tasso Scalabrone Rosato

### Prosecco

Adami
Le Colture

Bortolomiol
La Tordera

## SPAIN

From the time I started studying wine forty years ago, the wines of Rioja have always represented great value, especially their Crianzas and Reservas. The Tempranillo grape also shines in Ribera del Duero. From Ríax Bias, we have Albarinos and from Penedés we have the great Cavas (sparkling).

Here are some of my favorite Spanish producers and their value wines:

### Red

Alvaro Palacios Camins del Priorat
Beronia Rioja Reserva
Bodegas Beronia Reserva*
Bodegas La Cartuja Priorat
Bodegas Lan Rioja Crianza
Bodegas Muga Reserva*
Condado de Haza Ribera del Duero
CUNE Rioja Crianza "Viña Real"
Dinastía Vivanco Selección de Familia
El Coto Crianza and Reserva*
Hijos de Antonio Barcelo Viña Mayor Reserva*
Marqués de Cáceres Crianza
Onix Priorat
Urbina Rioja Gran Reserva

Baron de Ley Reserva
Bodega Numanthia Termes
Bodegas Emilio Moro "Emilio Moro"
Bodegas Lan Crianza
Bodegas Montecillo Crianza or Reserva*
Bodegas Ontañón Crianza
Conde de Valdemar Crianza and Reserva*
Descendientes de José Palacios
  Bierzo Pétalos*
Finca Torremilanos Ribera del
  Duero "Torremilanos"
Marqués de Riscal Proximo Rioja
Ontañón Crianza or Reserva

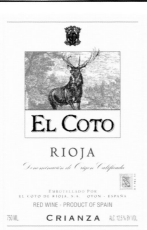

### White

Burgáns Albariño Rías Baixas
Condes de Albarei Condes
Legaris Verdejo Rueda
Licia Galicia Albariño

Castro Brey Albariño "Sin Palabras"
Do Ferreiro Albariño
 de Albarei Albariño

### Cava

Codorníu Brut Classico
Freixenet

Cristalino Brut
Segura Viudas

# ARGENTINA

Although the reputation of Argentina is made around the region of Mendoza and the Malbec grape, there are other grapes such as Bonarda, Cabernet Sauvignon, and Chardonnay that are great values.

Here are some of my favorite Argentinean producers and their value wines:

### Red

Achaval-Ferrer Malbec*
Alta Vista Malbec Grand Reserva*
Bodega Norton Malbec*
Bodegas Weinert Carrascal*
Catena Zapata Cabernet Sauvignon*
Cuvelier Los Andes "Coleccion"*
Domaine Jean Bousquet Malbec*
Kaiken Corte
Salentein Malbec
Salentein Malbec Gran Reserva*
Susana Balbo Cabernet Sauvignon*
Trapiche Oak Cask Malbec*

Alamos Malbec*
Bodegas Esmeralda Malbec*
Bodegas Renacer "Enamore"
Catena Alta Cabernet Sauvignon*
Clos de los Siete Malbec*
Cuvelier Los Andes Grand Vin
Kaiken Cabernet Sauvignon Ultra*
Miguel Mendoza Malbec Reserva
 "MMM"*
Susana Balboa Mendoza
 Malbec Signature
Valentin Bianchi Malbec*

### White

Alamos Chardonnay
Michel Torino Torrontés Don David Reserve

Catena Chardonnay

# CHILE

In my Wine School and when on the lecture circuit, I always say that the best value in the world for Cabernet Sauvignon is the country of Chile. Merlot, Carménère, and Sauvignon Blanc are also other grapes to look for.

Here are some of my favorite Chilean producers and their value wines:

### Red

Caliterra Cabernet Sauvignon or Merlot*
Casa Lapostolle "Cuvée Alexandre" Merlot*
Concha y Toro Puente Alto Cabernet
 Sauvignon*

Carmen Carménère*
Concha y Toro Marques de Casa Concha
 Puente Alto Cabernet Sauvignon*

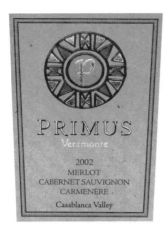

Cousiño-Macul Antiguas Reserva*
Errazuriz Cabernet Sauvignon
 Cabernet Sauvignon*
Los Vascos Reserve Cabernet Sauvignon*
Montes Cabernet Sauvignon and Merlot*
Veramonte Primus*
Veranda Pinot Noir Ritual

Cono Sur 20 Barrels Cabernet Sauvignon
Errazuriz Don Maximiano
 Single Vineyard
Montes Alpha Merlot Apalta Vineyard
Santa Carolina Reserva de Familia
 Cabernet Sauvignon
Viña Aquitania Lazuli Cabernet
 Sauvignon*

## White

Casa Lapostolle Sauvignon Blanc
Veramonte Sauvignon Blanc

Cono Sur "Bicycle Series" Viognier

# AUSTRALIA

Twenty-five years ago Australia took the world by storm with great wines at great prices, and that is still true today. The most famous red grape, Shiraz, is often blended with the classic Cabernet Sauvignon grape. But there are so many other wine regions throughout this big country that it is easy to find great Cabernet Sauvignons, Chardonnays, and Sauvignon Blancs that are sold at unbelievable prices.

Here are some of my favorite Australian producers and their value wines:

## Red

Alice White Cabernet Sauvignon*
Black Opal Cabernet Sauvignon or Shiraz*
D'Arenberg "The Footbolt" Shiraz*
Jacob's Creek Cabernet Sauvignon
 Coonawarra Reserve
Jim Barry Shiraz, "The Lodge Hill"
Lindeman's Shiraz Bin 50*
McWilliam's Shiraz*
Penfolds "Bin 28 Kalimna" Shiraz
Rosemount Estate Shiraz Cabernet
 (Diamond Label)*
Taltarni T Series Shiraz*
Yangarra Shiraz Single Vineyard

Banrock Station Shiraz*
D'Arenberg "The Stump Jump" Red
Jacob's Creek Shiraz Cabernet*
Jim Barry "The Cover Drive"
 Cabernet Sauvignon*
Kilikanoon "Killerman's Run" Shiraz
Marquis Philips Sarah's Blend*
Mollydooker "The Boxer" Shiraz
Peter Lehmann Barossa Shiraz*
Salomon Estate "Norwood"
Schild Shiraz*
Yalumba Y Series Shiraz Viognier
Yealands Pinot Noir

## White

Banrock Station Chardonnay
Grant Burge Chardonnay
Matua Valley Sauvignon Blanc
Rosemount Estate Chardonnay*
St. Hallett "Poacher's Blend" White
Trevor Jones Virgin Chardonnay

Bogle Sauvignon Blanc
Lindeman's Chardonnay Bin 65*
Oxford Landing Sauvignon Blanc
Saint Clair "Pioneer Block 3"
 Sauvignon Blanc
Yalumba Y Series Unwooded
 Chardonnay

# NEW ZEALAND

The two most important grapes of New Zealand are the Sauvignon Blanc for whites and Pinot Noir for reds. Its Sauvignon Blancs have become famous throughout the world with their "tropical" aromas and taste with a citrus finish. Even though the reputation of New Zealand is based on Sauvignon Blanc, it has entered the Pinot Noir arena for quality wines.

Here are some of my favorite New Zealand producers and their value wines:

## Red

Babich Pinot Noir
Crown Range Pinot Noir
Mt. Difficulty Pinot Noir
Saint Clair Pinot Noir "Omaka Reserve"
Stoneleigh Pinot Noir
The Crossings Pinot Noir

Brancott Estate Pinot Noir Reserve
Man O' War Syrah
Peregrine Pinot Noir
Saint Clair Pinot Noir "Vicar's Choice"
Te Awa Syrah

## White

Ata Rangi Sauvignon Blanc
Babich Unwooded Chardonnay
Cloudy Bay "Te Koko"*
Cru Vin Dogs "Greyhound"
    Sauvignon Blanc
Kim Crawford Sauvignon Blanc
Man O' War Sauvignon Blanc
Mt. Difficulty Pinot Gris
Oyster Bay Sauvignon Blanc
Peregrine Pinot Gris
Seresin Sauvignon Blanc
Te Awa Chardonnay*

Babich Sauvignon Blanc
Brancott Estate Sauvignon Blanc
Coopers Creek Sauvignon Blanc
Giesen Sauvignon Blanc
Glazebrook Sauvignon Blanc
Kumeu River Village Chardonnay
Mohua Sauvignon Blanc
Nobilo Sauvignon Blanc
Pegasus Bay Chardonnay
Saint Clair Sauvignon Blanc
Stoneleigh Chardonnay*
Te Mata "Woodthorpe"*

# SOUTH AFRICA

The diversity of the South African wines from Chenin Blanc and Sauvignon Blanc to Cabernet Sauvignon and Pinotage offers the consumer a lot of different wine choices at great value.

Here are some of my favorite South African producers and their value wines:

## Red

Boekenhoutskloof "Chocolate Block"
    Meritage
Jardin Syrah*

Doolhof Dark Lady of the
    Labyrinth Pinotage
Mulderbosch Faithful Hound*
Kanonkop Kadette Red

## White

Hamilton Russell Chardonnay*
Ken Forrester Sauvignon Blanc

Thelema Sauvignon Blanc

## UNITED STATES

I have tasted great value wines from states such as North Carolina, Pennsylvania, Virginia, New York, and many others. Unfortunately most of these wines are available only locally. California represents the major share of the U.S. market (90 percent) with great Sauvignon Blancs and Chardonnays for the whites and Cabernet Sauvignon, Merlot, Pinot Noir, Zinfandel, and Syrah for the reds. Washington State, the second largest producer in the United States, makes very good value Sauvignon Blancs, Merlots, Chardonnays, and Cabernet Sauvignons. And, yes, there are some Pinot Noirs and Chardonnays from Oregon that can be purchased at reasonable prices.

Here are some of my favorite American producers and their value wines:

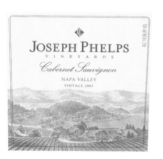

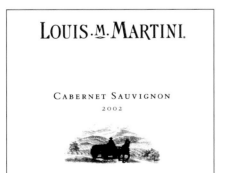

### Cabernet Sauvignon

Atalon*
B. R. Cohn Silver label
Bonny Doon "Le Cigare Volant"
Chateau Ste. Michelle*
Ex Libris*
Freemark Abbey
Gallo of Sonoma*
Hawk Crest*
Jordan*
Laurel Glen Quintana*
McManis*
Rodney Strong
Sebastiani*
St. Francis

Beaulieu*
Beringer Knights Valley*
Broadside "Margarita Vineyard"
Elements by Artesa
Forest Glen*
Frog's Leap
Geyser Peak Reserve*
Hess Select*
Joseph Phelps*
Louis M. Martini*
Provenance (Beckstoffer To-Kalon)
Rutherford Vintners*
Stag's Leap Wine Cellars "Hands of Time"
Trefethen Eshcol*

### Chardonnay

Acacia
Arrowood Grand Archer*
Bergström "Old Stones"*
Cambria "Katherine's Vineyard"
Chateau Ste. Michelle
Columbia Crest Sémillon-Chardonnay*
Estancia*
Fetzer Vineyard Valley Oaks*
Hawk Crest
Heitz Cellars*
Hogue Columbia Valley
Kendall-Jackson Grand Reserve*
Mer Soleil "Silver" (unoaked)
Simi*

Argyle*
Benziger*
Calera Central Coast*
Chateau St. Jean*
Clos Pegase Mitsuko's Vineyard
Covey Run*
Ferrari-Carano*
Francis Ford Coppola
   "Director's Cut"*
Hess Select*
Joel Gott*
Merryvale Starmont*
Rutherford Ranch*

## Merlot

Balboa
Benziger*
Chateau Ste. Michelle "Canoe Ridge"*
Columbia Crest*
Fetzer Vineyard Valley Oaks*
Frei Brothers*
Hawk Crest*
Markham*
Robert Mondavi
Souverain*
Waterbrook*

Beaulieu Coastal
Canoe Ridge
Clos du Bois Reserve*
Ferrari-Carano
Forest Glen*
Frog's Leap
Hogue*
Napa Ridge
Seven Hills
Swanson
Wolffer Estate

## Pinot Noir

Acacia
Artesa
Au Bon Climat
Buena Vista
Cambria Julia's Vineyard
Castle Rock
Cooper Mountain
Dutton-Goldfield "Dutton Ranch"
Heron
Saintsbury
Willamette Valley Vineyards

Argyle
A to Z Wineworks
Benton-Lane
Byron
Calera
Cloudline
Francis Ford Coppola "Director's Cut"
Garnet
Loring
Siduri

## Syrah/Shiraz

Cline
Fess Parker*
Justin*
Red Lava Vineyards*

De Martino*
Forest Glen*
Qupe Bien Nacido Vineyard
Zaca Mesa*

## Zinfandel

Bogle*
Joel Gott*
Ridge East Bench*
Seghesio Sonoma

Cline*
Ravenswood Old Vine*
Ridge Sonoma
St. Francis Old Vines*

## Pinot Gris

Cristom Vineyard
King Estate

Elk Cove Vineyards
King Estate "Signature Collection"

## Riesling

Chateau Ste. Michelle Eroica

Dr. Konstantin Frank

### *Sauvignon Blanc*

| | |
|---|---|
| Beaulieu Coastal | Beringer |
| Buena Vista | Chateau Montelena |
| Chateau St. Jean | Covey Run Fumé Blanc |
| Ferrari-Carano Fumé Blanc | Frog's Leap |
| Geyser Peak | Girard |
| Grgich Hills Fumé Blanc | Groth |
| Hogue Fumé Blanc | Honig |
| Joel Gott | Kendall-Jackson Vintner's Reserve |
| Kenwood | Mason |
| Matanzas Creek | Miner Family Viognier Simpson Vineyard |
| Ridge Santa Cruz | Rodney Strong |
| Sbragia Family | Silverado |
| St. Supéry | Tablas Creek Patelin de Tablas Blanc |

## GERMANY

The great value white wines of Germany are found in the Kabinett and Spätlese styles.

Here are some of my favorite German producers and their value wines:

Carl von Schubert Maximin Grünhäuser Herrenberg Riesling Kabinett
J. & H. A. Strub Niersteiner Ölberg Kabinett
J. J. Prüm Wehlener Sonnenuhr Kabinett or Spätlese
Josef Leitz Rüdesheimer Klosterlay Riesling Kabinett
Kurt Darting Dürkheimer Hochbenn Riesling Kabinett
Meulenhof Wehlenuhr Sonnenuhr Riesling Spätlese
Schloss Vollrads Riesling Kabinett
Scloss Saarstein Serriger "Schloss Saarsteiner" Riesling Kabinett
Selbach-Oster Zeltinger Sonnenuhr Riesling Kabinett
St. Urbans-Hof Riesling Kabinett
Weingut Johannishof Familien Eser Rüdesheimer Berg Rottland Riesling Spätlese
Weingut Max Richter Mülheimer Sonnelay Riesling Kabinett

## AUSTRIA

The two major white grapes of Austria are Grüner Veltliner and Riesling, perfect wines to serve with all kinds of foods, easy to drink, and readily available.

Here are some of my favorite Austrian producers and their value wines:

| | |
|---|---|
| Alois Kracher Pinot Gris Trocken | Forstreiter "Grand Reserve" |
| Hirsch "Veltliner #1" | Grüner Veltliner |
| Knoll Grüner Veltliner Federspiel | Nigl Grüner Veltliner Kremser Freiheit |
| Trocken Wachau Loibner | Salomon Grüner Veltliner |
| Salomon Riesling Steinterrassen | Salomon-Undhof Grüner Veltliner |
| Schloss Gobelsburg | "Hochterrassen" |
| Walter Glatzer Grüner Veltliner | |

# Frequently Asked Questions about Wine

## What happens when I can't finish the whole bottle of wine?

This is one of the most frequently asked questions in Wine School (although I have never had this problem).

If you still have a portion of the wine left over, whether it be red or white, the bottle should be corked and immediately put into the refrigerator. Don't leave it out on your kitchen counter. Remember, bacteria grow in warm temperatures, and a 70°F+ kitchen will spoil wine very quickly. If refrigerated, most wines will not lose their flavor over a forty-eight-hour period. (Some people swear that the wine even tastes better, although I'm not among them.)

Eventually, the wine will begin to oxidize. This is true of all table wines with an 8 to 14 percent alcohol content. Other wines, such as Ports and Sherries, with a higher alcohol content of 17 to 21 percent, will last longer, but I wouldn't suggest keeping them longer than two weeks.

Another way of preserving wine for an even longer period of time is to buy a small decanter that has a corked top and fill the decanter to the top with the wine. Or go to a hobby or craft store that also carries home winemaking equipment and buy some half bottles and corks.

Remember, the most harmful thing to wine is oxygen, and the less contact with oxygen, the longer the wine will last. That's why some wine collectors also use something called the Vacu-Vin, which pumps air out of the bottle. Other wine collectors spray the bottle with an inert gas such as nitrogen, which is odorless and tasteless, that preserves the wine from oxygen.

Remember, if all else fails, you'll still have a great cooking wine!

## Why do I get a headache when I drink wine?

The simple answer may be overconsumption! Seriously, though, more than 10 percent of my students are medical doctors, and none of them has been able to give me the definitive answer to this question.

Some people get headaches from white wine, others from red, but when it comes to alcohol consumption, dehydration certainly plays an important role in how you feel the next day. That's why for every glass of wine I consume, I will have two glasses of water to keep my body hydrated.

**WHAT KIND OF WINE BUYER ARE YOU?**

"Enthusiast"
"Image Seeker"
"Savvy Shopper"
"Traditionalist"
"Satisfied Sipper"
"Overwhelmed"

—FROM CONSTELLATION WINES U.S.

There are many factors that influence the way alcohol is metabolized in your system. The top three are:

1. Health
2. DNA
3. Gender

Research is increasingly leaning toward genetics as a reason for chronic headaches.

For those of you who have allergies, different levels of histamines are present in red wines; these can obviously cause discomfort and headaches. I myself am allergic to red wine and I "suffer" every day.

Many doctors have told me that food additives contribute to headaches. There is a natural compound in red wine called tyramine, which is said to dilate blood vessels. Further, many prescription medicines warn about combining with alcohol.

Regarding gender, due to certain stomach enzymes, women absorb more alcohol into their bloodstream than men do. A doctor who advises women that one glass of wine a day is a safe limit is likely to tell men that they can drink two glasses.

## Do all wines need corks?

It is a time-honored tradition more than two centuries old to use corks to preserve wine. Most corks come from cork oak trees grown in Portugal and Spain.

The fact is that most wines could be sold without using cork as a stopper. Since 90 percent of all wine is meant to be consumed within one year, a screw cap will work just as well, if not better, than a cork for most wines.

Just think what this would mean to you—no need for a corkscrew, no broken corks and, most important, no more tainted wine caused by contaminated cork.

I do believe that certain wines—those with potential to age for more than five years—are much better off using cork. But also keep in mind, for those real wine collectors, that a cork's life span is approximately twenty-five to thirty years, after which you'd better drink the wine or find somebody to recork it.

Some wineries now use a synthetic cork made from high-grade thermoplastic that is FDA-approved and also recyclable. These corks form a near-perfect seal, so leakage, evaporation, and off flavors are virtually eliminated.

SOME WINERIES, especially in California, are now using synthetic corks to seal their wine. Since 1993, St. Francis Winery in Sonoma has sealed its wine with a synthetic cork. And the Napa Valley's Plump Jack Winery released its $135/bottle 1997 Reserve Cabernet Sauvignon with a screw cap! Stay tuned for more.

They open with traditional corkscrews and allow wine to be stored upright.

But many wineries around the world use the Stelvin screw cap, especially in California (Bonny Doon, Sonoma-Cutrer, etc.), Australia, New Zealand, and Austria.

## What is a "corked" wine?

This is a very serious problem for wine lovers! There are some estimates that 3 to 5 percent of all wines have been contaminated and spoiled by a faulty cork. The principal cause of corked wine is a compound called TCA, short for 2,4,6-trichloranisole.

When we find such a bottle at the Wine School, we make sure that every student gets a chance to smell a "corked" wine. It's a smell they won't soon forget!

Some of my students describe it as a dank, wet, moldy, cellar smell, and some describe it as a wet cardboard smell. It overpowers the fruit smell in the wine, making the wine undrinkable. It can happen in a $10 bottle of wine or a $1,000 bottle of wine.

## How do I decant a bottle of wine?

1. Completely remove the capsule (protective sleeve) from the neck of the bottle. This will enable you to see the wine clearly as it passes through the neck.

2. Light a candle. Most red wines are bottled in very dark green glass, making it difficult to see the wine pass through the neck of the bottle. A candle will give you the extra illumination you need and add a theatrical touch. A flashlight would do, but candles keep things simple.

3. Hold the decanter (a carafe or glass pitcher can also be used) firmly in your hand.

4. Hold the wine bottle in your other hand, and gently pour the wine into the decanter while holding both over the candle at such an angle that you can see the wine pass through the neck of the bottle.

5. Continue pouring in one uninterrupted motion until you see the first signs of sediment.

6. Stop decanting once you see sediment. At this point, if there is still wine left, let it stand until the sediment settles. Then continue decanting.

NINEY-THREE PERCENT of New Zealand's bottles have screw caps, as do 75% of Australia's.

SCREW-CAP wines represent less than 5% of all bottled wine.

## What's that funny-looking stuff attached to the bottom of my cork?

Tartaric acid, or tartrate, is sometimes found on the bottom of a bottle of wine or the cork. Tartaric acid is a harmless crystalline deposit that looks like glass or rock candy. In red wines, the crystals take on a rusty, reddish-brown color from the tannin.

Most tartrates are removed at the winery by lowering the temperature of the wine before it is bottled. Obviously this does not work with all wines, and if you keep your wine at a very cold temperature for a long period of time (for example, in your refrigerator), you can end up with this deposit on your cork.

Cool-climate regions like Germany have a greater chance of producing the crystallization effect.

## Does the age of the vine affect the quality of the wine?

You will sometimes see on French wine labels the term *Vieilles Vignes* ("old vines"). In California, I've tasted many Zinfandels that were made from vines that were more than seventy-five years old. Many wine tasters, including myself, believe that these old vines create a different complexity and taste than do younger vines.

In many countries, grapes from vines three years old or younger cannot be made into a winery's top wine. In Bordeaux, France, Château Lafite-Rothschild produces a second wine, called Carruades de Lafite-Rothschild, which is made from the vineyard's youngest vines (less than fifteen years old).

As a vine gets older, especially over thirty years, it starts losing its fruit-production value. In commercial vineyards, vines will slow down their production at about twenty years of age, and most vines are replanted by their fiftieth birthday.

## What are the hot areas in wine?

It seems as if most countries are catching the wine craze. Here are some areas where I have seen major growth and improvement in quality, especially with certain grape varieties, over the last twenty years:

**Argentina:** Malbec
**Austria:** Grüner Veltliner
**Chile:** Cabernet Sauvignon
**Hungary:** Tokaji (one of the greatest dessert wines in the world)

*New Zealand:* Sauvignon Blanc, Chardonnay, and Pinot Noir
*Portugal:* Not just Port anymore! Try Bacca Velha and you'll see what I mean.
*South Africa:* Sauvignon Blanc, Pinot Noir, and Syrah

CHINA IS THE number-two grape producing country in the world, after Italy, and growing at a fast rate.

## And what will you be writing about in the year 2025?

Argentina, the United States, Australia, Chile, and China.

## What are the most important books for your wine library?

Thank you for buying my wine book, which I hope you have found useful for a general understanding of wine. As with any hobby, there is always a thirst for more knowledge.

I hope that you noticed that at the end of each chapter, I recommended specific wine books for the different wine regions.

The following is a list of general books I consider required reading if you want to delve farther into this fascinating subject:

*Oz Clarke's New Essential Wine Book*
*Oz Clarke's New Encyclopedia of Wine*
*Oz Clarke's Wine Atlas*
*Great Wine Made Simple,* Andrea Robinson
*Hugh Johnson's Modern Encyclopedia of Wine*
*World Atlas of Wine,* Hugh Johnson and Jancis Robinson
*The Wine Bible,* Karen MacNeil
*Wine for Dummies,* Ed McCarthy and Mary Ewing-Mulligan
*Keys to the Cellar* by Peter D. Meltzer
*Oxford Companion to Wine,* Jancis Robinson
*Sotheby's Wine Encyclopedia,* Tom Stevenson
*Parker's Wine Buyers Guide,* Robert M. Parker Jr.

Since the above volumes are sometimes encyclopedic in nature, I always carry with me one of these three pocket guides to wine:

*Hugh Johnson's Pocket Encyclopedia of Wine*
*Oz Clarke's Pocket Wine Guide*
*Andrea Robinson's Wine Buying Guide*

*In 2011, Kevin Zraly was awarded the Lifetime Achievement Award by the James Beard Foundation.*

## Where can I get the best wine service in the United States?

The James Beard Awards have recognized the following existing restaurants with the Outstanding Wine Service Award:

| | | | |
|---|---|---|---|
| 1993 | Charlie Trotter's, Chicago | 2006 | Aureole, Las Vegas |
| 1994 | Valentino, Santa Monica | 2007 | Citronelle, Washington, D.C. |
| 1997 | The Four Seasons, New York | 2008 | Eleven Madison Park, New York |
| 1999 | Union Square Café, New York | | |
| 2001 | French Laundry, Yountville, California | 2009 | Le Bernardin, New York |
| | | 2010 | Jean Georges, New York |
| 2002 | Gramercy Tavern, New York | 2011 | The Modern, New York |
| 2003 | Daniel, New York | 2012 | No. 9 Park, Boston |
| 2004 | Babbo, New York | 2013 | Frasca Food and Wine, Boulder, Colorado |
| 2005 | Veritas, New York | | |

The past winners for the James Beard Award for Wine and Spirits Professional of the Year are:

| | | | |
|---|---|---|---|
| 1991 | Robert Mondavi, Robert Mondavi Winery | 2004 | Karen MacNeil, Culinary Institute of America |
| 1992 | Andre Tchelistcheff, Beaulieu Winery | | |
| 1993 | Kevin Zraly, Windows on the World, New York | 2005 | Joseph Bastianich, Italian Wine Merchants, New York |
| 1994 | Randall Grahm, Bonny Doon Vineyard, Santa Cruz | 2006 | Daniel Johnnes, The Dinex Group, New York |
| 1995 | Marvin Shanken, *Wine Spectator* | 2007 | Paul Draper, Ridge Vineyards |
| 1996 | Jack and Jaimie Davies, Schramsberg Vineyards | 2008 | Terry Theise, Terry Theise Estate Selection |
| | | 2009 | Dale DeGroff, Dale DeGroff Co., Inc |
| 1997 | Zelma Long, Simi Winery | 2010 | John Shafer and Doug Shafer, Shafer Vineyards |
| 1998 | Robert M. Parker Jr., *The Wine Advocate* | | |
| 1999 | Frank Prial, *The New York Times* | 2011 | Julian P. Van Winkle, III, Old Rip Van Winkle Distillery, Louisville, Kentucky |
| 2000 | Kermit Lynch, writer | | |
| 2001 | Gerald Asher, writer | 2012 | Paul Grieco, Terroir, New York |
| 2002 | Andrea Robinson, author | 2013 | Merry Edwards, Merry Edwards Winery, Sebastopol, California |
| 2003 | Fritz Maytag, Anchor Brewing Co. | | |

## What's the difference between California and French wines, and who makes the better wines?

You really think I'm going to answer that? California and France both make great wines, but the French make the best French wines!

From production strategy to weather, each region's profile is distinct. California wines and French wines share many similarities. The greatest similarity is that both France and California grow most of the same grape varieties. They also have many differences. The biggest differences are soil, climate, and tradition.

The French regard their soil with reverence and believe that the best wines come from only the greatest soil. When grapes were originally planted in California, the soil was not one of the major factors in determining which grapes were planted where. Over recent decades, this has become a much more important aspect for the vineyard owners in California, and it's not unheard of for a winemaker to say that his or her best Cabernet Sauvignon comes from a specific area.

As far as weather goes, the temperatures in Napa and Sonoma are different from those in Burgundy and Bordeaux. The fact is, that while European vintners get gray hair over pesky problems like cold snaps and rainstorms in the growing season, Californians can virtually count on abundant sunshine and warm temperatures.

Tradition is the biggest difference between the two, and I'm not just talking about winemaking. For example, vineyard and winery practices in Europe have remained virtually unchanged for generations, and these age-old techniques—some of which were written into law—define each region's own style. But in California, where few traditions exist, vintners are free to experiment with modern technology and create new products based on consumer demand. If you've ever had a wine called Two Buck Chuck, you know what I mean.

It is sometimes very difficult for me to sit in a tasting and compare a California Chardonnay and a French white Burgundy, since they have been making wines in Burgundy for the last 1,600 years and the renaissance of California wines is not yet fifty years old.

I buy both French and California wines for my personal cellar, and sometimes my choice has to do totally with how I feel that day or what food I'm having: do I want to end up in Bordeaux or the Napa Valley?

## How long should I age my wine?

The *Wall Street Journal* recently came out with an article stating that most people have one or two wines that they've been saving for years for a special occasion. This is probably not a good idea!

More than 90 percent of all wine—red, white, and rosé—should be consumed within a year. With that in mind, the following is a guideline to aging wine from the best producers in the best years:

SOME WINES that are ready to drink immediately:
Riesling (dry)
Sauvignon Blanc
Pinot Grigio
Beaujolais

| WHITE | |
|---|---|
| California Chardonnay | 2–10+ years |
| French White Burgundy | 3–8+ years |
| German Riesling (Auslese, Beerenauslese, and Trockenbeerenauslese) | 3–30+ years |
| French Sauternes | 3–30+ years |

| RED | |
|---|---|
| California/Oregon Pinot Noirs | 2–5+ years |
| French Red Burgundy | 3–8+ years |
| California Merlot | 2–10+ years |
| Chianti Classico Riservas | 3–10+ years |
| Argentine Malbec | 3–15+ years |
| Brunello di Montalcino | 3–15+ years |
| California Cabernet Sauvignon | 3–15+ years |
| California Zinfandel | 5–15+ years |
| Spanish Riojas (Gran Reservas) | 5–20+ years |
| Barolo and Barbaresco | 5–25+ years |
| Hermitage/Syrah | 5–25+ years |
| Bordeaux Châteaux | 5–30+ years |
| Vintage Ports | 10–40+ years |

THE OLDEST bottle of wine still aging in Bordeaux is a 1797 Château Lafite-Rothschild.

There are always exceptions to the rules when it comes to generalizing about the aging of wine (especially considering the variations in vintages), hence the plus signs in the table above. I have had Bordeaux wines more than a hundred years old that were still going strong. It is also not unlikely to find a great Sauternes or Port that still needs time to age after its fiftieth birthday. But the above age spans represent more than 95 percent of the wines in their categories.

# Wine Resources

## Wine/Food/Spirits Publications

*Decanter*
www.decanter.com
800-875-2997

*Food & Wine*
www.foodandwine.com
800-333-6569

*Tasting Panel*
www.tastingpanelmag.com
818-990-0350

*Wine Advocate*
www.erobertparker.com
410-329-6477

*Wine & Spirits*
www.wineandspiritsmagazine.com
212-695-4660

*Wine Business Monthly*
www.winebusiness.com
800-895-9463

*Wine Enthusiast*
www.wineenthusiast.com
800-829-5901

*Wine Spectator*
www.winespectator.com
800-752-7799

**OTHER ONLINE WINE
AUCTION HOUSES:**

Auctionvine.com
brentwoodwine.com
munichwinecompany.com
spectrumwine.com
Winebid.com
winecommune.com

## Where to Sell Your Wine/Auctions

Aulden Cellars-Sotheby's Auction House
sothebys.com/wine
1334 York Avenue, 1st floor
New York, NY 10021
212-894-1990

Bonhams & Butterfields
bonhams.com
580 Madison Ave, 6th floor
New York, NY 10022
212-644-9001

Chicago Wine Company
tcwc.com
835 North Central
Wood Dale, IL 60191
630-594-2972

Christie's Auction House
christies.com
20 Rockefeller Plaza
New York, NY 10020
212-636-2000

Hart Davis Hart
hdhwine.com
363 W. Erie Street, #500
Chicago, IL 60654
312-482-9996

Morrell & Company
Morrellwineauctions.com
1 Rockefeller Plaza
New York, NY 10020
212-688-9370

Zachy's
zachys.com/auctions/
16 East Parkway
Scarsdale, NY 10583
866-922-4971

**CONSULT THE FOLLOWING RESOURCES
FOR WINE RATINGS AND PRICES:**

Beverage Tasting Institute, tastings.com
Parker's Wine Buying Guide,
Robert Parker Jr.
Snooth.com
Wine Price File
Wine-searcher.com
Wine Spectator's Ultimate Buying Guide

## Wine Storage Units and Wine Equipment

International Wine Accessories
www.iwawine.com
800-527-4072

Moving?
Western Carriers, Inc.
Wine Cellar Transportation
www.westerncarriers.com
1-800-631-7776

Sub Zero Freezer Company
www.subzero-wolf.com
800-222-7820

Wine Enthusiast Catalog
www.wineenthusiast.com
800-356-8466

## Wine Education

### Wine Certification Programs

*For the professional or those wishing
to become a sommelier:*

American Sommelier Association
americansommelier.com
580 Broadway, Suite 716
New York, NY 10012
212-226-6805

International Wine Center
internationalwinecenter.com
350 7th Avenue Suite 1201
New York, NY 10001
(212) 239-3055

Society of Wine Educators
www.societyofwineeducators.org
1319 F Street NW, Suite 303
Washington, DC 20005
202-408-8777

Sommelier Society of America
sommeliersocietyofamerica.org
P.O. Box 20080
West Village Station, NY 10014
212-679-4190

Wine & Spirit Education Trust
www.wsetglobal.com
Multiple locations

Wine Spectator Wine School
www.winespectator.com/school

*For a complete list of wine schools, go to the Society of Wine Educators website:
societyofwineeducators.org.*

### Consumer Education

Kevin Zraly's Windows on the World Wine Course
www.kevinzraly.com

Sherry-Lehmann/Kevin Zraly Master Classes
Contact 845-255-1456 or
kevin@kevinzraly.com for dates

## Further Reading

*The following are a list of books I consider required reading for those of you who want to delve further into this fascinating subject:*

*The Essential Wine Book*, Oz Clarke

*Exploring Wine*, Steven Kolpan, Brian H. Smith, and Michael A. Weiss

*The Food Lover's Guide to Wine*, Karen Page and Andrew Dornenburg

*Grapes & Wines*, Oz Clarke

*Great Tastes Made Simple* and *Great Wine Made Simple*, Andrea Immer

*Hugh Johnson's Modern Encyclopedia of Wine*

*Oxford Companion to Wine*, Jancis Robinson

*Perfect Pairings* and *Daring Pairings*, by Evan Goldstein

*The Ultimate Wine Companion*, Kevin Zraly

*Vino Italiano: The Regional Wines of Italy*, Joseph Bastianich and David Lynch

*The Wine Bible*, Karen MacNeil

*Wine for Dummies*, Ed McCarthy and Mary Ewing-Mulligan

*The Wine Lover's Guide to the Wine Country: The Best of Napa, Sonoma, and Mendocino*, Lori Lyn Narlock and Nancy Garfinkel

*World Atlas of Wine*, Hugh Johnson

*Since the above volumes are sometimes encyclopedic in nature, I always carry with me three pocket guides to wine:*

*Food & Wine Pocket Guide*

*Hugh Johnson's Pocket Encyclopedia of Wine*

*Oz Clarke's Pocket Wine Guide*

To order books: contact Barnes & Nobles at www.bn.com or the Wine Appreciation Guild at 1-800-231-9463.

## Bloggers

I like the *New York Times's* list of bloggers—go to dinersjournal.blogs.nytimes.com for the full list.

# Wine Consumer Events

*These are just select listings, check localwineevents.com for more events in your area. Please contact events directly for specific dates

Auction Napa Valley
napavintners.com/anv/
707-963-3388/1-800-982-1371

Boston Wine Expo, Winter
wine-expos.com
1-877-946-3976

Charlotte Wine & Food Weekend, every other year in the Spring
www.charlottewineandfood.com
704-338-9463

Epcot Food & Wine Festival
disneyworld.disney.go.com/parks/epcot/
407-939-3463

Finger Lakes Wine Festival
flwinefest.com
866-461-7223

Florida Winefest & Auction
floridawinefest.com
941-952-1109

Food & Wine Classic in Aspen
foodandwine.com/classic
1-877-900-WINE

Grand Wine and Food Affair (Texas)
fortbendwineandfoodaffair.com
281-491-0216

Naples Wine Festival, Winter
(Naples, FL), Winter
napleswinefestival.com
239-514-2239

Newport Mansions Wine & Food Festival
newportmansions.org
401-847-1000

New York Wine Experience
212-684-4224

New York Wine Expo
wine-expos.com
877-946-3976

Saratoga Wine and Food Festival
(Saratoga, NY)
www.spac.org
518-584-9330

South Beach Wine & Food Fest
sobewineandfoodfest.com
305-627-1741

Washington International Wine & Food Festival
wine-expos.com/
1-800-343-1174

# Trade Events

American Wine Society National Conference
www.americanwinesociety.org
888.297.9070

Society of Wine Educators Conference
www.societyofwineeducators.org/conference.php

# Best of the Best

I originally wrote this section a week before my fiftieth birthday. Ten years later, on the week of my sixtieth birthday, I'm editing my past Best of the Best selections. Some things have stayed the same, but there have also been many changes in the wine world over the last ten years. I have now spent forty years studying, writing, tasting, traveling, teaching, lecturing, and reading about wine. Bottom line: I have seen it all . . . wines, wine publications, wine writers, wine "experts," restaurant wine lists, wine controversies, wine events . . . I have seen a lot of them come and a lot of them go.

I've seen the wine world change and emerge from a select few wine drinkers to today, where great wines are produced around the world and wine has become the beverage of choice internationally.

For this edition, I have decided to share what I consider to be the "Best of the Best." I base my decisions on several factors—longevity, experience, worldwide impact, credibility, and also creativity.

I hope you enjoy my thoughts and reflections on wine, and remember, as it is with wine, these are all my *personal* selections.

## BEST WINE WRITERS IN THE WORLD

### Books: Hugh Johnson

When I started the study of wine in 1970, I began with three books, Alexis Lichine's *Wines of France*, Frank Schoonmaker's *Encyclopedia of Wine*, and Hugh Johnson's *Wine*. For most beginners, these books would be overwhelming. But in my case, I wanted more!

Alexis and Frank are no longer with us but Hugh Johnson has carried the torch with his *Modern Encyclopedia of Wine* (1997), *The World Atlas of Wine* (1994), *How to Enjoy Your Wine* (1999), and his thirty-fourth edition of the *Pocket Wine Book* (2011).

Three of my other favorite wine book writers are also Brits: Jancis Robinson, Clive Coates, and Oz Clarke. I also enjoy reading the books by Matt Kramer and the team of Ed McCarthy and Mary Ewing-Mulligan. For books on food and wine, my favorite writers are Andrea Robinson and Evan Goldstein.

### Newspaper: Eric Asimov, The New York Times

As we all know, the newspaper world has changed drastically over the last ten years. Wine writers have come and gone and many newspapers have discontinued having a weekly wine column, but for over thirty years, the *New York Times* has maintained theirs. For the first twenty-five years, the column was primarily written by Frank Prial, and for the last seven years by Eric Asimov. Eric writes about well-known wines and also shows his explorer attitude and searches out unknown wines. In most of his articles he is accompanied by food editor Florence Fabricant and two other wine personalities who taste and recommend wines and food-and-wine pairings.

My two other choices would be Jancis Robinson for the *Financial Times*; and most recently Lettie Teague and Jay McInerney, who share the responsibilities at the *Wall Street Journal*.

## BEST WINE TASTER IN THE WORLD

### Robert M. Parker Jr.

Robert Parker and I both started studying wines around the same time but took different paths. He has basically changed the way wines are tasted and rated in the world through his 100-point scoring system. I know of no other human being that has tasted more wines than Mr. Parker. Up until a few years ago, he would taste 10,000 wines a year; recently he told me he is down to 7,500. All of his reviews are published in the *Wine Advocate*, which has over thirty thousand subscribers, as well as on eRobertParker.com. Whether you like his assessments or not, you have to admire his stamina, perseverance, and red tongue!

Another wine taster I admire is Michael Broadbent. Through the Christie's wine department he has possibly tasted more older wines than Mr. Parker. Unlike Parker, he doesn't use a numbering system but describes wines in his British, poetic fashion.

Another American who is well respected is Stephen Tanzer, who has his own publication, *International Wine Cellar*.

There are many wine writers/tasters throughout the world who are experts on specific wines—Bordeaux, Burgundy, Tuscany, California—and I wish I could mention them all, but I do recommend their texts throughout the book.

## BEST WINE TO AGE

### The Great Châteaux of Bordeaux

There are many great wine regions on earth that produce red wines that will age for thirty or more years. But nowhere on earth is there a region that produces both red and white wines that you can drink 100 years later!

## BEST WINE PUBLICATION

**Wine Spectator**
*Runners-up:* **Decanter** *and* **Wine Enthusiast**

I remember meeting with Marvin Shanken when he purchased *Wine Spectator* in 1979. Back then it was a worthwhile publication with very few subscribers. Marvin is a better businessman than a wine guy and over the last thirty-three years has taken the magazine from a few hundred subscribers to now reaching 2.5 million people. It is a must-read for the consumer, and the articles and ratings are extremely important to all segments of the wine industry.

Marvin's ability to maintain his editorial staff of wine writers, many who have been with him for over twenty years, is a phenomenal accomplishment in this ever-changing world of wine.

My second favorite wine publication, with a totally different format and point of view, is *Decanter* magazine. This British publication includes feature articles by Brits Michael Broadbent, Steven Spurrier, Hugh Johnson, and Clive Coates, and Americans Brian St. Pierre and Linda Murphy.

Another important read is *Wine Enthusiast* magazine, created by entrepreneur Adam Strum, whose primary business is selling wine cellars, glassware, and wine accessories. Every year *Wine Enthusiast* gives out awards for the many aspects of the wine industry, including Best Wine Region in the World and Best Wine Retail Store.

## BEST RED WINE WITH FISH

*Pinot Noir*

It's light, it's easy, not overpowering, it usually has high acidity and low tannin, and blends in nicely with all different types of food. It's a "white wine" masquerading as a red. Pinot Noir is the perfect wine for a dinner of six or eight where everyone is having something different, from fish to poultry or meat.

Other choices include Chianti Classico and Spanish Riojas (Crianza and Reserva). For barbecued or grilled fish or shrimp in the middle of the summer, I opt for chilled Beaujolais-Village or Cru, especially from the 2009 vintage.

## BEST WHITE WINE WITH MEAT

*Chardonnay*

Whoever coined the phrase "white wine with fish" was probably thinking of Riesling, Pinot Grigio, and Sauvignon Blanc, since a vast majority of Chardonnays will overpower fish dishes, except possibly a tuna, salmon, or swordfish steak.

Chardonnay is a "red wine" masqerading as a white, especially the big, oaky, high-alcohol Chardonnays from California and Australia. Usually, the more expensive the Chardonnay, the more oaky it will be. With all of its flavor, weight, and tannin, the perfect match for Chardonnay is something like a sirloin steak!

## THE BEST "FUN" WINE CORK

### Frog's Leap Winery, Napa, California

I have great admiration for winemakers who produce great wine and can have fun at the same time. John Williams, the owner and winemaker of Frog's Leap, and one of the premier winemakers in California, adds humor to drinking wine with the inscription "Ribbit" on every Frog's Leap cork.

## THE BEST INVESTMENT FOR WINE

### The Great Châteaux of Bordeaux, France, and California Cabernet Sauvignons

My personal "portfolio" goes something like this: 25 percent stocks, bonds, and mutual funds; 25 percent real estate; and 50 percent wine. Probably not your average investor's portfolio.

For the last forty years, I've been "investing" in wine. Although I have never sold any of my wine collection, if I did I would realize a better return than any money market. Even if the market for wines goes south, I can still drink it!

From 2000 to 2010, the best wine ever was produced in Bordeaux, with great vintages in 2000, 2003, 2005, and 2009 and excellent vintages in 2001 and 2006, with all of the other vintages still being quite good.

It is getting harder to buy the best California Cabernet Sauvignons. By California, I mean specifically Napa Valley, where the Cabernet Sauvignon thrives. They have also been blessed with great vintages over the last ten years, especially the 2007 vintage and 2001, 2002, 2005, and 2006. You can buy many of these Cabernet Sauvignons for less than $50.

## THE BEST WINE TO HAVE IN A RESTAURANT

### Anything under $75!

Even though I've been in the restaurant business most of my life, I think it is one of the worst places to experiment with wine tasting. Restaurants are notorious for their markup on wines, sometimes double and triple what you will pay retail. It is easy for me to choose $100+ bottles of wine. But I find it more

interesting to find a $25 bottle of wine that tastes like a $50, a $50 bottle that tastes like a $100, and so on.

Last year while working with Nina and Tim Zagat I reviewed over 125 restaurant wine lists in New York City. Tim and I both agree that we don't normally spend more than $75 for a bottle of wine in a restaurant, unless someone else is paying! I was reviewing all of these wine lists to find out what the percentage was of wines under $50, under $75, and under $100. And to my surprise most of these restaurants had a large percentage of affordable wines! Restaurants with high-priced wines and very few wines under $75 do not get my credit card.

## THE BEST WINE TO CELLAR FOR YOUR CHILDREN'S 21ST BIRTHDAY OR FOR YOUR 25TH WEDDING ANNIVERSARY

First the bad news: there are not many wines that are made in the world that can age over twenty years (less than 1 percent). And the good news: sharing these aged wines with your loved ones is one of the greatest joys of collecting wine.

The best wines from the following regions and countries are the ones to look for:

2010    Bordeaux, Rhône Valley
2009    California Cabernet Sauvignon
2008    Bordeaux, Napa Valley Cabernet Sauvignon
2007    Sauternes, Southern Rhône, Napa Cabernet Sauvignon
2006    Bordeaux (Pomerol), Northern Rhône, Barolo, Barbaresco, Brunello di Montalcino, German (Auslese and Soave), Argentina Malbec
2005    Bordeaux, Sauternes, Burgundy, Southern Rhône, Piedmont, Tuscany, Germany, Rioja, Ribera del Duero, Southern Australia, Napa Cabernet Sauvignon, Washington State Cabernet Sauvignon
2004    Napa Cabernet Sauvignon, Piedmont
2003    Northern and Southern Rhône, Sauternes, Bordeaux, Port
2002    Napa Cabernet Sauvignon, Germany*, Burgundy**, Sauternes
2001    Napa Cabernet Sauvignon, Sauternes, Germany*, Rioja, Ribera del Duero** Grand Cru
2000    Bordeaux
1999    Piedmont, Rhône (North), California Zinfandel
1998    Bordeaux (St-Émilion/Pomerol), Rhône (South), Piedmont (Barolo, Barbaresco)

| | |
|---|---|
| 1997 | California Cabernet Sauvignons, Tuscany (Chianti, Brunello, etc), Piedmont, Port, Australian Shiraz |
| 1996 | Burgundy, Piedmont, Bordeaux (Medoc), Burgundy, Germany* |
| 1995 | Bordeaux, Rhône, Rioja, California Cabernet Sauvignon |
| 1994 | Port, California Cabernet Sauvignon and Zinfandel, Rioja |
| 1993 | California Cabernet Sauvignon and Zinfandel |
| 1992 | Port, California Cabernet Sauvignon and Zinfandel |
| 1991 | Rhône (North), Port, California Cabernet Sauvignon |
| 1990 | Bordeaux, California Cabernet Sauvignon, Rhône, Burgundy, Tuscany, Piedmont, Sauternes, Champagne, Germany* |
| 1989 | Bordeaux, Rhône, Piedmont, Rioja |
| 1988 | Sauternes, Rhône (North), Piedmont |
| 1987 | California Cabernet Sauvignon and Zinfandel |
| 1986 | Bordeaux, Sauternes, California Cabernet Sauvignon |
| 1985 | Bordeaux, Port, Rhône (North), Champagne, Piedmont |

*Auslese and above   **Grand Cru*

## THE BEST WINE REGIONS FOR A VACATION

### Napa Valley, California
### Tuscany, Italy
### Bordeaux, France

A great vacation for me is great wine, fabulous restaurants, perfect climate, proximity to the ocean, beautiful scenery (am I asking too much yet?), and nice people! These three wine regions fulfill my needs.

## THE BEST WINE GLASS

### Riedel

The Riedel family of Austrian glassmakers has been on a crusade for over the last thirty years to elevate wine drinking to a new level with specially designed varietal glassware. They have designed glasses to accentuate the best components of each grape variety, their opinion being that a Cabernet Sauvignon/ Bordeaux glass should be different from a Pinot Noir/Burgundy glass.

Riedel glasses comes in many different styles. There are wineglasses for special occasions and everyday wine usage. The top of the line is the hand-crafted Sommelier series. Next comes the moderately priced collection with the Vinum. For those of you who do not want to spend a tremendous amount of money on glassware, they also produce the least expensive series in the competitive line, the Ouverture.

## THE BEST PLACE ON EARTH FOR RIESLING

### *Germany*
### *Runners-up: Alsace, France, and the Finger Lakes District, New York State*

Many professionals and wine connoisseurs believe that the best white wine made in the world is Riesling. It is definitely one of the best wines to go with food, especially with lighter-style fish such as sole and flounder.

I still believe that the consumer is confused by the Riesling grape variety and thinks that all Rieslings are sweet. The reality is that 95 percent of all Alsace Rieslings are dry and I would classify most of the German Rieslings as off-dry or semisweet. In the Finger Lakes, they produce dry, semidry, and sweet Rieslings.

Even though I probably drink more Alsace Rieslings than I do German Rieslings, the diversity of style of the German wines—some being dry, off-dry, semisweet, and very sweet—is the reason I would rank German Rieslings as the best in the world.

## THE BEST PLACE ON EARTH FOR SAUVIGNON BLANC

### *Loire Valley, France*
### *Runners-up: New Zealand and California*

The Sauvignon Blanc produced in the Loire Valley is best known by its regional names, Sancerre and Pouilly-Fumé. The best of the New Zealand Sauvignon Blancs are sold under the producer's name.

The stylistic differences between the Sauvignon Blancs of the Loire Valley and New Zealand are striking. While both Sauvignon Blancs are medium in body with high acidity, and work well with fish and poultry, the New Zealand Sauvignon Blancs have what some would call a very tropical bouquet or aroma, which you either like or don't like, which continues in the taste. I like it! Sauvignon Blanc is the second-highest-quality white grape grown in California, after Chardonnay. In my opinion, the best Sauvignon Blancs are coming from the cooler climates, have no oak, and are lower in alcohol content.

## THE BEST PLACE ON EARTH FOR CHARDONNAY

### *Burgundy, France*
### *Runner-up: California*

As much as I like the best producers of California Chardonnay, the elegance and balance of fruit and acidity of a white Burgundy wine is unmatched in the world. From the non-oak-aged Chablis to the barrel-fermented and barrel-aged Montrachets, to the light, easy-drinking Mâcons and the world famous Pouilly-Fuissé, there is a style and a price for everyone.

As with Sauvignon Blanc, I believe the best Chardonnays of California are coming from the cooler climates such as Carneros and Santa Barbara. I am not a fan of high-alcohol, overly oaked Chardonnays, so make sure you tell your retailer that you are looking for a leaner, more elegant style of California Chardonnay.

## THE BEST PLACE ON EARTH FOR PINOT NOIR

### Burgundy, France
### Runners-up: Oregon and California

Burgundy is a region deep in history and tradition. Vines have been planted there for over a thousand years and the sensuous Pinot Noir is the only red grape allowed (except for Beaujolais).

The only problem with a great Pinot Noir from Burgundy is its price tag and availability. I believe that Oregon makes the best Pinot Noirs in the United States, and many refer to the wines of Oregon as the "Burgundy of the United States" since their emphasis is on Chardonnay and Pinot Noir. In California, the best Pinot Noirs are also grown in the cooler climates.

## THE BEST PLACE ON EARTH FOR MERLOT

### Bordeaux, France (St-Émilion, Pomerol)
### Runner-up: California

The number-one red grape planted in Bordeaux is Merlot, with Cabernet Sauvignon a distant second.

The great châteaux of St-Émilion and Pomerol produce wines made primarily of the Merlot grape. The major difference between the two is the price and availability of each wine region. There are only 1,846 acres in Pomerol, but St-Émilion has over 23,380 acres of vines in production. So for my money, I'd go with St-Émilion, based on its lower price and also the fact that today it is the most progressive of all the Bordeaux wine regions.

## THE BEST PLACE ON EARTH FOR CABERNET SAUVIGNON

### Bordeaux, France (Médoc)
### Runner-up: California; Best Value: Chile

In my opinion, the greatest wines of the world are the châteaux of Bordeaux. The primary grape of the Médoc is Cabernet Sauvignon and they are not only the best wines for investment, they are also some of the best wines to age. With some 7,000 châteaux, there's plenty of wine to choose from at all different price points.

The best Cabernet Sauvignon from California comes from the North

Coast counties, especially Napa and Sonoma. The Napa Cabernets usually have more intensity of fruit and body and the Cabernets from Sonoma generally are softer and more elegant.

The price of an acre of vineyard land in Chile is so far below that of Napa Valley and Bordeaux that you will find tremendous quality and value from the better producers of Chile.

## THE BEST THING THAT EVER HAPPENED TO THE CALIFORNIA WINE INDUSTRY

### Phylloxera

This might sound like a strange answer to many people, but it also proves in this case that good has come from bad. Over the last twenty-five years, this plant louse destroyed some of the best vineyards of California, costing over $1 billion in new plantings. So what's the good news?

There wasn't much thought in the early days of California grape growing about planting locations. Chardonnays were planted in climates that were much too warm and Cabernet Sauvignons were planted in climates that were much too cool.

With the threat of phylloxera, winery owners were forced to replant their vineyards, but this time had more information on matching the soil and climate with the grape varieties. It also gave the grape growers the opportunity to plant different grape clones. One of the biggest changes that came from using clones was in the planting density of the vines themselves. The traditional vine spacing used by most wineries up until phylloxera was somewhere between 400 and 500 vines per acre. Today, with the new replanting, it is not uncommon to have more than 2,000 vines per acre.

What does this all mean for the consumer and why is it good news? Bottom line: if you like California wines now, you will love them even more because the quality is already better and the costs are lower, making it a win-win situation for everyone.

## THE BEST FLYING WINEMAKER IN THE WORLD

### Michel Rolland

Over the last thirty years, the demand for high-quality wine around the world has exploded. As with any other business that hires consultants to help them, winemaking is no different. Known as the flying wine consultant, Michel Rolland, a Bordeaux native, works with over 100 wineries on four continents. His influence on the quality and style of wine produced all over the world is enormous.

## THE BEST WINE LIE

### *That all wines get better with age*

Think of all of the wines that you used to drink in high school and college. Now think about how much you used to pay for those wines! I'm sure they didn't stay around very long! Which is exactly the way it should be.

The reality is that 90 percent of all wines are meant to be consumed within one year and that another 9 percent of wines should not see more than five years of age. Which leaves us with less than 1 percent of wines made in the world today that can age over five years. So get out your corkscrews and start drinking the wines that you are "saving" for that special occasion.

## THE BEST WINE MYTH

### *That everyone tastes wine alike*

The fact is that no one tastes wine, or anything, alike. Sense of taste and smell are like your own fingerprint or a snowflake—no two are alike. The average person has 10,000 taste buds, which statistically speaking means that some people have 20,000 and some people have none! Since it is very difficult to measure how many taste buds one has, I can trust only my own judgment and no one else's. The sense of smell is even more important than the sense of taste. (We all know this from when we have a cold.) You can taste only five things in life, but the average person can smell over 2,000 smells, and there are some 200 smells in wine. Women have the upper hand here, since it is a fact that they have a better sense of smell than men. Other factors include age, medical injuries (deviated septum), and side effects from prescription medicine.

## THE BEST WINE FOR LAMB

### *Bordeaux or California Cabernet Sauvignon*

In Bordeaux they have lamb with breakfast, lunch, and dinner! Lamb has such a strong flavor that it needs a strong wine, and the big, full-bodied Cabernet Sauvignons from California and Bordeaux blend in perfectly.

## THE BEST WINE FOR CHICKEN

### *Anything*

Chicken is one of the best things to have with wine because it doesn't have an overpowering flavor. It can go with almost any wine—red or white, light, medium, or full.

THE 2004 NOBEL Prize in Medicine went to Richard Axel and Linda B. Buck for their discoveries of "odorant receptors and the organization of the olfactory system," part of which was recognizing about 10,000 different smells.

## THE BEST WINE FOR CHOCOLATE
### *Port*
For me, both chocolate and Port mean the end of the meal. They are both rich, sweet, satisfying, and sometimes even decadent together.

## THE BEST BOTTLE SIZE FOR AGING
### *Magnum*
This is not just my opinion, but my wine collector and winemaker friends say that their best wines will last longer and mature more slowly in a magnum (2 bottles) than in a 750 ml.

One of the theories for this difference in bottle-size aging is the amount of air that is in the bottle (the air between the wine and the cork) versus the quantity of wine. It's also more fun to serve a magnum at a dinner party.

## THE BEST TEMPERATURE FOR WINE STORAGE
### *55 degrees F*
This is the temperature at which all the great wineries store and age their wine. If you have a wine collection or are planning on collecting wines, you must protect your investment. Studies have shown that the best temperature for long-term wine storage is approximately 55 degrees F. The same studies have also shown that storing wine at 75 degrees ages wine twice as fast. Obviously, the optimum temperature is 55 degrees, but I would rather the wine be a consistent 65 degrees all year long than swing in temperature from 50 to 70 degrees. This is the worst scenario and can be very harmful to the wine. And, just as warm temperatures will prematurely age the wine, temperatures too cold can freeze the wine, pushing out the cork and immediately ending the aging process.

You can either buy a wine refrigerator, build your wine cellar with the proper air conditioning, or, as I have done at my own "château," build a passive wine cellar which I accomplished simply by building an insulated (R-factor 50) room in my cellar.

## THE BEST HUMIDITY FOR WINE STORAGE
### *75 percent relative humidity*
If you are planning to age your wines more than five years this is important. (If not, don't worry about it.) If the humidity is too low, your corks will dry out. If that happens, wine will seep out of the bottle. Again, if wine can get out, air can get in. Too much humidity and you are likely to lose your labels. Personally, I'd rather lose my labels than lose my corks!

## THE BEST CHEESE WITH WINE

### *Parmigiano-Reggiano*

Now we are really getting personal! I love Italian food, wine, and women (I even married one), but Parmigiano-Reggiano is not just to have with Italian wine. It also goes extremely well with Bordeaux, California Cabernets, and even the lighter Pinot Noirs.

## THE BEST WINE EVENT

### Wine Spectator's *New York Wine Experience*

There are many great wine events in the United States. In 2011, *Wine Spectator* celebrated its thirtieth anniversary of the New York Wine Experience. I have to admit a certain bias since I was the cofounder of the event. What makes this wine weekend the best is that it was founded on three principles: 1) only the best wineries of the world would be invited, 2) the winemaker or owner had to be present, and 3) proceeds would go to scholarships.

Thirty years later, this biannual event has maintained the highest quality of wines, seminars, and speakers of any wine event in the world.

## THE BEST WINE FOR A RECEPTION

### *Champagne*

One of the most versatile wines produced in the world is Champagne. Serving it at your reception—whether it be a wedding or dinner at home—has a magical effect on guests. Champagne still remains a symbol of celebration, romance, prosperity, and fun.

## THE BEST WINE FOR VALENTINE'S DAY

### *Château Calon-Ségur*

At one time the Marquis de Ségur owned Château Lafite, Château Latour, and Château Calon-Ségur. He said, "I make my wines at Lafite and Latour, but my heart is at Calon." Hence the label.

## THE BEST WINE FOR THANKSGIVING

### ?

This is one of the most asked wine and food questions that I get that I don't have a definitive answer for. The problem with Thanksgiving is that it's not just the turkey, but everything else that is served with it—sweet potatoes, cranberries, butternut squash, stuffing—that can create havoc with wine.

This is also the big family holiday in the United States, and do you really want to share your best wines with Uncle Joe and Aunt Carol? I suggest that you try "user friendly" wines: easy drinking, inexpensive wines from reliable producers. Check out the list on page 277 for more specific wines.

We have one tradition at our Thanksgiving family dinner, which is to serve an Amontillado Sherry after the turkey with a selection of nuts and fruits.

## THE BEST WINE FOR AFTER DINNER

### Port

You don't need to drink a lot of Port to get the full enjoyment. One glass of this sweet and fortified (20 percent alcohol) wine ends a meal with a satisfying taste.

I consume most Port, whether it be Ruby, Tawny, or Vintage, from September until March—the cooler months in the Northeast. The best way to have Port is when all the dishes have been washed, your children are tucked away into their dream worlds, you are sitting in front of your fireplace, it's snowing out, and your golden retriever is by your side.

## THE BEST RED WINE FOR LUNCH

### Pinot Noir

Since most of us have to go back to work after lunch, the light, easy drinking style of a Pinot Noir will not overpower your usual luncheon fare of soups, salads, and sandwiches.

## THE BEST WHITE WINE FOR LUNCH

### Riesling

Depending upon what you are having for lunch, you could go with the low-alcohol (8 to 10 percent) German Riesling Kabinett—its slight residual sugar will blend in nicely, especially with salads.

For those who prefer a drier style, an Alsacian, Washington State, or Finger Lakes Riesling are great choices.

# Afterword: Looking Back, with Gratitude

I will always remember:

- Working with and learning from John Novi at the Depuy Canal House, 1970–76
- My first visit to a winery, Benmarl, in 1970
- My first wine classes, in 1971 (one where I was a student and the other where I was the teacher)
- Hitchhiking to California to visit the wine country, in 1972
- Teaching a two-credit course as a junior in college (open only to seniors), in 1973
- Father Sam Matarazzo, my early spiritual leader
- Living and studying wine in Europe, 1974–75
- Planting my own vineyard (three-time failure), 1974, 1981, 1992; making my own wine, in 1984 (so-so)— still trying in 2011 (still praying)
- The excitement of opening Windows on the World, in 1976
- The support and friendship of Jules Roinnel, going back to our earliest days together at Windows
- Wine tastings with Alexis Bespaloff and friends
- Mohonk Mountain House in New Paltz, New York, where ideas come easy
- Curt Strand and Toni Aigner of Hilton International
- Evening, late-night, and early-morning wine discussions with Alexis Lichine in Bordeaux
- The adviser and great listener Peter Sichel, whose generosity of spirit inspired the way I teach and share my wine knowledge
- Sharing great old vintages with Peter Bienstock
- Jules Epstein, for his advice and sharing his wine collection
- Touring the world with wine expert Robin Kelley O'Connor
- Those who are no longer here to share a glass of wine: Craig Claiborne, Joseph Baum, Alan Lewis, Raymond Wellington, and my father, Charles
- Creating and directing the New York Wine Experience, 1981–91
- Witnessing the success of Michael Skurnik, who worked with me at Windows in the late 1970s and quickly rose to fame as a great importer of wines
- Watching my former student Andrea Robinson turn into a superstar wine-and-food personality and author
- The Food Network's *Wines A to Z*—together with Alan Richman

- Reading and enjoying the observations of the great wine writers and tasters (listed throughout the book)
- Having the opportunity to meet all the passionate winemakers, vineyardists, and owners of the great wineries of the world
- The wine events, wine dinners, and tastings around the country that I have had the privilege of attending
- All the groups that have invited me to entertain and educate them about wine
- Writing the first chapter of this book with Kathleen Talbert in 1983
- The original Sterling Publishing team of Burton Hobson, Lincoln Boehm, and Charles Nurnberg
- Marcus Leaver, former CEO of Sterling Publishing, for his tremendous support on all of my books
- The Sterling Publishing team and all of the staff
- All my editors over the last two decades, especially Felicia Sherbert, Stephen Topping, Hannah Reich, Becky Maines, and Mary Hern
- The Sterling team assembled for this edition—Becky Maines, Christine Heun, Lindsey Adams, Sal Destro, Jessie Leaman, Richard Leahy, and Hannah Reich
- Karen Nelson for twenty-five years of beautiful cover designs
- Mary Hern, for her diligent work and editing on so many of my books
- Jim Anderson, who designed the original edition; and Richard Oriolo for capturing my spirit in subsequent editions
- Barnes & Noble, for always supporting my books and ideas
- Carmen Bissell, Raymond DePaul, Faye Friedman, and Jennifer Redmond for their help with the Wine School
- All my pourers at the school over the last thirty-five years
- Having a great relationship with my New York City wine-school peers, especially Harriet Lembeck (Beverage Program) and Mary Ewing-Mulligan (International Wine Center)
- The twenty thousand students who have attended the Windows on the World Wine School, which celebrated its thirty-sixth anniversary in 2012
- The Baum-Emil team, who re-created Windows on the World in 1996
- Conducting the Sherry-Lehmann/Kevin Zraly Master Wine Class with Michael Aaron, Michael Yurch, Chris Adams, Shyda Gilmer, and Matt Wong
- Michael Stengel at the Marriott Marquis Hotel NYC, for his advice and support since September 11th
- My continuing grief at the loss of those friends and coworkers who lost their lives on September 11th

- Robert M. Parker Jr., who so generously donated his time and talents to aid the families of September 11th
- Alan Stillman, founder, chairman, and CEO of the Smith & Wollensky Restaurant Group
- Being honored for "loving wine"—receiving the 2011 Lifetime Achievement Award from the James Beard Foundation
- Teaching wine at Cornell University and the Culinary Institute of America
- Being a member of the Culinary Institute's Board of Trustees
- All the "special" wine friends who have "helped" me deplete my wine cellar over the years
- Those who have tried to keep me organized in my business life: Ellen Kerr, Claire Josephs, Lois Arrighi, Sara Hutton, Andrea Immer, Dawn Lamendola, Catherine Fallis, Rebecca Chapa, Gina D'Angelo-Mullen, and Michelle Woodruff
- My four best vintages: Anthony (1991), Nicolas (1993), Harrison (1997), and Adriana (1999)
- My mom, Kathleen
- My sisters, Sharon and Kathy
- Everyone who worked at Windows on the World, especially my colleagues in the wine department

## A Final Note

If this were an award-acceptance speech, I probably would have gotten the hook after the first three bullet points. Still, I'm sure I've forgotten to name at least one or two folks—an occupational hazard of consuming so much wine! So, to everyone I've ever known, from grammar school on: *May all your vintages be great!*

# Selected Glossary

**Acid:** One of the *components* of wine. It is sometimes described as sour or tart and can be found on the sides of the tongue and mouth.

**Acidification:** The process of adding acid, usually tartaric or citric, to grape *must* before fermentation in order to boost low levels of acidity, creating a more balanced wine.

**Aftertaste:** The sensation in the mouth that persists after the wine has been swallowed.

**Alcohol:** The result of *fermentation* whereby yeast converts the natural sugar in grapes to alcohol.

**AOC:** Abbreviation for Appellation d'Origine Contrôlée; the French government laws that control wine production.

**Aroma:** The smell of the grapes in a wine.

**Astringent:** The *mouthfeel* created by tannins in wine.

**AVA:** Abbreviation for American Viticultural Area. AVAs are designated wine-producing areas in the United States.

**Balance:** The integration of the various components of wine, such as acid, alcohol, fruit, and tannin. To be balanced, no one component should dominate the wine's taste.

**Barrel-fermented:** Describes wine that has been fermented in small oak barrels rather than stainless steel. The oak from a barrel will add complexity to a wine's flavor and texture.

**Biodynamics:** A type of holistic farming created by Rudolph Steiner in the 1920s based on principles similar to that of organic farming. Compost and manure are used instead of chemical fertilizers or pesticides.

**Bitter:** One of the three tastes of wine, found at the back of the tongue and throat.

**Blend:** A combination of two or more wines or grapes, to enhance flavor, balance, and complexity.

**Body:** The sensation of weight of a wine in the mouth. A wine high in alcohol feels heavier than a wine with low alcohol.

**Botrytis cinerea** ("bo-TRY-tis sin-AIR-e-a"): Also called "noble rot," *Botrytis cinerea* is a special mold that punctures the skin of a grape, allowing the water to dissipate, leaving a higher than normal concentration of sugar and acid. *Botrytis cinerea* is necessary in making Sauternes and the rich German wines Beerenauslese and Trockenbeerenauslese.

**Bouquet:** The smell of a wine, influenced by winemaking processes and barrel aging.

**Brix** ("bricks"): A scale that measures the sugar level of the unfermented grape juice.

**Brut:** A French term used for the driest style of Champagne and/or sparkling wine.

**Chaptalization:** The addition of sugar to the must before fermentation to increase the alcohol level of the finished wine.

**Character:** Refers to the aspects of the wine typical of its grape varieties, or the overall characteristics of the wine.

**Classified châteaux:** The châteaux in the Bordeaux region of France that are known to produce the best wine.

**Colheita** ("coal-AY-ta"): Means "vintage" in Portuguese.

**Components:** The components of a wine make up its character, style, and taste. Some components are: acidity, alcohol, fruit, tannin, and residual sugar.

**Cru:** Certain vineyards in France are designated *Grand Cru* and *Premier Cru*, the classification indicating level of quality.

**HERE IS A LIST OF RED-GRAPE VARIETALS, AND SOME OF THE REGIONS WHERE THEY CAN BE FOUND:**

Agiorgitiko (Greece)
Barbera (Italy, California)
Blaufränkisch (Austria)
Cabernet Franc (Bordeaux, Canada, Loire Valley)
Cabernet Sauvignon (Argentina, Australia, Bordeaux, California, Canada, Chile, Hungary, South Africa, Spain, Washington)
Cariñena (Spain)
Carménère (Chile)
Cinsault (Rhône Valley)
Concord (United States)
Gamay (Burgundy)
Garnacha/Grenache (Spain/France)
Kadarka (Hungary)
Kékfrankos (Hungary)
Malbec (Argentina)
Merlot (Argentina, Bordeaux, California, Canada, Chile, Hungary, Spain, Washington)
Monastrell (Spain)
Nebbiolo (Piedmont)
Petite Syrah (California)
Pinot Meunier (Champagne)
Pinot Noir (Austria, Burgundy, California, Canada, Hungary, New Zealand, Oregon)
Portugieser (Hungary)
Sangiovese (Tuscany)
St. Laurent (Austria)
Syrah/Shiraz (Argentina, California, Canada, Chile, Rhône Valley, South Africa, Spain, Washington/Australia)
Tempranillo (Spain, Argentina)
Xinomavro (Greece)
Zinfandel (California)

Albariño (Spain)
Assyrtiko (Greece)
Chardonnay (Argentina, Australia,
  Austria, Burgundy, Canada, Chile,
  Hungary, New Zealand, South Africa,
  Spain, United States)
Chenin Blanc (California, Loire Valley,
  South Africa)
Furmint (Hungary)
Gewürztraminer (Alsace, Germany)
Grüner Veltliner (Austria)
Hárslevelü (Hungary)
Macabeo (Spain)
Moschofilero (Greece)
Olaszrizling (Hungary)
Pinot Blanc (Alsace)
Pinot Grigio/Pinot Gris (Italy/Canada,
  France, Hungary, United States)
Riesling (Alsace, Austria, Canada,
  United States)
Roditis (Greece)
Sauvignon Blanc (California, Chile, Graves,
  Loire Valley, New Zealand, Sauternes,
  South Africa)
Sémillon (Australia, Graves, Sauternes)
Szürkebarát (Hungary)
Torrontés Riojano (Argentina)
Trebbiano (Italy)
Verdejo (Spain)
Vidal (Canada)
Viognier (California, Rhône Valley)

**Cuvée:** From the French *cuve* (vat); may refer to a particular blend of grapes or, in Champagne, to the select portion of the juice from the pressing of the grapes.

***Decanting:*** The process of pouring wine from its bottle into a carafe to separate the sediment from the wine.

**Dégorgement** ("day-gorzh-MOWN"): One step of the Champagne method (*Méthode Champenoise*) used to expel the sediment from the bottle.

**Demi-sec** ("deh-mee-SECK"): A Champagne containing a higher level of residual sugar than a *brut*.

**DOC:** Abbreviation for Denominazione di Origine Controllata, the Italian laws that control wine production. Spain also uses this abbreviation for Denominación de Origen Condado.

**DOCG:** Abbreviation for Denominazione di Origine Controllata e Garantita; the Italian government allows this marking to appear only on the finest Italian wines. The G stands for "guaranteed."

**Dosage** ("doh-SAHZH"): The addition of sugar, often mixed with wine or brandy, in the final step in the production of Champagne or sparkling wine.

***Drip irrigation:*** System for watering vines that applies water directly to the roots through a network of emitters or microsprayers; drip irrigation conserves water and nutrients and minimizes erosion.

***Dry:*** Wine containing very little residual sugar. It is the opposite of sweet, in wine terms.

***Estate-bottled:*** Wine that is made, produced, and bottled on the estate where the grapes were grown.

***Extra dry:*** Less dry than *brut* Champagne.

***Fermentation:*** The process of transforming sugar into alcohol in the presence of yeast, turning grape juice into wine.

***Filtration:*** Removal of yeast and other solids from a wine before bottling to clarify and stabilize the wine.

**Fino** ("FEE-noh"): A type of Sherry.

***Finish:*** The taste and feel that wine leaves in the mouth after swallowing. Some wines disappear immediately while others can linger for some time.

***First growth:*** The five highest-quality Bordeaux châteaux wines from the Médoc Classification of 1855.

***Fortified wine:*** A wine such as Port or Sherry that has additional grape spirits (brandy, for example) added to raise the alcohol content.

***Fruit:*** One of the components of wine that derives from the grape itself.

**Grand Cru** ("grawn crew"): The highest classification for wines in Burgundy.

**Grand Cru Classé** ("grawn crew clas-SAY"): The highest level of the Bordeaux classification.

***Gran Reserva:*** A Spanish wine that has had extra aging.

***Hectare:*** A metric measure of area that equals 2.471 acres.

***Hectoliter:*** A metric measure of volume that equals 26.42 U.S. gallons.

**Halbtrocken:** The German term meaning "semidry."

**Kabinett** ("kah-bee-NETT"): A light, semidry German wine.

***Maceration:*** The chemical process by which *tannin*, color, and flavor are extracted from the grape skins into the wine. Temperature and alcohol content influence the speed at which maceration occurs.

***Malolactic fermentation:*** A secondary fermentation process wherein malic acid is converted into lactic acid and carbon dioxide. This process reduces the wine's acidity and adds complexity.

**Mechanical harvester:** A machine used on flat vineyards. It shakes the vines to harvest the grapes.

**Meritage:** Trademark designation for specific high-quality American wines containing the same blend of varieties that are used in the making of Bordeaux wines in France.

**Méthode Champenoise** ("may-TUD shahm-pen-WAHZ"): The method by which Champagne, and sometimes sparkling wine, is made.

**Mouthfeel:** Sensation of texture in the mouth when tasting wine, e.g., smooth or *tannic*.

**Must:** Unfermented grape juice extracted during the crushing process.

**"Noble Rot":** See *Botrytis cinerea*.

**Nose:** The term used to describe the bouquet and aroma of wine.

**Phenolics:** Chemical compounds derived especially but not only from the skins, stems, and seeds of grapes that affect the color and flavor of wine. *Tannin* is one example. *Maceration* can increase their presence in wines.

**Oenology:** The science and scientific study of winemaking.

**Phylloxera** ("fill-LOCK-she-rah"): A root louse that kills grapevines.

**Prädikatswein** ("pray-dee-KAHTS-vine"): The highest level of quality in German wines.

**Premier Cru:** A wine that has special characteristics that comes from a specific designated vineyard in Burgundy, France, or is blended from several such vineyards.

**Proprietary wine:** A wine that's given a brand name like any other product and is marketed as such, e.g., Riunite, Mouton-Cadet.

**Qualitätswein** ("kval-ee-TATES-vine"): A German term meaning "quality wine."

**Residual sugar:** Any unfermented sugar that remains in a finished wine. Residual sugar determines how dry or sweet a wine is.

**Riddling:** One step of the Champagne-making process in which the bottles are turned gradually each day for weeks until they are upside down, so that the sediment rests in the neck of the bottle.

**Sediment:** Particulate matter that accumulates in wine as it ages.

**Sommelier** ("so-mel-YAY"): The French term for cellarmaster, or wine steward.

**Sulfur dioxide:** A substance used in winemaking and grape-growing as a preservative, an antioxidant, and also a sterilizing agent.

**Tannin:** One of the components of wine, tannin is a natural compound and preservative that comes from the skins, stems, and pits of the grapes and also from the wood barrel in which wine is aged.

**Terroir:** All of the elements that contribute to the distinctive characteristics of a particular vineyard site that include its soil, subsoil, slope, drainage, elevation, and climate, including exposure to the sun, temperature, and precipitation.

**Varietal wine:** A wine that is labeled with the predominant grape used to produce the wine. For example, a wine made from Chardonnay grapes would be labeled "Chardonnay."

**Vintage:** The year the grapes are harvested.

**Vinification:** Winemaking.

**Vitis labrusca** ("VEE-tiss la-BREW-skah"): A native grape species in America.

**Vitis vinifera** ("VEE-tiss vih-NIFF-er-ah"): The grape species that is used in most countries in the world for winemaking.

# INDEX

# Take Kevin's class!

Visit kevinzraly.com to enroll
and join 20,000 graduates of the
**Windows on the World Wine School!**

*Other books by Kevin Zraly:*